HSAs

The Tax-Perfect Retirement Account

William G. Stuart

Peter E. Randall Publisher
Portsmouth, NH
2019

ISBN: 978-1-942155-22-5

Library of Congress Control Number: 2019930299

Peter E. Randall Publisher
Portsmouth, NH 03801
www.perpublisher.com

Book Design: Tim Holtz

Printed in the United States of America

Table of Contents

Important Notes

This book does not constitute legal advice.

The author is *not* an attorney, nor is he a licensed financial planner, investment advisor, or retirement specialist. This book is *not* intended to offer legal, financial, investment or retirement advice to the reader.

Instead, this book is designed to introduce an additional option into retirement planning and provide information to stimulate the thought process as professional financial, investment, and retirement planners meet with their clients.

These clients know that licensed professionals are the best qualified people to discuss financial matters with them, and licensed legal or tax counselors are best qualified to review compliance and tax issues with them. A book—or any author or speaker—is *not* a substitute for a qualified licensed counselor who can deliver customized advice that captures all aspects of a client's financial and lifestyle situation.

This book uses the term *advising professionals*.

To avoid distracting references, this book refers to financial planners, investment professionals, and retirement advisors collectively as *advising professionals*. The reference is designed to capture the many men and women who provide invaluable services to their clients, regardless of the specific nature of their practices, their licenses, or their fee structures.

This book is intended for advising professionals, benefits advisors, employers, and HSA owners.

The information in this book is relevant to all advising professionals. Many have only begun to learn about the benefits that HSAs offer as financial accounts. They need to understand HSAs—not only basic compliance information, but also how HSAs may fit into specific clients' overall financial strategies.

At the same time, the book conveys information that is of value to benefits advisors, employers, and HSA owners. HSA owners need merely to substitute *I* or *me* for *you* or *your client* to absorb the full richness of the information presented. The principles are equally valid and relevant. Only the prism through which they're viewed changes.

Stay Updated

HSA rules change from time to time, either through legislative action, administrative guidance, or court decisions. To keep up-to-date on changes in the rules and general HSA information, please visit www.HSAunited.com and sign up for our newsletter. We provide regular updates via e-mail and post HSA-related content on the site, and we never sell, rent, or share our mailing list.

About the Author

William G. (Bill) Stuart has worked with Health Savings Accounts (HSAs) since their inception in 2004. He worked nearly two decades in a variety of roles at Harvard Pilgrim Health Care, a regional health services company named America's Best Health Plan every year between 2004 and 2013 by the National Committee for Quality Assurance (NCQA). During his last dozen years at Harvard Pilgrim, Bill managed the company's reimbursement program, including Health Flexible Spending Arrangements (FSAs), Health Reimbursement Arrangements (HRAs), and HSAs.

In 2016, Bill assumed the position of director of strategy and compliance at Benefit Strategies, LLC, a large, independent third-party administrator based in New Hampshire that serves clients throughout the country. Benefit Strategies manages Health FSAs, HRAs, and HSAs and offers commuter reimbursement programs, COBRA administration, direct billing solutions, and tuition and wellness reimbursement programs.

He is also the founder of HSAunited, an educational coalition of benefits advisors, financial professionals, and HSA owners. You can learn more at www.HSAunited.com.

Bill has worked closely with benefits advisors and delivered classroom training to more than 800 benefits advisors. He continued the education process through his highly acclaimed *CDH Guru* blog at Harvard Pilgrim and more recently with his *Health Savings Account GPS* blog (www.benstrat.com/blog). He speaks frequently at regional and national conferences on topics ranging from HSA rules and strategies to private marketplaces, medical insurance reform, and becoming and projecting as an expert in a field.

As a member of the American Bankers Association HSA Council, he is active in efforts to enhance HSAs and extend the concept as an option to

Medicare—and Medicaid-eligible individuals. This approach offers the potential to increase consumer choice, reduce claims costs, and limit taxpayers' financial responsibility.

Bill is active in the Employers Council on Flexible Compensation (ECFC). He is a licensed medical insurance broker, is active in the National Association of Health Underwriters (NAHU), and serves on the board of the Massachusetts chapter of NAHU. He meets with members of Congress, congressional staff members, and administration officials to provide information on reimbursement accounts and other issues affecting health-care consumers.

Bill's first book, *Health Savings Accounts: A Practical Guide for Accountholders,* published in 2012, is a reference book used by many benefits advisors, employers, and compliance professionals. An updated version is scheduled for publication in summer 2019 under the tentative title *Health Savings Account Guide for Account Owners and Employers.*

A graduate of Bowdoin College with an MBA from Duke University's Fuqua School of Business, Bill also studied at Ripon College and the University of Texas at Austin. He lives on the South Shore of Massachusetts with his wife and children. He is an Eagle Scout and serves as a Boy Scout leader.

Acknowledgments

Though I am responsible for the contents of this book, I could not have completed this undertaking without considerable help. Vin Capozzi and Scott Polansky at Harvard Pilgrim Health Care created the position of Consumer-Driven Health Product Specialist at the dawn of HSAs, hired me, invested in me, and offered me the flexibility and support to define the position and follow my passion. Cheryl Ierna provided invaluable support as I worked with the company to create my first book, *Health Savings Accounts: A Practical Guide for Accountholders.* That book, privately published and distributed, will be released in early 2019 under the tentative title *Health Savings Account Guide for Accountholders and Employers.*

Paul Smith, CEO, and Tom Smith, president, have supported my work since I joined Benefit Strategies, LLC, in 2016. They have provided me with the opportunity to contribute to national organizations advancing HSAs and the platform to blog biweekly (www.benstrat.com/blog) on topics related to HSAs, consumer-driven health (CDH) in general, and national political debates around medical care and financing.

My colleagues at the American Bankers Association HSA Council (under the direction of Kevin McKechnie and Jennifer Hatten) and the Employers Council on Flexible Compensation (led by Martin Trussell) constantly challenge me and support my work. These organizations focus on helping consumers manage the increasing out-of-pocket cost of medical care. Both attract committed volunteers who work tirelessly to educate elected officials, legislative staffers, and regulators on medical reimbursement issues and propose legislative and administrative enhancements to these programs. They have stellar reputations among elected and appointed federal officials as sources of unbiased information to help elected officials and staffers understand the complexities of these markets.

Brent Hunsberger, CFP (a financial advisor at Silver Oak Advisory Group in Portland, OR), Roy Ramthun (president of HSA Consulting Services, based near Washington, DC), and Chris Byrd (executive vice president of WEX Health based in Fargo, ND) provided meticulous feedback on my original manuscript. Their many suggestions have made the final product far superior to what I could have produced on my own.

Cynthia Moser, my editor, and I began our writing collaboration in 1983 as graduate students and have worked together intermittently since then. It's comforting to an author to have an editor who understands his thought process and his "voice." Cynthia has provided invaluable input to the manuscript in a manner consistent with my general thoughts and means of expression. I am indebted to this true professional and recommend her work highly.

My younger brother, Jon S. Stuart, inspired me. He worked for Lotus Software (now part of IBM) before starting a consulting and training business. I saw how his writing *Lotus Domino for Dummies* (published in 1997) set him apart in his field by validating his expertise. I wholeheartedly agree with his observation that putting one's thoughts on paper forces the writer to gain a deeper knowledge of his topic.

I'd like to thank Bob Macauley, Dan Perrin, John Young, Gary Fradin, Laine Brantner, Jason Cook, Jill Kelly, Dawn Murphy, Jody Dietel, Todd Berkeley, John Young, Doug Fisher, John Hickman, Carl Hall, Darcy Hitesman, Mark Gaunya, Dr. Steven Neeleman, former US Rep. Bill Archer, Ellen Kaplan, Nancy Rand, Ed Estey, and Dr. Bill West. Each of you has challenged me, inspired me, or added to my base of knowledge through formal training, informal conversations, or tough, real-life scenarios. And I can't neglect to mention Judith Hubbard, my high-school AP English teacher, who taught and demanded compositions that were well written and well reasoned. I hope I don't disappoint her.

Finally, I'd like to thank my family. My parents created a foundation upon which four children built successful lives that have included master's degrees, four (and counting) books, and a handful of patents. My wife Chris (who wanted me to call this book *50 Shades of HSGray* to boost sales) and my children—Mike, Matt, Nicole, and Cameron—keep life interesting (sometimes a little too interesting!) and worth living.

Foreword

As a nationally recognized expert on Health Savings Accounts (HSAs) and consumer-driven health care issues, I am passionate about expanding HSAs to millions more Americans while helping current HSA owners maximize the value of their accounts. Although HSAs have been around since 2004, many Americans are just learning about them for the first time. Others have had an HSA for a few years but are still learning the finer details. Bill Stuart embraces these issues and brings his knowledge and experience as a strategic benefits advisor to this important book. He shares his common-sense approach to applying the benefits of HSAs to our everyday lives with a specific focus on planning for the future.

My colleagues call me "Mr. HSA." I was there at the beginning of the program, having led the implementation of HSAs after they were enacted into law in 2003 while serving as the Senior Advisor for Health Initiatives to the Secretary of the U.S. Treasury Department. Since that time I have devoted my professional career to sharing my knowledge about HSAs, and I am a frequent speaker at conferences and seminars around the country. I currently serve as a consultant to the primary HSA industry group, the American Bankers Association HSA Council.

Bill Stuart is a member of this council and we have become good friends. We also share a Boy Scout connection. I consider Bill to be one of my most knowledgeable colleagues in the industry, in part because he shares my desire to understand the nitty-gritty details of HSAs. We have exchanged many questions and insights on the IRS guidance that frames the parameters of HSAs and sometimes debate its intent. He never hesitates to challenge my interpretation of the IRS rules. This keeps both of us on our toes and makes both of us feel more confident in our understanding of HSAs as a result.

HSAs: The Tax-Perfect Retirement Account provides a unique perspective on the "savings" aspect of an HSA by illustrating how Americans can use the tax advantages that HSAs offer to help them plan for their health care expenses during retirement. Study after study shows that Americans are not saving enough for retirement, let alone for health care expenses in retirement. Recent figures suggest couples retiring at age 65 in 2018 can expect to spend $280,000 on health care during their remaining years. While this is an astonishing figure, it represents out-of-pocket expenses *after* what Medicare covers *and* does not include long-term care expenses.

With this in mind, the book introduces the concept of "building medical equity," an uncommon term to many of us but a perfect choice for describing how funds in HSAs can be saved and invested similarly to the funds in our retirement plans. The book highlights the tax advantages that an HSA has over traditional retirement plans, which makes the HSA a clear winner for funding priority during our working years. For example, when you are faced with a choice of whether to contribute $4,000 to your 401(k) plan or your HSA, it doesn't seem like an easy decision. But when you understand that you could pay a $3,000 medical bill tax-free with a $3,000 withdrawal from your HSA yet paying the same expense from your retirement plan would require you to withdraw $4,000 so that you have $3,000 left after taxes (assuming a 25% tax rate), the choice becomes clearer. The difference is $1,000 that you can keep in your HSA instead of giving it to the government in the form of taxes. Did you know you can even transfer some of the funds in your retirement plan into your HSA? By reading this book, you will come to understand how you can use this and other strategies to build your own medical equity through an HSA.

For readers who want to learn more about the details of an HSA, Section II of the book goes into further detail so that you can learn about ways to use your HSA strategically, especially in the sometimes complicated world of employee benefits. Employers frequently offer other accounts similar to HSAs, such as Flexible Spending Arrangements (FSAs) and Health Reimbursement Arrangements (HRAs), that create confusion among employees and their families. Participation in an FSA or HRA may cancel an employee's eligibility to contribute to an HSA. No one wants that to happen, but it easily can.

HSAs may sometimes seem like they are too good to be true. Having been there in the trenches during the infancy of the program, I can say with authority that they are one of the best, if not **the** best, opportunities for Americans to save money on taxes while saving money for paying health care expenses. This is why I have devoted the latter part of my career to helping Americans understand the power of HSAs so that they can take full advantage of them. Although not a fan of vanity license plates, I have often considered getting one that says "MRHSA." But I'm too cheap to spend the extra money and I would rather put it in my HSA. Maybe it is because a Boy Scout is "thrifty."

Roy J. Ramthun, "Mr. HSA"
Founder & President, HSA Consulting Services
Silver Spring, Maryland
June 2018

A Whole New World

The tectonic plates are shifting. Though Health Savings Accounts (HSAs) have enjoyed steady growth during the past decade, they haven't dominated the employee benefits landscape. And they certainly haven't attracted the attention of professional advisors outside the group health plan space. Until now.

Consider these figures through the end of 2017:

- More than 25 million Americans were covered on HSA-qualified medical plans, most through their employers.
- HSA-qualified medical plans, which carry lower premiums and are the requisite coverage to open an HSA, are the overwhelming choices of buyers when they're spending their own money, either in the nongroup market or when their employer provides a flat-dollar contribution that employees can apply to one of several plans.
- There are more than 22 million HSAs today—a figure that grows by double digits annually.
- Those HSAs hold balances of about $50 billion—an amount that increases by at least 20% growth annually, even though the percentage growth in new accounts has recently settled in the low teens. This discrepancy reflects ever-higher balances as accounts age and owners realize the advantages of building medical equity, even though many are unfamiliar with the term itself.

HSAs are here to stay. What has changed is that people are now beginning to understand the concept of medical equity. And advising professionals are beginning to see the powerful benefit that HSAs offer to long-term savers—tax advantages superior to those offered by traditional retirement accounts.

The problem? Most advising professionals don't understand the nuances of HSAs—the opportunities, the strategies, and the rules. Like most of your colleagues, you're probably reluctant to advise clients without a comprehensive understanding of HSAs. And the concept of medical equity? Though it may not have entered your vocabulary yet, you'll grasp the idea and understand its financial power as you read this book.

Even if you do have a strong base of HSA knowledge, you probably don't have access to an HSA product or program to offer your clients that delivers a level of compensation commensurate with the time and skill that you devote to the effort. Expect this situation to change soon as existing and new players in the financial and reimbursement markets introduce new products and create new alignments that merge health and wealth.

Good news. This book includes all the information that you need to advise your clients. You'll discover strategies that you can recommend to your clients to maximize the financial benefits that they derive from opening and contributing to an HSA. You'll learn basic HSA rules about eligibility, contributions, and distributions. You'll discover the tricks, twists, and gotchas in the world of HSAs.

In short, you'll be able to discuss HSAs as part of your clients' overall financial, investment and retirement strategies with the same confidence that you discuss 401(k) plans, SEP IRAs, SIMPLE IRAs, strategies to reduce provisional income, retirement-account distribution strategies, and balancing long-term savings in taxable, tax-deferred, and tax-free buckets.

Armed with this knowledge, you will become even more valuable to your clients, and the advice that you provide will increase their financial well-being in retirement. You will take their financial future to a new level and experience the satisfaction of blending a powerful financial opportunity into their planning.

SECTION I

The Tax-Perfect Retirement Account

INTRODUCTION TO SECTION I

This section introduces you to Health Savings Accounts. You'll begin your journey with a brief history of HSAs—from their introduction as Medical Savings Accounts (MSAs) during the mid-1990s to their place today as reimbursement vehicles and financial accounts.

You'll then explore the interplay between medical coverage and HSAs. Because HSAs are tied to particular medical plans, it's important to understand how clients' decisions made during their employers' (or the *Affordable Care Act* marketplace's) annual open-enrollment period affect their finances.

Your journey then focuses on specific benefits that HSAs offer your clients. The items on this list appear throughout the book as you follow a deeper discussion about how HSAs can enhance your clients' financial planning.

Next, you'll be introduced to the concept of *medical equity*. The same sacrifice of current consumption during people's working years can produce very different levels of wealth available in retirement. Medical equity is the most efficient form of retirement savings.

Finally, you'll explore HSAs in the context of other common employer reimbursement programs: Health Flexible Spending Arrangements (Health FSAs) and Health Reimbursement Arrangements (HRAs). These plans play an important role in employees' lives today and will continue to do so in the future (absent negative changes in current laws). Though these plans compete with HSAs on some levels (federal tax law doesn't allow individuals to enroll in certain combinations of HSAs, Health FSAs, and HRAs simultaneously), they can be complementary when employers with foresight create combinations that maximize participating employees' current tax savings and long-term wealth building.

CHAPTER 1

The HSA Revolution

Welcome to a quiet revolution. In this chapter, you'll find

- a summary of the history of HSAs,
- a brief definition of HSAs,
- a high-level discussion of HSA rules, and
- the demographic profiles of HSA owners and how they've changed over time.

In late 2003, Congress passed and President George W. Bush signed the Medicare Prescription Drug, Improvement and Modernization Act. This bill was generally received favorably because it created a new program to help individuals age 65 and older manage their prescription drug costs. The law launched Medicare Part D, coverage for prescription drugs that Medicare-eligible individuals can purchase from private insurers regulated by the Centers for Medicare and Medicaid Services (CMS), a division of the US Department of Health and Human Services (HHS).

The Act also included a wholesale expansion of an idea piloted nearly a decade earlier to give people tax preferences if they chose coverage that left them with greater financial responsibility for their medical expenses in exchange for opening a tax-advantaged account to reimburse those expenses.

Archer Medical Savings Accounts (MSAs) were created as part of the Health Insurance Portability and Accountability Act of 1995 (sometimes called the Kennedy-Kassebaum Act, but known to every patient who's had to sign an acknowledgment of a medical provider's privacy statement simply as HIPAA). Archer MSAs were the brainchild of Golden Rule Insurance Company head Pat Rooney (with the support of Dan Perrin), National Center for Policy Analysis economist John Goodman and US Rep. Bill Archer (R-TX), then chair of the powerful House Ways and Means Committee. The Archer MSA program allowed employers to offer higher deductible insurance with lower premiums to their employees. In turn, the employer or employee could contribute to an account through which employees could reimburse their own and their family members' qualified medical expenses tax-free.

The Archer MSA program was limited to self-employed individuals and small business employees, had participation limits, and allowed contributions to MSAs by *either* employer or employee—but not both—up to a maximum that was lower than participants' deductibles. The plan proved to be a hit with financially savvy people, primarily the self-employed and others who were low utilizers of medical insurance, because the program offered lower premiums and tax advantages. Archer MSAs were less attractive to individuals with higher claims whose MSA contribution limits were less than the medical expenses for which they were responsible.

HSA Legislation, the HOPE Act, and the ACA

Seizing on MSAs as an idea worth expanding, key advisors in the George W. Bush White House, including Roy Ramthun, and influential members of Congress such as Archer, drafted legislation to enact a far broader program that was eventually attached to the Medicare prescription drug bill. The result: the birth of HSAs late in 2003, with implementation of the program beginning in 2004.

As HSAs were originally designed, employers *and* employees could contribute to HSAs (eliminating the MSA restriction of employer *or* employee contributions in a given year) up to a maximum amount. In the original legislation, that contribution limit was the *lower of* the medical-plan deductible or a statutory maximum annual contribution set annually by the Internal Revenue Service (IRS) to reflect general inflation during the prior year. People who became HSA-eligible mid-year had to pro-rate their contributions, even though their medical insurers rarely pro-rated their deductibles. HSA owners could reimburse tax-free a wide range of medically necessary medical, dental, and vision services; over-the-counter drugs, medicine, equipment, and supplies; and certain insurance premiums, including Medicare Part B, Part D, and Part C premiums.

In late 2006, Congress passed the *Health Opportunity Patient Empowerment (HOPE) Act*. The *HOPE Act* essentially turned HSAs from merely a triple-tax-free reimbursement account into a triple-tax-advantaged reimbursement *and long-term savings and investment account.*

The *HOPE Act* made HSAs more attractive in several ways.

First, individuals can contribute up to the statutory maximum annual contribution without regard to their plan deductibles. Thus, HSA owners who meet a low annual medical deductible still can contribute additional funds to pay for other qualified expenses or carry balances forward.

Second, individuals who become HSA-eligible mid-year can contribute to the statutory maximum, allowing them to reduce their taxable income immediately and build HSA balances to either (1) reimburse high qualified expenses that year, or (2) accumulate additional funds to use in the future.

Third, HSA owners can make a one-time rollover from an Individual Retirement Arrangement (IRA) to an HSA. This provision is important for tax-diversification purposes, as it allows an owner to move funds from an account whose distributions are always included in taxable income (a traditional IRA) to one whose withdrawals are tax-free when used for qualified expenses.

Fourth, employers could allow employees to roll over Health FSA or Health Reimbursement Arrangement (HRA) balances to an HSA to jump-start their HSA savings. Unfortunately, the design of this feature limited eligible beneficiaries to near zero, creating the frustration associated with unmet expectations. This provision of the law expired at the end of 2011.

Forward-thinking advising professionals are directing their clients to consider participation in an HSA program.

By enabling HSA-eligible individuals to increase their HSA contributions, the *HOPE Act* began the revolution that's coming to fruition today: Forward-thinking advising professionals are directing their clients to consider participation in an HSA program as a means of reducing medical premiums, diverting those saved premium dollars to an account that they own, and investing those balances to increase the account value and build medical equity.

The *Affordable Care Act* (ACA) of 2010 slightly changed two HSA advantages. Fortunately, these changes mean little to most owners and have no effect on the long-term value of these accounts as savings vehicles. The ACA disallows tax-free reimbursement for over-the-counter drugs and medicine unless the HSA owner has a valid prescription. And the penalty for withdrawals for non-qualified expenses—a levy that applies to owners who aren't age 65 or disabled—is increased from 10% to 20%.

The HSA revolution, once a secret known by few, is now in full force. And the advising professional who doesn't understand the power of these accounts isn't presenting to her clients the full menu of options to maximize their accumulation of effective wealth. The concept of effective wealth—or *medical equity*—is a frequent topic in this book.

What Is an HSA?

To clear up one misconception from the outset, an HSA is *not* an insurance product. When you hear people criticize HSAs, they're generally expressing dissatisfaction with the medical plan in which individuals must enroll to be eligible to open and contribute to an HSA. This criticism (often misguided) shouldn't be directed at this tax-advantaged financial account, any more than a worker at a minimum-wage job with no money left in his checking account after paying his monthly bills should criticize the bank that offers the checking account for his plight.

An HSA is a trust opened, owned, and managed by an individual. It's a triple-tax-free account designed to help certain people manage their current or future health-related out-of-pocket expenses by reimbursing those expenses with pre-tax dollars.

As an analogy, think of an HSA as a checking account. Even though it's structured differently (a typical checking account isn't legally established as a trust), an HSA is a financial account into which money flows and departs. The owner controls how much money goes into the account and directs when funds leave. Balances earn interest and are guaranteed by federal or state deposit insurance up to applicable limits of coverage. The owner can make withdrawals via debit card and can check balances by logging into a personal online account.

As with any tax-advantaged program, HSAs are subject to federal government rules regarding participation, such as who can own an HSA, limits on contributions, and restrictions on tax-free distributions. In this sense, HSAs are no different from retirement accounts like traditional and Roth IRAs, traditional and Roth 401(k) plans, SEP IRAs, and SIMPLE IRAs.

In Sections IV and V, you can dive into these restrictions in greater detail. In summary, they are:

Eligibility: To be HSA-eligible, your clients must be enrolled in a medical plan with a specific benefit design, including a broad up-front deductible. When a client is covered by more than one medical plan (such as a spouse's commercial plan, Medicare, Medicaid, or TRICARE), all plans must be HSA-qualified.

Contributions: The IRS places annual limits on contributions to an HSA. The 2019 figures are $3,500 for your clients who are enrolled in self-only coverage and $7,000 for those enrolled in family coverage. In addition, people who are age 55 or older and HSA-eligible can make an annual $1,000 catch-up contribution.

Distributions: A client's withdrawals from an HSA are tax-free only if the distributions reimburse qualified expenses incurred by certain family members after your client has established her HSA. Distributions for any other expenses are included in taxable income and possibly subject to penalties in the form of additional taxes.

Though most HSA owners participate in employer-based benefits and set up an HSA with an employer's chosen administrator, HSAs remain individually owned accounts. As such, they are completely portable—they go with their owner from job to job, from active employment to stay-at-home to return to the workforce, from job to extended unemployment to job again, and from work to retirement. HSA owners never lose their HSAs, their balances, or their ability to manage their HSA due to any changes in employment status, life events, or income.

Who Owns HSAs?

During the first half dozen years that HSAs were on the market, it was easy to identify who enrolled: the *healthy*, the *wealthy*, and the *wise:*

- *Healthy,* because they were in a position to minimize out-of-pocket costs. They enrolled in a medical plan with an up-front deductible, but they were unlikely to incur many expenses against that deductible. They paid a lower premium and directed the savings into their personal HSAs rather than continuing to give the higher premium to their insurer.
- *Wealthy,* because they had the discretionary income to fund their HSAs up to their applicable annual contribution limits.
- *Wise,* because, as with other tax-advantaged accounts, they understood the value of operating in a world without the friction of taxes.

Today, however, HSA owners reflect the population as a whole in terms of income, wealth, health, and education level. In fact, research by several trade associations indicate that the average incomes of families who participate in Health FSAs (traditionally thought of as the working family's tax-advantaged opportunity) and HSAs (viewed by many as accounts for wealthier people) is about $57,000 for both programs. Participation in one plan or the other is driven more by availability of one plan or the other through an employer, rather than a person's income, medical utilization, or weighing of the trade-off between current and future consumption.

What has changed? Well, several factors.

First, more employers who offered HSA programs as a third or fourth medical coverage option during the early years of HSAs now are consolidating coverage and sponsoring only one or two plans, including an HSA program. In this environment, more employees are enrolling in the low-premium coverage with an HSA, accepting a higher level of self-insurance (the deductible), and directing their premium savings to a tax-advantaged account to reimburse expenses for which they are financially responsible.

Second, a growing (but still small) number of employers are adopting a defined-contribution approach to funding their employees' medical insurance.

Employers often pay a percentage of the premium (defined benefit) of each plan that they offer. For example, an employer may pay 70% of the premium of each of two options priced at $1,500 and $1,700 per month for family coverage. The employee pays 30%. The employee pays $60 per month more for the more expensive coverage.

Today, more and more employers are paying a fixed-dollar amount to each employee. In the preceding example, whether the employer subsidy is $1,000 or $1,200 or $1,400, the employee who wants to "buy up" to the richer coverage must pay the entire $200 difference, rather than $60 under the defined-benefit approach.

Defined contribution accelerates adoption of HSA-qualified plans as more employees see the benefit of choosing the lower premium (usually the HSA-qualified plan with a higher deductible) and depositing their premium difference in an HSA to reimburse their out-of-pocket expenses tax-free.

Third, more people are purchasing coverage in the individual market, either directly from insurers or through ACA marketplaces. This situation is an extreme example of defined contribution, as discussed in the preceding paragraphs, since these consumers are responsible for the entire premium. These consumers, without a large employer subsidy, are more likely to "right-size" their insurance (balance premiums and out-of-pocket financial responsibility in a rational manner) than are individuals whose employers subsidize the difference in premium.

Fourth, because of ACA limitations on medical underwriting, insurers manage risk by offering plans in the individual and small-group markets with far higher cost-sharing than before. According to the Kaiser Family Foundation's annual survey, in 2018 the average cost-sharing based on enrollment in Silver (most popular) and Bronze (lowest premium) plans is:

	Silver	Bronze
Deductible—self-only	$4,033	$5,777
Out-of-pocket maximum—self-only	$6,863	$7,058
Deductible—family	$8,292	$11,555
Out-of-pocket maximum—family	$13,725	$14,115

With these levels of deductible and the introduction of in-network coinsurance—which increases patients' financial responsibility—people need HSAs to help them reduce the effect of their out-of-pocket costs by 30% on average.

As noted earlier, at the end of 2017 there were about 22 million HSAs holding balances of about $50 billion. These figures pale when compared to balances in retirement plans, which have a longer history and generally higher annual contribution limits. Viewed from a different angle, the $50 billion puts total HSA balances on par with the gross domestic product (GDP) of Alaska, which ranks 46th in state GDP, ahead of South Dakota, Montana, Wyoming, and Vermont.

The average HSA has a balance of about $2,000. Among account owners who invest (about one in 10 today), the average balance exceeds $14,000. So even though most current HSA owners use their HSAs as transactional accounts to reimburse current qualified expenses, a small, growing percentage of owners realize that HSAs are superior to other investment options because HSAs are tax-perfect. This figure is bound to increase as HSA adoption becomes more widespread, balances grow over time, and advising professionals add their voices to the choir hailing the investment virtues of HSAs. And HSA owners will strengthen their financial position as a result.

HSAs are entering the financial mainstream. Though total assets are a fraction of the wealth that individuals have accumulated in retirement plans, analysts who have studied the growth of IRAs (which began nearly three decades before the introduction of HSAs) and 401(k) plans observe an early growth pattern similar to that of HSAs.

HSAs won't overtake 401(k) plans in total assets. HSAs have more stringent eligibility requirements, their annual contribution limits are lower, and owners can enjoy immediate tax benefits with tax-free distributions for qualified expenses. What matters to you and your clients isn't the absolute size of the relative asset bases, but rather how your clients use HSAs to supplement their retirement savings, build medical equity, and diversify their tax liability.

The big question is whether you're prepared to counsel your clients about incorporating HSAs into their long-term financial strategy—or whether another advisor will!

CHAPTER 2

Coverage Determines the Opportunity

Not every one of your clients can contribute to an HSA under current law. That's unfortunate. It's important for you to be able to identify those clients who have this opportunity and to determine how they can make the most of it.

In this chapter, you can explore

- the information that you need to uncover from your clients to determine whether their employers offer a viable HSA program;
- how to assess coverage choices to determine which option helps clients best meet their immediate medical-coverage needs and their short- and long-term financial objectives;
- the basic design parameters of an HSA-qualified medical plan, as set by federal tax law;
- the differences in financial responsibility for coverage under a traditional medical plan and HSA-qualified coverage; and
- how to model out-of-pocket financial responsibility, premiums, and tax savings to evaluate options properly.

Most people who work for companies with more than 100 or so employees have access to workplace-based retirement programs, often with an employer match. Nearly every American under age 65 can open and contribute to an IRA—and many can make tax-deductible contributions. Many Americans have access to a Roth IRA, which allows tax-free distributions.

HSAs are different. For perhaps the first time, you need to provide your clients with some general guidance on their medical coverage. Your clients must understand the power of an HSA as a retirement savings account. They're unlikely to hear more than five minutes' worth of information about HSA basics during the typical 60- to 90-minute annual open-enrollment presentation on medical, dental, vision, life insurance, long- and short-term disability coverage options, and perhaps even the company retirement plan.

That simply isn't enough time to present the value of HSAs. And the handful of slides related to the benefits of HSAs typically focus on reimbursement of immediate expenses rather than positioning HSAs as opportunities to build medical equity.

In a best-case open-enrollment scenario, your clients have access to a live presentation or webinar perhaps an hour long that goes into detail on HSA rules about eligibility, contributions, and distributions (topics examined in depth in Sections IV and V of this book). They almost certainly don't learn anything about how to use their HSAs strategically as a long-term account to build medical equity.

That's unfortunate. As you'll learn throughout this book, HSAs represent a unique opportunity. Most people don't begin to realize the power of these accounts. You must don a new hat and begin to discuss medical-plan options with your clients to determine whether they have access to an HSA program.

You must don a new hat and begin to discuss medical-plan options with your clients.

You're not an insurance broker or benefits advisor. That's OK. You don't need the in-depth knowledge that these professionals have acquired about employee benefits. Good insurance brokers and benefits advisors are as knowledgeable within their professional sphere as you are within yours. And you shouldn't be expected to offer the level of counsel that they provide to their clients about benefit options.

You add value by providing your clients with essential information not about their medical coverage, but about the implications of that coverage. It's unfortunate when a well-intentioned and knowledgeable employee reviews her two medical options, estimates her utilization accurately, and chooses the plan that costs her $500 less per year in a year of high medical utilization while she contributes $15,000 to her traditional 401(k) plan. She could participate in an HSA program, reduce her traditional 401(k) plan contribution to $12,000, and contribute an additional $3,000 to her HSA for retirement medical costs.

And the $500 difference in total medical costs? That's a worst-case scenario. Unless she (or a family member) has a chronic condition or she has very accident-prone children, she's unlikely to reach her out-of-pocket maximum regularly and actually pay out an additional $500 every year.

By incorporating an HSA into her retirement planning and directing $3,000 of retirement savings into the account, she would immediately save $229.50 in payroll taxes (almost half the additional $500 worst-case cost of the plan). After 30 years and 6% annual investment gains, she would have an additional $4,200 in spending power for the same $3,000 contribution because (1) an additional $229.50 goes to work immediately and (2) her distributions for qualified expenses are untaxed in an HSA but subject to income taxes (this model assumes a 20% marginal income tax rate in retirement).

If she diverts $3,000 of retirement contributions from her traditional 401(k) plan to an HSA for 30 years with 6% annual growth and a 20% marginal income tax rate in retirement, her spending power for retirement medical services increases by more than $48,000 versus making the same $3,000 annual contribution to a traditional 401(k) plan or IRA.

This is precisely why it's so important for you to help your clients apply basic financial analysis to their choice of medical coverage. The same level of saving can produce dramatically different financial results based on nothing more than the account into which your client directs those savings.

Here is a common scenario: An employer offers two medical plans, one with a $1,000 deductible with an employee premium (payroll deduction) of $300 per month and another with a $3,000 deductible with a premium of $200 per month and a tax-free employer contribution of $100 per month to an HSA. Most employees don't bother to do the math. Instead, they look at the deductibles, think "I can't afford a $3,000 deductible if I get sick or hurt," and choose the low-deductible plan.

You can help this client evaluate the financial aspects of the two choices:

Feature	1000 Plan	3000 Plan	Dollar Difference
Deductible	$1,000	$3,000	–$2,000
Premium	$3,600	$2,800	$800
Employer contribution to HSA	$0	$1,200	$1,200
Cost with $1,000 claims	$4,600	$3,000	$1,600
Cost with $2,000 claims	$4,600	$4,000	$600
Cost with $3,000 claims	$4,600	$5,000	–$400
Cost with $1 million claims	$4,600	$5,000	–$400

Note: The dollar differences on the cost lines aren't adjusted to reflect tax savings, which increase the positive number by about 25% and reduces the negative numbers by a similar amount.

A benefits advisor can break down each plan with respect to benefits covered and referrals and authorizations needed to access certain care, prescription drug formularies, networks, and other distinguishing characteristics.

The value that you bring in guiding a client through the financial differences between the plans is important and unduplicated by anyone in the benefits-selection process. Employees typically renew their current plan during open enrollment (often with a passive enrollment, which means that the employer automatically renews the choices made last year unless the employee takes action). In fact, a recent AFLAC survey showed that 92% of employees re-enroll in their current election (or their inactions triggers an automatic renewal) with little engagement. Open enrollment is a period when employees make a number of decisions about health coverage without any thought to the long-term financial implications of their options and decisions.

It may make sense for an individual to remain enrolled in the plan with the $1,000 deductible for a variety of good medical and financial reasons. One individual may see doctors only infrequently but have several moderately priced prescriptions for a chronic condition that are covered with lower out-of-pocket costs on the plan with the $1,000 deductible. Another may be having a baby at a hospital and thus is certain to incur at least $3,000 in deductible claims, which makes the $1,000-deductible plan more attractive that year.

On the other hand, in many cases it makes financial sense for someone to enroll in coverage that offers a lower premium in exchange for more out-of-pocket responsibility when she incurs a claim. Consumers make this choice intelligently when they consider the premium-versus-deductible trade-off on their auto, homeowners, renters, and long-term disability insurance. They understand the nature of this trade-off when it comes to other insurance, but they typically don't apply the same *insurance* logic when it comes to employer-based medical coverage.

Your clients need your help blending the financial and medical. The difference between making the best decision with the information that they possess and the perspective that you can provide may be worth—literally—tens of thousands of dollars in retirement, as you'll see in later chapters.

HSA-Qualified Medical Coverage

Section IV takes a deep dive into HSA rules. In particular, Chapter 16, *HSA-Qualified Medical Plan,* provides detailed information about the design of these plans. HSA-qualified coverage is the foundational element of a client's ability to open and contribute to an HSA.

Here are the salient features of an HSA-qualified medical plan:

- All non-preventive services are subject to the deductible.
- The deductible can't be less than $1,350 for clients with self-only (individual) coverage or less than $2,700 for clients with family coverage (and is usually more) in 2018 or 2019. Family coverage is defined as a policy that covers two or more people, even if the insurer or employer defines a particular coverage level differently (such as *employee+spouse* or *employee+child[ren]*). These figures are adjusted annually to reflect price changes and consumer substitution of goods in the overall economy (chained CPI), not in medical costs (which rise, on average, at about twice the rate of overall consumer prices).
    - If the family deductible includes a per-person maximum (such as a $6,000 family deductible, with a cap of $3,000 on any family member's individual responsibility), the individual maximum can't be less than $2,700 in 2019.
- The total 2019 out-of-pocket maximum can't exceed $6,750 for self-only coverage or $13,500 for family coverage (and is nearly always less). These figures include all covered cost-sharing, including deductibles, coinsurance,

and copays. It applies to in-network services only and excludes the following: penalties, out-of-pocket costs for services not covered or services beyond plan limits, and charges in excess of allowable charges for services.

    - On a family contract, no family member can incur more than $7,900 of covered expenses, per a provision in the ACA. This figure is adjusted annually for inflation.

- Select preventive services can be covered below the deductible. Certain preventive services are covered in full through provisions of the ACA. Other preventive services can be covered in full, subject to lesser cost-sharing (such as a copay), or applied to the deductible. Preventive prescription drugs can also be covered below the deductible. The IRS has provided only limited guidance on this topic, and insurers take a range of different approaches to preventive prescription drugs.

Key Plan Design Elements

Though you aren't a benefits advisor, you can help your clients by identifying certain elements of the plan design that have a substantial effect on their out-of-pocket exposure. Two medical plans that look alike at first glance may have dramatically different potential out-of-pocket costs. And dissimilar plans may have total costs that make one plan look inferior at first glance but superior once you and your client calculate all costs.

> Example: *A plan offers $3,000/$6,000 deductible with 20% coinsurance up to $6,000/$12,000.*

This is a common thumbnail sketch of a benefit design. The deductible is $3,000/$6,000. The deductible for self-only coverage is $3,000. But it's not clear whether the family contract has an aggregate (umbrella) deductible of $6,000 (which means that any single family member or combination of family members can satisfy the entire $6,000 deductible alone) or whether each family member's deductible responsibility is capped at $3,000 (an embedded deductible) and the family has a $6,000 cap. Knowing whether the deductible is embedded or aggregate is important, particularly when the family has one high utilizer. The difference is a $3,000 or $6,000 deductible ceiling for that family member.

After the deductible, the insurer then shares allowable charges in an 80:20 ratio. So, in this plan, if a client with self-only coverage has a $20,000 hospital stay, she pays a $3,000 deductible, then is assessed 20% coinsurance on the remaining $17,000 balance, or $3,400. Since her out-of-pocket maximum is $6,000, she pays only $3,000 in coinsurance. Her insurer then pays all remaining covered expenses in full for the rest of the plan year.

Example: *Luca has two plan options for family coverage. Plan A has a $3,000 family deductible with 20% coinsurance to a $10,000 out-of-pocket maximum and a $700 monthly premium. It's not an HSA-qualified plan. Plan B, which is HSA-qualified, has a $6,000 family deductible with an out-of-pocket maximum of $6,000 and a $550 monthly premium. His gut tells him to choose the plan with the lower deductible. He says he's willing to spend a little more in premium each month to buy the plan with the lower deductible and thereby sleep more soundly at night.*

Most people facing these options choose Plan A because they don't know how they'd pay as much as $6,000 in deductible expenses in Plan B. This is where a good benefits advisor can provide perspective on claims utilization that you don't have. Nevertheless, you can provide a general financial perspective that goes something like this:

Worst-Case Scenario ($10,000 in covered expenses):

	Plan A	Plan B	Difference
Employee premium	$8,400	$6,600	–$1,800
Total exposure (worst case)	$10,000	$6,000	–$4,000
Total cost—worst case	**$18,400**	**$12,600**	**–$5,400**

So, in a worst-case scenario (say, cancer treatment or an extended inpatient hospital stay), the plan with the *higher deductible* is a *better* financial option in this example. And it's not just a little better—it's better by $5,400 per year, or $450 per month. That's a huge savings and funds an HSA nicely!

Now consider an ideal scenario.

Best-Case Scenario ($0 deductible expenses):

	Plan A	Plan B	Difference
Employee premium	$8,400	$ 6,600	–$1,800
Total exposure (best case)	$0	$0	$0
Total cost—best case	**$8,400**	**$6,600**	**–$1,800**

This scenario is somewhat unrealistic. In a typical year, only about 5% of families incur no deductible expenses (though more than a quarter of people with self-only coverage incur none). It's included to illustrate a point. What matters isn't just the value of the deductible, but also the premium. For employees whose share of their premium is deducted from their paychecks, the premium is often invisible to them—and thus often ignored.

Now let's move to more realistic scenarios—ones within a range that many of your clients with family coverage can expect to experience in a typical year.

Middle-Case Scenario 1 ($4,000 of Qualified Expenses):

	Plan A	Plan B	Difference
Employee premium	$8,400	$6,600	–$1,800
Total exposure	$3,200	$4,000	+$800
Total cost—middle-case 1	**$11,600**	**$10,600**	**–$1,000**

Middle-Case Scenario 2 ($8,000 of Qualified Expenses):

	Plan A	Plan B	Difference
Employee premium	$8,400	$6,600	–$1,800
Total exposure	$4,000	$6,000	+$2,000
Total cost—middle-case 2	**$12,400**	**$11,600**	**+$200**

You can play with the dollar values of middle-case scenarios all day. Depending on the dollar amount, one plan will be slightly better than the other. The math is going to vary depending on the cost-sharing elements of each option and the amount of premium paid by employees.

The point of this exercise is to focus on the *financial*, rather than the medical, consequences of choosing a particular plan. The two key financial variables to total cost of coverage are (1) the premium and (2) actual claims. One variable—the premium—is known up front and doesn't change during the year. The other—claims incurred—is unknowable for clients unless they have a chronic condition that's nearly guaranteed to satisfy the out-of-pocket maximum annually.

A third variable not introduced into the equation is tax savings. HSA contributions reduce the total cost of Plan B relative to Plan A because contributions aren't subject to federal payroll taxes, federal income taxes and (in most cases) state income taxes. Each $1,000 contributed to an HSA, whether to reimburse current qualified expenses or save for future qualified expenses, generates between $200 and $350 in tax savings. In typical "middle cases" this variable swings the financial advantage solidly to the HSA-qualified coverage.

HSA-Qualified Plans Versus Traditional Coverage

Defining *traditional* coverage is difficult. It's a moving target. A decade ago, traditional coverage meant a plan with either a low ($250/$500) or no deductible and copays for office visits, emergency services, and two or three tiers of prescription drugs. The no-deductible options frequently included higher copays for day surgery (often $250 to $500) and inpatient services (often $500 to $1,000).

Today, traditional coverage typically includes higher deductibles (often $1,000/$2,000 at larger companies and an average of more than $2,000/$4,000 at companies with 50 or fewer employees), copays for office visits, and copays or coinsurance (or both, depending on coverage tier) for five or six tiers of prescription-drug coverage.

Against this backdrop, HSA-qualified plans typically differ in the following ways:

- In traditional coverage, diagnostic ("sick") office visits are usually reimbursed in full by insurance after a flat-dollar copay on traditional coverage. In contrast, they are subject to the deductible on HSA-qualified plans. A growing number of traditional plans charge higher copays for specialty care. A patient with traditional coverage may pay $25 of a $145 primary-care visit and $50 of a $235 specialist visit. In contrast, a patient covered by an HSA-qualified plan pays the full $145 or $235 until she satisfies her deductible.
- Traditional plans typically cover prescription drugs in full after a copay (and, increasingly, coinsurance on higher tiers of coverage). These prescriptions are subject to the deductible on HSA-qualified plans. Some HSA-qualified plans cover certain preventive prescriptions below the deductible (typically with copays). After the deductible, HSA-qualified plans usually cover prescriptions either in full (higher deductible plans) or subject to copay (lower deductible plans).
- Either plan may impose in-network coinsurance after the deductible. This design was not common a decade ago, but increasingly it has become another tool to slow the rate of increase in premiums. In the small-group

market (fewer than 50 employees), coinsurance has become an important tool to help insurers keep their plan offerings within the narrow range of actuarial values permitted under the ACA.

- Traditional plans cover day surgery and inpatient services subject to either a copay (often $500 to $1,000) or a deductible. These services are always subject to the deductible on an HSA-qualified plan.

Again, your job isn't to become a benefits expert. The more that you can apply your financial expertise at the intersection of your clients' medical coverage and financial strategy, the better you can advise them in using *all* the tools at their disposal. Your recognition of this important tool—medical coverage—will help your clients understand the possibility that not just the investment, but also the medical coverage, decisions that they make today can have a profound effect on their long-term financial health.

CHAPTER 3

Ten Great Reasons to Own an HSA

It's difficult to overstate the benefits of owning an HSA. HSAs are incredibly powerful and flexible financial accounts that deliver benefits to your clients (and, ideally, to you as well) whether they want to enjoy the full range of tax advantages immediately or defer some tax savings until later in life.

HSAs straddle the fence between medical reimbursement programs such as Health FSAs and HRAs, and retirement accounts such as traditional and Roth IRAs and 401(k) plans. In doing so, HSAs offer owners the principal advantages that those reimbursement programs and retirement plans deliver. Though the other plans are geared toward *either* medical reimbursement *or* retirement savings, HSA owners can use their account to mimic *both* programs, with the flexibility to alter course at any time.

In this chapter, you'll read about

- characteristics of HSAs that make them popular, and
- how HSAs compare with other medical reimbursement and retirement options.

Here are 10 great reasons to own an HSA:

1. HSAs Are a Tax-*Perfect* Account

As the author sat next to a representative of one of the largest investment-management firms in the world several years ago, the conversation turned to HSAs. When the topic of the triple-tax advantages of an HSA came up, the mutual-fund representative stated, "We don't even use the word *tax-advantaged* to describe HSA, as we do with our retirement accounts. We simply refer to HSAs as *tax-perfect* accounts."

Tax-perfect. What a perfect description.

HSAs are unlike any other financial account to which individual investors have access. Let's look at the tax treatment of certain accounts to which Americans may contribute during their working years to see the power of HSAs:

Key Features of HSAs and Popular Retirement Plans

	Contributions	Account Growth	Distributions*
HSA	Tax-free	Tax-free	Tax-free
Traditional 401(k) plan	Income tax-free. Payroll taxes apply.	Tax-free	Income taxes apply.
Roth 401(k) plan	Income and payroll taxes apply.	Tax-free	Tax-free
Traditional IRA	Usually tax-free	Tax-free	Income taxes apply.
Roth IRA	Income and payroll taxes apply.	Tax-free	Tax-free
Health FSA	Tax-free	Not applicable.	Tax-free

* Many accounts place restrictions on distributions in order for them to qualify as tax-free.

Among these accounts, only HSAs allow individuals to make tax-free contributions, accumulate balances tax-free, *and* make tax-free distributions (for qualified expenses). The difference between a *triple*-tax-free and a *double*-tax-free account is enormous over time.

In Chapter 4, *Building Medical Equity*, you'll find models of the effect of tax friction on these various accounts. You'll see how HSA owners end up with more purchasing power in retirement than their contemporaries who make equal sacrifices of current consumption to invest in either traditional 401(k) IRA plans, or Roth 401(k) or IRA plans.

2. HSA Owners Don't Face a Year-End *Use-It-or-Lose-It* Choice

Many employees and advising professionals are familiar with a Health FSA. Employers offer these accounts to help employees manage their out-of-pocket financial responsibility for a wide range of health-related items. Health FSAs offer the same tax advantages as HSAs: Individuals contribute on a pre-tax basis and withdraw funds tax-free for qualified expenses.

A key difference is that Health FSAs are annual reimbursement programs, not long-term asset-accumulation accounts like HSAs. Participants must spend their Health FSA balances within the plan year or forfeit the balance back to their employer, the plan sponsor.

In recent years, changes to federal tax law have mitigated the effect of use-it-or-lose-it somewhat. Employers can offer a 2½-month grace period during which participants may continue to incur and reimburse qualified expenses. Think of the grace period as an opportunity to carry over *unlimited balances* for a *limited period of time.*

Alternatively, employers can amend their Health FSAs to allow participants to carry over up to $500 of unused balances into the following new 12-month plan year. Think of the carryover as an opportunity to carry over *limited balances* for an *unlimited period of time.*

Though these plan extenders help employees avoid or reduce balance forfeitures, they don't change the fundamental structure of a Health FSA. It remains an annual reimbursement program.

In contrast, HSAs aren't time-bound. Your clients can use them as they use a Health FSA—to reimburse current expenses now to enjoy immediate tax savings. In addition, they can use their HSA as a long-term account to build medical equity that they can tap tax-free in the future for the same wide range of qualified expenses. And best of all, they don't have to declare themselves a *spender* or a *saver* when they own an HSA. They are free to determine an appropriate strategy with each contribution and each expense that is qualified for tax-free reimbursement.

HSA owners don't need to be creative at the end of the year to find practical ways to spend their unused balances on qualified expenses, as Health FSA owners must often do. They can roll over unlimited balances to pay their portion of real medically necessary services in the future—whether the future is the following year or decades hence.

3. HSA Owners Can Change Contributions

One serious limitation of Health FSA is that participants must make a binding prospective election before the beginning of the plan year. They must estimate with a high degree of accuracy how much they expect to spend on Health FSA-qualified items during the following 12 months. Will they or a family member end up in the hospital or in need of an MRI, an expensive blood test, physical therapy, or a cardiac catheterization—or not? Will they or a family member need to replace a pair of expensive glasses—or not? Will they or a family member need major dental work like a root canal, crown, or implant (which even good dental insurance covers only in part—usually 50%)—or not?

Health FSA participants who make elections in excess of their needs risk forfeiting their remaining balance. In contrast, if they elect an amount less than the maximum and exhaust their funds before they reimburse all their qualified expenses, they don't forfeit balances, but they lose the opportunity to enjoy additional tax savings. Either way, they risk a loss.

Only two categories of Health FSA participants don't face these potential losses. One group includes those who know they'll incur expenses at least equal to their plan's maximum election, make that election, and actually incur the projected expenses. The other group includes the clairvoyant—and they'd be better served using their powers of prophecy to win big lottery jackpots rather than gain the equivalent of a fraction of those winnings in tax savings.

HSAs work differently. HSA owners aren't required to make a binding annual election. They can change their pre-tax payroll contributions as often as their employer allows. And they can make personal tax-deductible contributions at any time in any amount (up to their annual contribution limit). With this flexibility, HSA owners can increase their contributions when they incur higher expenses—they can even make the contributions after they know exactly how much they owe. And they can decrease them when they believe that they have adequate balances and want to redirect a portion of their HSA contributions to other personal financial priorities.

Health FSAs require participants to project their needs and can punish them when they're wrong. HSA owners don't have to be clairvoyant. Instead, they can adjust their balances up or down during the year as their expenses and savings goals change.

4. HSA Owners Don't Have to Provide Immediate Substantiation

The introduction of debit cards in the early 2000s has made Health FSAs much more popular and convenient for participants. The cards are coded by merchant category, connect in real-time to identify purchased items as FSA-qualified, and match medical copays and previously documented recurring payments. These measures ensure that participants spend funds on eligible items only. And some Health FSA administrators receive claims files from insurers that match card payments with qualified deductible and coinsurance expenses.

The system isn't perfect, however. A typical card allows payment at a dentist office or optical shop because those locations sell many products and services that are qualified expenses. But not all services and products at these locations constitute qualified expenses. For example, both teeth whitening and non-prescription sunglasses are considered cosmetic—not medically necessary—and therefore not qualified expenses.

HSA owners aren't required to make a binding annual election.

Health FSA administrators must ensure that all reimbursements are for qualified expenses. When your client swipes her debit card at a dentist's office or optometrist's shop, she may receive a request from the Health FSA administrator to substantiate the purchase. She must submit documentation showing the name of the patient, date of service, the actual service, and the amount paid.

Though these requests aren't common—typically fewer than 10% of total purchases require follow-up substantiation when the administrator uses all available technologies to limit requests—they tend to annoy typical Health FSA participants out of proportion to their actual frequency.

In contrast, federal tax law assigns responsibility for HSA compliance to individual HSA owners. They must know whether a distribution is for a qualified expense (tax-free) or not (included in taxable income and subject to an additional 20% tax if the HSA owner is under age 65 and not disabled). The HSA administrator won't ever request follow-up documentation.

HSA owners aren't off the hook, however. They self-report their activity on their personal income tax return. They should keep records (such as an insurer's Explanations of Benefits, detailed dental bills, receipts for prescription glasses and vision-correction surgery, and copies of detailed cash-register receipts) as they would to document any other tax deduction in case the IRS audits their personal income tax return.

Some HSA owners maintain meticulous files of paperwork. Others use the shoe-box method, stuffing all receipts and other paperwork into a box that they need to organize only if audited. Your millennial clients probably use a virtual shoebox method already for other financial items and can add HSA receipts to that system.

5. HSA Owners Face No Reimbursement Deadline

Some of the most anxious moments in Health FSA participants' lives occur in the last days of the third month after the end of their Health FSA plan year. That's normally the deadline for submitting all reimbursement claims for the plan year. (Employers can set shorter or longer reimbursement deadlines, but three months is the industry standard and default.)

Not only are Health FSA participants anxious themselves, but they're carriers of anxiety as well. Often, they must call an optical shop to have an invoice e-mailed to them, swing by the pharmacy to request a print-out of all prescriptions filled and the patient cost for each family member during the prior year, and ask their dentist or dental insurer for pre-treatment estimates and Explanations of Benefit to document their purchases of qualified expenses.

They have a lot at risk. Every dollar of reimbursement to which they're entitled but don't claim is a dollar lost. The financial stakes are high.

In contrast, HSA owners face no deadlines. Once they become HSA-eligible and establish their accounts, HSA owners can reimburse any subsequent qualified expense at any point in the future—the following month, the following year, or even decades later. This feature of an HSA ensures that owners who are good record-keepers never lose an opportunity to reimburse a qualified expense. And owners who aren't good at retaining receipts and Explanations of Benefits can use funds that could have reimbursed current qualified expenses on future qualified expenses because they don't forfeit balances and don't face a reimbursement deadline.

HSA owners can reimburse any subsequent qualified expense at any point in the future.

Some people may defend the substantiation time constraints imposed by a Health FSA. They could argue that such a deadline spurs participants to action during a time period when a merchant or health-care provider can reasonably be expected to maintain records that are accessible. In contrast, an HSA owner looking for the record of a qualified dental expense three years ago may find that the dentist has retired or installed a new patient-management information system.

6. HSA Owners Build Medical Equity

Because HSAs are personal financial accounts rather than annual reimbursement programs, they provide owners with an opportunity to build medical equity. What is *medical equity*? It's simply a term for assets (equity) that a person puts aside to pay for future qualified (medical) expenses.

Of course, financially responsible people can build equity many ways. They can build their own business, invest in public or private companies, invest in real estate, or lend their savings. And once they build their equity—receiving a return *on* and *of* their investments—they can spend the accumulated gains on medical expenses.

What's different about the medical equity that investors accumulate in their HSAs is that, as you've already learned, it's *never* subject to taxes. The triple-tax-free nature of HSAs ensures that your clients build medical equity in the most efficient manner possible, without experiencing the friction that taxes introduce to all other forms of building equity. HSAs give long-term savers and investors maximum future spending power for each dollar of contribution that they make to their HSAs.

Why is medical equity so important? In a January 2018 study, the Kaiser Family Foundation estimated that Medicare beneficiaries' average out-of-pocket spending on medical care will increase from 41% of their Social Security checks in 2013 to 50% by 2030. For many Americans, Social Security is their only (or by far their largest) source of retirement income to pay for housing, utilities, food, clothing, transportation, entertainment, and taxes. This survey suggests that they'll spend half their total monthly Social Security benefit on Medicare premiums and cost-sharing, dental, vision, and other health-related services.

To put these numbers in perspective, consider a projection by mutual-fund giant Fidelity®: Out-of-pocket medical costs for a couple retiring at age 65 in 2018 are projected at $280,000 in retirement. This number includes Medicare premiums, Medicare cost-sharing, and out-of-pocket payments for items that aren't covered, such as dental and vision services, and over-the-counter drugs, equipment, and supplies. It doesn't include nursing-home or long-term care costs, which can easily drive up the number by $100,000 or more for every year in those facilities.

That projected $280,000 figure is incomprehensible to most retirees. The concept is more manageable for those who plan ahead and can pay at least a portion of those expenses tax-free from an HSA rather than after-tax from a traditional IRA or 401(k) plan.

Building a triple-tax-free war chest must be a clear priority for your clients when they plan for retirement.

7. HSAs Are Portable

Health FSAs and HRAs are employer-sponsored notional accounts. Individuals can't participate in either program unless their employer offers a workplace program and they satisfy eligibility requirements. When they leave employment, they typically can't continue to participate in and benefit from these plans (unless they're eligible to continue their coverage by exercising their COBRA rights).

In contrast, an HSA is a financial account owned by an individual and not tied to an employer. This concept is confusing because most individuals are introduced to and enroll in an HSA program at work. An employer offers the HSA-qualified medical plan, typically chooses an HSA administrator with which to work exclusively, generally modifies its Cafeteria Plan to allow employees to make pre-tax payroll contributions to their HSAs, and often provides an employer contribution.

In these respects, an HSA looks like an employer-sponsored benefit plan. It's not, however. It's an account in the employee's (not the employer's) name that loses no value and places no restrictions on an individual who subsequently leaves employment. Former employees can keep their HSAs with their employer's preferred administrator partner (unless the administrator doesn't maintain HSAs that aren't employment based, which is rare) or move the balances to a different administrator that offers lower fees, more or better investment options, or better customer service. HSA owners make these decisions and arrangements without consulting a former employer, since HSAs aren't tied to or controlled by that former employer.

8. HSAs Are Flexible

As already noted, people must be employed to enroll in a Health FSA or HRA. This isn't true for an HSA. Eligibility for an HSA is based solely on requirements not related to employment. This feature is an especially welcome benefit to the millions of Americans who purchase their medical insurance in the nongroup market. An HSA is the only tax-advantaged medical reimbursement account that your clients can open and own if they're self-employed or covered by non-employer-based medical insurance.

Individuals must have earned income to contribute to a traditional or Roth IRA. No income, no contribution. In contrast, HSA owners can fund their HSA with investment income, rental income, gifts, savings, liquidated investments, proceeds from the sale of their baseball card collection, or legal gambling winnings.

A Health FSA can reimburse only current expenses. IRAs and 401(k) plans are designed to save money for retirement. HSA owners can choose for each qualified expense whether to enjoy all tax savings now—by reimbursing the expense tax-free—or later. If they pay for the qualified expense with personal funds now, they allow their HSA balances to grow tax-free for future tax-free distribution.

9. An HSA Is a Great Retirement Account Option

HSAs aren't retirement accounts, like traditional and Roth IRAs, traditional and Roth 401(k) plans, SEP IRAs, SIMPLE IRAs, and a handful of other programs designed to encourage individuals to save for retirement living expenses by extending some tax advantages to the accounts.

You've already seen many of the advantages that the triple-tax-free design of an HSA offers. Another important benefit is that HSA contributions saved for retirement don't count against the maximum that individuals can deposit annually into traditional retirement accounts. If married and not yet age 50, your forward-thinking clients can contribute up to $19,000 (2019 figure) into a 401(k) plan and still contribute another $7,000 (2019 maximum contribution figure for family medical coverage) to an HSA, even if they plan to use every dollar that they contribute to an HSA to build medical equity to reimburse qualified expenses in retirement.

HSAs also have three additional important characteristics that separate them from some retirement accounts.

- HSA contributions made on a pre-tax basis through an employer's Cafeteria Plan aren't subject to payroll taxes, as 401(k) plan contributions are.

Both employer and employee save 7.65%, then 1.45% each on income above $128,400 (2018 figure) when an HSA owner contributes a dollar to her HSA rather than her 401(k) plan. Note that this also means that the employer reports a lower income figure to the Social Security Administration for the purpose of calculating future Social Security benefits. The effect on your clients probably is, at most, minimal, but it's something to consider when evaluating where and how (pre-tax payroll or deductible contributions) your clients should invest their next dollar of retirement savings.

- HSAs don't have to make Required Minimum Distributions (RMDs) in the year that the owner turns age 70½, unlike tax-deferred accounts such as traditional IRAs and traditional 401(k) plans.

- Because HSA distributions are reimbursements, they are excluded from the calculation of provisional income. This figure determines how much of your clients' Social Security benefits are taxed. In most cases, this advantage doesn't apply to your clients, as you provide them with counsel that probably produces income streams greater than the $44,000 annually (a figure not indexed for inflation) at which 85% of total Social Security benefits are taxed.

10. HSAs Outlive Their Owners

An HSA is a trust. This structure is important because HSAs don't die when their owners do. Because an HSA is a trust, balances are never lost, and HSAs owners determine to whom the assets inside their HSAs pass upon their death.

When individuals open an HSA, they name a beneficiary (or multiple beneficiaries) to receive the balances upon their death. They can change a designated beneficiary whenever they choose when they're alive. If they're married at their time of death and named a spouse as beneficiary, their HSA passes directly to the spouse. The spouse enjoys the same tax advantages as they did, including tax-free account growth and tax-free distributions for qualified expenses. Spouses who are beneficiaries of an HSA and who are HSA-eligible themselves can make additional pre-tax or tax-deductible contributions as well.

If the owner names anyone other than a current spouse as beneficiary, the trust is dissolved, the assets are liquidated, and the balance goes directly to the named beneficiary (or beneficiaries). These beneficiaries may incur an income tax liability as a result of receiving the balance. Funds are no longer contained within an HSA, so beneficiaries enjoy no additional tax benefits. But they can spend the money on whatever they choose without restriction and without tax consequences, since they pay any tax liability when they receive the money.

Thus, an HSA, like any other financial asset, allows your clients to leave a legacy to their loved ones. As with everything else tangible in life, they can't take it with them. They can, however, determine who receives it and in what form.

CHAPTER 4

Building Medical Equity

The term *medical equity* may be new to you, but the concept isn't. One of the largest expenses in retirement for nearly all Americans will be medical expenses. And the reality of the cost of care in retirement will shock many of them, but not until it's too late for them to develop and execute a plan.

In this chapter, you'll find

- a discussion of estimates of the cost of medical coverage in retirement,
- a review of the most popular retirement savings accounts and how they treat distributions for medical expenses, and
- an analysis of why HSAs are the best way to save for these expenses.

The Cost of Medical Care in Retirement

How much will a typical retiree spend on medical expenses during the remainder of her lifetime? It depends on whom you ask. As noted in the previous chapter, Fidelity® publishes an annual estimate that reflects medical inflation, medical technology, changes in the law (full implementation of the ACA led to a decline in the estimate in 2014), and changes in longevity. For a couple retiring in 2018 at age 65, the projected out-of-pocket cost is $280,000.

That figure looks absurdly high at first glance. After all, people age 65 and older have access to coverage through Medicare, typically with no (Part A) or low (Parts B and C) monthly premiums. But Medicare also shifts some costs to patients and doesn't cover many services that traditional pre-retirement employer-sponsored medical, dental, and vision coverage reimburses.

For example, premiums for Part B and Part D coverage, plus a Medicare Supplement plan, may be $350 per month, or $4,200 annually for each spouse. Add out-of-pocket expenses of perhaps $2,000 annually for Medicare cost-sharing, $1,500 for dental expenses, and $500 for vision services, and suddenly out-of-pocket expenses climb to $8,200 annually, or $16,400 for a couple. Let's pretend that figure is too high; instead, the husband incurs an average of $7,000 and the wife $5,000 in out-of-pocket expenses per year. Factor in 5% inflation and, after 20 years, they will have spent almost $400,000 on medical care.

Is a 5% inflation figure too high? Let's run the same model with a 4% inflation factor. The 20-year total declines to just over $375,000. Is 3% more realistic? The figure drops to $357,000.

Are the out-of-pocket expenses too high? Let's give them a total of $10,000 in financial responsibility per year, again with 5% inflation. The total after 20 years is $330,000. At 4% inflation, the figure drops to $312,000. Projected inflation has to drop to 3% to move the 20-year total under $300,000, at a cool $296,500.

Still not convinced? *Barron's* magazine commissioned HealthView Services, a firm that analyzes medical claims to provide financial advisors with data and tools, to estimate retirees' out-of-pocket medical expenses based on claims. That study showed that retirees who fall into Medicare's high-income tier ($214,000 to $267,000 in annual retirement income) can expect to pay $565,000 in medical expenses. The higher figure is due to the phase-out of Medicare premium subsidies (paid by taxpayers from general tax revenues, not dedicated payroll taxes) for high-income individuals.

Any way you look at it, medical expenses will be either the second highest (after housing) or highest expenses that the average retiree incurs. And most are woefully unprepared to face them.

Recall that the 2018 Kaiser Family Foundation study estimated that Medicare beneficiaries had out-of-pocket medical expenses equal to 41% of the average Social Security benefit in 2013. The study projects that figure to rise to 50% by 2030.

Of course, Social Security benefits represent only a portion of total retirement income (with percentages that vary wildly among beneficiaries). The report estimated that, in 2013, one-third of beneficiaries in traditional Medicare (and one half of those with incomes below $20,000) spent at least 20% of their total income on medical-related costs. That percentage is expected to rise to 42% of all beneficiaries by 2030.

The figures are indeed sobering.

Medical Equity

Medical equity represents assets set aside to pay health-care expenses in retirement. Medical equity has two components:

- total amount contributed to relevant accounts, and
- tax treatment of contributions to and distribution from these accounts.

Thus, a statement such as "My client is saving $4,000 annually for 30 years toward retirement medical costs" tells us little more than that the client is sacrificing immediate consumption and making a genuine effort to meet his projected retirement medical expenses. It doesn't tell us about the spending power that he'll enjoy in retirement or the strain that medical costs will place on his total retirement savings.

HSAs play a key role in building medical equity. Because HSAs are free of tax friction, they represent the most efficient means of accumulating assets to pay for retirement medical expenses. People who decided to forego the same amount of immediate consumption to save for retirement medical expenses end up with far different effective spending power in retirement, depending on nothing more than their choice of accounts into which to direct those savings.

The Comparative Power of HSAs

Let's focus on three mythical triplets, Ashley, Brett, and Chris. All three are raised in the same home by parents who emphasize the importance of living below one's means, paying oneself first, and building a nest egg for retirement.

They all take this message to heart—there are no financial rebels in this household! All three meet with competent financial advisors at age 37 (after paying off their student loans), understand the importance of saving for retirement medical expenses, and make a commitment to a plan. Each commits to saving $3,000 of earned income beginning that year and to increase that amount by $50 annually for the next 30 years.

Ashley opens and contributes to a Roth IRA. She's focused on the concept of tax diversification and appreciates the fact that Roth IRA (and Roth 401(k) plan) distributions aren't taxed, nor are gains within the account. She's willing to sacrifice the immediate tax benefit (her contributions are after-tax, and she faces a tax rate of 30% with federal and state income taxes and payroll taxes). As a result of the up-front taxes imposed, Ashley's net contribution to her Roth IRA is $2,100 in Year 1 (increasing by $35 annually thereafter to reflect the $50 annual increase adjusted for taxes).

Brett sacrifices $3,000 of immediate consumption and increases his contributions to his employer's traditional 401(k) plan (he could choose a traditional IRA instead) to build his retirement medical savings. His contributions are free from federal and state income taxes, though they are subject to the 7.65% payroll tax. Balances grow tax-free. His distributions are taxable as ordinary income—a price he's willing to accept to reduce his taxable income today. Brett's net contribution to his 401(k) plan is $2,770.50 in Year 1 (increasing by $46.17 annually thereafter to reflect the $50 increase adjusted for payroll taxes).

Chris's employer has just introduced an HSA program. After speaking to her financial advisor, she commits to contributing an extra $3,000 annually (beyond distributions to reimburse immediate qualified expenses tax-free) to her HSA. Her contributions are free from federal and state income taxes (except in Alabama, California, and New Jersey, the three states that impose state income taxes on HSA contributions). Her balances grow tax-free. Her distributions are tax-free as long as she withdraws funds for qualified expenses. Chris's full $3,000 contribution goes to work immediately without any taxes applied.

How do their accounts grow over the next 30 years, assuming a 6% annual growth rate? As you can see in the following graph, Ashley has accumulated about $228,500 in her Roth IRA after three decades. Brett has a balance of $304,200 in his 401(k) plan. And Chris has a balance of $329,400 in her HSA.

Account Growth after 30 Years

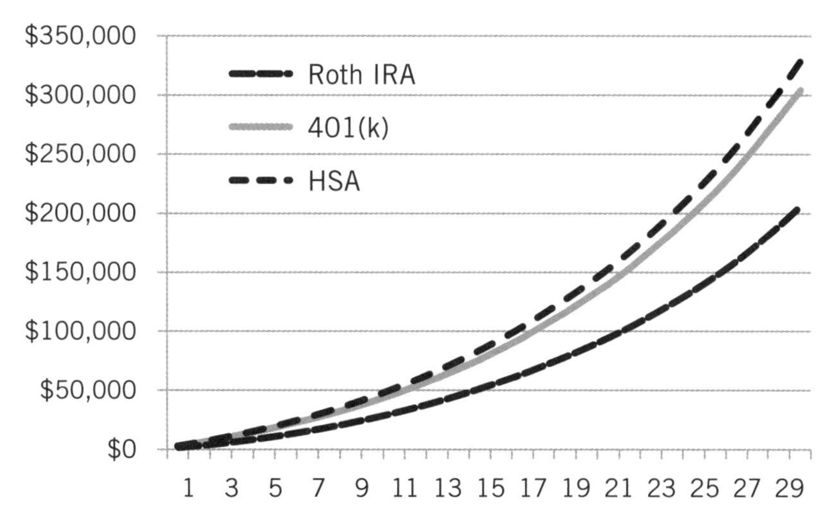

Note: Figures assume a $3,000 gross contribution in Year 1, increasing by $50 gross each year, and a 6% annual return. Marginal tax rate (federal and state income taxes, plus federal payroll taxes) is 30%.

But balances tell only part of the story. Remember, tax treatment is the second key variable in determining the spending power of each account at retirement.

After 30 years of building their balances, Ashley, Brett, and Chris all retire at age 67, their Social Security Full Retirement Age under current law. In retirement, they shed their previous professional commitments, but not the expenses of maintaining a lifestyle. Though they can reduce spending on certain items in their budgets (downsizing a home, purchasing less business attire, paying dues to fewer professional organizations, and driving less, for example), they have less control over the medical costs that they incur in retirement.

Most people's medical expenses rise as they age. Traditional Medicare covers fewer services than most employer-sponsored insurance and traditional Medicare cost-sharing is often higher (with no out-of-pocket limit on Part B). And older people, like older homes and older vehicles, on average cost more to maintain as they age.

This reality isn't news to Ashley, Brett, and Chris. In fact, it's why they made the commitment three decades earlier to focus part of their financial plan on building balances to pay their medical expenses in retirement.

What happens in retirement is fascinating. Let's assume that each sibling accumulates retirement medical expenses of $10,000 in Year 1, increasing by

5% per year, reflecting medical inflation, higher Medicare cost-sharing, and other factors. Let's also assume that the return on invested balances declines from 6% during the accumulation phase to 5% during the distribution phase as they shift assets to more conservative investments when return *of* the balance is more important than return *on* the balance.

In this scenario, all three siblings' balances grow initially as the 5% return exceeds annual withdrawals. Soon, balances in all three accounts begin an accelerating decline as the inflation-adjusted annual distribution to cover current medical expenses exceeds account growth.

Ashley continues to build the balance in her Roth IRA through her first four years of retirement, even after her initial $10,000 annual withdrawal (adjusted upward in subsequent years). She finally exhausts her balance in Year 24 of retirement, at age 91. At that point, her annual expenses have grown to more than $32,000.

Brett sees his 401(k) plan balance continue to increase through his first seven years in retirement. His beginning balance is nearly $75,000 more than Ashley's, so the 5% return on the higher asset base allows his account to continue to grow for two years longer than Ashley's.

Brett, however, must withdraw $12,500 in the first year to pay his $10,000 of expenses, since his distributions are subject to a 20% tax rate. Compounding inflation on this higher withdrawal figure takes its toll on Brett's balance. He depletes his account in Year 26 of retirement, at age 93, when his inflation-adjusted annual withdrawal has grown to more than $46,600.

That Ashley and Brett exhaust their account balances at about the same time is no surprise. Ashley's balance at the beginning of retirement was $75,000 lower because she paid taxes on her contributions, whereas Brett avoided income taxes (but not payroll taxes) on his contributions. When they began to distribute funds, the role of taxes reversed. Ashley enjoys tax-free distributions, whereas Brett's withdrawals are subject to taxes.

Why weren't the two accounts depleted at the same time? The assumptions were different: a 20% income tax rate on Brett's withdrawals in retirement and a net 23% difference in taxes on contributions for Ashley during her working years.

(Note: Ashley's tax rate was expressed as 30.65% to reflect an 18% federal income tax rate, 5% state income tax rate and 7.65% payroll tax rate. Both Ashley and Brett paid federal payroll taxes on their respective contributions to their Roth IRA and 401(k) plan, so the net rate that Ashley paid was 23%. A different assumption—such as Ashley's facing a 25% federal marginal income tax rate during her working years—would deplete Ashley's account far faster, since her annual after-tax contributions would be less.)

What about Chris? She has the highest balance of the three at retirement because her HSA contributions aren't subject to any federal or state income or payroll taxes. She continues to build her balance through her seventh year of retirement, at which point annual withdrawals (untaxed) exceed the return on remaining account assets. She finally exhausts her balance in her 34th year of retirement, at age 101.

The graph below illustrates Ashley's, Brett's and Chris's account growth and depletion from age 37 through the exhaustion of Chris's balance at age 101.

Account Growth and Exhaustion

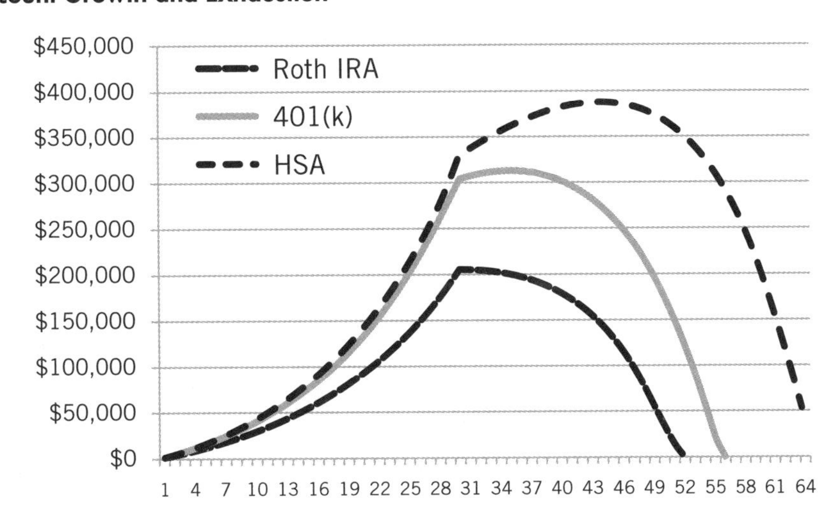

Why does Chris's balance last 10 years longer than Ashley's and eight years longer than Brett's?

Taxes. Pure and simple.

All other variables—gross contribution, rate of return, and annual retirement expenses—are held constant for all three siblings. The only difference is tax treatment of the three accounts. By choosing an account with no tax friction, Chris is able to reimburse more medical expenses tax-free than her brother or sister.

How much more? Here's where the analysis becomes even more interesting.

Let's assume that the triplets all live until age 101, the year that Chris exhausts her HSA. True, they probably all won't live that long (although the US population of centenarians has increased from more than 32,000 in 1980 to more than 50,000 in 2000 to more than 72,000 in 2014). But that's when Chris finally exhausts her HSA balance, so it's a logical point of comparison.

Let's look at the triplets' distributions for medical expenses beginning in the year that Ashley spends the last dollars of her retirement-account balance dedicated to medical reimbursement.

Total Withdrawals from Taxable Accounts after Designated Medical Equity Is Exhausted

Age	Expenses	Ashley	Brett	Chris
91	$27,860	$463		
92	$29,253	$36,556		
93	$30,715	$38,394	$23,553	
94	$32,251	$40,314	$40,314	
95	$33,864	$42,329	$42,329	
96	$35,557	$44,446	$44,446	
97	$37,335	$46,668	$46,668	
98	$39,201	$49,002	$49,002	
99	$41,161	$51,452	$51,452	
100	$43,219	$54,024	$54,024	
101	$45,380	$56,725	$56,725	$26,943
Total	**$395,796**	**$460,383**	**$408,513**	**$26,943**

Note: "Expenses" represents the total dollar cost of all medical-related expenses. The siblings' costs reflect the amount that they must withdraw from taxable accounts to net (after taxes) the amount necessary to pay their medical costs. In each case, the withdrawals of funds from a taxable account in their first year of distributions represent the net amount distributed after they exhausted their medical equity.

Ashley exhausts her Roth IRA balance during the year that she turns 91. She then has to pay her medical bills with after-tax dollars. To pay her bills through age 101, she must withdraw $460,000 from accounts with taxable distributions to net the funds that she needs to pay her expenses.

Brett's 401(k) plan balance is exhausted two years later, at age 93. He must withdraw more than $408,000 from accounts with taxable distributions to pay those bills and the taxes associated with the withdrawals.

Chris runs out of funds in her HSA midway through her 101st year. She incurs an additional $21,500 of expenses that year beyond her HSA total. She must withdraw nearly $27,000 from another account with taxable distributions to pay those bills.

Conclusion

All three siblings acted to forego the same amount of current consumption for 30 years to fund their medical (and other health-related) expenses in retirement. Because the triplets chose different accounts with different tax implications, however, they have very different financial experiences late in their lives.

- Ashley: $460,000 in taxable withdrawals from other funds.
    - $51,000 more than Brett.
    - $433,000 more than Chris.

- Brett: $409,000 in taxable withdrawals from other funds.
    - $51,000 less than Ashley.
    - $382,000 more than Chris.

- Chris: $27,000 in taxable withdrawals from other funds.
    - $433,000 less than Ashley.
    - $382,000 less than Brett.

Given these differences in outcome *from identical initial sacrifices of current consumption,* can you think of any more valuable counsel to give to your clients than to emphasize the importance of building medical equity to reimburse health-related expenses in retirement?

HSAs are a superior account in which to build medical equity.

An astute reader may want to challenge one or more of the assumptions in this model. Outside of the marginal tax rates prior to retirement (which affect Ashley's net contribution to her Roth IRA during each of 30 years) and after retirement (which affect Brett's distributions in retirement and Ashley's distributions after she exhausts her Roth IRA balance), the same assumptions apply to all three accounts. Changing any of the variables (such as tax rates during working years or in retirement) may affect slightly the difference in account values, but those changes don't produce meaningfully different outcomes.

In short, no matter the assumptions, HSAs are a superior account in which to build medical equity. As long as federal and state laws don't change negatively (imagine the positive change of no income taxes applied to contributions by residents of Alabama, California, and New Jersey), HSAs will remain the best option for individuals who want to maximize the purchasing power of their medical equity in retirement.

CHAPTER 5

Employer-Based Reimbursement Accounts

Employers have been offering tax-advantaged reimbursement accounts to their employees for decades. Before 2002, the only widely offered option was a Health FSA.

In this chapter, you'll find a review of

- the key features of a Health FSA and how they compare with an HSA,
- when a Health FSA offers superior short-term peace of mind, and
- the key features of an HRA and how they compare with an HSA.

Health FSA

Employees who participate in a Health FSA can reimburse qualified health-related expenses with pre-tax dollars. They make a prospective election, choosing to accept a portion of their compensation as pre-tax deposits into their Health FSAs. They then access these funds to pay for qualified medical, dental, vision, and over-the-counter medication and equipment expenses.

Health FSAs share important tax benefits with HSAs. Both allow individuals to make pre-tax contributions. Both allow tax-free distributions. Thus, from an annual tax perspective, the accounts are financially equivalent.

In practice, however, they operate very differently. HSAs offer a degree of flexibility and a time horizon that a Health FSA, despite its comparable immediate tax advantages, can't match.

Here are the key points of difference between Health FSAs and HSAs:

Time horizon: A Health FSA is an annual reimbursement plan that offers the immediate tax advantages of an HSA (pre-tax contributions and tax-free distributions for qualified expenses). It is, however, time-bound. Participants make a binding election at the beginning of each year and generally must spend their elections within that plan year, though recent changes in the law permit employers to extend plan years a little longer or allow participants to carry over small balances to reimburse future expenses.

In contrast, HSAs are lifetime accounts. Owners can reimburse this year's qualified expenses tax-free with this year's or a future year's contributions. Likewise, they can reimburse future qualified expenses tax-free with a prior year's, this year's, or future years' contributions. They face no reimbursement deadlines. Balances automatically carry over into future years.

Ownership: Health FSAs are employer-sponsored benefit plans under federal tax law. Participants choose their level of coverage with their annual election. They then pay their premiums in the form of pre-tax payroll deductions. They access their benefit when they swipe their debit cards or request manual reimbursement for qualified expenses. Individuals who aren't traditional benefit-eligible employees—like part-time workers, the self-employed, and those who constitute the growing population of Form 1099 workers in a burgeoning free-agent/gig economy—don't have access to Health FSAs.

In contrast, HSAs are individually owned accounts. Anyone who satisfies the eligibility requirements can open and contribute to an HSA, whether employed, self-employed, or unemployed. Employers aren't required to offer an HSA-qualified medical plan, so some of your clients may not have practical access (that is, an option that an employer sponsors and subsidizes) to an HSA program. Nevertheless, the HSA opportunity is available to millions more Americans than a Health FSA because the self-employed and unemployed have access to HSAs.

Contribution flexibility: Health FSA participants are locked into an annual election that they make before the beginning of the plan year. They can't change that election unless they have a qualifying event such as marriage, divorce, birth, adoption, or death of a family member covered under the plan. An unplanned medical, dental, or vision bill isn't a qualifying event.

Sometimes Health FSA owners can time their expenses to minimize this program limitation. They can, for example, accelerate or delay the purchase of prescription glasses or expensive dental work to fit the expenses in to the current or following year's election. It's more difficult to time treatment for a heart attack, cancer diagnosis, or a broken leg.

In contrast, HSA owners can adjust their contributions throughout the year as their reimbursement needs and financial priorities change. They can begin to contribute, stop contributing, adjust their payroll deductions up or down or make lump-sum contributions at any point during the year. This flexibility allows HSA owners to reimburse unexpected expenses tax-free, as well as to integrate their HSAs into their overall financial strategy for long-term saving and investing.

HSA owners can adjust their contributions throughout the year as their reimbursement needs and financial priorities change.

Carryover of unused funds: Health FSAs are annual reimbursement accounts that don't allow an unlimited carryover of unused funds (though employers can now elect one of two options that permit limited carryover). Health FSAs are designed to reimburse expenses during the relevant plan year only. The use-it-or-lose-it feature of Health FSAs discourages participation and limits elections, even though few participants who give thought to their annual elections actually forfeit balances at the end of the year. Many participants instead forfeit tax savings when they make prospective elections that are lower than their anticipated expenses.

In contrast, HSA owners can build balances in their HSAs—a concept referred to throughout this book as building *medical equity*—to pay current or future qualified expenses tax-free. An HSA is thus a lifetime account, not merely an annual reimbursement account.

Reimbursement deadline: Health FSA participants face a deadline—usually set by employers at three months after the end of the plan year—to reimburse qualified expenses. After that time, they lose the ability to reimburse those expenses from the Health FSA.

In contrast, HSA owners face no such deadline. They can reimburse tax-free at any point in the future any qualified expense that they incur after they become

HSA-eligible and establish their HSAs. This flexibility allows an owner with high medical claims to reimburse those expenses with future (or past) HSA contributions.

Portability: Because Health FSAs are employer-sponsored plans, participants have limited opportunities to continue coverage when they leave employment or otherwise lose eligibility. Participants may be entitled to continuation via COBRA, depending on their balance at the time that they lose eligibility. This opportunity generally isn't financially viable, however, so most participants aren't able to reimburse additional expenses that they incur after their last day of employment.

In contrast, HSAs are individually owned trust accounts and fully portable. Departing employees can maintain their HSAs with their current administrator (unless that administrator doesn't allow accounts that aren't associated with an employer, which is rare) or roll over their balances to an administrator of their choice without their former employer's involvement.

Account growth: Because Health FSAs are annual accounts with very limited carryover of unused funds, they don't offer participants the opportunity to build balances through either interest or investment income. Their financial value lies strictly in pre-tax contributions and tax-free distributions.

In contrast, HSAs are permanent accounts whose balances carry over from year to year. HSA owners typically earn interest on their balances. In addition, most robust HSA programs offer investment opportunities—typically a slate of mutual funds in which owners can place their balances beyond a certain cash threshold. Owners can manage their HSAs as they do their retirement plans for long-term asset growth, with the risk of market fluctuation.

Expenses reimbursed: Health FSAs reimburse qualified medical, prescription-drug, dental, vision, and over-the counter equipment and supplies expenses, as well as over-the-counter drugs and medicine with a valid prescription. Family members whose expenses qualify for reimbursement are the employee, her spouse, her tax dependents, and her children to age 26 (even if they're no longer her tax dependents or are enrolled in her medical plan). Expenses incurred by unmarried partners and ex-spouses aren't qualified expenses eligible for reimbursement.

In contrast, HSA owners can reimburse tax-free not only all the expenses that a Health FSA participant can, but also certain premiums for medical and long-term care policies. An HSA owner can reimburse her own, her spouse's, and her tax dependents' qualified expenses, but *not* those expenses incurred by children who are no longer their tax dependents, even if those children remain enrolled in the HSA owner's primary medical coverage. And she can't reimburse an unmarried partner's or ex-spouse's qualified expenses tax-free from her HSA.

Inheritability: Because Health FSAs are sponsored and owned by employers, a participating employee can't designate a beneficiary to receive balances upon her death. A spouse or child may have the right to continue the plan under COBRA, though this opportunity typically isn't financially viable.

In contrast, an HSA is a financial asset owned by an individual. The owner designates a beneficiary who receives the assets in her HSA trust upon her death either intact (beneficiary is her current spouse) or in cash from a liquidated HSA (beneficiary is anyone but her spouse).

Uniform coverage: Here is one characteristic that favors the Health FSA. As noted earlier, a Health FSA is an employer-sponsored benefit plan. Health FSAs follow several requirements of medical plans, including the provision that individuals covered by the plan can access their full benefits whenever they need them (rather than have insurers pro-rate benefits). Health FSA owners can spend their full annual election at any point during the plan year.

Thus, in addition to their tax benefits, Health FSAs offer cash-flow advantages for people who incur high expenses, such as an expensive drug, a hospitalization, major dental work, or vision-correction surgery, early in the plan year. They can tap their entire annual election, then reimburse their employer through their regular, level pre-tax payroll deductions during the remainder of the Health FSA plan year.

HSAs are permanent accounts whose balances carry over from year to year.

In contrast, an HSA works like a checking account with no overdraft protection. HSA owners can't withdraw more than the actual cash balance (though a growing number of administrators and employers offer programs that allow

HSA owners to use a line of credit or cash advance that's not secured by the account itself).

The reason for this disparity is that Health FSA owners make a binding election, so they are in effect borrowing against the promise of future repayment through their pre-tax payroll deductions. In contrast, HSA owners don't make binding contribution commitments and therefore can't receive a cash advance against a non-existent commitment.

But HSA owners do have the benefit of accumulating balances over time and reimbursing current qualified expenses tax-free with future years' contributions. This opportunity may more than compensate for the cash-flow advantage of Health FSAs.

Substantiation: Health FSA administrators must require substantiation for each reimbursement to ensure that the purchase is a qualified expense. The IRS allows autosubstantiation of some debit-card purchases, For example, if the transaction amount matches an insurance copay or is a recurring expense previously substantiated, or if the product code identifies a purchased item as a qualified expense, the administrator doesn't need to request follow-up documentation.

Otherwise, all debit-card purchases and any requests for direct reimbursement must be accompanied by paperwork showing the name of the patient, date of service, product or service purchased, and amount of purchase. If participants don't provide documentation, employers have the right to cease further reimbursements or disable debit cards. Employers can include any unsubstantiated reimbursements as taxable income on employees' Form W-2 statements at the end of the year.

In contrast, neither HSA owners nor employers can require substantiation, since HSA owners can use their balances for the purchase of any items (subject to taxes and penalties if the item isn't a qualified expense). HSA owners aggregate their distributions into qualified and non-qualified expenses and report these figures when they file their personal income tax return. They are advised, but not required, to maintain receipts in case the IRS audits their personal returns.

Here is a summary of the key characteristics of each account:

Key Features of HSAs and Health FSAs

Key Feature	HSA	Health FSA
Ownership	Individual	Employer
Contributions/elections	Contributions are pre-tax.	Elections are pre-tax.
Contributions/elections binding?	Contributions aren't binding.	Elections are binding except for certain qualifying life events.
Source of contributions/ elections	HSA owner/employee and often employer.	Typically employee only. Employers can (but rarely do) contribute.
Interest?	Yes	No
Investment opportunities?	Yes	No
Distributions	Tax-free for qualified expenses. Taxes and possible penalties for non-qualified expenses.	Tax-free for qualified expenses. No distributions for non-qualified expenses.
Whose expenses can be reimbursed tax-free?	Own, spouse's, and tax dependents'	Own, spouse's, tax dependents', and children's to age 26.
Substantiation	Not required. Activity self-reported on tax return. Record-keeping recommended.	Required by administrator during plan year.
Reimbursement deadline?	No	Yes
Spend entire contribution/ election at any time?	No	Yes
Portable?	Yes	Rarely—only via COBRA.
Inheritable?	Yes	No

Health Reimbursement Arrangement

An HRA is a self-insured, limited-benefit employer-sponsored benefit plan that typically is integrated with a high-deductible plan. It's *self-insured* because the employer alone funds the plan. It's *limited-benefit* because the plan has a ceiling on the total reimbursement to which any participant is entitled, regardless of total claims. It's an *employer-sponsored benefit plan*, and, although it doesn't behave like a medical plan, it is subject to some medical-plan rules.

Many employers who offer fully insured medical coverage have used HRAs to help balance premiums and employees' out-of-pocket responsibility. A typical plan that integrates medical coverage and an HRA looks like this:

- Employer reduces a renewal premium by purchasing a plan with a higher deductible, perhaps moving from a $2,000 to a $4,000 individual deductible.
- Employer also offers an HRA that reimburses the second half of the deductible, bringing the employees' maximum financial responsibility back to $2,000.
- Employer reimburses employees on a tax-free basis for all deductible expenses between $2,001.01 and $4,000.

Increasing the deductible and incorporating an HRA allow an employer (and employees, who typically pay a portion of the premium) to enjoy guaranteed premium savings compared to renewal of the current plan. By offering the HRA and assuming responsibility for all claims within a certain range, the employer in effect self-insures a portion of the medical coverage. The employer believes that the premium savings will more than cover the reimbursements and administrative costs associated with the HRA.

An HRA is a notional account. Employers don't prefund each employee's HRA, nor do they tie up funds equal to their potential HRA liability. Instead, employers in effect give each HRA participant an IOU that promises to reimburse certain claims. The employer works with an HRA administrator, which typically collects a portion of the maximum potential liability as a working balance from which to pay claims. The administrator then reimburses claims on a regular basis (usually weekly) from this balance and invoices the employer to replenish the account back to the working balance. Thus, a company with maximum liability of $100,000 (say, 50 employees, each with a $2,000 HRA) may deposit $8,000 into the working balance and then replenish the account to that balance as claims are paid.

Employers in effect give each HRA participant an IOU that promises to reimburse certain claims.

The following table illustrates this concept. The employer offers a low-deductible option (Plan A) and a high-deductible option (Plan B) with an integrated HRA to reduce employees' net deductible exposure. Under Plan B, the first $4,000 of expenses is self-insured. The employee is responsible for the first $2,000 (same as under Plan A). The employer reimburses any deductible expenses between $2001.01 and $4,000. The employer projects that the reimbursement and administrative costs of the integrated HRA will be less than the certain premium savings.

Plan Feature	Plan A	Plan B
Deductible	$2,000	$4,000
Annual premium (employer share)	$5,000	$3,800
Premium savings		$1,200
HRA value	$0	$2,000
Probable reimbursement (25%)	NA	$500
HRA administrative cost ($5/mo.)		$60
Total savings		$640

Though the employer can be thought of as *betting* that this arrangement will save money, it's not a blind wager. Deductible utilization information is available, so employers can predict with some accuracy their financial responsibility. The law of large numbers works in favor of bigger employers, but smaller companies also can predict a range into which their liability can be expected to fall. Even when claims exceed the expected amount, an employer's total liability is capped by the limits on reimbursements to each employee before the medical plan begins to assume responsibility for additional claims.

HRAs are a great way for employers to help manage medical costs. Since the IRS issued initial formal HRA guidance in 2002, millions of employers have offered HRAs to help employees manage increasing out-of-pocket costs. In recent years, a growing number of employers have phased out HRA programs in favor of HSAs. Their reasoning: Rather than assume responsibility for verifying employees' HRA-qualified claims each year (a function that employers typically assign to a plan administrator), employers can instead introduce an HSA program, make contributions to employees' accounts for several years to help employees build balances, and then shift responsibility for future claims to employees alone.

In some parts of the country, notably the Northeast, HRAs remain very popular—far more popular than HSAs. Employers appreciate being able to define certain key elements of an HRA program, such as:

- **Value of the HRA:** Employers determine the dollar value of employees' total qualified expenses they're willing to reimburse.
- **Qualified expenses:** Employers define (within federal limits) which expenses are HRA-qualified. Typically, they limit reimbursement to deductible expenses, other medical plan cost-sharing (like coinsurance for medial

services and separate deductibles, coinsurance and high copays for prescription drugs), or a combination of both.

- **Carryover of unused funds:** Employers choose whether to allow employees who don't use their balance in a given plan year to carry over part or all of those funds to use in a subsequent year and whether to cap the total carryover or total accumulated balance.

Another key feature of HRAs that is particularly attractive to employers is the expected payout. Though employer financial responsibility is a function of plan design, carryover decisions, group size, and claims, employers typically are responsible for between 25% and 60% of the total potential liability. In other words, if the employer offers a $2,000 HRA to each employee, it typically reimburses between $500 and $1,200 of an average participant's qualified expenses annually. So, the employer promises a $2,000 benefit but typically incurs cash costs of only $500 to $1,200 for that promise with an HRA. That's an attractive option for employers—as long as the actual reimbursement total and administrative fees are less than the premium savings.

Here are the main points of difference between HRAs and HSAs:

Time horizon: An HRA is designed as an annual reimbursement program, although employers have the option to extend the time horizon by allowing carryover of unused funds.

In contrast, an HSA is a lifetime account in which balances carry over automatically from year to year. Employers have no control over how much an employee accumulates in her HSA.

Ownership: HRAs are an employer-sponsored benefit plan. The employer owns the program. Employees merely enroll to receive benefits. People who don't qualify for employer-sponsored coverage—part-time workers, Form 1099 workers, the self-employed, and the unemployed—can't have an HRA.

In contrast, HSAs are individually owned financial accounts. People who purchase coverage on their own can choose an HSA-qualified medical plan and, if otherwise eligible, open and contribute to an HSA.

Contributions: There are no HRA contributions in the strictest sense. Instead, as you've already seen, employers simply pledge to reimburse certain expenses if employees incur applicable claims. The law bars employees from contributing, either directly or indirectly, to an HRA. Thus, HRAs don't provide participating employees with an opportunity to reduce taxable income (though many also participate in their employers' Health FSA programs to do so).

The IRS doesn't place a ceiling on the value of an HRA, so employers have side latitude in designing their program.

In contrast, HSA owners can contribute to their accounts up to the statutory limits set by the IRS (less any contributions from other sources and any adjustments based on month-to-month eligibility). Their contributions and those of their employer (if they receive company contributions) are made in cash and vest immediately.

Carryover of unused funds: Employers determine whether any unused HRA funds carry over for use in future plan years. Many employers don't allow carryover. Some do allow a limited carryover, usually to steer participants from receiving low-value care near the end of the plan year just to "use up their balances."

In contrast, HSA funds are placed in a permanent account that is individually owned. Funds not spent during the year that they're contributed are available for future use. HSA owners never face a financial incentive to seek care just to draw down their balances.

Reimbursement deadline: HRA reimbursement requests generally must be filed within 90 days of (1) the end of the plan year or (2) termination of coverage, if sooner. Employers can adjust this deadline to make it longer or shorter. Late reimbursement requests typically aren't accepted.

In contrast, HSA owners never lose the opportunity to reimburse a qualified expense tax-free—even years after they incur the expense.

Portability: HRAs are subject to several provisions that apply to employer-sponsored medical plans, including COBRA continuation. Former employees who have COBRA rights to maintain coverage after they're no longer benefit-eligible can choose to continue an HRA integrated with their medical plan. Employers often charge an additional premium for HRA coverage during the COBRA continuation period. For individuals with a high balance and expected expenses, paying the additional premium to continue their HRA may be a wise expenditure. Departing employees with no known future expenses may choose not to continue HRA coverage to avoid the additional premium.

In contrast, HSAs aren't employer-sponsored plans, nor do they follow regulatory requirements for medical plans. They're personal accounts owned by the participating employee. Former employees retain their HSAs when they separate from the company that provided the employer-sponsored medical coverage (which may be eligible for COBRA continuation). Companies often make a lump-sum contribution to employees' HSAs at the beginning of the year. They cannot recover a pro-rated portion of that contribution if the employee leaves the company mid-year.

Account growth: HRAs rarely pay interest on balances, since employees don't have a cash balance in a notional account. The typical exception is when an employer allows a carryover of unused funds into a separate HRA designated for retirement, in which case the balance may earn interest.

In contrast, HSA balances usually earn interest, and robust HSA administrators programs include investment options. HSA owners can invest a portion of their balances, at their discretion, in a variety of mutual funds.

Expenses reimbursed: Employers determine the expenses that the HRAs reimburse (within limits set by the tax code). HRAs integrated with medical plans typically reimburse only medical plan cost-sharing (some combination of deductibles, coinsurance, and copays).

In contrast, HSA owners can reimburse all qualified expenses under federal tax law tax-free and other expenses subject to taxes and possible penalties. Employers and HSA administrators can't limit distributions to a subset of qualified expenses allowed under federal tax law.

Inheritability: Because HRA programs are sponsored by employers, not owned by employees, they aren't inheritable. Spouses and children eligible for continuation of benefits under COBRA typically *can* remain covered on an HRA integrated with a medical plan (often at an additional premium).

In contrast, HSAs are individual trust accounts that are fully inheritable.

Uniform coverage: HRAs don't have a mandatory uniform coverage provision, so participants can't automatically access their entire balance at any point during the year. Employers typically make the entire balance available at the beginning of the year, however, to help employees with high out-of-pocket costs early in the year. Some employers, particularly those with transient workforces, may choose to allocate funds monthly.

In contrast, HSA owners can't draw funds in excess of their accrued balances. Some administrators and employers have eased potential cash-flow issues by introducing programs that allow HSA owners to draw on a line of credit not backed by the HSA itself or receive an advance of periodic employer contributions.

Substantiation: The IRS requires substantiation of all reimbursements through an HRA. In some cases, HRA administrators receive claims files directly from insurers, which they can use to substantiate and reimburse claims. Other reimbursement options—debit cards or manually submitted claims—trigger requests for paperwork showing the name of the patient, date of service, product or service, and cost. If participants don't provide documentation, employers have the right to cease further reimbursements or disable debit cards. Employers can include any unsubstantiated reimbursements as taxable income on employees' Form W-2 statements.

In contrast, neither HSA owners nor employers can require substantiation. HSA owners can use their balances for the purchase of any items (subject to taxes and penalties if the item isn't a qualified expense). HSA owners aggregate their distributions into qualified and non-qualified expenses and record these figures on Form 8889 of their personal income tax return. They are advised, but not required, to maintain receipts in case the IRS audits their personal income tax return.

Turn the page for a summary of the differences between HSAs and HRAs.

Key Features of HSAs and HRAs

Key Feature	HSA	HRA
Ownership	Individual	Employer
Contributions	Contributions are pre-tax.	No employee contributions permitted.
Contributions binding?	Contributions aren't binding.	No employee contributions permitted.
Source of contributions/ elections	HSA owner/employee and often employer.	Employer only.
Interest?	Yes	Typically no.
Investment opportunities?	Yes	Typically no.
Distributions	Tax-free for qualified expenses. Taxes and penalties for non-qualified expenses.	Tax-free for qualified expenses. No distributions for non-qualified expenses.
Whose expenses can be reimbursed tax-free?	Own, spouse's, and tax dependents'.	Own, spouse's, tax dependents', and children's to age 26.
Substantiation	Not required. Activity self-reported on tax return. Record-keeping recommended.	Required by administrator during plan year.
Reimbursement deadline?	No	Yes
Spend entire contribution/ election at any time?	No	Usually, but not required.
Portable?	Yes	Only via COBRA.
Inheritable?	Yes	No

Conclusion

Make no mistake. Health FSAs and HRAs play an important role in employee benefits. And they will continue to do so, assuming no changes in current law, even as employers increasingly offer HSAs instead. Health FSAs and HRAs offer many benefits to both employers and employees. Both programs are time-tested and easily managed by experienced administrators.

In many cases, HSAs are a superior account for employers and employees. HSAs give employees much more freedom and flexibility. HSAs allow employees to build balances—through contributions and investment returns—to reimburse future expenses tax-free. This accumulation of HSA balances gives employers the flexibility to reduce their contributions over time (as opposed to maintaining annual HRA funding).

As you'll see later, Health FSAs, HRAs, and HSAs aren't necessarily an "either/or" proposition. Federal tax law places some restrictions on combinations of these products for people who want to open and contribute to an HSA. Certain combinations of *limited* Health FSAs and *limited* HRAs allow employees to maximize their financial opportunities by participating in two and even all three of these programs.

Later chapters will discuss these strategies and products. After studying them, you'll be equipped to provide sound advice to your business-owner clients who sponsor benefits plans and your employee clients who have access to these innovative programs.

SECTION II

Using HSAs Strategically

INTRODUCTION TO SECTION II

Planning for retirement doesn't begin at age 65—or even at age 50. The ideal retirement planning, as you know, begins when your client is in his mid-20s (though, sadly, they usually aren't your clients then and typically are unaware of the time advantage that they enjoy). Decisions made and habits adopted at that age make a huge difference in his preparation for retirement. Although it's possible for him to "catch up" when he begins to plan for retirement at a later age, the path typically is much more perilous and the footing much less stable when his time frame is compressed.

This section outlines retirement-planning strategies that your clients should start to review as soon as you begin working with them. You know the Chinese adage that the best time to plant a tree for shade was 20 years ago—and the second best time is today. The sooner your clients begin to incorporate HSAs into their retirement strategy, the better.

Here, you'll find a discussion of the four broad strategies that HSA owners follow in managing their accounts. The good news is that owners aren't locked into a single approach. Rather, they can evolve, particularly as they build their HSA balances and their discretionary income. This section reviews your clients' potential sources for funding their HSAs, with a focus on pain-free funding that doesn't hurt their lifestyle. These strategies include using a Limited-Purpose Health FSA and executing a one-time rollover from an IRA to an HSA.

You'll learn more about building HSA balances through investment. Making regular contributions to an HSA helps your clients generate medical equity. So does investing those balances wisely. You'll find guidance on how to guide your clients on investments in a traditional HSA and be introduced to the concept of a self-directed HSA.

Most of this section focuses on building medical equity for retirement. The section ends with some guidance on managing an HSA optimally in retirement. Your clients have important decisions to make even when they're no longer contributing to their accounts. The final chapter in this section guides them through this process.

CHAPTER 6

Four Behavioral Types of HSA Owners

HSA owners don't behave much differently when managing their HSAs than they do when making other financial decisions. Some Americans take a long view and are willing to sacrifice something in the present (such as time, a larger house, lavish vacations, new cars every three years, or attendance at live sporting events) to secure a more prosperous financial future. Others stick to a shorter time horizon that reflects the "live for today, for tomorrow we may be dead" philosophy. This approach may send them to an early grave happy and fulfilled or may imprison them in old age without sufficient financial resources to live out the remainder of their lives as they had hoped. Still others fall somewhere in the middle, saving inadequately for the future to enjoy life today and hoping that something (such as an inheritance from an unknown source, lottery winnings, or a child's becoming a movie star or professional athlete) closes the financial gap between what they save and what they expect to spend.

Spoiler alert: As you know—but some of your clients may not—they have a better chance of spotting a unicorn than receiving an eight- or nine-figure lottery winning or a bequest from a relative whom they've never met. And the odds of a multi-year professional sports contract with an up-front bonus aren't much different.

In this chapter, you'll find

- a review of the four basic strategies that HSA owners follow, either consciously or unconsciously;
- a discussion of how owners move from one strategy to another over time; and
- an illustration of the differences in balances at retirement with each strategy.

HSA owners have a powerful financial account at their disposal. It's different from a Health FSA or HRA in that it's not an annual medical reimbursement account without the possibility of long-term asset accumulation. And it's different from a retirement plan, which owners understand is dedicated to building balances to fund their retirement and from which they therefore don't intentionally make premature withdrawals except when they face a financial crisis.

HSAs have important features of both a Health FSA and a retirement plan. Therein lies not only their power, but their temptation.

Each HSA owner, consciously or unconsciously, exhibits one of four long-term account management behaviors: Transactor, Unconscious Accumulator, Conscious Accumulator, or Maximizer. Regardless of behavioral type, people use the same kind of account. HSA administrators don't offer a *Conscious Accumulator* HSA to one client and a *Transactor* HSA to another (although some administrators do offer multiple HSA products with different fees, interest rates, and investment options to appeal to the budgets and strategies of different users). *Unconscious Accumulators* don't have support groups in all major metropolitan areas, and professional baseball teams don't honor the *Maximizer of the Year* (as they might a blood donor or public-school teacher) by allowing her to throw out the first pitch.

HSA owners fall into these types naturally. And, it's important to note, their behavior can change over time. Some who use HSAs like a Health FSA may subsequently begin to use their HSAs to build medical equity due to new information or a change in their financial situation (such as putting the last of their children through college or finally paying off their own student loans). At the same time, other owners may reduce their emphasis on building medical equity and use their HSAs more transactionally as their income changes or they become satisfied with their level of medical equity.

Transactor

Transactors take advantage of the HSA provision that allows owners to fund their accounts *after* they incur an expense (as long as they incur the expense after they become HSA-eligible and establish their accounts—see Chapter 19, *HSA Distributions*). They understand that an HSA is more flexible than a Health FSA, which requires participants to make a prospective binding annual election before the beginning of the plan year.

Transactors typically make small pre-tax contributions to their HSAs through their employer's Cafeteria Plan. To minimize the effect on their take-home pay, they often redeploy funds that they would have contributed to a Health FSA or the difference between their payroll deductions for their former medical plan and the lower deductions for an HSA-qualified plan. As they incur qualified medical, dental, and vision expenses, Transactors increase their HSA contributions to build sufficient balances to pay their bills. It's not uncommon for the financially savvy (or desperate) among them to approach providers to negotiate payment terms (like prompt-pay discounts and schedules for expensive services) to help them manage their cash flow. Incidentally, the practice of negotiating repayment terms with providers, including prompt-pay discounts, is a very underutilized practice across all four behavioral types.

They may supplement their HSA with a Limited-Purpose Health FSA (more on this strategy in Chapter 9, *Utilizing a Limited-Purpose Health FSA Strategically*) to reimburse dental and vision expenses. They typically do so for cash-flow advantages rather than to reduce their taxable income further (although the latter result is a happy byproduct of their action). They probably understand that they can access their entire Health FSA annual election at any point in the year as they pay level deductions each payroll period.

If they know during open enrollment that they will incur a specific dental or vision expense (or know their general spending history for these services), they can use a Limited-Purpose Health FSA to pay those expenses in full.

Transactors often don't take advantage of this feature of the Limited-Purpose Health FSA for the same reason that more than two-thirds of employees at most companies don't participate in any Health FSA programs: They're paralyzed by fear of forfeiting unused balances. Yet the risk is minimal—and often reduced further by employers who add a grace period or limited carryover of unused funds.

> Even though Transactors don't maximize the long-term value of their accounts, they still derive value from their HSAs.

Transactors never build balances in their HSAs. Rather, as the label implies, they use their HSA strictly as a transactional account. Their balance at the beginning of the year is zero (first year) or very small (subsequent years), and their balance at the end of the year is typically very small as well.

Even though Transactors don't maximize the long-term value of their accounts, they still derive value from their HSAs. This benefit is often overlooked by HSA critics in politics and academia who underrate the financial effect of HSAs on Transactors. These observers point to low average HSA balances over time, particularly among households with incomes of, say, $75,000 or less.

Though snapshots of account balances show no long-term asset accumulation, the tax savings can be meaningful for these HSA owners. A household with $75,000 in income and $3,000 in out-of-pocket medical, dental, and vision expenses can save between $750 and $900 in taxes by running these costs through an HSA. For a family of four with $75,000 in income, this tax savings may produce a happier Christmas, pay tuition to a summer STEM camp for an aspiring student, or cover the cost of three replacement windows to reduce home heating costs.

Although Transactors don't gain long-term asset-accumulation advantages from their HSAs, they derive financial benefit from their accounts.

Unconscious Accumulator

Unconscious Accumulators have a little more disposable income, a little more knowledge, or a little more financial savvy than Transactors. They employ a strategy that doesn't take full advantage of the long-term financial benefits of an HSA.

Like Transactors, Unconscious Accumulators want to maximize their take-home pay. Unconscious Accumulators are more proactive in making pre-tax payroll deductions to reimburse their anticipated qualified expenses for the year. And like Transactors, they fund their HSAs primarily from former Health FSA contributions and differences in the premium.

Unlike Transactors, Unconscious Accumulators project their annual expenses and make pre-tax payroll contributions to cover those anticipated expenses, even if it reduces their take-home pay slightly. They prefer to receive take-home pay that reflects their anticipated discretionary income after medical, dental, and vision expenses, rather than adjust their payroll deductions with each new medical bill, dental procedure, or new package of contact lenses.

Unconscious Accumulators are more likely than Transactors to participate in a Limited-Purpose Health FSA because they seek to stabilize their take-home pay. The consistent deductions paycheck-to-paycheck provide a pool from which they can reimburse dental and vision expenses without adjusting their HSA payroll deductions.

Neither Transactors nor Unconscious Accumulators are focused on building medical equity in their HSAs. The term means nothing to Transactors and little to Unconscious Accumulators. The difference is what happens at the end of the year. Because Unconscious Accumulators project expenses and set their contribution levels accordingly rather than react to each bill with a deposit, they may end up with a balance at year-end. They may overestimate their expenses by $50 or $500.

> Unconscious Accumulators are more proactive in making pre-tax payroll deductions.

When they end the year with a balance, Unconscious Accumulators retain it and don't factor it in when planning the following year's contributions. Let's say they finish the year with $300 in one spouse's HSA. They anticipate $1,000 in qualified expenses the following year. They base the next year's HSA contributions on $1,000 (about $20 per week), not on the net new $700 that they project as their need (about $14 per week). The difference is subtle when the amounts are small, but funds accumulate over time. These seemingly small annual decisions make a big difference in the total medical equity that they accumulate over a lifetime.

More important, this discipline prepares them to advance to the next level of HSA management, which dramatically increases the accumulation of medical equity. The step from Transactor to Unconscious Accumulator is large philosophically because it involves a shift in focus from the immediate to keeping one eye on the present and one on the future. Moving from Unconscious Accumulator to the next behavioral type is more subtle and involves only strengthening the vision in the eye that's looking over the horizon.

At the same time, a shift from Transactor to Unconscious Accumulator isn't dramatic financially because the family's disposable income at the end of the year may not be all that different (even though the accumulation over time may be). Moving to the next behavioral type, however, requires a different level of financial commitment to support the increased focus on the future.

Conscious Accumulator

For individuals who evolve along the behavior spectrum, moving from Unconscious Accumulator to Conscious Accumulator represents the largest leap. Though moving from Transactor to Unconscious Accumulator is the equivalent of fording a small brook on foot, moving from Unconscious Accumulator to Conscious Accumulator can be like crossing a fast-moving river on a rope bridge suspended above the rapids. It's a safe crossing, but your clients' degree of preparation, level of knowledge, and experience in making similar crossings all factor into the trepidation with which they consider the crossing.

Conscious Accumulators contribute to their HSAs up to the IRS maximum every year, rather than limit contributions to what expenses they have incurred (Transactors) or expect to incur (Unconscious Accumulators) during that year. This is a major financial commitment. At first glance it's outside the financial reach of most HSA owners (which is why moving to this behavioral type appears initially to be so daunting). This is where a second glance comes in handy, because many HSA owners of ordinary means who focus on the future can adopt this strategy.

Conscious Accumulators typically aren't people with an income in the top 5% or early investors in Berkshire Hathaway stock. They find money to contribute to their HSAs rather creatively. The key to their success with this behavior is that they've already established a pattern of substantial annual contributions to a retirement plan long before they open an HSA.

Here's how they reconfigure their existing level of retirement savings to become Conscious Accumulators:

- First, they continue to contribute to their retirement plan up to the full employer match. This allocation is critical, since receiving the full employer contribution to which they're entitled represents an immediate 50% (half match) to 100% (full match) return on their savings. This strategy accelerates accumulation of their retirement savings and increases the base that grows over time. Leaving no employer money on the table is the best way to turbocharge long-term tax-advantaged accumulation.
- Second, once they've contributed enough to receive the full employer match, they contribute to their HSAs to the IRS limits.

- Third, once they've reached the HSA contribution limit, they shift contributions back to the retirement plan. They add to this contribution the equivalent of their former Health FSA elections (if they don't participate in a Limited-Purpose Health FSA) and the difference in payroll deductions for premiums—and more if they can afford it, up to the IRS contribution limits on the retirement plan.

Example: *Kalani's employer matches 100% of her first $4,200 of 401(k) plan contributions. She's covered on a family medical contract and plans to save $6,000 for retirement in her HSA. Kalani plans to contribute a total of $16,200 to all retirement plans in 2018 in equal installments throughout the year (24 pay periods). Here is her allocation:*

$4,200 ($175 per pay period) to receive the full employer match to her 401(k) plan.
$6,000 ($240 per pay period) into her HSA.
$6,000 ($240 per pay period) additional into her 401(k) plan.

Kalani sets her payroll deductions so that her employer deducts $415 ($175 plus $240) for her 401(k) plan and $240 for her HSA each pay period.

Conscious Accumulators also retain all receipts for qualified expenses that they incur from the date that they establish their HSAs. This simple step can yield some important advantages. It provides them with documentation in case the IRS audits their personal income tax return and questions whether the amount distributed from the account in a given year represents reimbursement for qualified expenses.

And since the IRS imposes no deadlines for reimbursing qualified expenses tax-free from an HSA, a Conscious Accumulator can use her accumulated medical equity to reimburse any qualified expenses incurred since establishing the HSA. This feature of the program is both an opportunity and a risk.

It's an opportunity in that a Conscious Accumulator can pay a qualified expense incurred after establishing her HSA with personal funds to retain HSA balances in a tax-advantaged account, then make withdrawals years later from the account without tax consequences. This flexibility in the timing of reimbursements is a major advantage of HSAs over other reimbursement accounts, which place a time limit on when an expense can be reimbursed. This feature is particularly attractive to an account owner who uses an HSA as a reimbursement account rather than an investment account or who starts out as an

Unconscious Accumulator or Conscious Accumulator and then has an unexpected need for cash.

It also represents a risk. The downside of this flexibility in the timing of reimbursements is that a Conscious Accumulator may be tempted to view an HSA as a quick source of funds when she faces a cash-flow crunch. She must resist the temptation to tap HSA balances—even when she has incurred enough qualified expenses not otherwise reimbursed to make the distribution tax-free—unless the distribution fits with her overall financial strategy (a rare situation).

Conscious Accumulators enjoy several additional financial benefits.

First, HSAs provide additional tax savings that retirement plans don't. All retirement plans offer either pre-tax contributions and taxable distributions (traditional 401(k) plans and traditional IRAs) or post-tax contributions and tax-free distributions (both 401(k) plans and Roth IRAs). HSAs offer both tax-free (or tax-deductible) contributions *and* tax-free distributions for a wide range of qualified expenses. Your clients can build medical equity in an HSA without tax friction. In contrast, their tax-advantaged retirement accounts are subject to income taxes either when they (1) contribute (Roth plans) or (2 make distributions (most traditional plans).

Second, HSAs aren't subject to Required Minimum Distributions at age 70½, unlike 401(k) plans and traditional IRAs, which means that owners can choose the amount and timing of distributions to meet *their* needs, rather than the IRS's. For some individuals, particularly those still employed at age 70½ or who draw a large income from investments, preserving funds in an account without RMDs represents a huge financial benefit.

HSA owners don't have a silent financial partner (the IRS) that demands a share of all distributions.

Third, distributions from HSAs for qualified expenses are considered reimbursements, not income. As such, HSA distributions aren't included in calculating provisional income, which in turn determines how much of your clients' Social Security check is taxed. HSA owners don't have a silent financial partner (the IRS) that demands a share of all distributions from the account, as traditional 401(k) plan and IRA owners do.

Example: *Jamaal, who is single, receives $20,000 annual Social Security benefit. He supplements his retirement income with $12,000 from his traditional IRA. His provisional income is below $34,000, so 50% of his Social Security benefit ($10,000) is included in his taxable income. Jamaal incurs a $3,000 medical bill late in the year. If he withdraws funds from his HSA, the transaction doesn't affect his provisional income.*

In contrast, if he makes an additional $3,000 distribution from his IRA, that transaction pushes his provisional income up to $35,000. With provisional income above $34,000, Jamaal must now include 85% of his Social Security benefit ($17,000) in his taxable income. At a 15% marginal federal income tax rate, the additional provisional income results in an extra $1,050 of federal income taxes owed.

The keys to executing this strategy successfully are *knowledge* and *discipline*, the same personal attributes that are most important in creating and following a sound long-term financial plan. Individuals must know and understand how and why to follow this approach—the subject of this book. The second trait—the ability to practice discipline—can't be taught by a book. Rather, it's like a muscle that individuals must develop and then maintain.

Why discipline? Because it's easy to go off the tracks when something unexpected happens.

Example: *Esoleta saves $15,000 annually in her traditional 401(k) plan. She reads this book and decides to become a Conscious Accumulator. She contributes $5,000 to her 401(k) plan to receive a 60% employer match ($3,000, or an instant 60% return on her contribution). She contributes the next $3,500 (2019 HSA maximum contribution for self-only coverage) to her HSA. Finally, Esoleta contributes the balance of her $15,000 ($6,500) to her 401(k) plan, along with the $1,000 that she formerly contributed to her Health FSA and the $500 premium difference with her lower payroll deductions for medical insurance.*

Esoleta can spend $1,500 from her HSA and still contribute a net total of $15,000 to retirement savings because she contributed a total of $16,500 between the two accounts.

Here's where discipline comes in. A Conscious Accumulator like Esoleta remains on track with her long-term savings plan as long as she spends, in our example, $1,500 or less from her HSA. What if she incurs a high medical expense, needs a dental crown, or wants to undergo vision-correction surgery and enjoy the immediate tax advantages of her HSA? If her total expenses are $2,500 and she distributes that amount from her HSA, her distributions create a $1,000 deficit in her long-term savings plan. She contributed a total of $16,500 and spent $2,500 from her HSA, leaving her with only $14,000 in long-term savings versus her target of $15,000 savings. That deficit may not seem like much, but when this move is repeated annually for 25 years, it creates a gap in retirement assets of nearly $54,000, assuming 6% annual account balance growth.

A Limited-Purpose Health FSA is an important ally to an HSA owner who wants to pursue this strategy and anticipates dental and vision expenses. The Limited-Purpose Health FSA election is made with personal funds not connected to the long-term savings target. Thus, an HSA owner can remain on track with this strategy and enjoy immediate tax advantages (and cash-flow benefits) from the Limited-Purpose Health FSA.

You've probably figured out why this group is called the *Conscious* Accumulators. Unlike the Unconscious Accumulators, who just let HSA balances grow on their own when contributions exceed distributions, Conscious Accumulators fuel balance growth by contributing to the IRS limits and then minimizing their distributions for qualified expenses.

Because this is the first user behavior introduced thus far that incorporates contributions to both an HSA and a retirement plan, it has more moving parts to understand. Most important, it's the first strategy that can result in *decreased* total retirement savings for an HSA owner with high out-of-pocket expenses that are qualified for tax-free distribution from an HSA. If a Conscious Accumulator can't manage those expenses with personal funds and yields to the temptation to use HSA balances for immediate cash flow and tax advantages, she robs herself of what otherwise would be a retirement asset.

If she doesn't have an HSA, but instead places all her retirement savings in a retirement account with penalties for early withdrawals, she probably maintains her retirement contribution target and finds personal funds to pay her out-of-pocket medical expenses. Because the HSA offers both immediate and long-term tax benefits, it's easy to derail the long-term saving plan to meet an immediate need. That's why knowledge and discipline are more important in executing this strategy successfully than for any of the other three behavioral types.

Maximizer

Maximizers are very similar to Conscious Accumulators. The difference is that they never spend a dime from their HSAs during the accumulation phase. Instead, they contribute to the maximum in their HSAs without touching their growing medical equity—except to move it from their HSA cash account to the investment platform. They pay for all their qualified expenses with personal funds (or dental and vision expenses from a Limited-Purpose Health FSA, if their employer offers this program).

Maximizers retain their receipts for all qualified expenses incurred after they establish their HSAs. This step is an important part of the overall strategy because they can reimburse those expenses tax-free at any point in the future. Rather than reimburse $2,000 per year for 20 years, they let that money accumulate at 6% and achieve a balance of $73,500 at the end of 20 years. They then can withdraw the original $40,000 tax-free to reimburse those qualified expenses. And they still have an additional $47,700 to reimburse other qualified expenses tax-free, whether they incurred those expenses in the past (on or after the date that they established their HSAs) or incur them in the future.

At this point, you can bring the time value of money into the equation. You can factor in inflation estimates and projected tax rates at various points in your clients' lives. Those factors are relevant, but they unduly complicate the analysis.

> Delaying tax-free distributions during your clients' working years, may be a reasonable price to pay to reimburse future qualified expenses tax-free.

The goal of this chapter is to show the simplified power of accumulation and deferred reimbursement. In conducting your analysis, don't forget to include one of the central theses of this strategy: People often have—or perceive that they have—more disposable income during their working years than they do during retirement. Delaying tax-free distributions during their working years, when they're more likely to have the flexibility to do so without diminishing their lifestyle, may be a reasonable price to pay for the security of higher tax-free balances to reimburse future qualified expenses tax-free.

Different Strategies, Very Different Results

Each of these HSA user behaviors is a viable strategy, and each offers immediate tax advantages, long-term tax-advantaged asset accumulation, or a combination of the two. There is no single right strategy for all HSA owners, any more than there is a single best strategy for retirement savings.

What's important to understand is that with HSAs, behavior today can have a huge impact on balances tomorrow. Clients willing to forego the immediate tax advantages of tax-free distributions can build substantial medical equity to help them pay future expenses—particularly in retirement, when they may be living on a tighter budget with limited earned income.

Let's look at the differences in account balances after 20 years:

HSA Balances after 20 Years by HSA User Behavioral Type

Balance at the End of Year . . .	Transactor	Unconscious Accumulator	Conscious Accumulator	Maximizer
5	$0	$6,400	$29,500	$41,300
10	$0	$16,700	$70,800	$98,500
15	$0	$31,800	$127,500	$176,600
20	$0	$53,600	$205,000	$282,600

Note: Figures based on 2018 statutory maximum annual contribution of $6,900 and a $100 annual increase, with earnings of 6% annually. Unconscious Accumulators accumulate $1,000 in additional balances annually. Conscious Accumulators contribute the maximum and spend $2,000 annually. Maximizers contribute the maximum and don't make any distributions.

As you can see, the three strategies that include some form of savings and investment all provide HSA owners with balances that grow annually. But the choice of strategy makes a huge difference in the balance accumulated. Unconscious Accumulators choose to enjoy immediate tax advantages and find themselves with a balance of more than $50,000 after 20 years. Conscious Accumulators limit their immediate tax advantage and, in exchange for enjoying immediate maximum tax advantages when paying for qualified expenses, accumulate nearly four times as much as Unconscious Accumulators to spend on future health-related expenses. The Maximizers, who reduce their taxable income each year but pay for all qualified expenses with personal funds, accumulate $75,000 more than the Conscious Accumulators.

Which strategy is best? That's where your expertise guides your clients. You may advise some clients to enjoy immediate tax savings—a sure thing—because of uncertainty around their physical or financial future and projected tax rates, or because they have sufficient assets to fund the retirement that they desire. Those clients should become Unconscious Accumulators.

You may advise others to hedge their bets by enjoying some tax benefits now and deferring some tax benefits to build long-term savings. In these cases, they should assume the role of Conscious Accumulators.

And you may have other clients who should reduce taxable income immediately and are in a position to defer the benefits of tax-advantaged distribution in order to build wealth in the form of medical equity. They are candidates to become Maximizers.

When determining the best strategy, note the difference between Conscious Accumulator and Maximizer. Let's imagine a client with $6,000 in annual expenses qualified for tax-free reimbursement in each of 20 years. The Conscious Accumulator reimburses $2,000 tax-free and pays the balance with personal funds. The Maximizer pays all $6,000 with personal funds. And let's assume your client is in the 35% tax bracket (federal and state income taxes, plus federal payroll taxes).

In this case, the Conscious Accumulator saves $700 annually in taxes, or $14,000 over 20 years, by reimbursing $2,000 of qualified expenses immediately from her HSA. That $14,000 tax savings comes at the expense of an additional $75,000 in medical equity available after 20 years. And remember, $75,000 in an HSA has the same spending power as $90,000 to $100,000 in a traditional IRA or 401(k) plan. Looked at in this light, the Conscious Accumulator strategy appears to offer limited immediate financial advantages at the expense of long-term asset accumulation.

As a final point, let's not neglect the Transactor. This individual probably isn't a client of any financial advisor. He lives paycheck-to-paycheck and has little in the way of retirement savings. He's the person to whom HSA critics point when they claim that HSAs benefit only the wealthy. And the savings table certainly reinforces that notion.

This analysis couldn't be more wrong, however, as noted previously. Though the Transactor doesn't accumulate any long-term balances, he benefits from his HSA through its immediate tax benefits. Let's say he has $2,500 in qualified expenses annually. By contributing $2,500 to his HSA and then paying those expenses with tax-free distributions, he saves about $700 in taxes (assuming an

18% federal marginal income tax rate, 7.65% payroll tax and 6% state income tax). For someone living on the edge, an additional $700 can be a godsend.

In addition, the tax advantages of an HSA give him the incentive to make regular contributions to build his HSA balance. In effect, the HSA program serves as a savings discipline tool. That's critically important to individuals with limited saving. Though some medical expenses are regular (a monthly prescription, for example), many large expenses come all at once (maternity care, accident, major illness, or emergency services, for example). Surveys show that more than half of all Americans have less than $500 in liquid assets to face an emergency. Contributing $25 per biweekly paycheck (or $1,300 annually) reduces take-home pay by about $20 (or $1,040 annually). Even that figure may be offset by lower employee contributions to the premium, which may result in little effect on the employee's net paycheck. Should he incur a sudden, large expense, he has $1,300 to pay his bill or make a down payment as he arranges terms with the provider.

This HSA owner is using his HSA like a Health FSA—accumulating balances through regular contributions with minimal effect on his take-home pay. No politician or pundit criticizes Health FSA programs because participants end the year with a zero balance. Nor should commentators aim the same criticism at HSAs, as they often do.

Counseling Your Clients

- ✓ Help your clients understand and apply the power of HSAs as retirement savings and investment accounts. They need to appreciate the value of medical equity, regardless of the ultimate role that you and they determine for medical equity in their financial strategy.
- ✓ Work with your clients to determine the right mix of current tax savings versus account balance growth and future tax savings when determining how to use their HSAs strategically.
- ✓ Create for and with each client a strategy for allocating retirement savings money between retirement plans and HSAs.

CHAPTER 7

Funding an HSA

One of the more common barriers to individuals' participating in an HSA program is that they lack—or perceive that they lack—the funds to take full advantage of the account.

In this chapter, you'll explore

- four sources of HSA contributions, and
- how these sources affect net pay and lifestyle.

First Source: Difference in Premium

In many cases, individuals who switch from more traditional coverage to an HSA-qualified plan realize a substantial reduction in premium. This difference is especially pronounced among your clients who purchase coverage in the nongroup market. In these cases, they pay the full premium (no employer contribution), so a difference of, say, $3,000 in the premium provides them with a true savings of $3,000 that they can deposit in an HSA without otherwise affecting their family budget.

In contrast, a client with employer-sponsored insurance may see the employer pay 75% of the premium. In that case, the employer has a $2,250 premium reduction; your client's premium cost goes down by only $750. Unless the employer shares a large portion of its savings in premiums via an employer HSA contribution, your client may struggle to make the numbers work in her favor.

A growing number of employers are addressing this issue by moving to a defined-contribution approach to funding employees' premiums, a concept to which you were introduced briefly in Chapter 1, *The HSA Revolution*. Under a defined-contribution (or flat-dollar) approach, the employer gives each employee a fixed dollar amount (typically adjusted for self-only or family coverage). Following is an example when your client faces a choice between a plan with a $2,000 family deductible (Option A) and a $6,000 deductible (Option B):

Scenario 1: Defined Benefit (Standard Percentage-of-Premium Funding)

	Option A	Option B
Deductible	*$2,000*	*$6,000*
Premium (monthly)	$2,400	$2,000
Premium (annual)	$28,800	$24,000
Employer	$21,600 (75%)	$18,000 (75%)
Employee	$7,200 (25%)	$ 6,000 (25%)
Difference	**$1,200**	

In this scenario, an employee faces a net increased potential deductible responsibility of $4,000 (from $2,000 to $6,000), with only a $1,200 employee savings in premium, if she chooses Option B. Unless the employer is sharing much of its $3,600 premium savings or the employee is very healthy and willing to place a leveraged bet on continued low claims, the employee usually chooses Option A.

Scenario 2: Defined Contribution (Fixed-Dollar Funding)

	Option A	Option B
Deductible	*$2,000*	*$6,000*
Premium (monthly)	$2,400	$2,000
Premium (annual)	$28,800	$24,000
Employer	$20,000	$20,000
Employee	$8,800	$ 4,000
Difference	**$4,800**	

Now, it costs the employee $4,800 net to buy down the deductible by $4,000 (from $6,000 to $2,000). In this scenario, employees have a financial incentive to choose Option B.

Scenario 2 simply reflects the cost of coverage more accurately to employees.

To apply this concept to funding HSA contributions, let's say the employer funds coverage under Scenario 1 this year. Your client chooses Option A and has $7,200 deducted from her paycheck on a pre-tax basis. Next year, she switches to the HSA-qualified Option B and has only $4,200 (assuming a 5% year-over-year premium increase) deducted from her paycheck—again on a pre-tax basis. She can deposit the difference ($3,000) into her HSA on a pre-tax basis over the course of the year without reducing her paycheck. She simply diverts $3,000 in funds that she once paid to the insurer (on a pre-tax basis) into her HSA (on a pre-tax basis) to cover qualified expenses as she incurs them or to build medical equity.

A growing number of employers are moving to a defined-contribution approach. It is an important step, since it forces employees to come to grips with the full relative cost of differences in premium. When the company pays a percentage of the premium, employers give employees who "buy up" a blank check to spend the employer's money in a manner that is in no way tied to the employees' productivity or value. A defined-contribution approach

- allows employers to set their benefits budgets in advance (since employee coverage choices don't affect the budget),
- provides employers with future cost certainty (since employer contributions don't need to change in proportion to premium increases),
- reflects accurately the cost difference in different coverage options, and
- shifts that cost difference from a shared function between employer and employee to the employee alone.

Second Source: Current Health FSA Contributions

The employees who are typically the most enthusiastic early adopters of an HSA program are those who participate in a Health FSA. They understand the concept of reducing taxable income and of paying for qualified expenses with tax-free dollars. They appreciate that they save about 25% on every qualified item that they purchase through their Health FSA. HSAs offer the same immediate tax benefit.

As will be discussed in Chapter 17, *HSA Eligibility,* individuals who are enrolled in their employer's general Health FSA (or have a spouse who participates in his employer's general Health FSA) aren't eligible to open or contribute to an HSA immediately. They're locked into their Health FSA for the balance of the plan year, even if they've spent their entire election already. This creates enrollment issues when the Health FSA and medical plan renewal dates aren't aligned.

When their general Health FSA plan year ends, they can open and contribute to an HSA. Though they can't renew their participation in the general Health FSA election, they can redeploy the equivalent of their former Health FSA elections to their HSA going forward. Since both Health FSA and HSA payroll deductions are pre-tax, your clients can redirect this money to an HSA without reducing their net paycheck or losing any immediate tax advantages.

Third Source: Retirement Funds

As discussed in Chapter 6, *Four Behavioral Types of HSA Owners,* some of your clients will grasp the concept of using their HSAs as a retirement account to build medical equity. For them, diverting funds that they otherwise would contribute on a pre-tax basis to a 401(k) plan or other retirement account allows them to fund their HSAs without reducing their net paycheck.

Of course, your clients who really understand this concept and want to maximize their retirement savings and minimize their current income tax liabilities are more likely to contribute up to the maximum permitted by law to both their retirement plans and their HSAs.

Fourth Source: Other Resources

It may sound flippant to identify *other resources* as a source of funds. On a practical level, however, individuals who incur out-of-pocket expenses for medical, dental, or vision products or services must pay their providers, whether or not they own an HSA. The question is how. Tap a home-equity line of credit? Secure a loan from a friend or relative? Borrow funds saved in the vacation or children's education account? Sell a fishing boat or pop-up camper? Take a second job? Create an online business? Monetize a hobby?

In each case, individuals rearrange some aspect of their financial lives to raise the funds necessary to pay bills that they've incurred or are about to incur. In each case, if they run these funds through their HSA rather than pay the provider directly, they gain a tax advantage.

Obviously, these resources don't result in an increase in long-term assets in the HSA, since they're designed to meet an immediate need. Nevertheless, they remain a source of HSA funding because they represent assets that your clients can monetize and deposit in their HSAs for tax-free distributions for qualified expenses.

Bonus: Savvy Shopper Savings

This isn't a source of contributions to an HSA, but it's an important way of maintaining account balances. Smart consumers of medical services can reduce their medical costs, which in turn reduces total distributions from their accounts. This source is particularly attractive because it has no impact on a client's personal budget.

How do savvy shoppers save?

- They consult reputable online sources to research a particular ailment. They may not be able to self-diagnose, but they often gain insight that helps a practitioner diagnose an injury, illness, or condition quickly and accurately.
- They self-treat many simple conditions with over-the-counter medications, elastic bandages, rest, and other treatments.
- They determine the proper site of service. Is their condition likely a simple injury or illness that a nurse practitioner at a retail clinic (a treatment center located in a drug store) can diagnose? Might it require x-rays or a higher level of professional judgment, in which case a free-standing urgent-care center with a physician on staff is appropriate? Is it a condition that can wait for a PCP to diagnose or treat tomorrow? Does it warrant a visit to the emergency department of a local hospital? These venues have very different cost structures and therefore very different prices.
- They negotiate balances due with providers. Many hospitals and some doctors offer prompt-pay discounts. A patient who owes a hospital $2,000 for services subject to the deductible may be able to negotiate a prompt-pay discount of $1,200. The insurer still records $2,000 of deductible satisfied and the HSA owner retains the additional $800 in his HSA.
- They negotiate repayment terms with providers. If they owe the same $2,000 above and the provider doesn't negotiate discounts, patients and providers can often agree to a repayment schedule—perhaps $100 per month for 20 months. This schedule might allow a patient to make payments with

new payroll deductions contributed to the HSA, rather than liquidating investments at an inopportune time.

Counseling Your Clients

- ✓ Work with your clients to identify how they can redeploy existing payroll deductions to build HSA balances without reducing net pay.
- ✓ Help your clients identify other sources of funds to minimize current taxes and maximize the value of their HSA balance as retirement funds.

CHAPTER 8

Rolling an IRA Balance to an HSA

Your clients who are eligible to make contributions to their HSAs can make a once-per-lifetime rollover from an IRA to an HSA. This strategy may make sense for some of your clients. For others, the opportunity cost or risk of remaining eligible through a testing period (defined later in this chapter) may outweigh the advantages.

In this chapter, you'll

- review the rules around rolling IRA balances to an HSA,
- determine when a rollover makes sense—and when and why it may not—and
- discuss whether the rollover should come from a traditional or Roth IRA.

Let's dive right into the rules and issues when you consider which of your clients may be candidates to execute a rollover.

Rollovers must come from a traditional or Roth IRA only. Your clients can't transfer funds from any other type of retirement account except a traditional or Roth IRA. No transfers are allowed from a 401(k) plan, SEP IRA, SIMPLE IRA, or other individual or employer-based retirement plan. If a client has assets in one of these accounts and can roll over those funds to an IRA, she can do so and then execute the rollover from that IRA to an HSA.

Rollovers must come from a single IRA. Your clients can't transfer balances from multiple small IRAs to an HSA. A client must consolidate the IRAs into a single account and then transfer the funds from that account to her HSA.

Rollovers count against annual contribution limits. This provision prevents HSA owners from moving large sums of retirement savings from tax-deferred accounts (with distributions included in taxable income) to tax-free HSAs (with no tax liability for qualified distributions). You and your clients must weigh the benefits of moving funds from a taxable to a tax-free distribution stream against the opportunity cost of not reducing taxable income through contributions in the year of the rollover.

And since withdrawing any of the rollover funds constitutes *eating the seed* (spending money previously designated as a long-term asset), your client shouldn't spend the rollover funds to reimburse current expenses. HSA rules don't prohibit spending the rollover funds immediately—HSA funds are fungible once they enter the account—but a prudent HSA owner whose goal is to maximize retirement assets by consciously building medical equity shouldn't roll over funds merely to spend them. Doing so reduces assets.

Your client shouldn't spend the rollover funds to reimburse current expenses.

Because HSAs provide the opportunity to enjoy tax savings either now or in the future, the temptation to distribute balances to pay for current expenses can be strong. For this reason, a successful rollover that preserves total retirement requires either (1) a level of discipline or (2) recognition of lack of discipline and subsequent opening of a second HSA with self-limited access to balances to preserve medical equity.

Rollovers are limited to once per lifetime. Because HSA owners can execute a rollover from an IRA only once per lifetime, they must be careful to use this opportunity to maximize the financial effect of a rollover. Here are some considerations for clients who

- *are covered on a self-only contract and foresee coverage on a family plan in the future.* They may want to delay making a rollover until they are enrolled in family coverage, when their annual contribution limit (and thus maximum rollover amount) approximately doubles. Foreseeing a marriage, birth, or adoption is an important planning skill in this context.
- *are approaching age 55.* It may make sense to wait until the year that they turn 55 to execute their rollover, since their annual contribution limit increases by $1,000 to reflect the catch-up contribution. They should weigh this additional contribution maximum against remaining HSA-eligible longer

into the future by considering job security and personal situations that may affect future HSA eligibility.

- *gain HSA eligibility late in the calendar year.* This timing creates an ideal opportunity to use the Last-Month Rule. This concept allows individuals who become HSA-eligible as late as Dec. 1 to make a full (not pro-rated) contribution for that year (for further discussion, see Chapter 18, *HSA Contributions*). Your clients can roll over up to their maximum contribution from an IRA to their HSA. Then, at the beginning of the following year, they can begin to make pre-tax or tax-deductible contributions for that year to reduce their taxable income and reimburse tax-free any qualified expenses incurred since they became HSA-eligible and established their HSAs.

There is one exception to the "once per lifetime" limit. An individual with self-only coverage who executes a rollover and then switches to a family contract later that year can make a second rollover so that the total rollover is equal to the maximum contribution to which she's entitled under family coverage (less any contributions that also apply to the annual limit). She must make the second contribution for that year before the due date of her personal income tax return for that year.

Individuals must remain HSA-eligible through a *testing period.* The testing period begins the month after the rollover and lasts for 12 full months. (Note that this period is different from the testing period associated with the Last-Month Rule, which extends to the end of the following calendar year and thus may be as long as 23 months.) If your client rolls over funds from an IRA to her HSA and subsequently loses eligibility, her entire rollover becomes a premature withdrawal from her IRA. She must include the entire distribution in her taxable income. And unless the distribution occurs during the year that she turns age 59½ or later or she is disabled, she pays an additional 10% tax as a penalty for a withdrawal for non-qualified expenses.

HSA owners can execute a rollover from an IRA only once per lifetime.

Funds can be rolled over from a traditional or Roth IRA. Though individuals can roll over funds from either type of IRA, you'll probably recommend that your clients roll over funds from a traditional IRA only.

Traditional IRA: Your client probably made pre-tax contributions to this account, whether those contributions were made directly to an IRA or to a 401(k) plan that she later rolled over to an IRA. Her subsequent distributions are included in her taxable income, whether they're used for health-related or general expenses. By rolling over funds from a traditional IRA to an HSA, she realizes these benefits:

- Distributions for qualified items are tax-free. Her spending power increases by about 30% when she makes distributions for qualified items from an HSA rather than a traditional IRA.
- She isn't subject to Required Minimum Distributions from her HSA, as she is with traditional IRA balances no later than the year that she turns age 70½. She can preserve funds in her HSA to spend when she actually needs the money rather than creating an immediate tax liability with RMDs that she must make whether or not she needs the funds.
- Her HSA distributions don't count against her provisional income and thus don't influence whether none, 50%, or 85% of her Social Security benefits are subject to income taxes. Having only 50% rather than 85% of a $20,000 annual Social Security benefit subject to taxes saves about $800 on federal income taxes alone at the 12% marginal income tax rate (plus additional savings if her state or local government imposes income taxes as well). Reducing provisional income is desirable for some individuals, though your clients probably have (or will have) retirement income that exceeds $34,000 (single filers) or $44,000 (joint filers). Thus, they have 85% of their Social Security benefit taxed regardless of whether the next dollar to reimburse qualified medical expenses comes from an IRA or an HSA (though the tax treatment of the distribution itself remains favorable to the HSA).

It's always to your client's advantage to have funds in an HSA rather than in a traditional IRA if she's reimbursing qualified expenses.

At worst, at age 65, tax treatment for non-qualified items is identical (included in taxable income, but no additional tax as a penalty) for both an HSA and a traditional IRA. And it's always to your client's advantage to have funds in an HSA rather than in a traditional IRA if she's reimbursing qualified expenses. The only situation in which it doesn't make sense is to make distributions for non-qualified expenses between the years that she turns age 59½ and age 65 when she isn't disabled. During that period in her life, distributions from traditional IRAs are taxable but no longer subject to a penalty for premature withdrawal, but HSA distributions for non-qualified expenses are included in taxable income and subject to an additional 20% tax as a penalty.

It always makes sense for her to make the distribution when she spends the funds on qualified items.

Roth IRA: Your client made after-tax contributions to her Roth IRA. She already paid taxes on the contributions in exchange for the promise of tax-free distributions for any purpose. In contrast, an HSA allows tax-free distributions only for qualified expenses. If she rolls over funds from a Roth IRA to an HSA, she loses distribution flexibility by exposing all non-qualified expenses to taxes (and penalties if she's under age 65 and not disabled). It's difficult to think of a single advantage of converting a Roth IRA to an HSA.

Don't eat the seed. Farmers who struggle to find enough to eat during a long hard winter know that they risk death if they grind the seeds that they plan to plant during the spring to make bread in February. That action is called *eating the seed*. Retirement savers must exercise the same discipline. When they transfer funds from an IRA (whose rules impose penalties for premature withdrawal as an incentive for owners to preserve balances) to an HSA (with no taxes or penalties for withdrawals for qualified expenses), they may be tempted to spend the money to alleviate a short-term cash-flow crunch.

You must help your clients resist this impulse, whether you help them build financial discipline or encourage them to open a second HSA whose balances they can't withdraw easily. Retaining balances is critical. Individuals who spend a long-term asset on current expenses typically suffer a financial setback equal to many times the amount of the withdrawal, since those funds no longer grow long-term in a tax-free environment.

For more information on rollovers, see *IRS Notice 2008-51,* which appears in the back of this book as Appendix D. The notice is devoted exclusively to this topic.

Counseling Your Clients

- ✓ Review each client's situation (such as financial resources, enjoying a tax break now versus creating a tax benefit in retirement, and risk aversion) to determine whether a one-time rollover from an IRA to an HSA makes sense.

- ✓ If a rollover is a prudent financial move, determine whether a change in the law (for example, proposed higher HSA contribution limits) or a client's personal situation (transitioning from self-only to family coverage or vice versa, nearing age 55, or preparing to enroll in Medicare, for example) allows a client to roll over a greater or lesser (or no) sum in the future. Timing a rollover optimally can make a difference of thousands of dollars at the time of the rollover and tens of thousands of dollars in accumulated medical equity in retirement.

- ✓ Make sure your clients understand that spending any of the money rolled over from an IRA on pre-retirement expenses diminishes their wealth. Your clients must understand the don't eat the seed mantra, which is especially important with an HSA (as opposed to a retirement account) because the law extends tax benefits to HSA owners for immediate or future distributions for qualified expenses.

CHAPTER 9

Utilizing a Limited-Purpose Health FSA Strategically

A Limited-Purpose Health FSA is one of the more underutilized tools that HSA owners can deploy to build their HSA balances and enjoy additional and immediate tax benefits. Limited-Purpose Health FSAs have already been mentioned, but not from a strategic perspective.

In this chapter, you'll

- review the definition of a Limited-Purpose Health FSA,
- identify the expenses that can be reimbursed tax-free from a Limited-Purpose Health FSA and how that list differs from a general Health FSA and HSA, and
- learn how an HSA owner who can't reimburse certain children's qualified expenses tax-free from her HSA can enjoy tax benefits through a Limited-Purpose Health FSA.

Individuals who participate in a general Health FSA—sponsored by either their own or their spouse's employer—aren't eligible to open or contribute to an HSA until the end of the Health FSA plan year

. . . even if they're enrolled in an HSA-qualified plan,

. . . even if they've exhausted their Health FSA election, and

. . . even if they promise not to file a claim for reimbursement.

Though a Health FSA may be thought of as a benefit plan, it is subject to some areas of the tax code that apply to group medical plans. One instance is determining HSA eligibility. Employees who participate in a general Health FSA aren't HSA-eligible unless all applicable coverage—medical coverage and benefit plans like a Health FSA or an HRA—satisfy the requirements of an HSA-qualified plan.

The key qualifier in the preceding statement is *general.* Here, *general* refers to a Health FSA that reimburses (1) all qualified expenses (2) for all family members (3) without a deductible. A general Health HSA is the most common Health FSA offered to employees because it offers the largest list of qualified expenses and doesn't impact an employee's ability to participate in any other employee benefit except an HSA.

Limited Health FSAs

With the introduction of HSAs in 2004, the IRS defined two distinct Health FSA designs that allow your clients to remain HSA-eligible and enjoy the benefits of a Health FSA. These benefits include additional tax savings, immediate access to their entire elections, and the ability to preserve HSA balances as they reimburse qualified expenses through a second tax-advantaged program. The two HSA-qualified limited Health FSA designs are a Limited-Purpose Health FSA and a Post-Deductible Health FSA. You can read more about these plans in *IRS Rev. Rul. 2004-45.*

Limited-Purpose Health FSA. This design reimburses dental and vision expenses only, plus select preventive services that aren't covered in full. Participating in a Limited-Purpose Health FSA program is a great option for your clients and their family members who want to undergo vision-correction surgery, purchase glasses, complete orthodontia treatment, or repair or replace teeth. They can reimburse these expenses tax-free from a Limited-Purpose Health FSA without reducing their HSA balances and enjoy the same immediate tax benefit.

This plan design doesn't affect HSA eligibility because dental and vision expenses are permitted coverage under HSA rules and select preventive care services can be covered below the deductible on an HSA-qualified plan. Enrolling in dental-only or vision-only coverage doesn't disqualify your clients from becoming HSA-eligible.

Post-Deductible Health FSA. This design begins to reimburse all Section 213(d) expenses after your clients have met a deductible no less than the statutory minimum annual deductible for an HSA-qualified plan. This design doesn't affect HSA eligibility because both the medical plan and the limited Health FSA satisfy the statutory minimum annual deductible requirements of an HSA-qualified plan.

Pure Post-Deductible Health FSAs aren't common. The design is incorporated into a growing number of limited Health FSAs that blend both *Limited-Purpose* and *Post-Deductible* characteristics into a single limited Health FSA (which some administrators may call a Post-Deductible Health FSA). Here's how this hybrid plan works for a family in 2018 and 2019:

- Vision and dental expenses—qualified for reimbursement.
- Medical, prescription drug, and over-the-counter equipment and supplies (and over-the-counter drugs and medicine with a prescription)—qualified for reimbursement once your client certifies that he has met at least $2,700 of his medical-insurance deductible (the 2018 and 2019 statutory minimum annual deductible for an HSA-qualified plan). The applicable minimum deductible on the Post-Deductible Health FSA for someone with self-only coverage on an HSA-qualified medical plan is $1,350 both years.

The benefits to this hybrid approach are that it

- reduces the likelihood that participants forfeit unused balances, since the range of qualified expenses expands beyond the Limited-Purpose Health FSA list for those who incur higher medical expenses; and
- allows HSA owners to enjoy immediate tax benefits through tax-free distribution for qualified expenses while they preserve HSA balances as medical equity for future tax-free distribution for qualified expenses.

Employers offering limited Health FSA programs have the option to add a grace period or limited carryover to reduce the likelihood that participants forfeit unused balances at the end of the plan year. A grace period gives participants an additional 2½ months to incur expenses (see Chapter 17, *HSA Eligibility,* for further discussion). Think of the grace-period provision as an *unlimited carryover* of unused funds for a *limited period of time.*

The limited carryover allows participants to carry over up to $500 of unused funds for use during the next plan year. Think of it as a *limited carryover* of unused funds for an *unlimited period of time.*

These provisions aren't automatic, and participants themselves can't choose one option or the other. The employer chooses a grace period or a limited carryover, or neither. Because the Health FSAs are limited, neither the grace period nor the carryover affects a participant's HSA eligibility during the following plan year. In contrast, grace periods and carryover provisions attached to general Health FSAs may disqualify someone from opening and contributing to an HSA if the participant has a balance to carry over.

Many employers offer limited Health FSAs, but many others don't. Employers who offer a general Health FSA to employees who aren't concerned with HSA eligibility often add a Limited-Purpose Health FSA, since the incremental cost of expanding the Health FSA program to include a limited Health FSA is typically small. In contrast, employers who don't offer a general Health FSA or believe that their employees won't come close to maximizing their HSA contributions and therefore can reimburse dental and vision expenses from their HSAs generally don't offer a limited Health FSA.

Ask your clients about the availability of a limited Health FSA through their employers (or through their spouses' employers). You and your client can then determine whether the benefits of immediate access to the entire limited Health FSA balance, the opportunity to further reduce taxable income, and the ability to build medical equity make participation in a limited Health FSA a sound financial strategy.

Adult Children

There's another reason why some of your clients should consider enrolling in a Limited-Purpose Health FSA. Even though Health FSAs are benefit plans, they must comply with some requirements of employer-sponsored medical plans under federal tax law. Included is the provision that children to age 26 can receive reimbursements through a parent's Health FSA for qualified expenses, whether or not they are your clients' tax dependents.

Children to age 26 can receive reimbursements through a parent's Health FSA for qualified expenses, whether or not they are your clients' tax dependents.

This is different from the rules governing HSAs. Your clients can't reimburse any expenses that a child incurs after the date that the child ceases to become a tax dependent.

Example: *Jack, age 24, remains covered on his father Dont'a's medical plan. Jack works full-time and is no longer his father's tax dependent. Dont'a can't reimburse any of Jack's qualified expenses tax-free from his HSA, since Jack is no longer Dont'a's tax dependent. On the other hand, if Jack undergoes vision-correction surgery or a restorative dental procedure, Dont'a can reimburse the expense from his Limited-Purpose Health FSA.*

It's not uncommon for a young adult who has recently (or not yet) joined the full-time workforce not to have discretionary income sufficient to cover a large medical, dental, or vision expense. In these cases, your client may cover the cost of the service. If your client has a Limited-Purpose Health FSA and the adult child's expense is a dental or vision service, your client can reimburse it on a tax-free basis from his Health FSA.

In contrast, if your client has an HSA only, he can't make a tax-free distribution for the non-dependent child's qualified expense. Any withdrawals for expenses incurred by the non-dependent child are included in your client's taxable income, and unless your client is at least age 65 or disabled, he pays an additional 20% tax as a penalty.

Alternatively, your client can help the child open his own HSA if he's HSA-eligible (enrolled in an HSA-qualified plan—he doesn't have to be the plan subscriber—and not enrolled in disqualifying coverage and not someone else's tax dependent). In that case, if your client contributes to his son's HSA, the son—not your client—receives the tax deduction. Yes, the tax deduction is far more beneficial to the higher income parent, but at least someone in the family enjoys a tax benefit.

The key point is that a Limited-Purpose Health FSA may provide your client with an opportunity to receive tax advantages when reimbursing a non-dependent child's expenses from his Limited-Purpose Health FSA. Your client doesn't receive the same benefit when reimbursing the same expenses from his HSA.

Counseling Your Clients

- ✓ Ask your clients whether they have—or their spouses have—the option to participate in a Limited-Purpose Health FSA.

- ✓ If they have access to a limited Health FSA, discuss the merits of making an election into that Health FSA. In many cases, the advantages (additional tax savings, immediate access to the full election, and coverage for children to age 26) outweigh the risks (forfeiting unused balances).

- ✓ Be sure to ask them about adult children who aren't tax dependents. Your clients may be able to help them enjoy tax advantages and build equity through their own HSAs, even if your clients don't gain a tax break.

CHAPTER 10

Investing HSA Balances Traditionally

Most HSA owners are former Health FSA participants. They understand the tax advantages of depositing pre-tax money in an account and making tax-free withdrawals for qualified expenses. Their world-view is somewhat narrow. As a result, only about 10% of HSA owners hold any portion of their balances in equities. But that figure is rising and will continue to grow as more HSA owners understand the benefits of investing and have built sufficient balances to do so.

In this chapter, you'll find a discussion of

- investment options typically available in an HSA,
- HSA administrator rules about investment options, and
- investment strategies.

HSA owners experience an immediate positive return when they contribute to their HSAs because they save on federal income and payroll taxes. In addition, if they live anywhere other than Alabama, California, and New Jersey, they avoid state income taxes as well.

And when an employer contributes to an HSA, as many do, the initial rate of return on those funds is infinite.

For most HSA owners, the returns end there. In today's interest environment—with returns typically less than 20 basis points (0.2%)—balances grow slowly. Even in an era of low inflation, balances don't keep up with general inflation. They fall far short of medical inflation, which has run at about twice the rate of general inflation in the economy since the introduction of Medicare and Medicaid—the federal government's first wide-scale involvement in medical coverage and finance—in 1965.

Investment Basics

Most new HSA owners are unlikely candidates for investing. Administrators generally require that they build an initial cash balance of $1,000 to $2,500 before they can invest. If they dip into their cash balances to make distributions, they must replenish the cash balance back to that threshold before they can purchase more investment instruments. The stated rationale for these thresholds is to ensure that owners have sufficient funds to reimburse expenses without being forced to liquidate investments during a market downturn and thus compound the effect of the distribution.

A more cynical view is that the financial institution that holds the cash balances can pool those funds and lend a multiple of the total cash assets. That opportunity evaporates with each dollar that moves from the FDIC-insured cash portion of the HSA to the investment account.

It typically takes Unconscious Accumulators and Conscious Accumulators (remember these behaviors from Chapter 6, *Four Behavioral Types of HSA Owners*?) several years to build balances sufficient to invest. For Maximizers, the decision point may come as soon as three or four months into their owning and contributing to an HSA.

Most HSA administrators offer a select menu of mutual fund options. The typical menu has between 24 and 48 options. This size reflects the concern that too few options leave investors frustrated and too many choices leave some HSA owners with a "paralysis by analysis" complex. These individuals become so overwhelmed with the prospect of choosing the right investments from a long list that they end up not investing at all.

Most HSA administrators offer a select menu of mutual fund options.

The list typically includes representative funds in categories such as large-cap growth, large-cap blend, large-cap value, mid-cap growth, mid-cap blend, mid-cap value, small-cap growth, small-cap blend, and small-cap value, as well as several international, bond, and money-market funds. They may also include target funds similar to those in retirement account portfolios so that your clients themselves don't have to change the ratio of equity-to-fixed-income investments in their investment portfolios as they draw closer to retirement.

Investment Mechanics

Though some HSAs sponsored by financial institutions (particularly small savings banks and credit unions) offer only certificates of deposit as an investment option (mirroring their IRA product), larger HSA administrators integrate an equity trading platform with their HSA. HSA owners can move funds easily from their cash accounts to the investment portal, though they may need to leave their HSA portal and log into the investment account to begin to allocate funds into specific funds.

As with an IRA, your clients must understand the cost of investing. Some administrators charge a monthly fee to access the investment platform. Others offer free access, then charge a fee for each transaction. Still others charge no fees for access or specific trades, but the funds themselves include high administrative fees that go to the fund-management firm or other fees that are collected by the fund managers and then distributed to the HSA administrator. You and your clients need to understand the cost structure to ensure that their investment gains aren't absorbed by high fees or their losses in a down market aren't magnified by these fees.

Your clients can allocate the pool of funds that they've moved to the investment platform to the funds that they choose. This is a one-time allocation that they can adjust at any time (subject to any limits imposed by the administrator or fund manager and subject to possible transaction costs).

In addition, many HSAs offer a *sweep* option. As long as the account maintains the minimum cash balance, new contributions are swept directly into the investment account. The new contributions are invested according to the HSA owner's instructions (which may or may not reflect the current allocation of existing investments).

The allocation within existing investments is dynamic and changes with market-driven changes in the value of the underlying investments. The allocation can be rebalanced by either reallocation of existing investments or a different investment ratio for new investments. The allocation of future contributions is constant in percentage terms unless altered prospectively by your client.

> These two dynamics are the levers that HSA owners control to manage their investment portfolios.

These two dynamics—which reflect the same tools that retirement plan participants have available to them—are the levers that HSA owners control to manage their investment portfolios.

Example: *Hadley allocates one-third of her portfolio to each of the following equity investments: large-cap growth, mid-cap blend, and small-cap value. After a year, with changes in market value, large-cap growth represents 45%, mid-cap blend 45%, and small-cap value 10% of the portfolio. Rather than rebalance the allocation immediately, Hadley can either execute two trades (selling large-cap growth and mid-cap blend and buying small-cap value) or change the allocation of future contributions in perhaps a 15%, 15%, and 70% ratio to rebalance the portfolio slowly.*

Investment Strategies

Some HSA owners may be dissatisfied with the range, quality, or cost of the investment options within the HSA that their employer has chosen. Remember, employers can—and almost always do—choose a single HSA administrator with which to work and typically won't deposit employer or employee pre-tax payroll contributions to HSAs managed by other administrators.

If your client is dissatisfied with her investment policies, options, or costs (or any other feature of the product) of her employer's HSA administrator, she can open a second HSA and make a one-time—or frequent—trustee-to-trustee transfer from her HSA with her employer's preferred administrator to her preferred HSA. Though the trustee-to-trustee transfer process may seem daunting, it's not complicated. It is, however, one more task to remember to complete unless it can be automated through the receiving HSA platform.

A semi-annual or quarterly schedule of trustee-to-trustee transfers may satisfy you and your client. That way, she dollar-cost averages her investments two to four times annually rather than monthly or biweekly. This type of schedule may be a reasonable compromise between the desire to dollar-cost average more often and the work required to schedule a manual transfer.

What about the investment portfolio itself? Some HSA owners want to create a balanced portfolio within their HSAs. These owners may be dissatisfied with their employers' preferred HSAs and their investment options. They may search for an HSA administrator that offers more investment options or includes funds from a family with which they're familiar—perhaps the funds family available in their 401(k) plan.

Other owners may see their HSAs as a part of their overall retirement portfolios and seek to balance the total portfolio. For example, they may dislike most of their HSA administrators' funds but see value in, say, the international growth fund and the mid-cap blend fund. In that case, your clients can concentrate their investments in those two funds to create an unbalanced HSA portfolio that becomes part of a balanced overall retirement portfolio.

You may or may not be concerned with your clients' adopting this approach. Though the overall portfolio is balanced, the HSA isn't. A collapse of the international growth or the mid-cap blend segment could leave your client with a reduced balance in her HSA, even as her 401(k) plan balance grows. This imbalance isn't an issue in two 401(k) plans, since the money is all subject to the same market forces and the tax treatment is identical.

On the other hand, 401(k) plan and HSA balances aren't interchangeable. If a bad market wipes out half the value of the HSA, your client can't rebuild that balance by merely transferring funds from the 401(k) plan to the HSA. That value is gone forever, and your client is left with less medical equity from which to reimburse future health-related expenses tax-free.

It's important to consider these issues when advising your clients on a proper overall investment strategy, platform, fund choices, and management.

One HSA or Two?

This question has already been addressed in the context of features of the products offered by an employer's preferred HSA administrator. When product features don't meet your client's needs, then your client should open a second HSA.

Chapter 6, *Four Behavioral Types of HSA Owners,* touched on another reason that a second HSA may be appropriate: lack of discipline. If you are or your client is concerned that she may spend balances that you both had pegged for long-term savings in an HSA, a second HSA may make sense.

> Example: *Mariana, age 56 and single, and her advising professional determine that she should save $3,500 annually in her HSA. Her maximum contribution*

in 2019 is $4,500 with her catch-up contribution, which leaves her with $1,000 to reimburse current qualified expenses tax-free. If Mariana faces a $1,400 bill, her temptation may be to pay it with her HSA balance (thus dipping into $400 of balances designated for savings). She may figure that she can make it up next year.

A solution is for Mariana to set up two HSAs. Funds flow into the HSA of her employer's chosen administrator. She then makes trustee-to-trustee transfers to move all contributions above $1,000 to the second HSA. Mariana cuts up the debit card associated with the second HSA to make sure she's not tempted to dip into it to pay for a current expense.

The second-HSA approach just illustrated may be more important when other family members have access to the HSA. When your client, her husband, and her daughter in college all have debit cards, it may be difficult for your client to ensure that no more than the designated distribution amount is withdrawn from the account in a given year. Moving balances beyond that amount into a second HSA to which other family members don't have access ensures that funds designated as medical equity are segregated and thus not spent.

To Invest or not to Invest?

You and your clients must consider this question. The answer is simple for many clients when dealing with a retirement account that won't be tapped for decades. In that case, the best long-term strategy is to invest in equities, ride out market fluctuations, and count on a return approaching the historical average of 7% to 9% annually.

HSAs differ in that the funds can be used to reimburse today's expenses tax-free or retained to grow and reimburse tomorrow's expenses—or today's expenses at a future point in time—tax-free. This increased flexibility requires a fresh look at the benefits of investing. If your clients are using their HSAs as a fund in which to accumulate and build medical equity for retirement medical expenses, they must invest in equities merely to keep up with general and medical inflation. Today, no HSA trustee—indeed, no financial institution—offers a no-risk investment with returns that equal or exceed medical inflation.

In most cases, HSA owners today are reluctant to invest or are simply unaware of this option. Many who've participated in a Health FSA don't understand that they can invest HSA balances, since that wasn't an option with Health FSAs. Others delay investing until they build sufficient cash balances to feel confident that they will be able to reimburse their anticipated expenses without regard to whether their equity investments are up or down. You may have some clients who take the same approach to retirement account investing and have accumulated high-five-figure or low-six-figure cash balances in their 401(k) plans that they plan to invest at some point during the 20 years before retirement.

You can apply the same educational approach to your clients for HSAs as you do for their retirement equity investing—though admittedly the lower balances in the HSA may lead to a different mix of cash and equities and a more conservative allocation of risk in the HSA.

Counseling Your Clients

- ✓ Understand each client's level of discipline to dedicate a portion of HSA contributions and balances to medical equity accumulation, not to be spent on current—even unanticipated high current—expenses. Your client may need to open a second HSA.
- ✓ Review with your client the terms and conditions of the investment option within her HSA. You need to understand the menu of investments, investment costs, and other characteristics to determine whether a particular HSA fits into an overall investment strategy. Again, a second HSA may be optimal.
- ✓ With your client's input, determine whether the appropriate investment strategy is to have a diversified HSA investment portfolio or to let the HSA itself lack diversification as long as her overall retirement portfolio (retirement plan and HSA) is diversified.

CHAPTER 11

Self-Directed HSAs

HSA owners have the option to open and invest in a true self-directed account. Few HSA owners have adopted this strategy because (1) it's riskier than traditional equity investing and (2) few know about this approach with traditional retirement plans, never mind HSAs.

In this chapter, you'll find

- the definition of a true self-directed HSA,
- a discussion of the investment options available within a self-directed HSA, and
- a review of some potential benefits and risks inherent in investing through these accounts.

In most investors' eyes, a self-directed IRA/HSA is a brokerage account that allows them to select from a wide range of mutual funds, stocks, and debt instruments rather than a short list of mutual funds offered in the typical 401(k) plan or bank-based IRA/HSA program. Indeed, a major financial incentive cited by retirees in moving funds from an employer's 401(k) plan to an IRA is the greater range of investment options.

Although the type of self-directed IRA/HSA that most investors picture does provide additional investment options, it remains limited to the types of investments that the sponsor offers. Since most self-directed IRAs are offered by brokerages and mutual-fund companies (and most HSAs are offered by financial institutions or administrators and have only a narrow range of investment options), investment options are typically limited to stocks, bonds, mutual funds, and exchange-traded funds.

In contrast, a true self-directed IRA/HSA opens the range of investments to a much wider selection of money-making opportunities. These options include

- stocks, bonds, mutual funds, and exchange-traded funds

- self-storage facilities

- commercial and residential real estate. Owners can purchase and flip or maintain single-family rental homes, multi-family housing units, retail space, warehouses, factories, and other real property.

- personal and commercial lending. Owners can lend funds to real-estate investors (an acquaintance who rehabilitates housing units), businesses (such as a neighbor or fellow parishioner who runs a landscaping company and needs to purchase new equipment), and personal borrowers (such as a co-worker who fails to qualify for a traditional mortgage).

- precious metals, most commonly gold and silver

Investors can't purchase the following items in a self-directed IRA/HSA:

- works of art. The basic rule is that if you can enjoy looking at, touching, or displaying a physical piece of property, it's more than a pure financial investment and therefore not permitted. Examples include framed artwork, sculpture, and musical instruments.

- antiques, gems, stamps, coins, alcohol, and other tangible property

- insurance contracts. Since these contracts provide additional benefits outside capital appreciation, they aren't permitted.

In addition, investors can't comingle their self-directed HSA balances in pools that take the form of a common trust or common investment. See *IRC Section 223(d)(1)(D)* and *IRS Notice 2004-50, Q&A 66* for more information on this important topic.

Though the concept of a true self-directed HSA is new, hundreds of thousands of savvy investors have been using true self-directed IRAs for years to build their balances. Self-directed accounts require a high degree of management and compliance effort, so they're not for the casual investor. The typical investor who benefits from these arrangements is someone who has time, expertise, and connections:

- *time* to manage a business, because this type of investing is a business. The time commitment varies with the number and types of investments.

- *expertise*, because, in most cases, only people with specific skills benefit from this intense level of investing. Most individuals are better off leaving investing to professional money managers (either active traders or passive indexers). Some investors with special knowledge in a particular industry or expertise in a specific sector of the economy, on the other hand, may benefit from leveraging that information to generate investment income, just as they benefited during their career.

- *connections*, because often these investments are private and involve knowing people who need cash to fund a business launch or expansion. These opportunities usually aren't advertised to the public.

Even with clients who possess this expertise, you'll probably warn them of the danger in investing solely in areas of their personal expertise if they derive their incomes from that same industry. They run the same risk as an employee who purchases stock in his company for his retirement portfolio. If the company struggles, his income *and* his retirement are placed at risk simultaneously.

Assessing the Benefits

Why do some investors move funds to a true self-directed account? They may do so to:

- reduce overall portfolio risk. By placing a portion of their savings in investments other than those tied to the general stock market, they can diversify their risk.

- force appreciation. By adding value directly (by owning) or indirectly (by lending with input) to a particular investment (for example, rehabilitating real estate), they can directly increase the value of the asset rather than rely on others (for example, CEOs of publicly held corporations) to do so.

- assume control. Self-directed account owners want to be at the helm of their investment strategy, rather than sit back and let professionals manage their portfolios. They love being *in the game* and want to remain engaged.

Weighing the Risks

Though the self-directed opportunity offers some clear benefits, it also exposes investors to a higher degree of risk than simply investing in professionally managed securities. The risks include

- prohibited transactions. Federal tax law places restrictions on allowable investments (described very generally on the preceding page), the level of personal involvement and potential partners (restrictions on investing in opportunities with certain family members). The account administrator does not assume any responsibility for vetting the legality or HSA compliance issues of any investment opportunity, so the investor must have a good legal team to verify compliance with federal law.

- greater downside risk. Though an investor with specialized knowledge can build more wealth in a self-directed account than through publicly traded securities, self-directed investments typically also carry higher risk of total loss. Balances typically are invested heavily in one or a handful of similar opportunities, reflecting the investor's knowledge. In contrast, mutual funds and a broad-based stock portfolio are invested in a wider range of markets, thus creating a level of diversity that helps insulate investors against large losses.

- costs. Self-directed accounts are much more expensive to maintain than traditional IRAs or HSAs. The expenses include an up-front fee to establish the account and high annual maintenance fees, often assessed as a percentage of the value of the account. Self-directed investors incur legal, tax preparation, and accounting fees as well.

The pros and cons of self-directing investments in an HSA are the same as the rewards and risks associated with self-directed IRAs. The advice that you provide your clients with respect to the latter are appropriate for the former.

HSA owners who choose the self-direct route must take steps to manage compliance, since their investments may not be regulated and administrators of self-directed HSAs don't offer compliance services. If the IRS finds that a self-directed HSA engaged in a prohibited transaction or investments, the HSA is liquidated immediately. The entire balance is deemed a premature withdrawal and subject to income taxes and potential penalties.

The best way to minimize risk is to consult with a tax attorney who is well versed in the rules and can vet each investment. That guidance is expensive, but far less expensive than the penalties for engaging in a prohibited transaction. The higher costs that self-directed HSA owners face in both account administration and legal fees reduce the amount of the actual investment gain.

The best way to reduce the potential cost of a prohibited transaction is to create a new self-directed HSA for each investment. If your client invests in three rental buildings, for example, she can create three self-directed HSAs and place one building in each account. That way, if the IRS determines that one transaction is prohibited—requiring immediate liquidation of the self-directed HSA, with tax and penalty implications—the other two investments aren't affected.

Clearly, self-directed HSAs aren't for amateurs. Regular HSAs, with their registered investment options, provide a safer alternative with a much lower compliance risk. Self-directed HSA ownership should be recommended only to individuals who have a particular expertise (or who work with someone with a particular expertise and a need for an equity or lending partner) and are willing to accept more concentration, business, and compliance risk and higher costs in exchange for potentially higher returns than traditional investment options inside a regular HSA.

Counseling Your Clients

- ✓ Make sure that your clients understand the risks inherent in self-directed investing. They typically understand the benefits (though often with unrealistic understanding and expectations), but fail to grasp the level of expertise and commitment of time needed to manage these investments.

- ✓ Counsel your clients on the importance of securing competent legal and accounting resources to ensure that they structure their investments correctly, avoid prohibited transactions, and properly account for all activity. The penalty for a prohibited transaction is disqualification of the entire HSA balance. The balance must be included in that year's taxable income (with additional penalties possible as well).

- ✓ Emphasize to your clients the importance of maintaining multiple self-directed accounts or refer them to legal or tax counsel to discuss this issue. In most cases, each investment should be made through a separate account to minimize the financial exposure if the IRS successfully challenges the legality of a single investment. The pain of making a $3,000 prohibited transaction is multiplied when your client makes that investment within a self-directed HSA with a $75,000 balance. The result is an additional $75,000, rather than $3,000, included in taxable income and subject to potential penalties.

CHAPTER 12

Using an HSA in Retirement

Retirement is the easiest period of HSA management. When your clients are no longer HSA-eligible, they aren't concerned with HSA eligibility or contributions. The contribution door is shut and locked permanently. They can now focus on what happens within the HSA and what funds go out the distribution door.

They continue to use the HSA as they always have—to reimburse qualified expenses tax-free. The tax treatment of qualified expenses doesn't depend on whether your client is or isn't HSA-eligible. As long as it's a qualified expense incurred by your client, her spouse, or her tax dependents after your client opened the HSA, the reimbursement is tax-free.

In this chapter, you'll find a discussion of

- tax treatment of distributions from an HSA in retirement,
- what questions you need to ask your clients to determine whether their current HSA is their best option in retirement, and
- whether your clients should reimburse old expenses or retain HSA funds for future retirement expenses.

Your clients don't need to be HSA-eligible to make tax-free distributions from their HSAs. Eligibility is necessary to contribute to an HSA, but not to build balances tax-free or make tax-free distributions for qualified expenses.

> Example: *Tomas retired five years ago and enrolled in Medicare. He can't contribute to his HSA any longer because Medicare doesn't offer an HSA-qualified plan option. Tomas can spend his $52,000 balance on qualified expenses with no tax consequences.*

Your clients can reimburse their own, their spouse's, and their tax dependents' qualified expenses tax-free, as long as this relationship exists at the time that the expenses are incurred.

Example: *Maya, a 72-year-old widow, ceased contributing to her HSA when she lost her HSA eligibility at age 66. She recently remarried. Her new husband, Sage, incurs a $500 dental expense. Maya can reimburse that expense tax-free from her HSA because Sage is her spouse at the time of the expense. This is true even though Maya wasn't married to Sage when she was HSA-eligible and contributing to her account.*

Medicare Part B, Part C, and Part D premiums are qualified expenses (as are Part A premiums for those who worked fewer than 40 employment quarters). Your clients can reimburse these expenses tax-free from their HSAs beginning in the month that they turn age 65.

Example: *Bridget's Part B premium is deducted automatically from her Social Security check. She can reimburse herself (her HSA administrator can provide direction) for that expense from her HSA, making it tax-free.*

Your clients can reimburse tax-free qualified expenses that they incurred years ago, as long as they have proper documentation and the expense was incurred by someone who was a spouse or tax dependent at the time that the expense was incurred.

Example: *Violet is 70 years old and was HSA-eligible between the ages of 46 and 68. When she was 48, she paid $4,000 for her then-teenage daughter's orthodontic work, which she didn't reimburse from a tax-advantaged account. Even though her daughter is no longer her tax dependent, Violet can reimburse herself for that expense today because her daughter was her tax dependent then and orthodontia is a qualified expense that she incurred after she opened and funded her HSA. Violet needs to have retained detailed paperwork—showing the name of the patient, date of service, the service, and the cost—to document this tax-free withdrawal if the IRS audits her personal income tax return for the year that she reports the distribution.*

One quirk in the law is that an HSA owner can reimburse tax-free her spouse's out-of-pocket qualified expenses, but she can't reimburse her spouse's Medicare premiums until she—the accountholder—reaches age 65.

Example: *Brinley is age 62. Her husband, Kellen, is 66 and recently enrolled in Medicare Part A and Part B. Brinley can't reimburse Kellen's Part B premiums tax-free from her HSA until she herself reaches age 65. She can reimburse Kellen's other qualified expenses—medical, dental, or vision copays; deductibles; and coinsurance—regardless of her or his age.*

The basic rules set forth in the preceding discussion cover the tactics of using an HSA at age 65 and beyond.

Your clients also face strategic decisions that are important when attempting to maximize the value of an HSA within a personal financial plan. And they need your continued counsel to ask and explore the answers to these questions:

"Is this still the right HSA for me?" During their working years, your clients probably worked with the HSA administrator that their employer chose. Though HSA owners are free to work with any administrator at any time, employers usually choose a single provider for ease of administration.

Think of an HSA as a grocery store. Most of your clients have a choice of a handful of grocery stores within a reasonable geographic area. And at first glance, grocery stores are pretty generic. They're nothing more than four walls and a roof to protect food for sale against the elements. They all offer the same basic services, with similar formats, shopping carriages, and check-out experiences.

Yet your clients probably have a favorite grocery store. Beyond grocery stores' similarities, your clients see differences that attract them to that particular store. The prices are lower in their preferred store. Or the produce is fresher. Or the workers are friendlier and more helpful.

On one level, HSAs are all the same. All have the same general features—a cash account that's FDIC-insured, a debit card, online accounts, annual tax statements. The similarities typically end there. Most, but not all, offer investment options, and among those who do, the investment line-ups are different. Some still issue paper checks. Some charge a monthly administrative fee regardless of balance. Others waive the fee with a minimum balance. Some offer free electronic bill-pay services through which the owner requests that payment be sent directly to the provider. Others either don't offer this service or charge a fee for it.

Your client needs to assess his current HSA administrator and its product, particularly if his employer paid the monthly administrative fee for active employees but doesn't cover the cost for former employees.

"Do I need to consolidate HSAs?" You may have advised some clients to establish a second HSA during their working years. They opened one through their employer so that they could receive the employer's tax-free contribution and their own pre-tax payroll contributions. They then opened a second HSA because the investment options were better or they wanted to segregate funds that they planned to dedicate to building medical equity.

Now that the HSA no longer receives contributions from the former employer, it may be time to consider consolidating by closing the account with the employer's HSA administrator and rolling those funds into the second HSA—or even closing both accounts and rolling funds to an entirely new HSA.

"Which expenses do I reimburse with my HSA funds?" This question may seem strange. After all, your clients have been contributing to their HSAs for years and building medical equity to pay for their qualified expenses tax-free in retirement. They understand that they can pay a $1,000 medical bill with a $1,000 distribution from an HSA or make a distribution of $1,250 or so from their traditional 401(k) plan or IRA to pay the $1,000 bill and the taxes due on all distributions from a non-Roth retirement account.

For most clients, the discussion ends there.

On the other hand, you may have clients still working after age 70. They must make a Required Minimum Distribution from their retirement accounts during the year that they turn age 70½ or face a penalty equal to 50% of the RMD.

Let's put this in perspective.

Example: *Casey has $3,000 of medical expenses. He has an RMD of $10,000 from his 401(k) plan. He's still active at work and has no need for funds from his 401(k) plan.*

If he distributes $3,000 from his HSA to cover his qualified expenses, he saves roughly $1,000 in taxes and depletes his account by $3,000. He still must *withdraw $10,000 from his 401(k) plan and incur a $3,000 or so tax bill or keep the money in his 401(k) plan and pay a $5,000 penalty.*

In this case, he's better off keeping the $3,000 in his HSA growing tax-free, since he never faces RMDs from his HSA. He can withdraw the $3,000 from his 401(k) plan and actually pay less in taxes (about $1,000) than he'd pay if he kept the funds in his 401(k) plan and paid the 50% penalty ($1,500).

Your clients need to understand this concept. Sometimes it's better to make a taxable distribution from a retirement account and pay taxes to avoid a penalty. The good news is that the funds remain in the HSA as medical equity. They continue to grow in value through investments. And if your client passes away with a balance, the funds pass to his designated beneficiary.

"Should I reimburse old expenses with HSA funds now?" Many HSA owners choose to be *Conscious Accumulators* or *Maximizers* (as you remember from the discussion in Chapter 6, *Four Behavioral Types of HSA Owners*). They incurred expenses that they could have reimbursed from their HSAs but chose to pay with personal funds at the time, deferring an immediate tax benefit to build medical equity.

HSA owners never lose the opportunity to reimburse their qualified expenses tax-free, as long as they incurred the expenses after they opened their HSAs. It's not unusual for an HSA owner (like the author) to have accumulated $25,000 or more in such expenses, with documentation to substantiate a tax-free distribution if the IRS inquires.

So, the answer to this question is probably "no."

It may make sense to distribute funds from an HSA to reimburse old qualified expenses and pay current living expenses if your client is close to the top of a tier of provisional income.

Example: *James receives $20,000 in Social Security benefits, has withdrawn his entire RMD of $23,500 from his traditional IRA, and still has a $2,000 auto-repair bill that he and his wife need to pay by the end of the year.*

He should consider withdrawing funds from his HSA to pay the mechanic's bill. If James withdraws the funds from his IRA, his provisional income increases to $45,500, and he must subject 85% (rather than 50%) of his Social Security benefit *to income taxes. That's a difference of subjecting $17,000 instead of $10,000 to income taxes.*

At a 20% marginal tax rate, James saves $1,400 in taxes that he otherwise would pay on the increased provisional income. He also saves $400 in income taxes that he otherwise would pay if he withdrew funds from his IRA instead of his HSA (when the HSA distribution is matched with a prior qualified expense not reimbursed). The combined tax savings of $1,800 nearly covers the $2,000 mechanic's bill. In other words, he effectively pays only $200 of that $2,000 bill out of his own pocket once the impact of all tax consequences is considered.

Otherwise, unless a client is on the cusp of a higher threshold of provisional income, the decision comes down to balances in the respective accounts and projected future needs for funds.

"I don't have long to live. What steps should I take with my HSA?"
Ideally, nothing, because your client knows that continued living isn't a given and has engaged in proper estate planning. Because her HSA is a trust, she designates an HSA beneficiary when she's alive and can change the beneficiary at any time. She can name multiple beneficiaries, as well as one or multiple contingent beneficiaries who receive the funds upon her death.

When your client names her spouse as the beneficiary, the HSA passes intact. The spouse transfers the assets from her HSA to his without tax implications. He then manages the HSA as your client managed it during her lifetime, reimbursing his own, his tax dependents', and potentially a future spouse's qualified expenses tax-free. He enjoys all the benefits and is constrained by the same rules that applied to your client when she was alive and owned the HSA.

Example: *Viktoriya named her husband Stefan as her beneficiary before she died. When she passed away, her HSA passed to Stefan. Stefan can withdraw funds tax-free for qualified expenses that he and his tax dependents incur. If he's HSA-eligible, Stefan can contribute to the account as well.*

If your client leaves her HSA to anyone else—for example, a child, a friend, or a charity—the HSA is liquidated and the proceeds are distributed to the beneficiary. The recipient, if subject to income taxes, must pay taxes on the proceeds. Since the funds are no longer in an HSA, the beneficiary enjoys no tax advantages and isn't constrained by any HSA rules.

Example: *Arjun named his niece, Divya, as the beneficiary of his HSA with a $10,000 balance. When Arjun died, Divya received $10,000 in cash, which she then included in her income when she filed her personal income tax return. She spent the funds on college tuition with no penalties or additional taxes.*

If your client doesn't designate a beneficiary, the HSA is liquidated and included in her estate. It passes to her heir or heirs according to her estate plan or the estate laws of her state of residence.

One step that your client can take before her death, or the executor of her estate can take within a year of her death, is to reimburse any qualified expenses that she—or any family members with qualified expenses—incurred prior to her death.

Counseling Your Clients

- ✓ Remind your clients that nothing changes with respect to their distributions for qualified expenses in retirement. These withdrawals remain tax-free for qualified expenses.
- ✓ Discuss with clients whether it makes sense for them to withdraw funds for non-qualified expenses, now that those distributions are included in taxable income (like a traditional 401(k) plan or a traditional IRA) but not subject to an additional 20% tax. It usually doesn't, but sometimes clients can save on total taxes by withdrawing the next dollar for a non-qualified expense from an HSA rather than another account.
- ✓ Review with your clients the terms of their HSA agreement, particularly if they maintain their balances in an HSA chosen by a former employer. Those terms (for example, services, fees, minimum balances, and investment options) may not be appropriate in retirement.
- ✓ Make sure your clients have named a beneficiary and that the beneficiary and executor of their estate are aware of the HSA.

SECTION III

Medicare Considerations

INTRODUCTION TO SECTION III

Medicare is a very complicated program, and some benefits advisors focus their practices exclusively on this topic. Even they often find it difficult to keep up with legislative and administrative changes in the program as elected officials and CMS administrators attempt to keep pace with changes in medical payment, medical delivery, and federal budget constraints.

The purpose of this section isn't to make you an expert in all aspects of Medicare. Rather, the focus is on the intersection of Medicare and HSAs. Most workers are eligible to enroll in Medicare beginning at age 65. Enrolling in Medicare when first eligible is mandatory for some individuals, including anyone collecting certain retirement benefits and many employees who work for small employers.

For others, the decision whether to remain on employer-sponsored coverage only, employer-sponsored coverage and one or more Parts of Medicare, or Medicare only involves many issues. Among the more important are the quality and source of their current coverage and the potential application of penalties and coverage gaps when they delay Medicare enrollment.

This section sorts through these issues by reviewing how Medicare works, Medicare premiums, Medicare out-of-pocket responsibility, Medicare penalties, and other considerations that influence your clients' timing of their Medicare enrollment.

You won't become a Medicare savant after reading this section. But you will enhance your knowledge so that you can guide your clients through a discussion of the financial implications of the timing of their enrollment in Medicare. For nearly all of your clients, you probably will be the most informed advisor to whom they have access—more knowledgeable or more accessible than their employer's benefits advisor, their insurer's account executive, their employer's benefits team, or customer-service representatives at CMS.

Your advice to these clients will be invaluable.

CHAPTER 13

Understanding Medicare

HSAs can be confusing. Medicare can be very confusing. When you put the two of them together, life becomes very complicated. Medicare touches HSAs, particularly in the form of HSA eligibility. HSAs touch Medicare, particularly in the form of HSA distributions.

Unfortunately for most individuals enrolled in Medicare or nearing the age of eligibility to enroll in Medicare, answers are difficult to find. In fact, many don't know the questions to ask if they want to weigh the advantages of and potential issues associated with continuing their participation in an HSA program versus enrolling in Medicare when they're first eligible. And even if they understand the questions to ask, they probably won't find correct answers if they call Medicare customer service. Representatives may be well versed in Medicare rules, but they may not understand how Medicare intersects with HSA eligibility and the financial effect of the choices that individuals like your clients may make. Medicare representatives are paid to answer questions that callers ask. They don't provide advice about approaches and considerations that may benefit callers financially.

Fortunately, your clients have an advocate who can navigate these tricky waters for them. If you read, absorb, and understand the key concepts in this chapter, you can help them determine the best course of action to maximize their long-term financial position.

In this chapter, you'll find a review of

- when a client is automatically enrolled in Medicare, and when she isn't;
- when she's subject to penalties for not enrolling during her Initial Enrollment Period;
- what a Special Enrollment Period is, how your client can quality for one, and what it means for her effective dates of coverage and penalties;

- what happens if your client delays enrollment and isn't eligible for a Special Enrollment Period; and
- what Medicare Creditable Coverage is and why it may or may not be important to your client.

[Note: This chapter isn't an exhaustive discussion of Medicare. It explores just enough of the program for you to understand how it interacts with an HSA owner's opportunity to continue to contribute to an HSA. Every year, CMS updates its excellent guide, *Medicare and You*, which goes into great detail on how the Medicare program works. Several books published by experts not affiliated with CMS also provide a wealth of information to people who want to understand Medicare options and coverage.]

Medicare Part A explained. Part A (sometimes called Hospital Insurance, or HI) covers inpatient care in hospitals and skilled nursing facilities, as well as hospice and home health care. People who have worked more than 40 employment quarters receive this benefit premium-free after paying a 2.9% payroll tax (divided equally between employer and employee) during their working years. Part A has a deductible of $1,364 (2019 figure) per benefit period. A benefit period begins with admission to a hospital and ends 60 days after discharge from an inpatient facility. Thus, individuals can experience more than one benefit period annually and apply to multiple deductibles within a single year.

Part A has a deductible of $1,364 (2019 figure) per benefit period.

Patients have no cost-sharing after the deductible for the first 60 days of inpatient confinement, then pay (in 2019) $341 daily for days 61-90 (up to $10,230 total). After 90 days of hospitalization during a benefit period, patients pay the entire bill (except that they can use 60 lifetime reserve days at a cost to them of $682 daily, or a total of up to $40,920).

Medicare Part B explained. Part B (sometimes called Medical Insurance, or MI) covers services delivered by physicians and other providers, outpatient care, home health care, durable medical equipment (items like wheelchairs, hospital beds, and crutches), and many preventive services. Enrollees pay a monthly premium as low as $135.50 (though Social Security recipients may pay a few dollars less) and as high of $460.50 (2019 figures, depending on income). The premium is based on income from two years prior (which typically represents the last filed personal income tax return).

Services are subject to an annual deductible ($185 in 201'
are covered at 80%. Patients are responsible for the remai
with *no annual or lifetime cap* on their financial responsi

Part A and Part B are often referred to as *original Med*
the two Parts that were signed into law by President Johnson in Ju.,
ushering in federal coverage for seniors' medical care. The program was designed with two distinct parts—hospital and medical insurance—that don't have a single deductible because in 1965, that was the standard structure of coverage. Blue Cross (hospital coverage) and Blue Shield (outpatient coverage), for example, didn't merge as a single entity with a unified benefit design that incorporated both inpatient and outpatient services until 1982.

Medicare Part D explained. Part D traces its history to late 2003, when Congress passed and President George W. Bush signed a law that created a prescription drug program for Medicare recipients (and, coincidentally, created HSAs as well). The federal government doesn't offer Part D coverage. Instead, private companies sell prescription drug programs approved by CMS. The private market offers many different products (with variations in prescriptions covered, premiums, and patient cost-sharing). The average premium is $35.02 in 2019.

The federal government doesn't offer Part D coverage. Instead, private companies sell prescription drug programs approved by CMS.

These choices can be confusing. Large pharmacy chains often have specialists who can review a patient's prescription history and recommend a plan whose cost and coverage may work best for that patient.

Individuals must be enrolled in Part A or Part B (or both) to enroll in Part D. They can't enroll in Part D only. Individuals enrolled in Part C (discussed next) can't enroll in Part D unless their Part C plan doesn't offer prescription drug coverage.

Medicare Part C (often called Medicare Advantage, or MA) explained. About 30% of all Medicare enrollees—a figure that grows annually—choose to enroll in a Medicare replacement program run by private companies and approved by CMS. These plans look like the traditional medical coverage (HMOs with copays, a single deductible for inpatient and outpatient services, and a broad range of preventive services and value-added programs). Medicare Advantage is an especially popular option with younger Medicare enrollees, who have been enrolled in similar managed employer-sponsored coverage for decades. CMS makes a fixed monthly payment (which varies by enrollee, depending on geography, medical condition, and other factors) to the private insurer. The insurer in turn assumes all financial responsibility for the patient's claims. An insurer may charge individuals a premium on top of what it collects from Medicare to provide coverage.

Medicare Supplement plan: A Medicare Supplement plan is *not* Medicare coverage. Rather, it's a policy that individuals covered by traditional Medicare can purchase from private insurers to supplement their benefits. Medicare enrollees can choose from 10 specific plan designs identified by letters (A, B, C, D, F, G, K, L, M, and N). Though each plan design is different, all products within each letter plan design are identical, allowing consumers to shop for coverage based on price and perceived service alone.

These plans provide an important level of financial protection to traditional Medicare enrollees. All designs allot an additional 365 days of hospital coverage beyond the 60 lifetime reserve days that traditional Medicare offers. Most designs also pay Part B coinsurance and copays and Part A hospice and skilled-nursing cost-sharing. Some provide coverage for treatment outside the country.

Perhaps most important, Medicare Supplement plans cap Part B expenses with an annual ceiling on out-of-pocket financial responsibility. Part B has no ceiling on out-of-pocket expenses, in stark contrast to commercial coverage, which must set a limit on a patient's total annual financial responsibility. A Medicare enrollee who undergoes outpatient cancer treatment can easily run up a bill of $200,000 or more. After the $183 annual deductible, the patient pays 20% of the bill under Part B, with no ceiling. On a $200,000 bill, 20% represents $40,000 (or more than a dozen years of premiums under a typical Medicare Supplement plan). Medicare Supplement policies provide insurance against such catastrophic losses.

Medicare Supplement plans are available only to individuals who enroll in Part A and Part B. Part C enrollees aren't permitted to purchase a Medicare Supplement plan. A supplement plan is unnecessary for Part C enrollees, since Part C provides benefits and financial protections beyond what traditional Medicare offers.

Enrolling in Medicare

Individuals don't have to enroll in Part A and Part B at age 65, unless . . . Though most Americans are eligible to enroll in the various Parts of Medicare when they turn age 65, only individuals who receive Social Security or Railroad Retirement benefits are automatically enrolled in Part A and Part B when they begin to collect benefits through one of these retirement programs and turn age 65. More than half of all Social Security recipients (56% of men and 64% of women, according to the Center for Retirement Research) begin to collect Social Security or Railroad Retirement benefits *before* they turn age 65. And age 65 is still a year short of their Full Retirement Age, so they accept a reduced Social Security benefit for the remainder of their lives. These individuals are enrolled in Part A and Part B automatically. They can waive Part B, and usually do when they remain active at work and enrolled in employer-sponsored coverage. They can't waive Part A, which disqualifies them from making (or accepting from their employer) additional HSA contributions at the later of the month that they turn age 65 or that they enroll in any Part of Medicare.

> Only individuals who receive Social Security or Railroad Retirement benefits are automatically enrolled in Part A and Part B.

Your clients who don't enroll in Medicare when they're first eligible may be subject to certain penalties, which will be discussed later.

Individuals don't have to enroll in Part D at age 65 or any age, period. Enrollment in Part D—the prescription drug program—is always optional. Individuals are eligible to enroll in Part D at age 65, but they're not required to enroll at any age—even if they begin to collect Social Security or Railroad Retirement benefits or enroll in Part A or Part B (or both). They risk paying a permanent penalty if they delay enrollment without qualifying coverage and later enroll, however, as discussed later.

Individuals don't have to enroll in Part C at age 65 or any age, period. Medicare Advantage is an alternative to traditional Medicare. Medicare-eligible individuals who choose to enroll in Medicare (or are automatically enrolled in the program) have the option of replacing Part A, Part B and Part D with a Medicare Advantage product. They pay their Part B premium to the federal government, which in turn pays the private insurer from whom they buy their Medicare Advantage plan a fixed monthly fee reflecting their age, general health condition, and location.

Medicare Secondary Payer Rules

When individuals are enrolled in more than one coverage, the insurance industry has very specific rules about which insurer is the primary payer and which is the secondary payer. Insurers coordinate benefits so that your client receives benefits up to the amount that the richer plan pays, but no more. When your client remains active at work past age 65 ("working senior") and is covered on her employer's plan and Medicare, the number of employees working for the company (more in a moment) determines whether Medicare is the primary or secondary payer.

Workers covered by an employer's medical plan and Medicare present both cards to their provider at the time of service. Ideally, the patient tells the provider which coverage is primary and which is secondary. The provider then submits a claim to the primary payer. The primary payer pays according to its benefit schedule and issues a statement reflecting its responsibility. The provider then submits a claim and the primary payer's statement to the secondary payer for possible additional payment up to—but no more than—the secondary payer's benefit schedule less the primary payer's payment.

> Example: *Mohamed is enrolled in Medicare Part A. He's also covered by his employer's plan with a $4,000 deductible and no coinsurance responsibility after the deductible. He has incurred no expenses so far this calendar year. Mohamed then spends three days in the hospital. The employer's plan is the primary payer. The hospital submits the claim to the primary payer, which pays the entire bill less the $4,000 deductible. The hospital submits the claim and the primary payer's statement to Medicare, which pays all but $1,340 (the Part A deductible in 2018) of the remaining $4,000 responsibility (total $2,660 paid by Part A). Mohamed pays the $1,340 balance due from personal funds or his HSA.*
>
> *In this case, the patient receives no more coverage than what the richer plan pays (the $1,340 Part A deductible). The two insurers coordinate benefits so that neither pays more to Mohamed or his providers than the terms of its policy dictate.*

Medicare and employers with 19 or fewer employees. If your client works for a company with 19 or fewer employees, Medicare is the primary payer. So, using the facts in the preceding example, the hospital claims go to Medicare first. Medicare pays all but $1,340 of the claim. The secondary payer subsequently pays nothing, since it covers inpatient services only after a $4,000 deductible.

Though Medicare rules don't require someone who isn't receiving Social Security or Railroad Retirement benefits to enroll in Medicare, an employer's insurer may require employees who are Medicare-eligible and enrolled in the employer-sponsored plan to purchase Part A and Part B. Alternatively, it may give employees the option not to enroll in Medicare but pay no more than it would if the employee were enrolled in Medicare.

An employer's insurer may require employees who are Medicare-eligible and enrolled in the employer-sponsored plan to purchase Part A and Part B.

Example: *The same situation for Mohamed (from the previous example), except that Medicare is the primary payer. The employer's insurer doesn't require Medicare enrollment, but its rules are clear that it won't reimburse any more than its responsibility as the secondary payer. Mohamed isn't enrolled in Part A and has a $25,000 hospital stay.*

Medicare Part A would have paid all but $1,340 of the cost if he were enrolled. The employer's insurer, with a $4,000 deductible, pays nothing. Mohamed is responsible for the $25,000 bill. Because Mohamed isn't enrolled in Part A, his financial responsibility jumps from $1,340 (his Part A deductible) to $25,000 (total cost borne by Mohamed, who is the primary payer).

Medicare and employers with 20 or more employees. When the company has 20 or more employees, Medicare is automatically the secondary payer. Unless the employer's plan has a deductible exceeding the $1,340 Part A deductible, Medicare probably won't pay any benefits unless an inpatient stay exceeds Medicare's standard 60-day limit per benefit period. If all services—including outpatient, such as physician, lab tests, imaging, and outpatient therapy—are subject to the deductible (as they are in an HSA-qualified plan), Part B may reimburse some expenses as a secondary payer with a low deductible and then coinsurance.

Most individuals who remain employed and covered on their employers' medical plans don't enroll in Part B, however, because they would pay a monthly Part B premium in addition to the premium for their employer's coverage. They typically derive little benefit from Part B as secondary coverage. Any potential Part B benefit is typically far less than the Part B premium. And remember that Part B premiums are based on income as reported on an individual or joint tax return. A working senior may pay more than the standard $135.50 Part B premium. A married working senior with a household income of $125,000, for example, faces a monthly premium of $270.90 in 2019, for example.

When to Enroll in Medicare

Counsel your clients on the right time to enroll in Medicare. If they're not enrolled in an HSA program, their decision usually is simple:

- Enroll in Part A when first eligible because it's premium-free.
- Delay enrollment in Part B as long as they remain enrolled in employer-sponsored coverage.
- Enroll or delay enrollment in Part D (depending on their employer coverage and potential penalties discussed later).
- Enroll in Part B (and Part D, if previously deferred) during a Special Enrollment Period immediately after terminating employer-sponsored coverage.

That formula is tried and true and is appropriate for anyone who remains enrolled in employer-sponsored coverage with prescription drug coverage at least equal to the Part D benefit (a concept that will be explored later).

> People enrolled in an HSA program need to weigh the benefits of continuing HSA tax advantages against potential penalties and gaps in coverage.

People enrolled in an HSA program, however, face a more difficult decision. They need to weigh the benefits of continuing HSA tax advantages against potential penalties and gaps in coverage when they finally enroll in certain Parts of Medicare. These decisions are complicated.

Medicare Enrollment Periods

Your clients can enroll in Medicare during one of three enrollment periods.

Initial Enrollment Period. This time frame extends from three full months before the month of their 65th birthday until three months after that milestone—a total of seven months. During this time, anyone who's Medicare-eligible can join, regardless of whether she has any coverage prior to enrolling. It's the equivalent of your client's being offered benefits when she starts a new job. It's a once-in-a-lifetime opportunity around her 65th birthday only.

If she enrolls before her 65th birthday, her coverage begins as of the first day of the month of her 65th birthday (unless her birthday falls on the first day of the month, in which case she's enrolled as of the first day of the *prior* month). If she enrolls during the three months after her birth month, her coverage begins on the first day of the first month following her successful enrollment.

Special Enrollment Period. Your clients who delay enrollment in Medicare at age 65 can trigger a Special Enrollment Period during the eight months immediately following their disenrollment from group coverage. A key term here is *group* coverage. As long as they had employer-based coverage immediately before they enroll in Medicare, they're entitled to a Special Enrollment Period. If they had nongroup coverage—including individual coverage that they bought directly from an insurer, through an ACA marketplace, or through another intermediary; or continued group coverage through COBRA—immediately before enrolling in Medicare, they're not entitled to a Special Enrollment Period. They can't sign up for coverage until the next General Enrollment Period and won't be covered until the effective date of coverage of that Part of Medicare.

The Special Enrollment Period is the equivalent of a qualifying life event—such as a spouse's loss of coverage—that allows your client who is eligible for employer-based coverage to enroll outside of her employer's annual enrollment period.

General Enrollment Period. The General Enrollment Period is the once-a-year opportunity to enroll initially or change Medicare coverage. For Part A and Part B, this period extends from Jan. 1 through March 31 with an effective date of coverage of July 1. For Part C and Part D, the general open enrollment period begins Oct. 15 and ends Dec. 7, with an effective date of coverage of Jan. 1.

The General Enrollment Period is akin to the annual enrollment period in the world of employer-based coverage. If your client isn't eligible for a Special Enrollment Period (because she's not covered by a group plan immediately before seeking to enroll in Medicare), she may experience a gap in coverage if the termination of her old coverage doesn't line up with the General Enrollment Period for any Part of Medicare.

She can bridge the gap by continuing her employer-based coverage through COBRA. COBRA coverage doesn't entitle her to a Special Enrollment Period because it's not considered group coverage, as noted earlier, but it may allow her to continue coverage until the next General Enrollment Period. She also may be able to purchase coverage through an ACA marketplace. These plans, however, are age-rated and thus expensive for an older enrollee unless her income is sufficiently low that she qualifies for an advance premium tax credit.

Penalties for Delayed Enrollment

Medicare assesses penalties for people who delay enrollment and don't have acceptable coverage—or any coverage—before enrolling in any Part of Medicare. It's important to understand these penalties when you are advising your clients about the opportunities and risks of delaying enrollment in Medicare.

Part A penalty. Almost no one incurs penalties for delaying enrollment in Part A. Individuals who work 40 employment quarters (and spouses or ex-spouse's of individuals who worked at least 40 quarters) and earn a certain amount per employment quarter (the 2018 figure is $1,320 per quarter, and prior years' minimum earnings are lower) pre-pay their Part A premiums for life through their FICA taxes during their working years. The tax is 2.90% of earnings, split evenly (1.45% each) between employee and employer, with no annual ceiling. Individuals who have worked fewer than 40 employment quarters pay a sliding premium, based on the number of employment quarters that they paid into the system, to receive Part A benefits.

Medicare penalties take the form of premium surcharges. Your clients who don't pay a premium for Part A coverage don't pay a penalty for delaying enrollment in Medicare. For the very few people who do pay a premium and didn't have group coverage before enrolling in Part A, a penalty applies. The Part A penalty is equal to a 10% monthly premium surcharge for double the number of years that they delayed enrollment.

Example: *Cara worked only 20 employment quarters (five years) before retiring at age 62. She felt great and went without insurance for five years, missing her Initial Enrollment Period because she didn't want to pay for coverage that she didn't think she needed. She then signed up for Part A during the General Enrollment Period at age 67. Since Cara delayed Part A enrollment for two years after she was initially eligible (at age 65), she pays a penalty equal to 10% of her Part A premium for four years (twice the number of years that she delayed enrollment). In 2018, her premium would be $422 per month, so the penalty would add an additional $42.20 to her total due each month (total $462.20). After four years, the penalty ends and Cara reverts to her standard Part A premium for the rest of her covered life.*

Part B penalty. Individuals who fail to enroll in Part B when first eligible and who aren't enrolled in employer-based coverage face a penalty when they enroll in Part B during a General Enrollment Period. Since Part B enrollees always pay a premium, they always have the potential to pay a penalty. The penalty is equal to a *permanent* 10% premium surcharge for every 12-month period that they delayed Part B enrollment without group coverage. This penalty is different from the *temporary* levy on individuals who don't enroll in Part A when first eligible and don't maintain employer-based coverage. Part B enrollees pay the surcharge every month that they remain enrolled in Part B coverage.

Part B enrollees pay the surcharge every month that they remain enrolled in Part B coverage.

Example: *Cara (from the preceding example) also enrolls in Part B at age 67. Let's assume that she went two years and five months between age 65 and her effective date of Part B coverage. Thus, she had a gap of two full years (partial years don't count when calculating the surcharge penalty). Cara pays an additional 20% premium surcharge as long as she remains enrolled in Part B. The standard premium for Part B in 2018 is $134. Cara thus pays an additional $26.80 (20% of $134) for a total monthly premium of $160.80. As the Part B premium increases in future years, the 20% penalty represents an increasing dollar amount.*

Few Part B enrollees pay the penalty. In fact, the Congressional Research Service reported that in 2014, fewer than 2% of all Part B enrollees paid the penalty. Among those who did, the average penalty was a 29% premium surplus.

Most people who are Medicare-eligible enroll in Part B as soon as they terminate employer-sponsored coverage. There are exceptions, though.

Example: *Garreth works until age 64½, then is diagnosed with cancer and liver disease. He retires from work. Rather than enroll in Medicare, Garreth continues his employer's coverage through COBRA to ensure that he has access to his current specialists. Eighteen months later, he recovers, at which time he drops his COBRA coverage and enrolls in Medicare.*

When he signs up for Medicare, he learns that he doesn't have group coverage and thus isn't entitled to a Special Enrollment Period. He must wait until the next General Enrollment Period to enroll in Medicare. His COBRA continuation stops after 18 months. He faces a potential gap in coverage until the next effective dates of the various Parts of Medicare. Because he delayed his enrollment when first eligible at age 65 without qualifying group coverage, he pays a permanent Part B penalty when he finally enrolls in coverage.

In a case like Garreth's, you can help your clients balance the immediate premium savings of delaying Part B enrollment against the long-term effect of Part B penalties and potential gap in coverage.

Part D penalty and Medicare Creditable Coverage (MCC). The Part D penalty is completely different from the Part A and Part B levies. Medicare makes no distinction between employer-based and individual coverage (including COBRA continuation) when determining whether an enrollee is subject to Part D penalties and potential gaps in coverage. What matters isn't the *source* of coverage, but its *perceived quality.*

Here is where Medicare Creditable Coverage comes into play. MCC refers to the actuarial value of commercial prescription drug coverage versus a Part D plan. If the commercial plan offers coverage that's at least as rich as Medicare, no penalty applies to people who delay enrollment in Part D when they're first eligible to enroll.

Who determines the relative value of a commercial plan versus Medicare prescription drug coverage? Every year, CMS releases a formula to evaluate commercial prescription drug benefits. Insurers test all their prescription drug riders, using the formula and their (the insurers') applicable population (members enrolled in the insurers' Medicare programs or members age 65 or older). If the commercial plan delivers the same drugs as Medicare for no more than the out-of-pocket cost of a Part D plan, the commercial coverage is *creditable.* If commercial members pay more out-of-pocket than Medicare enrollees do, the commercial plan is *non-creditable.*

To avoid penalties, your client who waives Part D coverage during her initial eligibility period when she turns age 65 must be enrolled continuously in prescription coverage that is deemed MCC from her 65th birthday until she enrolls in Part D. For every month that she doesn't maintain MCC, she is assessed a permanent premium surcharge equal to 1% of the national base beneficiary premium ($35.02 in 2018). The premium surcharge is a percentage of this national figure, not the actual premium attached to the Part D plan that she subsequently chooses (unlike the Part B surcharge).

> Example: *Moses doesn't have MCC prescription drug coverage during the 30 months since his 65th birthday, when he chose to delay enrollment in Medicare. He enrolls in Part A and Part B effective July 1, the effective date of coverage following a General Enrollment Period. The Part D General Enrollment Period, and thus the Part D effective date, is six months later, which means that Moses won't have creditable coverage for a total of 36 months. Moses pays an additional $12.60 (36% of $35.02, rounded up to the nearest dime) on top of his regular Part D premium. As the national base beneficiary premium increases in future years, so does Moses's penalty.*

Chapter 14, *Timing Medicare Enrollment,* builds on this base of knowledge to prepare you for discussing when your clients should enroll in Medicare. There is no right answer for everyone. In Chapter 14, you'll read about some scenarios and the pros and cons of each. The discussion is intended to lead you and your clients to consider the right factors to make the optimal decision for them.

Counseling Your Clients

- ✓ Begin conversations about future medical coverage with your clients long before their 65th birthday. They need to plan this aspect of their life carefully to ensure continuous coverage and balance the costs of paying premiums before they need Medicare coverage against paying penalties if they delay enrolling.

- ✓ Be sure your clients understand that they avoid permanent Part B penalties and are entitled to a Special Enrollment Period after age 65 (thus preventing a potential gap in coverage) only if they're continuously enrolled in group coverage from their 65th birthday.

- ✓ Help your clients determine whether they're subject to permanent Part D penalties if their commercial prescription drug coverage after their 65th birthday isn't MCC. It may make sense for them to incur penalties (as discussed in more detail in the next chapter) and remain HSA-eligible. Additionally, you and they need to run the numbers before they're subject to penalties to determine the right strategy for them to build medical equity.

CHAPTER 14

Timing Medicare Enrollment

Chapter 13, *Understanding Medicare,* presents information about the structure of Medicare, enrollment periods, and potential penalties for failure to enroll at age 65. Some people who read that chapter may become confused and determine that the best option for them to avoid any compliance issues or future penalties is simply to enroll in Medicare during their Initial Enrollment Period around their 65th birthday and be done with it. And for many of them, particularly those who aren't enrolled in employer-sponsored coverage at age 65 or who have a non-MCC prescription program or who aren't interested in becoming or remaining eligible to open and contribute to an HSA, enrolling in Medicare when first eligible is the right move.

For others, however, the right option isn't as easy to determine. Your clients are probably more likely than the average person to remain productively employed past age 65, continuing to do meaningful work that stimulates and fulfills them and keeps them mentally focused. For many of them—particularly those who are enrolled in employer-sponsored coverage at age 65 and who have an MCC prescription drug program or who are interested in becoming or remaining eligible to open and contribute to an HSA—enrolling in Medicare during their Initial Enrollment Period doesn't make sense for financial and coverage reasons.

In this chapter, you'll learn

- how your clients can avoid most penalties and gaps in coverage through proper timing of their transition from employer-sponsored insurance to Medicare,
- when it makes sense to incur penalties for delayed enrollment, and
- how an HSA can help minimize the effect of penalties.

Quick Medicare Review

Medicare Part A. Part A covers inpatient services and hospice after a $1,340 deductible per benefit period. People who have paid FICA taxes for 40 employment quarters receive Part A coverage premium-free for the rest of their lives, beginning as early as age 65 (or sometimes earlier with a disability, but the focus here is on becoming eligible based on age). Unless your client is collecting Social Security or Railroad Retirement benefits, she can waive coverage and enroll later. She faces no penalty as long as she has worked long enough not to pay a premium.

Medicare Part B. This Part covers outpatient services like physician visits, imaging, lab tests, and outpatient therapy. CMS sets the premium each year, and the premium is tiered so that it rises with higher incomes. In 2018, the base premium is $134, though it can rise to as much as $428.50 for high-income enrollees (taxable income above $160,000 for single filers and $320,000 for joint filers). Enrollees are responsible for the first $183 of allowable charges, then pay 20% of remaining allowable charges with no out-of-pocket maximum.

Your clients who delay enrollment at age 65 and don't have qualifying group coverage pay a Part B penalty equal to a permanent 10% premium surcharge on their applicable premium for every 12-month period of non-qualifying group coverage. They also may face gaps in coverage, since they must wait until the following July 1 as the effective date of coverage. Individuals who receive Social Security or Railroad Retirement benefits are enrolled automatically as of the first day of the later of (1) the month of their 65th birthday or (2) the first month thereafter that they receive Social Security or Railroad Retirement benefits. People who are automatically enrolled when they begin to receive these retiree benefits can waive Part B coverage. Most who remain enrolled in group (employer-sponsored) coverage, especially those whose companies have 20 or more employees, waive Part B coverage to delay the monthly premium.

Medicare Part D. Part D is a prescription drug program offered by private insurers regulated by CMS. These private companies offer different formularies (drugs covered), cost-sharing, and premiums. Your clients who are enrolled in Part A or Part B (or both) are eligible to purchase Part D. It pays to shop! Individuals who waive coverage when first eligible must maintain coverage at least as rich as Medicare (Medicare Creditable Coverage). If they don't, they face a potential gap in coverage and a permanent surcharge on their monthly premium equal to 1% of the national base beneficiary premium (not their actual premium) for every month that they don't have creditable coverage after age 65. In 2018, that penalty results in a surcharge of about $0.35 for each month that they're enrolled in a non-MCC prescription drug plan after turning age 65. The figure is expected to decline to about $0.33 in 2019.

Medicare Part C (Medicare Advantage, or MA). Medicare Advantage is a program offered by private insurers and replaces coverage offered by traditional Medicare. Your client enrolls in Part A and Part B, pays the Part B premium (plus Part A premium in the unlikely event that your client hasn't worked 40 employment quarters) and chooses a Medicare Advantage plan. The plan covers all Medicare services, extends some benefits limited by Medicare, and offers value-added programs like vision services and gym discounts. The insurer often charges an additional premium. In most cases, this additional premium is less than the monthly cost for Part D prescription-drug coverage and a Medicare Supplement plan that pays most of Medicare's patient cost-sharing.

Medicare Advantage is a program offered by private insurers and replaces coverage offered by traditional Medicare.

Most individuals fall into one of three categories:

- **not eligible for Medicare.** They can't enroll in Medicare because they haven't attained age 65, aren't disabled, or aren't eligible for some other reason.

- **eligible for Medicare and still covered on a group medical plan.** They are often labeled *working seniors* because they remain employed after the traditional (though outdated) retirement age of 65. They're eligible to enroll in Medicare and must carefully choose whether or not to (1) remain on their group medical plan only, (2) disenroll from group coverage and enroll in Medicare only, or (3) maintain group coverage and enroll in Medicare.

- **eligible for Medicare and no longer have access to group coverage.** They almost universally enroll in Medicare, which typically offers the most cost-effective—and sometimes the only—option.

Delaying Enrollment in Medicare

Most Americans become eligible to enroll in Medicare when they approach their 65th birthday. That milestone birthday triggers their seven-month Initial Enrollment Period, which begins three months prior to their 65th birthday and continues three months after their birth month.

If their 65th birthday falls any time after the first day of the month, they can enroll in Medicare as of the first day of their birth month. If it falls on the first day of the month *(example: Nov. 1)*, they can enroll in Medicare as of the first day of the *prior* month *(example: Oct. 1)*.

If they sign up during the last three months of the Initial Enrollment Period (the three months after their 65th birthday), they are enrolled as of the first day of the month after their enrollment is complete.

Individuals aren't required to enroll in Medicare at age 65 unless they're collecting Social Security or Railroad Retirement benefits.

Individuals aren't required to enroll in Medicare at age 65 unless they're collecting Social Security or Railroad Retirement benefits. If they're collecting these benefits, they're automatically enrolled in Medicare Part A and Part B (but can waive Part B, which requires paying a premium if they enroll) either at age 65 (if they begin to collect Social Security or Railroad Retirement benefits prior to this age) or after age 65 when they begin to receive retirement benefits through either program.

Key issue: Source of coverage. The first factor in determining when to enroll in Medicare is current coverage. If your client has employer-sponsored coverage, he can delay enrolling in Medicare when he's first eligible and not risk any future Part A or Part B penalties (though Part D penalties may apply).

If he has nongroup coverage (purchased directly from an insurer, through an ACA marketplace or other intermediary, or by exercising his COBRA continuation rights), he is a good candidate to enroll in Medicare Part A, Part B, and Part D during his Initial Enrollment Period. Otherwise, if he delays, he won't be entitled to a Special Enrollment Period (off-anniversary enrollment) when he wants to drop his current coverage. He needs to remain on that coverage until the next applicable Medicare General Enrollment Period and subsequent effective date of coverage (July 1 for Part A and Part B and Jan. 1 for Part C and Part D).

Key issue: Quality of coverage. People who delay enrolling in Part A and Part B when first eligible must be enrolled in employer-sponsored coverage to trigger a Special Enrollment Period and transition off-anniversary into one or both of those Parts of Medicare. The actuarial value of the plan doesn't matter. Whether the plan has no deductible or a $10,000 family deductible is irrelevant when you're assessing the quality of coverage. As long as the coverage is through a group medical plan, it satisfies this criterion.

The quality of coverage does make a difference for individuals who delay Part D enrollment. If their prescription drug rider is deemed less rich than Medicare (non-MCC coverage), they're assessed a penalty (described earlier) for the remainder of their time enrolled in Part D. The penalty, as illustrated in the next example, is annoying if applicable, but it may not be a prohibitive financial barrier for your clients who want to continue to enjoy tax savings and build medical equity in their HSAs.

Key issue: Expiration of coverage. Individuals who are covered by COBRA (for example, early retirees) and delay enrolling in Medicare face a potential gap in coverage in addition to potential Part B and Part D penalties. Because COBRA isn't considered employer-sponsored coverage, individuals with COBRA coverage aren't entitled to a Special Enrollment Period when they want to enroll in Medicare. If their COBRA coverage expires (usually 18 months after the event that triggered the right to continue coverage) before the next Medicare General Enrollment Period, they face a potential gap in coverage.

Individuals with COBRA coverage aren't entitled to a Special Enrollment Period.

The source of the coverage (employer-sponsored or individual) is *not* a factor in determining potential penalties for Part D coverage. The Part D penalty is based on whether their coverage is MCC or not, rather than whether it's employer-sponsored. COBRA coverage may result in a gap in coverage, however. Individuals can't enroll in Part D if they're not enrolled in Part A or Part B (or both). This can lead to a gap in coverage, since Part A and Part B have a July 1 effective date of coverage and Part D has a Jan. 1 effective date of coverage.

> Example: *Ewell's COBRA coverage expires in August 2018. He can't enroll in Part D effective Jan. 1, 2019, and then enroll in Part A or Part B (or both) effective July 1, 2019. Instead, he can enroll in Part A or Part B (or both) effective July 1, 2019, watch his prescription drug coverage expire as his COBRA coverage ends, and experience a gap in prescription coverage until Jan. 1, 2020, when his enrollment in Part D becomes effective. Ewell faces a lifetime Part D penalty when he finally enrolls in Part D.*

How Long to Delay Medicare Enrollment?

Your clients can delay Medicare enrollment forever. *Forever* probably isn't the right strategy. It may, however, make financial sense to delay enrolling in Medicare for a period of time after age 65, even if the delay results in penalties in the form of permanent premium surcharges, particularly for Part D coverage.

Determining when to receive Social Security benefits is a very complex topic because it can involve drawing from someone else's (such as a deceased or divorced spouse's) benefit. You should consider those factors when advising your clients (or refer them to private Social Security advisors with sophisticated software who specialize in analyzing the hundreds of factors that influence a client's lifetime payout). For the sake of simplicity, the following discussion focuses on individuals who can draw on only their own earned benefit.

As you've counseled your clients, they can delay Social Security benefits when they reach Full Retirement Age. Full Retirement Age follows this schedule:

Born between 1943 and 1954:	66 years and no months
Born in 1955:	66 years and two months
Born in 1956:	66 years and four months
Born in 1957:	66 years and six months
Born in 1958:	66 years and eight months
Born in 1959:	66 years and 10 months
1960 and later:	67 years and no months

You've doubtless counseled most of your clients not to apply for Social Security benefits before they reach Full Retirement Age. For those clients who remain active at work and earning sufficient income, it often makes financial sense to delay applying for Social Security benefits until age 70. Every full year of delay increases their future monthly benefits by about 8%. So, a client whose Full Retirement Age is 66 years and two months (born in 1955) can earn roughly an additional 30% monthly benefit by not applying for benefits before she turns age 70.

At age 70, the benefit of further delaying Social Security benefits evaporates. Does it make financial sense for her to forego perhaps $22,000 in Social Security benefits to remain HSA-eligible and contribute $8,000 to an HSA? That contribution reduces her taxable income by about 30% if she lives in a state with a personal income tax. So, that's $2,400 of tax savings.

The opportunity cost, however, is $22,000 of foregone Social Security benefits. Under current tax law, she probably pays taxes on 85% of that figure, or about $18,700. At the same 30% tax rate, she pays about $5,600 in taxes, netting her about $16,400 in spendable income after taxes.

It probably isn't worth giving up $16,400 in post-tax income to save $2,400 in taxes and deposit $8,000 in a tax-advantaged account. On the other hand, if Congress changes the law and allows higher HSA contributions—perhaps to the statutory out-of-pocket maximum for an HSA-qualified medical plan—your recommendation may change. It's unlikely that even higher HSA contribution limits would make it more attractive for your client to delay enrolling in Social Security benefits past age 70, but it's certainly worth monitoring and recalculating should any of the variables change.

It's unlikely that even higher HSA contribution limits would make it more attractive for your client to delay enrolling in Social Security benefits past age 70.

The Effect of Penalties

Let's examine the effect of penalties for individuals who don't enroll in Medicare during their Initial Enrollment Period. You probably have some clients who associate *penalty* with *doing something wrong*. They always strive to follow the law and obey the unwritten rules of respectable society. To them, penalties are bad and are to be avoided. Even if the term is *surcharge* or *assessment,* some people have an aversion to acting in a way that extracts money from them involuntarily.

The penalties described below are arranged from most common to least common.

Part D penalty. This is where your value to your clients comes in. Are the same clients who have an aversion to paying a Part D penalty unwilling to accept an assessment of, say, 35% on a $100,000 financial windfall? Probably not. They understand that they receive a net benefit, even after they pay taxes. The same can hold true for the Part D penalty.

Here's an illustration of the effect of delaying enrollment in Part D by three years, beginning in 2018. Your client can contribute $7,900 to his HSA in 2018. Let's increase that figure by $100 annually for the next two years (a conservative estimate) and assume earnings of 4% (reflecting more conservative investments; assume contributions are made regularly throughout each year). During this three-year period, he builds his HSA balance by about $25,000 and saves about $7,000 in taxes (at a 30% tax rate) and about $1,350 in Part D premiums. The effect of three years of additional contributions is shown below.

Age	HSA Contribution	Earnings	Ending Balance	Tax Savings
65	$8,000	$160	$8,160	$2,400
66	$8,100	$488	$16,748	$2,430
67	$8,200	$834	$25,782	$2,460
Total	**$24,300**	**$1,454**	**$25,782**	**$7,290**

The model assumes
(1) a $100 annual increase in family contribution limits in 2020 and 202, and
(2) contributions are made evenly through the year, so that the 4% return is applied to the average contribution (reducing the first-year growth to 2%.

After three years (36 months), he drops his HSA-qualified coverage and enrolls in Medicare. His annual Part D premium at age 68 is $500, a figure that increases 5% annually. His penalty is a permanent Part D premium surcharge of 36%, or $180 on a $500 annual premium at age 68. This figure increases annually as his Part D premium rises. He continues to earn a 4% annual return on his HSA balances.

Age	Beginning Balance	Earnings	Part D Premium	Part D Penalty	Ending Balance
68	$25,646	$1,019	$500	$180	$25,802
69	$25,802	$1,032	$525	$189	$26,121
70	$26,121	$1,045	$551	$199	$26,416
71	$26,416	$1,057	$579	$208	$26,685
72	$26,685	$1,067	$608	$219	$26,926
73	$26,926	$1,077	$638	$230	$27,135
74	$27,135	$1,085	$670	$241	$27,309
75	$27,309	$1,092	$704	$253	$27,445
76	$27,445	$1,098	$739	$266	$27,538
77	$27,538	$1,102	$776	$279	$27,585
78	$27,585	$1,102	$814	$293	$27,580
79	$27,580	$1,103	$855	$308	$27,521
80	$27,521	$1,101	$898	$323	$27,400
81	$27,400	$1,096	$943	$339	$27,214
82	$27,214	$1,089	$990	$356	$26,956
83	$26,956	$1,078	$1,040	$374	$26,621
84	$26,621	$1,065	$1,091	$393	$26,201
85	$26,201	$1,048	$1,146	$413	$25,691
86	$25,691	$1,025	$1,203	$433	$25,082
87	$25,082	$1,003	$1,264	$455	$24,367
88	$24,367	$975	$1,327	$478	$23,537
89	$23,537	$941	$1,393	$502	$22,584
90	$22,584	$903	$1,463	$527	$21,498
91	$21,498	$860	$1,536	$553	$20,270
92	$20,270	$811	$1,613	$581	$18,887
93	$18,887	$755	$1,693	$610	$17,340
94	$17,340	$694	$1,778	$640	$15,616
95	$15,616	$625	$1,867	$672	$13,702
96	$13,702	$548	$1,960	$706	$11,584
97	$11,584	$463	$2,058	$741	$9,249
98	$9,249	$370	$2,161	$778	$6,680
99	$6,680	$267	$2,269	$817	$3,861
100	$3,861	$154	$2,383	$858	$775

The account balance actually grows through age 78 (or 10 years after he begins to draw balances to pay his Part D premiums) before distributions exceed account growth. The account depletion accelerates until he finally exhausts this windfall balance in the third month after his 100th birthday.

In graph form, the account balance looks like this:

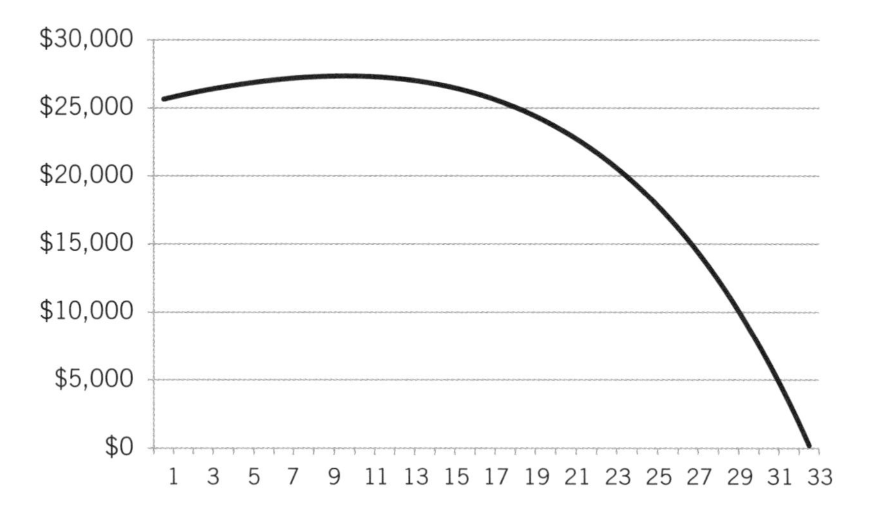

Imagine how this client would have fared if you weren't his advising professional. He probably would have enrolled in Medicare during his Initial Enrollment Period to avoid penalties. He would have given up three years of HSA contributions totaling $24,300. Those three years of additional contributions paid his *entire* Part D premium—both the base premium and the penalty in the form of a 36% surcharge—through age 100. His total penalty was about $14,400, or slightly less than half the total lifetime earnings on the additional contributions that he made in the three years between age 65 and 68.

As with any model, assumptions matter. This model assumes that his account balance grows by 4% annually and the Part D inflation adjustment is 5%. If the account balance grows by 5% and Part D premiums by 4%, the three years' additional HSA contributions fund Part D premiums and penalties through age 116. If the account balance and Medicare premiums both grow by 5%, the additional contributions cover Part D premiums and penalties into age 106. Assumptions matter, but small changes don't materially affect the model until it has run at least three decades.

Part B penalty. The Part B penalty is much greater—not in percentage terms (10% per full 12-month period for Part B, versus 12% per 12 months for Part D), but in magnitude. The Part B premium is currently about four times as high as the national base beneficiary premium on Part D. The good news is that very few individuals actually face a Part B penalty. Why?

If your client is active at work, she probably is enrolled in employer-sponsored coverage. Your client's group plan doesn't have to satisfy any minimum actuarial value or be richer than Medicare. As long as it's a group plan and she remains enrolled until she activates a Special Enrollment Period to sign up for Medicare, she faces no Part B penalty.

If she's age 65 (the age at which the penalty is activated) and not enrolled in employer-sponsored coverage, her best move financially probably is to enroll in Medicare. At a $134 premium per month for Part B, perhaps a $50 monthly premium for Part D, and maybe an additional $150 to $200 monthly to purchase a Medicare Supplement plan, Medicare options cost far less than COBRA premiums when the employer doesn't contribute to the COBRA premium.

Medicare options cost far less than COBRA premiums when the employer doesn't contribute to the COBRA premium.

The most common scenario that may lead to Part B penalties is when your client stops working because of an illness and wants to continue his group plan through COBRA until he completes a course of treatment. After completing treatment, he plans to enroll in Medicare, a program in which his specialist might not participate. In this case, because Medicare doesn't recognize his COBRA continuation as qualifying group coverage, he is subject to a penalty. Depending on the application of some complex rules, he may have to discontinue his COBRA coverage before its normal (18-month) course.

[Note: COBRA premiums are group-based, so your client pays the same premium as all employees if the plan is composite-rated (one blended rate for all participants, rather than an age-rated pricing allocation in which premiums vary by age band, thus increasing as enrollees grow older). Still, even though the COBRA premium is lower than comparable coverage in the individual market (where plans are age-rated), your client pays the entire premium, which could easily cost $500 to $900 *per month* in many geographic areas.]

Consider the effect of delaying enrollment for three full years, as illustrated in the Part D example earlier. Your client makes $24,000 in additional contributions, saving more than $7,000 in taxes and about $5,000 in Part B premiums. That's a pretty solid initial return.

According to the same model, the additional HSA balances cover a little more than a decade of Part B premiums and penalties, as shown below:

Age	Beginning Balance	Earnings	Part B Premium	Part B Penalty	Ending Balance
68	$25,464	$1,019	$1,608	$482	$24,392
69	$24,392	$976	$1,688	$507	$23,173
70	$23,173	$927	$1,773	$638	$21,689
71	$21,689	$868	$1,861	$670	$20,025
72	$20,025	$801	$1,955	$704	$18,168
73	$18,168	$727	$2,052	$739	$16,103
74	$16,103	$644	$2,155	$776	$13,187
75	$13,187	$553	$2,263	$815	$11,292
76	$11,292	$452	$2,376	$855	$8,513
77	$8,513	$341	$2,495	$898	$5,461
78	$5,461	$218	$2,619	$943	$2,117

The real test, however, is the effect of the penalties themselves. If the additional HSA balance is dedicated to paying Part B penalties only, your client doesn't exhaust the balance until after his 101st birthday, as illustrated below.

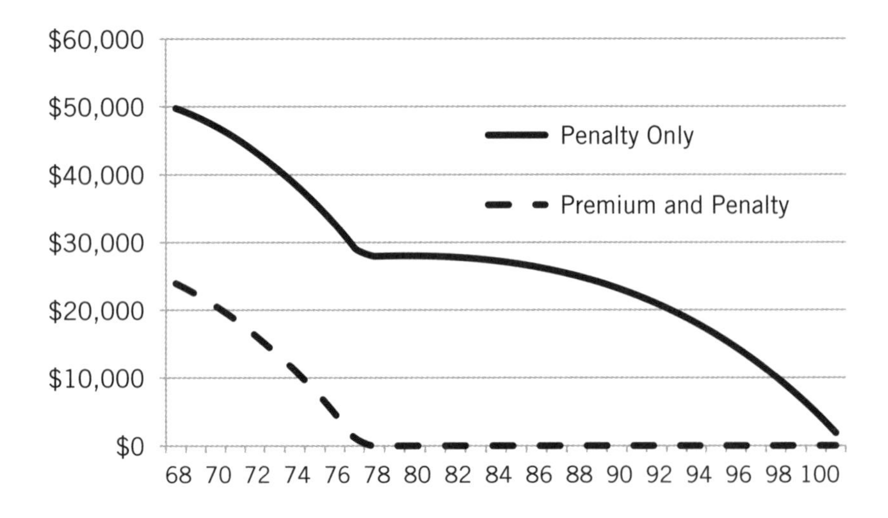

Again, as with the analysis of delaying enrollment in Part D, the purpose of this illustration isn't to determine a *right* or *wrong* approach to enrolling during the Initial Enrollment Period or delaying Medicare enrollment for a period of time. The point is that even though delaying enrollment has a negative consequence in the form of permanent penalties, it also creates a financial upside in the form of initial premium savings and greater accumulation of medical equity. It's up to each client (and you as the advising professional) to weigh these two factors.

Part A penalty: Individuals must work a total of 40 employment quarters and earn at least a certain amount per employment quarter. The 2018 figure is $1,320. The earnings figure is indexed annually for inflation (so that minimum earnings are less in prior years). The earnings figure is indexed and changes annually.

Individuals who have worked at least 40 employment quarters pay no premium and therefore face no penalty if they delay enrollment in Part A without continuous employer-sponsored coverage. After all, the penalty is a surcharge to the premium, and these individuals face no premium to which to apply a surcharge.

Individuals who have not worked 40 employment quarters must pay a premium to receive Part A coverage. The 2018 premium is $422 for those who worked fewer than 30 employment quarters and $232 for those who worked between 30 and 39 employment quarters. The penalty for not enrolling when first eligible and not having creditable coverage is a 10% premium surcharge for double the number of months with non-qualified coverage.

> Example: *Natalie starts working later in life and accumulates only 28 employment quarters before she retires. She didn't have employer-sponsored coverage during her last two years of employment.*
>
> *She pays a monthly premium of $422 in 2018, plus an additional $42.20 surcharge (total penalty of $462.22 annualized). The penalty remains at 10% of the premium, and the total surcharge changes (usually increases) as the Part A premium changes during the following three years. She pays the surcharge for a total of four years (twice the length of time that she didn't have qualifying coverage after her Initial Enrollment Period) before reverting to the standard premium with no surcharge.*

Strategies to Avoid Penalties

Though the penalties are often palatable because individuals can accumulate more tax-advantaged savings in an HSA than they pay in penalties, it's ideal when your clients can delay their enrollment in Medicare, continue to contribute to their HSAs, and pay no penalties when they subsequently enroll in Medicare. Here are some strategies that your clients can use if they don't want to enroll in Medicare during the Initial Enrollment Period:

Part A: Work 40 employment quarters. As long as your client works 40 employment quarters and earns at least $1,320 per quarter (since the figure is indexed, this figure is lower in prior years), she faces no penalty when she enrolls in Part A.

Part B: Remain enrolled in group coverage. Your client avoids penalties as long as she remains enrolled in a group plan until she signs up for Part B coverage. When she drops her group coverage, she triggers a Special Enrollment Period during which she can enroll in Part B with no penalty and no gap in coverage.

Part B: Return to work. If your client doesn't have group coverage as she approaches age 65, she may benefit from returning to the workforce until she's ready to enroll in Medicare. That way, she can pick up group coverage and retain it, which eliminates penalties and allows her to elect a Special Enrollment Period to sign up for Medicare coverage. Absent group coverage, she isn't allowed to enroll in Part B (or Part A) until the next General Enrollment Period.

The Part B penalty is assessed only when an individual doesn't have group coverage for 12 consecutive months. Your client could delay returning to the workforce past her 65th birthday, as long as she enrolled in coverage by age 65 and 11 months.

Part D: Retain MCC coverage. If your client remains covered on an MCC plan every month beginning with the month of her 65th birthday and ending when she enrolls in Part D, she faces no penalty. The coverage can be through a group plan, COBRA continuation of coverage, or a nongroup plan. What matters isn't the source of coverage (as it does with Part B), but rather the quality of the coverage (a prescription-drug plan at least as rich as Medicare offers).

Part D: Retest non-MCC coverage. As mentioned earlier, insurers test their prescription drug riders annually against a formula supplied by CMS. Insurers figuratively pull each rider off the shelf, test it, and put it back on the shelf. They then notify individuals enrolled in the plan whether it represents MCC. The insurer also passes this information along to CMS, which can then apply penalties.

What insurers don't do is "field-test" a pharmacy rider as it's deployed in real life. Here's an illustration of this issue.

Example: *Ronan is enrolled in self-only HSA-qualified coverage with a $5,000 deductible. All prescription drugs apply to the deductible. This rider fails his insurer's MCC test. Ronan's employer includes a Post-Deductible HRA that reimburses the final $3,500 of deductible expenses, bringing his net deductible to only $1,500. Most prescription-drug plans with a $1,500 self-only deductible satisfy the MCC standard.*

Do you see the problem here? The insurer is testing a $5,000 deductible and determining that the prescription drug coverage isn't MCC. The net deductible after the employer-funded HRA is only $1,500. A plan with the first $1,500 of medical and prescription drug expenses may well satisfy the MCC standard. So, what's a client to do?

Employers can hire an independent actuary to run the MCC calculation on the employer's prescription drug coverage. Medical actuaries have access to the CMS formula and can find a pool of claims from individuals age 65 and older to plug into the formula. If the plan as designed by the employer represents MCC, the actuary or employer can report this information to CMS and provide covered employees with a letter for their records certifying that the plan satisfies MCC standards. That way, employees avoid penalties for non-MCC coverage after their 65th birthday when they finally enroll in Part D.

If the employer won't arrange independent testing—the price may be high if only a few employees are affected—employees themselves can hire an actuary to conduct the test. It may cost, say, $2,000 split among three employees—a hefty sum, but small in comparison to the years of penalties to which they're subject if they delay enrollment in Medicare and are reported to have non-MCC coverage.

Your clients' coverage on a non-MCC prescription drug plan is irrelevant before age 65. The penalty applies only to non-MCC coverage after an individual's 65th birthday.

Part D: Delay enrollment. At first glance, this idea may seem silly. After all, many older people have multiple prescriptions, and Part D is a godsend to those who save money by shifting some of their financial risk to insurers.

On the other hand, a number of seniors are healthy and take few if any prescription drugs. For them, it may make sense to delay enrollment in Part D. Sure, penalties accumulate the longer they aren't enrolled in Medicare prescription drug coverage, but every year that they let the General Enrollment Period pass by without enrolling, they save perhaps $600 in premiums. If they remain HSA-eligible during this time and contribute $8,000 or more to their HSAs, they reduce their taxable income (saving up to $2,400 in taxes) and build their tax-free HSA balances for future tax-free distributions.

If they suddenly face the prospect of purchasing prescriptions before they can enroll in a Part D plan during the next General Enrollment Period, they may find value in purchasing a drug-discount card, downloading a coupon from a site like GoodRx, or comparing prices at various retail pharmacies. These efforts don't constitute insurance, but a discount card, coupon, or discount price may save them 25% to 50% on prescriptions that they purchase with personal funds until the next General Enrollment Period. At that time, they can evaluate the merits of enrolling in Part D versus continuing to pay for prescriptions with personal funds and a drug-discount card or coupons.

Too few patients actively shop for prescriptions. This is a good exercise even with coverage. Prices vary widely from pharmacy to pharmacy for the same prescription. Many chain-drug and mass-merchant stores fill one-month or three-month prescriptions at below-cost prices (typically in the range of $3 to $4 per month and $10 to $12 per three-month supply). Why? They want your clients to fill a shopping cart while roaming the aisles as they wait for the prescription. These merchants don't mind losing a few dollars on the prescription if customers in turn purchase higher-margin items while waiting.

The option to delay enrollment isn't mentioned as a strategy to minimize the effect of Part B penalties. Though this strategy is equally applicable to Part B in theory, it's much more costly. Part B premiums generally run three to four times a typical Part D penalty. Delaying enrollment in Part D for five years results in a 60% penalty on perhaps a $40 Part D premium ($24 per month, or $288 the first year). The same delay in enrolling in Part B generates a 50% penalty on a Part B premium of $134 ($67 per month, or $804 per year).

Retroactive Medicare Enrollment

Medicare rules were written originally in 1965—nearly four decades before Congress authorized HSAs. Since no other employer-sponsored or nongroup coverage is part of a program for which eligibility is tied to Medicare enrollment, Medicare rules' interaction with other coverage never created an issue.

HSAs changed that. Beginning in 2004 and continuing today, various features of the Medicare program affect individuals' eligibility to continue to contribute to an HSA. One of the most damaging rules to continued HSA eligibility is the retroactive Medicare enrollment policy.

> One of the most damaging rules to continued HSA eligibility is the retroactive Medicare enrollment policy.

Here it is in a nutshell: When your client delays Medicare enrollment when first eligible (during the Initial Enrollment Period) and later enrolls in Part A, her Part A enrollment is retroactive six months (but in no case does it extend prior to age 65). If she has prefunded her HSA, she may have to withdraw funds to avoid exceeding the pro-rated contribution limit imposed by her retroactive enrollment in Part A.

Example: *Calvin (who is HSA-eligible) and Inge (who isn't), a couple, decide on a whim to retire at the same time, in September 2019. Calvin is 66 years old, and Inge turned age 65 two months ago. Both sign up for Medicare during their respective Special Enrollment Periods. Because they've turned age 65, their enrollment in Part A is retroactive. Calvin's Part A enrollment is retroactive six months, and Inge's is retroactive only two months—back to the first day of the month of her 65th birthday.*

Calvin contributed up to the $8,000 maximum (including catch-up contribution) to his HSA early in 2019. His retroactive enrollment in Part A makes his coverage effective April 1, 2019. Calvin must withdraw 9/12 of his contribution ($6,000) - 3/12 for October through December when he isn't covered by his employer's HSA-qualified plan and 6/12 due to his retroactive Part A *coverage—and any earnings on that contribution. He must then include that amount as taxable income on their 2019 joint income-tax return..*

The retroactive-enrollment provision is especially annoying to anyone who has continuous commercial coverage before enrolling in Medicare and wants to maximize HSA contributions. When your client enrolls in Medicare after her 65th birthday, the Part A retroactive enrollment provision always applies.

You can help your clients by advising them of this provision and working with them to stop their HSA contributions six months before enrolling in Part A. That way, they minimize the work and rework that they—and perhaps their employers—must do to remain in compliance.

Beware of COBRA

As noted several times, COBRA isn't group coverage, even though a former employee (or spouse or dependent of a former employee) is continuing coverage on an employer-sponsored (group) medical plan. A COBRA policy provides the same coverage as employees receive, but it's not considered group coverage. That designation has important implications for your clients who delay enrollment in Medicare when they're first eligible.

Example: *Brianna just turned age 64 and is covered on an MCC group medical plan. She could leave the workforce today and be comfortable. Instead she plans to retire at age 65 and move to another part of the country to be closer to her daughter and her growing family. Then, her son Michael becomes ill and his wife is overwhelmed caring for Michael and their three children. Brianna accelerates her retirement plan. She elects to continue her group plan via COBRA to bridge the gap to age 65, when she qualifies for Medicare coverage. With all the chaos in Michael's home, Brianna forgets to enroll in Medicare until age 65½, when her COBRA coverage ends.*

When Brianna completes her paperwork to enroll in Medicare, she's informed that she can't enroll in any Part of Medicare until the next applicable General Enrollment Periods and that she may face a Part B penalty when she does enroll.

What happened? COBRA coverage isn't group coverage, so Brianna isn't entitled to a Special Enrollment Period when she wants to sign up for Medicare. If she misses her Initial Enrollment Period (three months before and three months after the month of her 65th birthday), she can't enroll until the next

General Enrollment Period. In the meantime, her COBRA coverage expires (the maximum period of COBRA coverage is 18 months in most situations), which means that she experiences a gap in coverage before the Medicare General Enrollment Periods for Part A and Part B (effective date of coverage: July 1) and Part D (effective date of coverage: Jan. 1).

Brianna may be forced to purchase an age-rated (very high premium) nongroup plan through an ACA marketplace or directly from an insurer to cover the gap between the end of her COBRA coverage and her enrollment in Medicare. Fortunately, commercial coverage rules are different from Medicare. The loss of *any* qualified coverage is a qualifying event that allows an individual to pick up new coverage.

COBRA coverage isn't group coverage.

The key point, which is worth emphasizing again, is that your clients need to be familiar with these rules and requirements, or you need to be familiar with them and your clients need to tell you their plans. If Brianna had been working closely with you, you—removed from the distractions that Brianna was experiencing—would have counseled her about the need to enroll in Medicare at age 65. She would have enrolled during her Initial Enrollment Period, which is triggered by her 65th birthday. She would face no coverage gap and no penalty.

Options for Working Seniors

Many people who continue to work after their 65th birthday and haven't started collecting Social Security or Railroad Retirement benefits don't enroll in Medicare when they turn 65. Most have three distinct options available to them:

- Remain enrolled in the group medical plan and delay enrollment in Medicare.
- Remain enrolled in the group medical plan and enroll in one or more Parts of Medicare as additional coverage.
- Disenroll from group coverage and enroll in one or more Parts of Medicare as sole coverage.

Here are the implications of each strategy:

Remain enrolled in the group medical plan and delay enrollment in Medicare: In this scenario, your clients can disenroll from group coverage at any time. They need to be careful, however, as they must time their disenrollment from the group medical plan to coincide with a window of opportunity to enroll in Medicare. If they remain actively employed and enrolled in an MCC group medical plan, they can enroll in Medicare at any time. If their coverage doesn't satisfy specific Medicare rules—either because it fails the MCC test or they continued coverage by exercising their COBRA rights—they may have to delay enrollment until the next General Enrollment Period and may be subject to Part B and Part D penalties.

Key questions that your clients must ask:

- **"Have I had continuous group medical coverage since turning age 65?"** If so, no Part B penalties apply. Your client disenrolls from that coverage and uses her Special Enrollment Period to sign up for Part A and Part B.

- **"Has my insurer determined that my prescription drug coverage meets the MCC standard?"** If so, as long as your client maintains that coverage continuously from his 65th birthday until he enrolls in Part D, he doesn't face a Part D penalty or gap in coverage.

- **"If my prescription drug coverage doesn't meet the MCC standard according to the insurer's testing, has my employer (or have I) hired an independent actuary who has determined that the plan is creditable when factoring in my employer's HRA contribution to reduce my net financial responsibility?"** If so, and if your client has continuous coverage since age 65 on an MCC prescription drug plan, he can delay Part D enrollment without facing a penalty or gap in coverage.

- **"If my coverage doesn't satisfy the MCC standard, am I willing to pay a permanent penalty in the form of a premium increase of 1% of the national base beneficiary premium for every month after my 65th birthday that I don't have MCC coverage?"** The penalty for delaying three years (36 months) on the 2018 national base beneficiary premium ($35.02) is $12.60 per month, or about $150 for the year. The dollar value of the Part D penalty increases over time as the national base beneficiary premium increases, resulting in $14,400 in penalties for an individual enrolling in Part D at age 68 and remaining covered until age 100 (assuming an annual 5% increase in the national base beneficiary premium).

- **"Does my employer-sponsored plan offer superior coverage compared to Medicare so that it makes financial sense for me to risk future penalties to enjoy financial and medical benefits of the group plan today?"** Your client needs to consider his share of employer-sponsored coverage premiums, out-of-pocket responsibility, services covered, participating providers, and value-added programs to determine whether his current coverage is better than what Medicare offers. It may make sense for him to maintain his employer-sponsored coverage and risk future Medicare penalties.

- **"How much additional money can I accumulate in my HSA and what tax savings can I enjoy now to offset the financial effect of penalties and other qualified expenses in the future?"** An individual delaying Medicare enrollment from 2016 through 2018 would have contributed up to $13,200 (self-only) or $23,400 (family) to the account during those three years. Those contributions alone—even before factoring in anything but minimal investment growth on the self-only contribution—are more than sufficient to pay the permanent penalties.

Remain enrolled in the group medical plan and enroll in one or more Parts of Medicare as additional coverage: To avoid potential future penalties, employees can try to capture the best of both worlds by remaining enrolled in their employer's medical plan and also enrolling in Medicare Part A, Part B, and Part D. There are several advantages to your clients who adopt this approach:

- They retain group coverage, which typically covers more services with fewer daily and lifetime limits than Medicare, has a wider network of physicians and other providers, and offers various members savings programs on everything from glasses and hearing aids to gym memberships and vision-correction surgery.

- They retain group coverage, ensuring that they receive at least that level of benefits for all services.

- They retain group coverage, which entitles them to a Special Enrollment Period—and thus no gap in coverage—when they finally enroll in Medicare.

- They receive the benefit level of the richer plan, which may vary from service to service.

Can individuals be covered for services on two different policies? Absolutely. Millions of Americans are enrolled in more than one coverage. A common example is children covered on both divorced parents' policies. When someone is covered on two different policies, insurers work together in a process called *coordination of benefits* to ensure that the patient receives the full reimbursement of the more generous plan without being reimbursed by two different policies for the same benefit.

Example: *Lily turns 65, remains covered on her employer's group medical plan, and also enrolls in Medicare. If the company has 20 or more employees, her group insurance is the primary payer and Medicare is the secondary payer.*

She ends up in the hospital Jan. 2 and incurs a bill of $27,000. She gives the hospital billing office copies of her group medical plan and Medicare cards and tells the billing agent that the group plan is the primary payer. (If she doesn't happen to know the coordination of benefits rules, the hospital will ask her how many people the company employs to determine which coverage is primary.) The hospital bills the group plan. The group plan processes the claim. In this case, let's say the contracted rate for the services that she received is $20,000 and she has a $4,000 deductible. The group medical plan sends the hospital $16,000 and tells Lily and the hospital that she owes the $4,000 deductible.

The hospital then bills Medicare. Part A has a deductible of $1,340 per benefit period, with no additional cost-sharing for the first 60 days of hospitalization. Medicare pays the hospital a total of $2,660 of the $4,000 remaining balance, leaving Lily with a $1,340 deductible for which she's responsible.

As you can see from this example, no one—neither Lily nor the hospital—is paid more than what the richer plan (in this case, Medicare) pays. Had Lily been covered by Medicare only, Medicare would have paid the entire bill less the $1,340 deductible. The real winner in this example is Medicare, which pays the $2,660 gap between its deductible and the point at which the group plan begins to pay, rather than assume responsibility for the entire bill above the $1,340 Part A deductible.

The rules on which plan is the primary payer and which is the secondary payer when Medicare coverage is involved are written into federal law. The group medical plan is primary when the company has 20 or more employees. The unit of measure is *employees* rather than full-time equivalents (FTEs). The group plan for a company with two full-time and 20 half-time employees is primary because it has 22 employees, even though it has only 12 FTEs.

In contrast, when the company has 19 or fewer employees, Medicare is primary. The intent of this law is to protect working seniors at smaller companies; these employees otherwise might represent an insurance liability to the company. A firm with six employees is probably less able than a 60-employee company to absorb the higher claims costs of an older worker.

You've seen the benefits of having dual coverage composed of a group medical plan and Medicare. There are some disadvantages as well:

- Your client pays extra premiums. She pays a portion of her group medical plan premium (and her employer pays the balance). She's also responsible for paying her Part B and Part D premiums. Though the Part B monthly premium is $134 for most enrollees, that figure rises to $187.50 monthly with adjusted family income of $170,000 and $267.90 if her adjusted family income is $214,000. The premium is based on her income two years earlier, so she may pay a higher premium for three years before her premium declines to reflect her retirement income.

- It's more complicated. She must present two cards to providers and reconcile statements from two insurers—the group plan and Medicare. Her providers also face a more complicated claims-submission process.

- She loses her eligibility to contribute additional funds to her HSA, which means that she forfeits an opportunity to reduce her taxable income and begins to deplete her medical equity to reimburse qualified expenses. She can make up for part of this loss by participating in a general Health FSA to reimburse her out-of-pocket medical, prescription drug, dental, vision, and certain over-the-counter expenses with pre-tax funds if her employer offers this coverage.

Key questions for your clients to ask themselves—and for you to follow up on:

- **"How similar is my group medical insurance plan's benefits to Medicare's?"** If the coverages are similar, your client pays two sets of premiums without gaining a real advantage in terms of additional coverage.

- **"How similar are the two networks?"** Your client's group plan may have a much broader network of providers from whom he prefers to receive care.

If so, he won't have to deal with primary and secondary payers because only his group insurance pays for services from providers who aren't part of the Medicare network. If this is the case, why would he pay Medicare premiums for benefits that he won't access?

- **"How much do I pay for my group insurance premium?"** Unless your client's group plan premium is very inexpensive, dropping the group coverage and directing the money that he pays for that premium toward Medicare premiums and out-of-pocket costs may leave him better off financially.

- **"Is my group insurance prescription drug benefit MCC?"** If so, he doesn't face any penalties if he defers enrollment in Part D when he's first eligible. If not, calculate the additional HSA contributions, tax advantages, and medical equity accumulated versus Part D penalties.

Disenroll from group coverage and enroll in one or more Parts of Medicare as your client's sole coverage: This option relieves your client of the first two disadvantages of remaining enrolled in group coverage and enrolling in Medicare. She no longer pays group premiums and doesn't have to complicate her own life and her providers' lives with dual coverage.

This option doesn't relieve your client of the third disadvantage—losing her ability to contribute additional funds to build medical equity in her HSAs. The good news is that her take-home income increases when her employer no longer deducts her share of pre-tax medical premiums and her pre-tax HSA contributions from her paycheck. If she used to pay $4,000 in premiums and contribute $6,000 to an HSA, her net income increases by about $6,500 to $7,000 ($10,000 gross, less taxes). On the other hand, she can't contribute $6,000 to her HSAs to pay her current or future medical expenses.

Key questions for your clients to ask themselves—and for you to follow up on:

- **"What benefits do I lose when I drop my group coverage and utilize Medicare as my sole coverage?"** Considerations include services covered by the medical plan, cost-sharing, network, special programs (disease management, chronic care), and non-medical benefits (member savings and discount programs). And, group coverage is governed by the ACA and imposes an out-of-pocket maximum financial responsibility, whereas Part A and Part B place no ceiling on out-of-pocket financial responsibility. The higher the cost-sharing in the group plan, the less likely that it provides meaningful benefits compared to Medicare after coordination of benefits.

- **"Does my spouse rely on my coverage?"** If your client drops her medical plan, her spouse probably can continue the group medical plan via COBRA. COBRA rights extend for a limited time, so she must consider how close her spouse is to Medicare eligibility. Also, if her spouse pays the entire COBRA premium (no employer contribution), the full cost of that coverage may be more than if she continues family coverage on the group plan (when her employer's contribution to premium is factored in).

Part A and Part B place no ceiling on out-of-pocket financial responsibility.

More and more Americans are joining the centenarian club every year. Between 1980 and 1999, about 17 Americans joined each week. In the first 14 years of this century, the number increased to more than 30. Talk about a growth stock! (Perhaps the candles explain global warming, at least in part.) Only about half the population is disproportionately affected, as 80% of centenarians are women. Men are less likely to outlive reasonable net present value savings and investing to pay their Medicare penalties over a long lifetime.

This longer lifespan has important implications for retirement planning, as you've pointed out to your clients. Those implications affect HSAs. When you review with your clients their financial needs in retirement, be sure to extend this conversation to include HSAs.

Counseling Your Clients

- ✓ Counsel your clients before they apply for Social Security or Railroad Retirement benefits. You already do so, for a range of reasons that go beyond continued HSA eligibility. Now, the effect of this action on HSA eligibility is another financial factor for them to consider before enrolling.

- ✓ If your clients aren't actively at work at age 65, it's almost always best for them to enroll in Medicare during their Initial Enrollment Period. They lose their ability to continue contributing to an HSA, but it makes little financial sense to forego coverage or enroll in a nongroup plan if eligible (premiums of perhaps $500 to $900 monthly) when most clients can enroll in Medicare Part A (no premium), Part B ($134 monthly premium for most enrollees), and Part D (average national premium of less than $40). Even adding a Medicare Supplement plan for an additional $200 per month may still make Medicare a lower-cost option.

- ✓ If your clients are actively at work at age 65 and haven't applied for Social Security or Railroad Retirement benefits, be sure to engage them in a discussion about their current and future financial plans to determine what strategy makes the most sense for them.

- ✓ If your clients are approaching age 70 and haven't applied for Social Security or Railroad Retirement benefits, it's time for another discussion. The financial calculus changes when they can't increase their monthly Social Security retirement benefit further by delaying enrollment.

- ✓ Counsel your clients that penalties associated with delayed enrollment in Part B and Part D aren't really penalties (negative connotation), but rather taxes (a levy that applies only when they first make money or build wealth). Their path to increased personal wealth may lead them to pay penalties when they subsequently enroll.

CHAPTER 15

Beginning at Age 60 . . .

Though it's common to think of age 65 as a milestone birthday—and it is, thanks to the politics of certain federal entitlement programs—individuals who wait until that age to consider serious retirement decisions limit their options and suffer adverse financial consequences. They should begin to contemplate myriad issues related to when they end their careers, how they then occupy their time, how they manage their income and expenses, and how they maintain their health in retirement long before then.

And your clients undoubtedly do, as you probably have worked with them for years and helped them see over the horizon to a more fulfilling and financially stable retirement. For those who haven't engaged in this activity, the 60th birthday is about as late as they should begin to think about these issues.

In this chapter, you'll

- explore important questions that you and your clients must discuss as part of the planning process, and
- review some answers and how they influence coverage and financial decisions that affect the rest of their lives.

Beginning in their early 60s, your clients face a number of important age milestones. Their actions—or inaction—at these key points have a major effect on their future financial and coverage experience. These are the key decision points:

- At age 62, individuals can begin to receive reduced Social Security benefits. Doing so disqualifies them from making further contributions to an HSA beginning at age 65, when they're automatically enrolled in Part A and Part B.

- At age 65, individuals are eligible to enroll in Medicare, though only some are required to enroll in any Part of the program on that birthday. Enrolling affects HSA eligibility, as noted in the previous point.
- Somewhere between ages 66 and 67 (varies by birth year), people who haven't yet enrolled can sign up and receive their full Social Security benefit. When they begin to collect Social Security benefits, they're automatically enrolled in Part A and Part B (retroactively six months in Part A, which may result in having to correct excess HSA contributions). They can then disenroll from Part B (to avoid the premium, particularly if they have other coverage), but not Part A.
- Between Full Retirement Age (between ages 66 and 67) and age 70, individuals who haven't yet signed up for Social Security can enroll and receive an enhanced monthly Social Security payment. When they begin to receive Social Security benefits, they're automatically enrolled in Parts A and B and face the retroactive Part A issue, which reduces their HSA contributions and may require refiling their personal income tax return.
- In the year that they turn age 70½, they must begin to take Required Minimum Distributions from their retirement accounts, whether or not they need these funds. RMDs may create additional income tax liability, particularly if your clients have other sources of income (such as a salary from ongoing employment).

During this period in your clients' lives, their work plans also are interrelated and affect Social Security, group medical coverage, COBRA coverage, and Medicare. It's all very confusing, and some decisions that don't seem related have an effect on HSA owners.

Key questions that your clients need to ask and answer themselves annually beginning at age 60—and for you to follow up on:

"How much longer do I plan to work in my current job/company/industry?" The question used to be "When will I retire?" Today, a growing number of workers are retiring from a career or a company and then engaging in other income-producing activity to maintain a flow of earned income and fill their time meaningfully. That work may be related to their career (for example, part-time consulting or writing, perhaps with their current employer or a trade organization) or completely different (a move from plastics engineer or sales representative to seasonal assistant harbormaster or free-lance photographer).

The focus is on "job/company/industry" because career positions are typically associated with employer-sponsored medical coverage, whereas part-time work in retirement often doesn't include access to a group medical plan. The availability and attractiveness of employer-sponsored coverage are key determinants of when an individual's best coverage option is to enroll in Medicare.

"How large is my current employer?" This question is very important because of its medical-coverage implications. As discussed, if the company has 19 or fewer employees, Medicare becomes the primary payer when your client enrolls. Neither Medicare nor an employer can require someone to enroll in Medicare at any age. The employer's insurer, however, can stipulate that an employee who is Medicare-eligible can't remain on the group plan if he doesn't enroll in Part A and Part B as well.

Neither Medicare nor an employer can require someone to enroll in Medicare at any age.

At issue here are Medicare secondary payer rules. If the employer has 20 or more workers, the group medical plan is the primary payer. An employee enrolled in Medicare has secondary coverage; Medicare pays, at most, only a portion of the bill that the primary insurer doesn't pay. With small groups, in contrast, Medicare is the primary payer. The group plan pays only, at most, a portion of the bill that Medicare doesn't cover.

Your clients who want to remain active at work and remain eligible to contribute to an HSA need to understand the financial implications of enrolling (and losing HSA eligibility) or not enrolling in Medicare at age 65. Again, if they work for an employer with 20 or more employees, it's not an issue, because the group plan is the primary payer. But if a client works for a smaller firm, where the group medical plan is the secondary payer even when the employee doesn't enroll in Medicare, the financial exposure for your client can be severe. Remember, absent Medicare enrollment, your client becomes the primary payer with no ceiling on his financial exposure.

"How does my spouse play into this strategy?" Now it gets interesting. Let's say the company has fewer than 20 employees and the group insurer is the secondary payer. Your client—even if she's healthy at the moment—is all but forced to enroll in Medicare to prevent a huge level of personal financial responsibility if she, in the absence of Medicare, becomes the primary payer. Her financial liability could run into six figures for a serious illness or condition.

Once she enrolls in Medicare, she can't contribute to her HSA any longer. But wait. Does she cover her husband on her employer's plan? If her husband isn't yet age 65, the group insurance remains his only coverage. If he satisfies HSA eligibility requirements, he can contribute up to the family limit (as long as the two of them are enrolled in the group plan, even if she's also enrolled in Medicare) in his own HSA.

Thus, the family achieves just what it wanted all along: The couple makes the maximum contribution to an HSA that reimburses the husband's and wife's qualified expenses tax-free. The employee has both primary and secondary coverage, reducing her financial responsibility. The husband remains covered on his wife's group medical plan. The husband makes his $1,000 catch-up contribution in addition to the $7,000 (2019 figure) HSA contribution maximum for a family contract.

The couple does lose a little financially. The employee can no longer make a catch-up contribution to her HSA. And if the company provides tax-free employer contributions to her HSA, those payments cease once she's no longer HSA-eligible. Her employer can make an after-tax contribution to her husband's HSA that the couple can then deduct on its personal income tax return. Her employer isn't required to contribute to a spouse's HSA, and most employers don't. Doing so typically requires modifying the company's Cafeteria Plan documents and communicating this benefit to all employees.

"What are my costs and coverage under my current employer plan?"
If the group medical plan has a high deductible and the employer requires employees to share a large portion of the deductible, your client may be better off foregoing the tax advantages of HSA contributions and instead enrolling in Medicare.

On the other hand, the cost and coverage may be similar enough that your client can gain several thousands of dollars of tax advantages in exchange for little or no difference in premiums and out-of-pocket costs if she remains covered on the group medical plan rather than enroll in Medicare.

"Is my current pharmacy plan considered Medicare Creditable Coverage?" This is a key issue for Part D. Your client may want to work until age 68 at a large company and remain covered on the group medical plan. If he enrolls in Medicare during a Special Enrollment Period (coverage effective immediately after he disenrolls from the employer-sponsored plan), he avoids any Part B penalties. Part B penalties are assessed only when the coverage after age 65 isn't considered group coverage.

On the other hand, Part D penalties are triggered by the quality of prescription-drug coverage beginning at age 65, regardless of whether that coverage is group or nongroup. To avoid a penalty, your client must have continuous MCC coverage beginning at age 65. The penalty is 1% of the national base beneficiary premium ($35.02 in 2018) for every month of non-creditable coverage after your client's 65th birthday.

Part D penalties are triggered by the quality of prescription-drug coverage beginning at age 65.

The benefits of remaining enrolled in non-MCC coverage and enjoying the tax advantage associated with contributing to an HSA may outweigh future penalties. Or they may not. Your clients need to calculate the financial and psychological effect of the penalties.

"What is my time horizon? What is my tolerance for risk?" If your client weighs a strategy that involves future penalties, she needs to evaluate her comfort with paying the levies. Some people are uncomfortable with paying penalties, as the term implies that they've done something wrong. Others prefer to think of the penalties as *surcharges* and then view them unemotionally as one factor in a financial equation.

Time horizon is important as well. Does your client expect to live another 10 years? Another 35 years? The Part B and Part D penalties are *permanent.* They remain in place for the rest of your client's life. And since penalties are calculated as a percentage of each year's Part B and Part D premiums, they vary (almost always increasing) over time. For example, a client who doesn't enroll in Medicare when first eligible and has non-creditable coverage pays a lifetime penalty of about $4,000 during 30 years of Part D coverage for every 12 months that she was covered on a non-MCC prescription drug plan between age 65 and her enrollment in Part D.

But she can also contribute to her HSA $4,500 (2019 figure, adjusted annually for inflation) or more every year if she has self-only coverage and $8,000 (2019 figure, adjusted annually for inflation) or more if she has family coverage. And those contributions grow over time to easily pay the penalty and provide additional funds to reimburse other qualified expenses tax-free.

"Will I need coverage to bridge the gap between when I leave my employer and when I enroll in Medicare?" This situation can take one of two common forms. The more common is that an employee retires before reaching age 65 and becoming eligible to enroll in Medicare. The less common situation is when an employee is eligible to enroll in Medicare but wants commercial coverage for other reasons, such as access to a broader provider network when receiving ongoing care with providers who don't accept Medicare.

In both cases, your clients may be eligible to continue coverage by exercising their COBRA rights. Alternatively, they can purchase coverage in the nongroup market or enroll in a spouse's plan.

These decisions are important because COBRA and nongroup plans aren't group coverage, as discussed already. People who enroll in *non*group coverage understand this concept, but it often strikes them as counterintuitive that continuing coverage on a *group* medical plan through COBRA doesn't constitute group coverage.

Individuals who become eligible to enroll in Medicare and defer enrollment at the time of their Initial Enrollment Period must maintain continuous group coverage to avoid Part B penalties and potential gaps in enrollment in all Parts of Medicare. For example, if your 66-year-old client's COBRA rights expire March 31, she can't enroll in Part A and Part B until the July 1 General Enrollment Period effective date. She can't enroll in Part D coverage until the following Jan. 1 General Enrollment Period for that Part of Medicare.

In this situation, she must either roll the dice and forego coverage or purchase expensive age-rated coverage in the nongroup market to bridge the gap until the next General Enrollment Periods for Medicare coverage. Nearly all nongroup plans carry much higher premiums and impose much higher out-of-pocket costs than Medicare (except for Part B, which places no ceiling on a patient's financial responsibility). And your client could end up increasing her financial responsibility. She may satisfy her deductible on her COBRA coverage, incur high out-of-pocket costs during her brief coverage on a nongroup plan, and then face a whole new set of deductibles and coinsurance on her Medicare coverage—all within the same calendar year.

And she faces potential Part B and Part D penalties because of the gap in coverage. Note the word *potential.* The Part B penalty is assessed only for a full 12-month period of not being enrolled in group coverage. If her gap in group coverage since turning age 65 is less than 12 months, she faces no penalty. If her prescription-drug coverage is MCC, she faces no Part D penalty.

"Does my company offer retiree coverage?" In a bygone era, many large employers offered generous retiree medical benefits to their employees. Coverage typically consisted of a Medicare Supplement plan that paid most of the out-of-pocket costs that Medicare charges. These plans remain a standard in some states' public employee populations (sometimes including spouses), but fewer and fewer private employers still offer this coverage.

Instead, employers who offer retiree coverage have moved to a defined-contribution approach. They commit a monthly or annual dollar sum to retirees, often through an HRA so that retirees receive the stipend on a pretax basis. They typically contract with a private marketplace through which employees can shop for a Medicare Supplement plan. When the contribution is in the form of an HRA, employees may have the option to spend the funds on Medicare Supplement plan premiums or direct reimbursement of out-of-pocket medical, prescription drug, dental, and vision expenses.

If your client's employer (or former employer) offers retiree coverage, that extra boost may influence his retirement timeline. He may choose to leave his employer at age 65 and enroll in Medicare and a Medicare Supplement as he pursues the next chapter in his life without thinking about the medical coverage linked to this new professional venture, hobby, volunteer service, or other activity.

On the other hand, if he has no retiree coverage or stipend options and thus is faced with remaining active at work on the group plan or leaving the company (or coverage) with traditional Medicare as his best option, he may choose to remain at work longer. When he remains at work and HSA-eligible, each month that he delays Medicare enrollment represents another opportunity to make additional contributions to his HSA to build medical equity and reduce his taxable income.

Obviously, this exercise takes some time. It's time well spent, however. When your clients spend two hours per year beginning at age 60 (ideally before) reviewing these questions and their evolving answers, they're prepared to integrate their medical coverage with other aspects of their transition from full-time work to the next chapter in their lives.

Sadly, all too many people—not your clients, of course, thanks to your counsel—make decisions in isolation and only afterwards realize the financial implications of their decisions. Those mistakes can be costly. Spending five or 10 hours a year thinking through these issues can be a very smart investment—with no tax consequences!

Counseling Your Clients

- ✓ Emphasize to your clients the importance of a holistic approach to the transition from their current careers to the next chapters in their lives. They need to consider the financial effect of medical coverage along with fulfillment, income, and other factors.
- ✓ Review the questions in this chapter annually with your clients. The questions plant unconscious seeds that may influence your clients' approach to designing their post-career lives.
- ✓ Monitor year-to-year changes in your clients' answers. A different answer to a particular question may affect not only their future medical coverage, but other financial considerations as well. Be prepared to walk with them wherever the new path leads and assess the terrain with them.

SECTION IV

HSA Compliance Basics

INTRODUCTION TO SECTION IV

If you believe that you know what you need to know about HSA compliance, you're welcome to skip to Appendix A *and complete the test. Warning: The test is pretty comprehensive and detailed. The questions aren't designed to trip you up or embarrass you, but rather to test the depth of your knowledge.*

If you don't do well, don't be discouraged. The author would have failed this exam not long ago. If you read Section IV *and* Section V *and then retake the exam, you'll be amazed at how much you've learned. And you'll know where to look to find detailed explanations around the concepts that you haven't yet mastered.*

In this section, HSA rules are the focus. The first of these chapters deals with concepts on which you typically don't advise your clients: medical coverage. It's important to do so, however, for several reasons.

First, your clients need to be enrolled in specific medical coverage to be eligible to open and contribute to an HSA. This isn't the only requirement, any more than oxygen is the single requirement needed to remain alive. In both cases—HSA eligibility and sustainability—a key ingredient must be present before an individual can satisfy the other requirements.

Second, medical premiums and cost-sharing (the portion of all care for which the patient is responsible) continue to grow. It's not unusual for individual coverage to carry a premium of $5,000 to $9,000 annually, with premiums for family coverage often between $15,000 and $28,000. And that's the premium only. These plans then shift some of the cost of treatment to patients through up-front deductibles, coinsurance, and copays for office visits, diagnostic services, treatments, and prescription drugs.

Your clients need to plan for these expenses. Even when an employer pays 75% of a family premium, some—or perhaps even many—of your clients are paying a combined total of $10,000 or more in premiums and out-of-pocket costs. Premiums are generally paid with pre-tax dollars through an employer's Cafeteria Plan. This simple arrangement pulls employees' share of premiums from their paychecks before federal income taxes, state and local income taxes (if applicable), and federal payroll taxes are applied. Employees typically save about 25%. An employee who has to pay $6,000 toward his medical insurance premium sees his take-home pay decline by only $4,200—not the full $6,000—when he faces a marginal tax rate of 30% and pays through a Section 125 Plan.

Your goal as an advising professional is to find ways that your clients can pay their remaining $1,000 to $4,000 of out-of-pocket medical costs, as well as additional dental and vision expenses, with minimal tax friction.

A key strategy for you to explore with your clients is opening and contributing to an HSA. You and your clients need to understand the rules to ensure that they seize the opportunity to establish an HSA and remain in compliance with all rules and regulations so that they can continue to enjoy the tax savings associated with their HSA.

This section introduces you to all relevant rules and regulations around HSA eligibility, contributions, distributions, and other issues. In each case, you'll see a description of the rule and a citation. You can turn to the appendices to read some of the original document on which the information in these chapters is based. And you'll find a comprehensive list of resources in Appendix G.

CHAPTER 16

HSA-Qualified Medical Plan

The first step in becoming eligible to open and contribute to an HSA is to be covered on an HSA-qualified medical plan. Congress and the IRS refer to these plans as *high deductible health plans* in the original legislation and guidance. They are often called *High Deductible Health Plans* or *qualified High Deductible Health Plans* today. The *qualified* label is necessary because many of today's medical plans with high deductibles don't satisfy the requirements to allow your clients to become HSA-eligible.

This book refers to these plans as *HSA-Qualified* plans (or *HSA-qualified* coverage). This isn't a government-sanctioned phrase. But it distinguishes HSA-qualified plans from other high-deductible medical coverage that requires high patient cost-sharing without qualifying the individuals covered on the plan to open and contribute to an HSA.

In this chapter, you'll find a discussion of

- the minimum deductible and maximum out-of-pocket cost levels that plans must satisfy to be HSA-qualified;
- which services must apply to the deductible, and which can be offered with no cost-sharing at the point of service;
- how the ACA, passed more than six years after Congress authorized HSAs, affects HSA-qualified medical plans;
- the difference between an embedded and aggregate family deductible and your clients' financial responsibility under each design; and
- how prescription drugs are covered, whether integrated into the medical plan or offered by a separate pharmacy manager.

Defining an HSA-qualified medical plan. An HSA-qualified plan must satisfy certain requirements:

1. All services except select preventive care are subject to a broad deductible.

2. The deductible is no less than the figure that the IRS calculates each year to reflect general inflation.

3. The out-of-pocket maximum for in-network services does not exceed a figure that the IRS calculates each year to reflect general inflation.

[See IRS Notice 2004-2, Q&A 3 and *IRS Publication 969* for updated dollar figures.*]*

The product chassis doesn't—and does—matter. Insurers can design an HMO, PPO, or POS plan to be HSA-qualified. An HMO plan typically requires a patient to work with a primary-care physician (PCP), often (but not always) requires a referral from the PCP to visit most specialists, and limits non-urgent/non-emergency care to network providers. A PPO plan typically allows a patient to self-refer to any provider within the network at any time and gives access to providers who aren't part of the insurer's network (usually with higher financial responsibility), with an increased burden on patients to follow plan rules or face potential penalties. A POS plan typically is a hybrid between an HMO and PPO—essentially an HMO (with a designated PCP and often requiring referrals for specialty care) and an out-of-network level of benefits with greater cost-sharing and patient responsibility.

PPO members typically can self-refer to any specialist or facility, which gives them a great deal of flexibility to shop for care based on quality and price. In contrast, HMO and POS members who need a referral for specialty care often are at the mercy of their PCP and their (or their physician group's) willingness to refer outside the physician groups. HMO and POS members can't get more cost-effective care if they can't self-refer to specialists. And a patient with a regularly occurring condition that requires specialty care may have to visit a PCP first (at a cost of $100 to $225) just to receive the referral to the specialist who can actually deliver treatment.

Funding arrangement doesn't matter. An HSA-qualified plan can be either fully insured (your clients and their employer pay a fixed premium to an insurance company, which assumes all claims risk) or self-insured (an employer hires an insurance company to administer the plan, but the employer pays all claims). The plan design is the critical design feature in determining an individual's HSA eligibility. The funding arrangement is irrelevant.

Today, more than half of all employees covered by their employers are enrolled in self-insured plans. Employees typically don't notice the difference, since these plans are often administered by local or national insurers with whom the employees are familiar and who offer fully insured products as well. Self-insured plans don't have to incorporate state-mandated benefits and typically have different processes to appeal denial of services. *[See IRS Notice 2004-2, Q&A 7.]*

Self-insured plans don't have to incorporate state-mandated benefits.

All services except select preventive care must apply to a deductible. An HSA-qualified plan covers all diagnostic and treatment services subject to a deductible. Some examples are non-preventive office visits; non-preventive lab work; high-tech imaging (such as X-rays, MRIs, and CT scans); outpatient physical, occupational, speech, and cardiac therapy; chiropractic care (if covered); surgery; inpatient care at an acute or rehabilitation hospital; home health services; durable medical equipment (like wheelchairs, C-PAP machines, crutches, and walking boots), and prescription drugs.

A patient is financially responsible for all services up to the deductible. After that point, the insurer begins to pay claims in part or in full. *[See IRC Section 223 (c)(2)(A)(i)* and *IRS Notice 2004-2, Q&A 3.]*

Select preventive care is covered outside the deductible. The United States Preventive Service Task Force (USPSTF), an independent, volunteer panel of national experts in prevention and evidence-based medicine, evaluates a wide range of preventive tests and services based on their ability to identify diseases and conditions in their early stages so that patients can receive follow-up care before the disease or condition becomes more acute. Preventive services given a grade of A or B are covered in full under federal law. Insurers can cover other preventive services either subject to the deductible, in full, or via another cost-sharing arrangement (such as a copay or coinsurance).

See the end of this chapter for specific information on coverage of preventive prescription drugs. *[See IRC Section 223(c)(2)(C)* and *IRS Notice 2004-23.]*

Not all services in a routine annual physical are considered preventive. The USPSTF list determines which services are covered outside the deductible. Any service *not* included on that list *must* apply to the deductible on an HSA-qualified plan. Some physicians order tests (such as a resting electrocardiogram to monitor a patient's heart) that aren't medically appropriate for an asymptomatic patient (a person with no symptoms of underlying heart disease). On an HSA-qualified plan, electrocardiograms are covered as a diagnostic service and thus are subject to the deductible.

And it's not unusual for a patient to discuss an illness, injury, or condition while undergoing a routine physical. In that case, if the doctor diagnoses or treats (or even discusses) that condition, any resulting tests or treatment is subject to the deductible. In this case, the patient may receive care that includes a routine physical and several preventive tests that are covered in full, plus an office visit and diagnostic test that are subject to the deductible. *[See IRS Notice 2004-23.]*

Minimum deductible. The IRS reviews the statutory minimum annual deductible each year and adjusts it in $50 increments to reflect increases in the Consumer Price Index (CPI, the economy-wide—not medical—inflation). Medical costs have increased at about twice the rate of the overall CPI.

As a result of the *Tax Cuts and Jobs Act of 2017*, the IRS now calculates minimum deductibles using chained CPI. Chained CPI tracks changes in the consumer price index and factors in consumer substitution (for example, when the price of steak increases by 25%, consumers don't experience a 25% increase in their meat expenditures—because they substitute other protein such as hamburger, hot dogs, or beans—for part of the quantity of steak that they once consumed). Chained CPI rises more slowly than CPI (and much more slowly than medical CPI).

The statutory minimum annual deductibles in both 2018 and 2019 are:

Self-only contract	$1,350
Family contract	$2,700

[See IRC Section 223(c)(2)(A)(i), Section 223(c)(4), and *Section (g)(1); IRS Rev. Proc. 2017-37;* and *IRS Rev. Proc. 2018-30.]*

Rating tiers and minimum deductibles. The IRS recognizes only two tiers of coverage: self-only (your client covers only herself) and family (the policy covers more than one person). Though insurers and employers may offer additional rating tiers (such as *employee+spouse*, *employee+1*, *employee+child*, and *employee+children*), any policy that covers more than one person follows the rules established for a family contract. *[See IRC Section 23(c)(2)(i)* and *IRS Notice 2004-50, Q&A 12.]*

Aggregate and embedded deductibles—deductible design matters. Insurers can design their family policies with either an *aggregate* or *embedded* deductible. It's important to know how a policy works, since aggregate and embedded deductible designs can result in very different out-of-pocket responsibility, particularly if only one member of a family receives services subject to the deductible.

<u>Aggregate (umbrella)</u>: The family has a single deductible toward which all family members' claims accumulate.

> Example: *Meghan's employer's medical coverage has a $6,000 family deductible that must be met before the insurer begins to reimburse claims.*

<u>Embedded (per-person)</u>: Each family member has an individual deductible and the family itself has a ceiling on total family deductible responsibility.

> Example: *Andrew's employer's coverage has a $6,000 family deductible, but it caps each family member's deductible responsibility at $3,000.*
>
> *After a family member incurs $3,000 of deductible expenses, the insurer begins to reimburse that individual's claims in whole or in part. If members of Andrew's family collectively reach the $6,000 family deductible (whether or not a single family member reaches the individual deductible), the deductible is satisfied.*

If the family plan has an embedded deductible, the individual family member deductible can't be less than the statutory minimum annual deductible for a *family* contract, or $2,700 in 2018 and 2019. This design feature ensures that the policy never begins to pay benefits for non-preventive services until the family has incurred deductible expenses at least as great as the statutory minimum annual deductible for a family contract. If the individual deductible were, say, $2,000, one family member who incurred the family's first deductible expenses of the plan year would have all her claims covered after she reaches the $2,000 threshold. If the insurer assumes responsibility for any portion of any non-preventive claim below $2,700 in 2018 and 2019, the policy is *not* an HSA-qualified plan. *[See IRS Notice 2004-2, Q&A 3* and *Rev. Proc. 2017-37.]*

Financial responsibility after the deductible. Post-deductible cost-sharing varies by plan. The most common approaches are

- *coinsurance*, which means that your client and the insurer share the cost of each claim (with patient responsibility typically between 10% and 50% of the allowable charge).

- *copay*, which means that a patient pays a fixed dollar amount. Copays often apply to physician visits, imaging (like an MRI or CT scan), inpatient services, and prescription drugs.

- *an additional deductible on select services*, often applied to specialty prescription drugs.

- *full coverage*, which means that the insurer reimburses the provider for the full amount of the allowable charges and patients have no out-of-pocket financial responsibility.

Ceiling on out-of-pocket expenses for covered services. The out-of-pocket maximum is the most that an individual or family pays for covered expenses in a plan year before the insurer is responsible for paying all claims for covered services in full for the balance of the plan year. The IRS reviews this figure annually and adjusts it in $50 increments to reflect general, not medical, inflation.

The *Tax Cuts and Jobs Act of 2017* changes the calculation by introducing chained CPI (see a description under *Minimum Deductible* earlier). The result of this change is that the out-of-pocket maximum will rise more slowly in the future than it did with traditional CPI (and even more slowly than the rise in overall medical costs as measured by medical CPI).

The statutory out-of-pocket maximum figures are:

	2018	2019
Self-only contract	$6,650	$6,750
Family contract	$13,300	$13,500

[See IRC Section 223(c)(2)(A)(ii), Section 223(c)(4), and *Section 223(g)(1); IRS Rev. Proc. 2017-37;* and *IRS Rev. Proc. 2018-30.]*

The out-of-pocket maximum doesn't apply to *all* services. Your client could end up paying more than the statutory out-of-pocket maximum for one or more of the following reasons:

- The out-of-pocket maximum applies to in-network services only. If the policy offers coverage for out-of-network services, the insurer can impose higher limits. The HSA rules don't mandate an upper limit, though individual states may impose restrictions.

Example: *Piper's PPO plan has a $3,000 deductible and a $6,000 out-of-pocket maximum in-network. If she receives care outside the network, she has a separate $12,000 deductible and $24,000 out-of-pocket maximum.*

- It applies to covered services only.

Example: *Lionel's plan limits chiropractic care to 20 visits.*

Any amounts that Lionel pays for additional visits beyond 20 aren't applied to his out-of-pocket maximum. Furthermore, because the additional visits are beyond the coverage limit, Lionel's chiropractor can charge whatever he wants, rather than the contracted rate. Lionel can negotiate an arrangement directly with the chiropractor (perhaps at the insurer's contracted rate).

- It doesn't include *balance billing*. Balance billing represents the amount above the insurer's allowable charge that a non-network provider charges a patient.

Example: *Mikayla receives care from a doctor not contracted with her insurer. The doctor charges $400 for an office visit. The insurer allows only $300 as its maximum reimbursement for that service in that geographical market.*

The extra $100 isn't applied to Mikayla's deductible or out-of-pocket maximum. Mikayla is responsible for paying that difference to the provider as billed.

- It doesn't include penalties for failing to follow plan rules. Some policies require patients to secure an authorization for hospitalization, surgery, and expensive imaging received outside the network. The insurer can impose penalties ranging from a dollar figure for not securing the authorization to denying the claim because the service wasn't appropriate for a patient in a given medical situation. Insurers typically don't include these penalties when tracking the out-of-pocket maximum.

Example: *Raphael undergoes knee surgery at an out-of-network hospital and has a two-day inpatient stay. He doesn't secure an authorization before surgery. His insurer reviews the claim and determines that under its plan rules, the surgery doesn't require hospitalization.*

Raphael's insurer assesses a $500 fine for failure to preauthorize the service and then pays the balance of its allowable charge for the surgery. Raphael is responsible for the cost of inpatient care. Neither the penalty nor the inpatient charges are applied to the deductible or out-of-pocket maximum.

[See IRC Section 223(c)(2)(D); IRS Notice 2004-2, Q&A 4; and *IRS Notice 2004-50, Q&A 19, Q&A 20,* and *Q&A 21.]*

Aggregate and embedded out-of-pocket maximums. As with the deductible, insurers can design the out-of-pocket maximum to be aggregate or embedded. Regardless of whether the out-of-pocket maximum is aggregate or embedded, no family member can face out-of-pocket financial responsibility for covered services higher than the ACA out-of-pocket maximum. That figure is $7,900 in 2019 and is different from the out-of-pocket maximum for self-only coverage on an HSA-qualified plan, which is $6,750 in 2019.

No family member can face out-of-pocket financial responsibility for covered services higher than the ACA out-of-pocket maximum.

If a policy has an aggregate family out-of-pocket maximum of $6,000, any one family member alone can reach the $6,000 figure, after which the insurer pays all covered claims for the balance of the year. If a policy has a family out-of-pocket maximum of $9,000, the out-of-pocket maximum must be embedded so that no family member's total out-of-pocket responsibility exceeds $7,900 in 2019. *[See Department of Health and Human Services publication* 2018 Benefit Payment Parameters *and 45 FR 94058.]*

Prescription drug coverage. Prescription drugs are subject to the deductible. Once the deductible is satisfied, a plan can cover prescriptions subject to other forms of cost-sharing—typically copays or coinsurance—up to the policy's out-of-pocket maximum or a separate prescription drug out-of-pocket maximum. A plan can also cover prescriptions in full after the deductible.

For many people, this prescription drug plan design is their introduction to the real cost of pharmaceuticals. Patients often pay only a copay for prescriptions, while the insurer pays the balance (though more recently, more insurers have introduced coinsurance for specialty drugs, which usually exposes patients to more of the cost). When paying a copay, patients don't know (and have no incentive to know or care) whether their $30 copay is covering 50% or 5% of the insurer's negotiated cost of the prescription. When prescriptions are subject to the deductible, costs are more transparent. Your clients have a financial incentive to look for alternatives that are less costly. *[See IRS Publication 2004-2, Q&A 3.]*

Preventive prescriptions. Some insurers offer prescription drug programs that classify certain prescriptions as *preventive* and cover these drugs outside the deductible—typically subject to a copay. Neither the IRS nor the USPSTF nor any other federal agency has issued a list of preventive prescriptions or other guidance to determine whether a drug or a specific prescription for that drug is preventive in nature. Insurers take different approaches to prescriptions. Some cover all prescriptions subject to the deductible. Others offer pharmacy benefit designs that classify certain drugs as preventive and cover those prescriptions outside the deductible (often subject to copays). *[See IRC Section 223(c)(2)(C)* and *IRS Publication 2004-50, Q&A 27.]*

Counseling Your Clients

- ✓ Make sure your clients' medical coverage is HSA-qualified, especially if they're buying a policy in the individual market (rather than through an employer). The issuing insurer should provide this information. Many insurers include HSA in the product name to make this step easy, though increasingly they use terms like Value Plan or Saver Plan without mention of HSAs. Be careful not to rely on the representations of anyone other than the insurer. Others can make mistakes. (The author even saw a state-based ACA marketplace mislabel a non-qualifying plan as HSA-qualified.) Seek an answer in writing. You usually can find correct information in an insurer's plan documents.

- ✓ Help your clients identify whether the plan is an HMO, a PPO, or a POS and understand the plan rules (particularly when they're responsible for securing authorization for certain services). Otherwise, they may incur costs that aren't applied to their deductible or out-of-pocket maximum. These costs include penalties or outright denial of coverage for services that weren't authorized in advance by the insurer and didn't satisfy the insurer's requirements for coverage. Most of these additional charges are qualified for tax-free reimbursement through an HSA. But when your clients incur them, they have greater financial pressure to withdraw funds to pay the expenses—rather than retain balances for tax-free growth and distribution to reimburse future qualified expenses tax-free.

- ✓ If the plan is an HMO or a POS and patients are required to secure a referral for specialty care, have your clients call their PCPs to see whether the doctor (1) makes referrals to *any* specialists within the insurer's network or (2) restricts patients to the PCP's network. If PCPs restrict access, your clients must work within their PCPs' medical groups. Though those providers may deliver excellent care, they may not provide the most cost-effective care or deliver continuity of care when an old injury or illness resurfaces years later.

- ✓ If a client covers more than just herself on the plan, make sure that she checks to see whether the deductible is aggregate or embedded. This information is critical! She needs to understand this important plan feature before she enrolls—and certainly as she budgets for care. Does the description of a "$3,000/$6,000 deductible" mean that family policy has a deductible limit of $3,000 per family member? Or does the $3,000 figure apply to one-person contracts only, meaning that the family is covered by an umbrella $6,000 deductible? The Schedule of Benefits or Summary Plan Description should spell out this provision. But insurers aren't always clear in their language. Their documents should state per member when the deductible is embedded and per contract when the deductible is aggregate. You and your clients can't rely on this language alone, however. Check plan documents for specific examples of how the deductible works or have your clients call their insurers for more information. Be sure to advise your clients to log all calls (date and time, representative's name, summary of conversation) to strengthen their position in the event of a subsequent dispute.

- ✓ Determine how services are covered once your client reaches the deductible. Some plans impose additional cost-sharing (like copays or coinsurance for office visits, emergency-room visits, day surgery, or inpatient stays) up to the out-of-pocket maximum. This post-deductible cost-sharing could add an extra $5,000 or more to a family's financial responsibility in the case of a serious medical condition like a hospitalization or cancer treatment.

- ✓ Find out whether the policy covers select preventive prescription drugs outside the deductible. This provision may save $100 or more in monthly cash flow.

- ✓ Review your clients' potential financial responsibility (deductible, out-of-pocket maximum, penalties for failing to follow plan rules) if they receive care from outside the network. Policies often have different deductible and out-of-pocket maximum thresholds for in-network and out-of-network services, and the out-of-pocket maximums set by the federal government cover only in-network services.

✓ Remind your clients that they are consumers and should apply to their purchase of medical services the same shopping skills that they hone and apply to other purchases. Granted, it's more difficult for your clients to find accurate cost and quality information about MRIs, physical therapists, and meniscus-tear diagnoses and treatments than it is information about automobiles, cruise lines, and smart phones. Nevertheless, asking providers about alternative treatments, shopping for prescription drug prices, leveraging technology (including telemedicine and respected medical Web sites), and using insurers' online shopping tools can result in less expensive alternative treatments and sites of service.

What's Wrong with These Plans?

Each of the plans listed below fails to satisfy all requirements to be labeled an HSA-qualified plan. Can you identify the problems with each?

	Plan A	Plan B	Plan C	Plan D
In-network deductible	Aggregate $2,000 self-only $4,000 family	Embedded $2,500 individual $5,000 family	Aggregate $3,000 self-only $6,000 family	Embedded $2,750 individual $5,500 family
In-network out-of-pocket maximum	Aggregate $6,000 self-only $12,000 family	Embedded $5,000 individual $10,000 family	Aggregate $7,000 self-only $7,350/member $14,000 family	Embedded $7,000 individual $14,000 family
Out-of-network out-of-pocket maximum	Aggregate $9,000 self-only $18,000 family	Embedded Combined with in-network	Aggregate Combined with in-network	Embedded $9,000 individual $18,000 family
Prescriptions	Preventive covered in full	All subject to deductible	All covered subject to $25/$50/$100 copays	Preventive subject to $50/$75/$90 copay, others subject to a separate $500 prescription deductible before copays are applied

Answers:

Plan A:

- The deductible isn't embedded, so the family pays the first $4,000 of expenses, regardless of who incurs them. That's OK.
- The in-network out-of-pocket maximum is below the statutory limit, but the aggregate family maximum of $12,000 is greater than the ACA individual limit of $7,350. Under this plan, one family member's financial responsibility doesn't stop at $7,350 as the plan is written. The insurer can impose a $12,000 family out-of-pocket maximum as long as it configures an embedded $7,350 individual out-of-pocket maximum. **This feature violates ACA guidelines set by HHS (not the HSA rules set by the IRS).**
- The out-of-pocket limits don't apply to the out-of-network out-of-pocket maximum, so this figure is OK.
- Preventive drugs can be covered outside the deductible, making this benefit OK.

Plan B:

- The deductible is embedded and begins to pay claims at $2,500, which is less than the statutory minimum annual deductible of $2,700 in 2018 and 2019. **This feature disqualifies individuals enrolled from opening or contributing to an HSA.**
- The out-of-pocket maximum is compliant, since no one in the family pays more than $5,000.
- The out-of-pocket limits don't apply to the out-of-network out-of-pocket maximum, so this design is OK.
- Insurers can, but aren't required to, cover preventive prescription drugs outside the deductible, so this design is OK.

Plan C:

- The aggregate deductible is compliant.
- The higher embedded out-of-pocket maximum for an individual family member brings the plan into compliance.
- The out-of-pocket limits don't apply to the out-of-network out-of-pocket maximum, so this design is OK.
- The plan covers non-preventive prescription drugs subject to a lower deductible, then copays. All non-preventive services must apply to the deductible on an HSA-qualified plan. **This cost-sharing feature makes the plan non-compliant.**

Plan D:

- The embedded individual deductible on a family contract is above the $2,700 statutory minimum, so this deductible design is compliant.
- The out-of-pocket maximum ensures that no family member incurs more than $7,000 in out-of-pocket expenses, which keeps it in compliance.
- The out-of-pocket limits don't apply to the out-of-network out-of-pocket maximum, so these levels of responsibility are OK.
- Non-preventive prescriptions are subject to a separate $500 deductible, which means that anyone in the family with $500 or more of prescription charges could begin to receive reimbursement for subsequent purchases. **Reimbursing any non-preventive expenses below the statutory minimum deductible of $2,700 disqualifies the plan.**

CHAPTER 17

HSA Eligibility

As with all other programs that allow participants to reduce their taxable income, HSAs come with restrictions. Individuals must satisfy eligibility requirements set initially by Congress and subsequently by administrative rules drafted chiefly by the IRS with periodic guidance issued by other federal regulatory agencies.

In this chapter, you'll explore a host of issues around HSA eligibility. Your clients' enrolling in an HSA-qualified plan is a *necessary* first step, but not *sufficient* to ensure that they can open and contribute to an HSA.

This chapter reviews how your clients' HSA eligibility is affected by

- other major medical coverage, such as their enrollment in a spouse's medical plan, Medicare, or Medicaid;
- non-insurance coverage such as receiving care through the Department of Veterans Affairs (VA) or Indian Health Services (IHS);
- their participation in other reimbursement programs administered by their own or a spouse's employer; and
- their access to other services that their employers may offer, such as wellness programs, Employee Assistance Programs (EAPs), and work-site medical clinics.

HSA eligibility is determined month-to-month. A situation that disqualifies an individual for one month may not be present the following month. And your clients can begin a year being HSA-eligible and then lose eligibility, even though they remain enrolled in an HSA-qualified medical plan.

As with any program, your clients (with your guidance) must know, understand, and follow the rules to become and remain HSA-eligible.

Eligibility requirements at a high level. To open and contribute to an HSA, your clients must satisfy each of the following requirements:

- they are enrolled in an HSA-qualified plan;
- they don't have any other coverage that's not HSA-qualified, unless it's permitted coverage; and
- they don't qualify as someone else's tax dependent.

[See IRC Section 223(c) and *IRS Notice 2004-2, Q&A 2.]*

First-day-of-the-month rule. Individuals are HSA-eligible for any month during which they satisfy all eligibility requirements as of the first day of the month, regardless of whether they lose eligibility later that month. Your client who enrolls on his employer's HSA-qualified plan as of Nov. 1, then leaves employment and disenrolls from the medical plan Nov. 2 is HSA-eligible for November. The new employee who replaces him Nov. 3, enrolls in the employer's HSA-qualified plan, and is eligible immediately for benefits doesn't become eligible to open or contribute to an HSA until Dec. 1. *[See IRC Section 223(c)(1)(A)(i); IRS Notice 2004-2, Q&A 21;* and *IRS Notice 2004-50, Q&A 11.]*

Coverage on more than one medical plan. Your clients who are enrolled in (or eligible to receive benefits from) more than one type of coverage can become or remain HSA-eligible only if *every* plan in which they're enrolled meets the requirements of an HSA-qualified plan In a moment, we explore how this requirement affects their enrollment in Medicare, Medicaid, a Health FSA, and an HRA, as well as their receiving care through the VA or IHS, a disease management program, an Employee Assistance Program, an onsite clinic, or via telemedicine. [*See IRS Notice 2004-2, Q&A 5* and *Q&A 6.]*

HSA eligibility isn't limited to subscribers. HSA eligibility is determined on an individual basis. It's not uncommon for more than one person (such as a spouse or a child who's no longer a tax dependent but still eligible for coverage on your client's or spouse's medical plan) to satisfy all HSA eligibility requirements. This provision may be important when a client has enrolled in Medicare Part A (disqualifying coverage) but maintains coverage on an HSA-qualified medical plan that also covers a younger spouse who's not enrolled in Medicare. *[See IRC Section 223(c)(1)(A)* and *IRS Notice 2004-2, Q&A 2.]*

Coverage that doesn't affect HSA eligibility. Your clients are allowed to enroll in some other forms of permitted coverage that's not medical related without losing HSA eligibility. This coverage includes

- dental insurance;
- vision insurance;
- discount cards for prescription drugs, dental, and vision;
- accident insurance (pays a fixed amount per accident);
- critical illness insurance (typically pays a fixed amount per diagnosis of, for example, cancer); and
- hospital insurance (typically pays a fixed amount for hospitalization or daily amount for each day of hospitalization).

In addition, they don't lose HSA eligibility if another person or entity is responsible for paying their medical expenses. Common examples include automobile, homeowners, and business liability insurance. And if another party is required to pay medical expenses as a result of a legal verdict, those payments don't affect an individual's HSA eligibility. *[See IRC Section 223(c)(1)(B)(ii)* and *Section 223(c)(3)*, and *IRS Notice 2004-2, Q&A 6.]*

Government Coverage and HSA Eligibility

Medicare is disqualifying coverage. Medicare doesn't offer an HSA-qualified medical option. Your clients are *not* HSA-eligible during any month in which they're enrolled in any Part of Medicare. ***It is vital that you conduct proper Medicare planning with your clients to weigh all factors—including continuing to contribute to an HSA to reduce taxable income and build triple-tax-free retirement savings—before determining the optimal time for them to enroll in Medicare.*** Section III of this book guides you in this evaluation. *[See IRC Section 223(b)(7); IRS Notice 2004-2, Q&A 2;* and *IRS Notice 2004-50, Q&A 2.]*

Your clients are *not* HSA-eligible during any month in which they're enrolled in any Part of Medicare.

Individuals who receive Social Security or Railroad Retirement benefits are enrolled in Medicare automatically at age 65. Today, about 56% of men and 64% of women begin to collect Social Security benefits before age 65. At age 65, they're automatically enrolled in Medicare Part A and Part B. (They can opt out of Part B, and many do so to avoid the $134 monthly premium in 2018 if they have other coverage, such as an employer-sponsored plan.) These individuals can't contribute to their HSAs for any month after the date that their Medicare coverage becomes effective. *[See* Medicare and You, 2017 edition, *p. 21-22.]*

Individuals who don't enroll in Social Security or Railroad Retirement benefits are *not* enrolled in Medicare at age 65. Your clients who defer enrollment in the Social Security or Railroad Retirement program must proactively enroll in Medicare to receive benefits. They control the timing of their enrollment and can choose whether to remain on an employer-sponsored plan (and contribute to an HSA if they're otherwise HSA-eligible), enroll in both the employer plan and Medicare (and lose HSA eligibility), or enroll in Medicare coverage only (and lose HSA eligibility). *[See* Medicare and You, 2017 edition, *p. 21-22.]*

HSA eligibility when family members are enrolled in Medicare. Medicare issues individual policies only. Your clients can't access benefits under anyone else's Medicare policy. Thus, a spouse's enrollment in any Part of Medicare doesn't affect your client's HSA eligibility. Family members, however, aren't eligible to open or contribute to their own HSAs once enrolled in Medicare. Chapter 19, *HSA Distributions,* explains that a client can still reimburse all of her spouse's and many family members' qualified expenses (except perhaps Medicare premiums, depending on her age) tax-free from her HSA, even when she and her eligible family members can no longer contribute to their HSAs. *[See IRS Notice 2008-59, Q&A 11.]*

A spouse's enrollment in any Part of Medicare doesn't affect your client's HSA eligibility.

Medicaid is disqualifying coverage. Medicaid, the government program designed primarily for individuals who are poor, are elderly, or have been diagnosed with certain conditions, doesn't offer an HSA-qualified option. Anyone enrolled in and eligible to receive benefits through Medicaid isn't HSA-eligible.

Note that *Medicaid*, the federal government name for the program, may have a different name in your state. For example, Tennessee offers TennCare, SelectCommunity, and CoverKids, all of which are Medicaid programs.

In addition, CHIP (Children's Health Insurance Program) plans offered by states are a form of Medicaid and thus disqualify children enrolled in those plans—but not their parents—from opening an HSA. Most children who qualify for CHIP plans aren't HSA-eligible since they typically qualify as a parent's tax dependent under Section 152 of the IRC. *[See IRC Section 223(c)(1)(A)(ii).]*

HSA eligibility when family members are enrolled in Medicaid. Like Medicare, Medicaid issues only individual policies. Since individuals can't receive benefits from their spouse's or children's enrollment in Medicaid, they don't lose their HSA eligibility based on family members' enrollment in the program. *[See IRS Notice 2008-59, Q&A 11.]*

Enrollment in TRICARE and HSA eligibility. TRICARE is the federal program that covers active and retired military personnel and their families. TRICARE doesn't offer an HSA-qualified option. Thus, active and retired members of the armed forces who are enrolled in (and entitled to receive benefits under) TRICARE can't open or contribute to an HSA—even if they're enrolled in an HSA-qualified medical plan as well and don't file claims for reimbursement through their TRICARE coverage. *[See IRS Notice 2004-50, Q&A 6.]*

VA care and HSA eligibility. People who are enrolled in an HSA-qualified medical plan don't lose their HSA eligibility merely because they're *eligible* to receive care through the VA medical system. They can even obtain certain care—select preventive services and treatment for a service-related condition—without losing their HSA eligibility. If they receive other care through the VA, they lose their HSA eligibility for the three months immediately following the conclusion of that treatment.

This three-month eligibility gap may or may not affect their HSA contribution limits that year, depending on the timing of their VA services and their contribution strategies. This issue is discussed in detail in Chapter 18, *HSA Contributions. [See IRS Notice 2004-50, Q&A 5* and *IRS Notice 2015-87, Q&A 20.]*

Indian Health Services care and HSA eligibility. Many Native Americans are eligible to receive care through IHS, a federal program. Like the VA, IHS doesn't offer HSA-qualified coverage. Individuals who receive any IHS care other than select preventive services lose their HSA eligibility for the three full months following the conclusion of treatment. This temporary loss of eligibility may or may not affect their maximum contribution to their HSA, depending on the timing of their treatment. *[See IRS Notice 2012-14.]*

Reimbursement Programs and HSA Eligibility

HSA eligibility when enrolled in an employer's Health FSA program. A general Health FSA allows individuals to receive a portion of their income tax-free when they elect to receive it through a Health FSA to reimburse certain health-related expenses. They then draw funds from the Health FSA to pay for medical, prescription drug, dental, and vision services, and some over-the-counter items. A general Health FSA is a benefit plan that doesn't apply a deductible and therefore violates the eligibility rule that all coverage must be HSA-compliant. Clients who participate in a general Health FSA aren't HSA-eligible for the duration of the plan year, even if they spend their entire balance prior to the end of the plan year.

This issue applies to *Health* FSAs only. Many employers also offer a Dependent Care FSA (also called Dep Care or DCRA) that allows employees to receive a portion of their income tax-free to pay for qualified day care, preschool, after-school, and adult day care services for certain qualifying family members. Participation in a Dependent Care FSA does *not* affect HSA eligibility, since these programs don't reimburse medical or other health-related expenses. *[See IRS Rev. Rul. 2004-45.]*

HSA eligibility when a spouse is enrolled in an employer's Health FSA program. Under federal tax law, a Health FSA automatically covers an employee, the employee's spouse, and the employee's children to age 26 (whether or not the children are tax dependents as defined in Section 152 of the IRC). Your client's spouse's employer can restrict coverage (for example, by offering a Health FSA that reimburses only its employees' qualified expenses), but employers *rarely* do so. Thus, if your client's spouse is enrolled in a general Health FSA, your client isn't HSA-eligible during the Health FSA plan year. This is true even if the spouse exhausts her balance prior to the end of the plan year or even if your client pledges not to seek reimbursement from his spouse's Health FSA. *[See IRS Rev. Rul. 2004-45.]*

If your client's spouse is enrolled in a general Health FSA, your client isn't HSA-eligible.

Employers can design certain limited Health FSAs that allow employees to participate without affecting their HSA eligibility. Following are examples.

Health FSA designs that are HSA-qualified. Employees enrolled in certain limited Health FSAs don't lose their HSA eligibility as a result of their participation in a:

- **Limited-Purpose Health FSA**: This design reimburses only dental and vision expenses, as well as select preventive care services that aren't covered in full. Dental and vision coverage aren't disqualifying insurance, and select preventive care can be covered outside a plan deductible. If your client's *only* Health FSA coverage (her own or a spouse's) is a Limited-Purpose Health FSA, she (and her spouse, if otherwise HSA-eligible) won't lose HSA eligibility. Limited-Purpose Health FSAs are a popular and attractive part of a robust HSA program, as discussed in Chapter 9, *Utilizing a Limited-Purpose Health FSA Strategically*. They allow your clients to reduce their taxable income further and preserve HSA balances for future use without foregoing immediate tax advantages.

- **Post-Deductible Health FSA**: This design reimburses all medical, prescription drug, dental, and vision and select over-the-counter items and services once your client has paid up to at least the statutory minimum annual deductible ($1,350 for self-only coverage and $2,700 for family coverage in 2018 and 2019). Employers can set a higher deductible figure. Employers don't commonly offer Post-Deductible Health FSAs.

Many Health FSA administrators combine these two features. They offer a Limited-Purpose Health FSA that reimburses dental, vision, and preventive services only, then allow participants to reimburse medical and prescription drug expenses once they certify that they've met the statutory minimum annual deductible (not their particular medical plan deductible, which typically is higher). *[See IRC Section 223(c)(1)(B)(ii)* and *IRS Rev. Rul. 2004-45.]*

HSA eligibility when an individual is enrolled in an employer's HRA program. As you'll recall, an HRA is an employer-funded reimbursement account typically designed to offset a portion of employees' out-of-pocket expenses when integrated with a medical plan. An HRA that pays the first portion of cost-sharing constitutes coverage that's not HSA-qualified. Because individuals with access to reimbursements through an HRA are enrolled in at least one coverage that isn't HSA-qualified, they aren't HSA-eligible if they're covered by a general HRA design. As with Health FSAs, however, certain HRA plan designs are HSA-qualified and therefore don't affect HSA eligibility (as you'll discover in a moment). Employers can deploy these limited HRAs to increase deductibles, thereby decreasing premiums, while reimbursing some or all of their enrolled employees' increased financial responsibility. *[See IRS Rev. Rul. 2004-45.]*

HSA eligibility when a spouse is enrolled in an employer's HRA program. This situation is less common than being enrolled in a spouse's Health FSA because HRAs typically are integrated with an employer's medical insurance plan (particularly under reform provisions of the ACA). If your client's spouse isn't enrolled in his employer's insurance plan, he is unlikely to be enrolled in that employer's HRA program. *[See IRS Rev. Rul. 2004-45.]*

HRA plan designs that are HSA-qualified. Employers can preserve employees' HSA eligibility through one of two designs:

- **Post-Deductible HRA**: This HRA doesn't begin to reimburse any qualified expenses until your client assumes responsibility for an amount equal to at least the statutory minimum annual deductible ($1,350 for self-only coverage and $2,700 for family coverage in 2018 and 2019). The employer can set a higher deductible. This design is common among employers who want to increase medical plan deductibles to reduce premiums without increasing (or increasing only slightly or gradually) employees' financial responsibility for out-of-pocket medical costs.

- **Limited-Purpose HRA**: This design is not common. It limits reimbursement to dental and vision expenses. Employers usually offer a dental-only or vision-only HRA in place of dental or vision insurance, not as a means of keeping employees HSA-eligible. If an HRA limits reimbursements to these expenses, employees enrolled in the plan don't lose HSA eligibility.

In addition, if an HRA has a carryover feature that allows participants to spend unused balances in subsequent plan years, an employer can establish one of two HRA designs so that employees who want to become HSA-eligible can retain their notional balances for future use:

- **Suspended HRA**: Funds carry over into an HRA that employees can't tap during the plan year, but can draw down at a specified future date (at which point they won't be HSA-eligible unless the funds are deposited in a Post-Deductible or Limited-Purpose HRA).

- **Retirement HRA**: Funds carry over into an HRA that employees can't tap until they separate from the company and satisfy other requirements. An employer may set requirements such as age, number of years of service, and a minimum balance that must be met before they have access to these funds.

[See IRC Section 223(c)(1)(B)(ii) and *IRS Rev. Rul. 2004-45.]*

Health-sharing ministries and HSA eligibility. More than a million Americans are now covered by health-sharing ministries programs. Under these arrangements, a group of people with similar religious beliefs agree to cover all medical bills incurred by all active participants in the program. Members pay a monthly fee (not unlike a premium) and are responsible for a certain amount of personal medical expenses (not unlike a deductible). Members send claims in excess of their personal responsibility to the administrator, which pays the bills from the ministry balances funded by the monthly fees up to a certain limit.

Health-sharing ministry plans don't constitute insurance. And they don't cap members' financial responsibility, as HSA-qualified plans must. An individual covered by a health-sharing ministry program isn't covered by an HSA-qualified plan and is thus not eligible to open or contribute to an HSA.

Association Health Plans (AHPs) and HSA eligibility. President Trump issued an executive order in October 2017 asking administration officials to draft regulations to expand the use of AHPs. AHPs are a form of group insurance sponsored by a number of companies that are connected in some way—such as industry, geography, or purpose. For example, a local chamber of commerce, an automobile dealers association, or a number of independent local restaurants can band together to purchase group insurance. The benefit to them is that the association may be eligible to purchase a wider range of plan designs and enjoy lower premiums than if each small entity bought coverage on its own.

AHPs have existed for decades, but under long-standing rules the businesses had to be formed for a business purpose other than purchasing insurance (as were the chamber and auto dealers association in the example). They couldn't organize solely to purchase insurance (as did the independent restaurants in the example). The proposed Trump administration rules permit small businesses to band together for the sole purpose of offering group coverage.

The source of the insurance is irrelevant to HSA eligibility. As long as an individual is enrolled in HSA-qualified coverage and satisfies other eligibility requirements, she can open and contribute to an HSA.

Non-Disqualifying Coverage

Dental or vision coverage and HSA eligibility. Individuals can access benefits through a dental or vision insurance or reimbursement plan without affecting their HSA eligibility. This is the same provision in the law that allows employers to design Limited-Purpose Health FSAs and HRAs (mentioned earlier) that don't affect HSA eligibility. *[See IRC Section 223(c)(2)(B)(ii)* and *IRS Notice 2004-2, Q&A 6.]*

Hospital, accident, and critical illness policies and HSA eligibility. Your clients don't lose their HSA eligibility when they enroll in coverage that pays a fixed amount per accident or occurrence of cancer or other specified illness, or that pays a certain daily benefit during hospitalization. In fact, these policies, particularly hospital and accident coverage, can help individuals pay their out-of-pocket financial responsibility without using HSA funds. This coverage doesn't affect HSA eligibility because the policies don't reimburse medical expenses. Instead, these policies pay a fixed amount that individuals can spend on living expenses (since people often suffer a loss of income when they or a family member ends up in the hospital or is injured in an accident). *[See IRC Section 223(c)(3)* and *IRS Notice 2004-2, Q&A 6.]*

Limited-duration coverage and HSA eligibility. President Trump's October 2017 executive order also directed his administration to expand the availability of limited-duration coverage. These plans offer coverage for a defined period of time only and are ideal for individuals who need temporary coverage to bridge a gap between employer-sponsored plans or other interruptions in traditional coverage.

The Obama administration limited the duration of these plans to three months. The proposed Trump administration rules allow coverage up to 12 months. These plans are attractive because they do not need to comply with all ACA benefit mandates and other requirements and are therefore less expensive than ACA-governed coverage.

Individuals enrolled in limited-duration coverage are eligible to open and contribute to HSAs as long as their plans are HSA-qualified and they satisfy all other eligibility requirements.

Discount cards and HSA eligibility. Some non-insurance companies sell drug discount cards (or perhaps discount cards for medical services, though prescription drug discount cards are more common) for a modest fee (often $25 to $50 annually). These companies have negotiated discounts with retail pharmacies to provide a percentage discount off the retail price of prescriptions. The program may offer a single discount (such as 20% off all medications) for all prescription purchases, or it may have a tiered discount (such as 15% off generic drugs and 20% off brand-name medications). Sometimes consumers purchase these cards directly. Other times employers subscribe to the service and issue cards to all employees. These cards don't affect HSA eligibility because they're not insurance. The retailer discounts the cost of the drug and foregoes that revenue; no third party reimburses the pharmacist for the difference between the discounted price and the full retail price.

> These policies, can help individuals pay their out-of-pocket financial responsibility without using HSA funds.

Your clients can shop to determine whether a prescription medication is less expensive when taking advantage of the insurer's discount or the drug card. The less expensive option may vary from drug to drug. Retailers and insurers often negotiate contracts that call for prices that reflect a percentage discount off the average wholesale price (AWP), which varies over time and sometimes from store to store or region to region within a single chain.

Prescriptions purchased with a drug discount card aren't processed through insurance. Depending on the insurer, your clients may or may not be able to apply the purchase to their deductible. Some insurers allow members to file a claim to apply the purchase price to the deductible; others don't. It's important that your clients balance the impact of a lower cost for a prescription drug against not having the purchase apply to the deductible or out-of-pocket maximum. Because the discount card doesn't constitute insurance, an individual who uses a card doesn't have conflicting coverage. *[See IRS Notice 2004-50, Q&A 9.]*

Retailer promotions and HSA eligibility. It's not unusual for large drug and mass-market retailers to offer promotional pricing on prescription drugs. They may advertise a $4 cost to consumers for a one-month supply and $10 for a three-month supply. Their rationale is simple: While your clients wait for the prescription to be processed, they're likely to spend time shopping for other items. Prescription drugs with promotional pricing become "loss leaders," sometimes literally selling for less than the retailer's cost, as a means of increasing sales of other goods.

Taking advantage of this promotional pricing doesn't affect HSA eligibility. The retailer absorbs the cost of the discount and no third party pays a portion of the cost.

These purchases may or may not be processed through your clients' insurance coverage. Clients should ask at the time of purchase. If not, their insurer may or may not accept a manual claim submission to apply the amount paid to the plan deductible or out-of-pocket maximum.

Potentially Disqualifying Services

Telemedicine. This is an area of concern in HSA compliance. The IRS hasn't issued definitive guidance on telemedicine. Since the IRS issued its last comprehensive guidance in 2008, more and more people have access to this benefit, either as part of their insurance coverage or as a stand-alone benefit offered by their employer. Absent guidance, it seems prudent to treat a telemedicine consultation as a physical interaction with a physician. That service must apply to the deductible if it's non-preventive. If the telemedicine benefit is a free-standing option not tied to the medical plan, the cost to your client must represent the market rate for that service.

For example, a program offered by an employer that covers telemedicine consultations subject to a $10 copay or a program that covers three consultations in full probably disqualifies an individual from HSA eligibility. Alternatively, a stand-alone program that covers telemedicine visits subject to a $49 fee with no third-party payment to the consulting physician is more likely to be viewed as reflecting the market rate for that service and thus may not disqualify that patient.

In the absence of guidance or a safe harbor, your clients should be very careful about signing up for or utilizing a telemedicine benefit that appears to offer a benefit below the fair market value of the service. Best practices for employers for whom employees' HSA eligibility is a concern are to offer a telemedicine benefit integrated with the medical coverage or one that offers the service only at fair market value.

Onsite clinics. A growing number of employers offer some medical services at large work sites. These clinics can treat minor injuries incurred at work and provide care for other issues for which employees otherwise seek care offsite during working hours. The IRS has indicated that merely having access to free or discounted care at an employer's onsite clinic isn't disqualifying if the clinic doesn't provide "significant benefits in the nature of medical care." But the IRS hasn't defined "significant benefits." It's reasonable to assume that de minimus care (Acetaminophen? A bandage?) doesn't disqualify your client from opening or contributing to an HSA, but what about two stitches to close a cut suffered at work? What about crutches after twisting an ankle tripping on the office carpet?

> Absent guidance, it seems prudent to treat a telemedicine consultation as a physical interaction with a physician.

The preventive safe harbor ensures that services like a flu shot, routine physical, or mammogram through a mobile unit don't disqualify your client from opening or contributing to an HSA. Onsite medical services outside de minimus diagnosis and treatment and preventive care are potentially disqualifying. *[See IRS Notice 2008-59, Q&A 10.]*

Discount/free services. Your clients who work in medical facilities must be careful not to jeopardize their HSA eligibility by receiving a blood test, MRI, or other non-preventive service with a fee discount or waiver that a non-employee doesn't receive. The IRS hasn't issued formal guidance on this issue, but it's prudent for individuals who want to become or remain HSA-eligible not to accept such care.

Employee Assistance Program. Many employers offer their employees access to an EAP. EAPs help workers navigate family issues (such as child care and elder care), financial issues (for example, improving credit scores or securing a mortgage), and social services. The services are generally available to employees at no cost.

One area of concern is employees' use of some types of EAP services—for example, counseling for employees facing a personal crisis such as the potential dissolution of a marriage; a child or spouse with substance-abuse issues; or a family member in hospice care. The IRS hasn't provided clear guidance on whether accessing some EAP services may disqualify an individual from HSA eligibility. In most cases, it's prudent for such individuals to move quickly from an EAP-provided service to a professional counselor to manage these life situations. A transition to receiving counseling through HSA-qualified medical coverage minimizes HSA eligibility issues. *[See IRS Notice 2004-50, Q&A 10, Example 1.]*

Disease Management Programs. Insurers offer disease management programs to members who have chronic conditions like diabetes, COPD, and liver disease. A typical program includes monitoring by a nurse case manager via regular communication with members and their providers. As long as the program facilitates communication and coordinates care, it doesn't provide services that affect HSA eligibility. If it offers at no cost (or a discounted cost) services that otherwise are subject to the deductible, the program probably disqualifies a participant from opening or contributing to an HSA. Examples might include no-cost annual podiatric and ophthalmic visits for a diabetes patient. Absent new IRS guidance on the topic, coverage below the deductible for these services is likely to be disqualifying. *[See IRS Notice 2004-50, Q&A 10, Example 2.]*

Wellness programs. Many employers are committed to their employees' health and offer wellness programs to help employees lead more healthy and active lifestyles. These programs range from nutrition education, flu shots, and monitoring vital signs to gym membership reimbursement and smoking cessation programs. Most services offered through these programs are either preventive care (such as nutritional counseling, flu shots, vital-sign monitoring, or smoking cessation) that can be covered in full under HSA-qualified coverage or goods and services (such as gym memberships, pedometers to participate in a walking challenge, or a complimentary entry into a corporate challenge 5K road race) that aren't medical services. If the wellness program offers services that otherwise are subject to the deductible on an HSA-qualified medical plan (such as behavioral counseling to address the issues driving an employee to excess alcohol consumption or in-house physical therapy so that an employee can get back to the company gym sooner), the services are likely to be disqualifying. *[See IRS Notice 2004-50, Q&A 10, Example 3.]*

Eligibility Checklist

Your clients are **not** HSA-eligible . . .

- ✓ during any month that they don't satisfy all HSA eligibility requirements as of the first day of the month,
- ✓ if they're enrolled in any Part of Medicare (although a family member's enrollment doesn't affect their HSA eligibility),
- ✓ if they're enrolled in Medicaid (although a family member's enrollment doesn't affect their HSA eligibility),
- ✓ if they participate in their employer's Health FSA program or if their spouse participates in an employer's Health FSA unless all applicable Health FSAs are HSA-compliant,
- ✓ if they're enrolled in their employer's HRA program or their spouse is enrolled in an employer's HRA unless all applicable HRAs are HSA-compliant,
- ✓ for three months after the completion of treatment if they received non-preventive care not related to a service disability through the VA medical system,
- ✓ for three months after the completion of treatment if they received non-preventive care through Indian Health Services, or
- ✓ if they're enrolled in TRICARE, even if they don't receive reimbursement for any services through TRICARE.

Counseling Your Clients

- ✓ Be sure your clients understand the eligibility rules. Remember, they must satisfy all eligibility requirements to be eligible to open and contribute to an HSA.

- ✓ Learn which actions by a client's spouse may affect his HSA eligibility (such as a spouse's making an election into her employer's general Health FSA program) and which actions have no impact on the client's HSA eligibility (such as a spouse's enrolling in Medicare).

- ✓ Understand how your clients can benefit from enrollment in an HSA-qualified plan even if they have disqualifying coverage. If a spouse is HSA-eligible (remember, individuals don't have to be the medical plan subscribers to be HSA-eligible), the spouse can open an HSA. And as you'll see in the next two chapters, your client and spouse can then contribute up to the family maximum to the spouse's HSA to reduce taxes and maximize HSA balances—and also reimburse your client's and her spouse's qualified expenses tax-free.

CHAPTER 18

HSA Contributions

Contributions to HSAs aren't included in federal taxable income or state taxable income (except in Alabama, California, and New Jersey). They're also exempt from federal payroll (FICA) taxes. Thus, HSAs are a great way for your clients to reduce their personal tax liability.

With this benefit, however, come restrictions. This chapter acquaints you with the rules and regulations around HSA contributions. As with other aspects of HSA compliance, HSA owners are responsible for knowing whether they're eligible to contribute to an HSA (key topics covered in Chapter 17, *HSA Eligibility*). HSA administrators can provide guidance on contributions, and those who have adopted industry best practices should have a process in place to warn HSA owners when total contributions exceed the maximum. But this guidance and process don't guarantee that your clients won't exceed their maximum contribution. Your clients need to understand the rules.

In this chapter, you'll find a review of

- the maximum contributions that your clients can make to their HSAs when they're HSA-eligible all year or for less than 12 months,
- deadlines to contribute for a given tax year,
- pre-tax payroll contributions versus tax-deductible personal contributions, and
- timing of contributions and changing contribution amounts during the year.

Determining eligibility to make contributions. Review Chapter 17, *HSA Eligibility*, with your clients to determine whether they're HSA-eligible. If they satisfy all eligibility requirements as of the first day of a month, they're eligible to make a contribution for that month (even if they lose eligibility a day later). If they don't satisfy the eligibility requirements as of the first day of the month, they're not HSA-eligible for that month (even if they satisfy all eligibility requirements as of the second day of the month). *[See IRC Section 223(c)(A)(i).]*

Tax treatment of HSA contributions. If employers allow employees to make pre-tax payroll deductions through a Cafeteria Plan, your clients' HSA contributions are deducted from their paychecks before taxes are assessed. The full value of the contribution goes to work immediately, and your clients avoid payroll taxes, federal income taxes, and, if applicable, state income taxes (except in Alabama, California, and New Jersey).

Your clients also can make personal contributions outside the payroll system. In this case, they deposit post-tax dollars into their HSAs and then deduct the contribution when they file their personal income tax return. The income taxes that your clients paid on the money when they earned it are applied against the income tax owed to each level of government that exempts HSA contributions from income taxes.

Neither your clients nor their employers receive a credit for payroll taxes when they make contributions outside pre-tax payroll. That's a net loss of 7.65% *each* for employee and employer on all taxable income below $128,400 (2018 figure). Above that amount, only the Medicare payroll tax (1.45% apiece by employer and employee) applies. Thus, individuals reap the full tax benefits associated with an HSA only when they make pre-tax payroll contributions. *[See IRS Notice 2004-2, Q&A 17* and *Q&A 20.]*

Contribution Limits

HSA minimum contributions. The IRS doesn't impose minimum contributions. Individuals eligible to open an HSA don't have to do so (though your clients will contribute, per your guidance), and individuals who have opened HSAs and are eligible to contribute don't have to make deposits (though again, your clients will). Employers can't force employees, even those eligible to open and contribute to an HSA, to make any level of contributions as a condition for participating in an HSA program and receiving employer contributions.

Maximum contribution based on contract size. HSA contributions are based on the size of the contract—self-only (covering only your client) or family (your client and at least one other person covered). This concept is widely misunderstood. Your clients are entitled to make the maximum contribution for a family contract as long as they cover at least one family member besides themselves on their contracts, even if your client is the only person covered on the contract who's HSA-eligible.

Examples:

- *Magena covers herself and her husband, Akule, who's disabled and has been enrolled in Medicare for more than a decade, on her employer's plan.*

Akule isn't HSA-eligible because he's enrolled in Medicare. Magena can contribute up to the family maximum contribution because she's enrolled in a family contract, even though only she is HSA-eligible.

- *Marguerite is a single mother with three teenage children. Only she is HSA-eligible.*

Marguerite can contribute up to the family maximum because she's enrolled in family coverage, even though no other family member is HSA-eligible.

- *Gustavo and his wife, Izabel, are enrolled in his nongroup family plan. Izabel disenrolls Jan. 1, 2018, and enrolls in Medicare. Gustavo switches from family to self-only coverage.*

Gustavo can contribute up to the self-only contribution limit in 2018 because he's enrolled in self-only coverage.

- *Iris covers herself and her husband, Dag, on her employer's plan. Dag turns age 65 and enrolls in Medicare effective May 1. He also remains covered on Iris's plan.*

Iris can continue to contribute to the family maximum because she remains enrolled in family coverage, even though Iris is the only HSA-eligible family member on the contract.

[See IRC Section 223(b)(2) and *IRS Notice 2008-59, Q&A 16.]*

HSA maximum contributions. The IRS sets the statutory maximum annual contribution limits to an HSA, indexing the figure annually in $50 increments to reflect general (not medical) inflation.

The statutory maximum annual contribution limits are:

	2018	2019
Self-only contract	$3,450	$3,500
Family contract	$6,900	$7,000

[See IRC Section 223(b)(2) and *Section 223(g), IRS Rev. Proc. 2017-37, IRS Rev. Proc. 2018-18, IRS Rev. Proc. 2018-27,* and *IRS Rev. Proc. 2018-30.]*

Catch-up contribution amount. HSAs, like retirement plans, include a catch-up contribution, though the HSA version isn't as substantial. Your clients can make an additional $1,000 HSA contribution annually once they reach age 55. This figure isn't indexed for inflation and won't increase without legislative action. *[See IRC Section 223(b)(3)* and *IRS Notice 2004-2, Q&A 14.]*

Catch-up contribution caveat. Under current law, catch-up contributions must be deposited in an HSA owned by the individual eligible to make that contribution. Families in which both spouses are age 55 or older and both are HSA-eligible must have two HSAs—one owned by each spouse—in order for each spouse to make a $1,000 catch-up contribution.

Example: *Pedro, age 57, and his wife, Regina, age 54, are enrolled in his employer's HSA-qualified medical plan. Both are HSA-eligible. Pedro contributes up to the statutory maximum annual contribution for a family contract into his HSA each year. He also deposits his $1,000 catch-up contribution.*

When Regina turns age 55 next year, she becomes eligible to make a catch-up contribution. Regina must open her own HSA to make the contribution.

[See IRS Notice 2008-59, Q&A 22 and *Q&A 28.]*

Employer contributions and annual contribution limits. The statutory maximum annual contribution includes contributions from all sources (typically account owners and their employers, but also gifts from relatives and any other source of funds). Thus, any employer contributions reduce your clients' opportunity to decrease their taxable income through their own pre-tax or tax-deductible contributions. On the other hand, employer contributions represent additional compensation and can be seen as freeing up funds that your client would otherwise contribute to an HSA. These funds can instead be deposited in a retirement plan to increase long-term savings. *[See IRC Section 223(a)* and *IRS Notice 2004-2, Q&A 12.]*

Impact of HSA contribution on retirement account contribution limits. HSA contributions are independent of your clients' contributions to any other type of tax-advantaged account. Your clients can contribute to their HSAs and build medical equity without offsetting contribution limits to retirement accounts, thereby turbocharging total retirement savings.

Contribution period. HSA contributions are tracked on the calendar year, regardless of the anniversary date of the medical insurance plan or when your client gains or loses HSA eligibility. *[See IRC Section 223(b)(1)* and *IRS Notice 2004-2, Q&A 12.]*

Contribution Limits and Partial-Year Eligibility

Losing HSA eligibility during the year. Most life changes don't occur Jan. 1. It's not uncommon for some of your clients to change jobs, choose different medical coverage during open enrollment, or enroll in Medicare during the year. When individuals lose HSA eligibility during the year, they must pro-rate their contributions by dividing their statutory maximum annual contribution by 12 and multiplying by the number of months that they are HSA-eligible (remembering that they're eligible for the month only if they satisfy all eligibility requirements on the first day of the month).

> Example: *Elisa is under age 55 and covered on a self-only contract. She changes jobs as of May 6, 2019, and enrolls in a non-HSA-qualified plan as of that date.*
>
> *Elisa is HSA-eligible as of the first day of January, February, March, April, and May, so she's eligible to make a contribution of 5/12 of the statutory maximum of $3,500. Divide $3,500 by 12 to arrive at a monthly contribution maximum of $291.67. Multiply that figure by five months to calculate Elisa's maximum contribution of $1,458.33.*

[See IRS Notice 2004-2, Q&A 12 and *Q&A 13; IRS Publication 2008-59, Q&A 19;* and *IRS Publication 969.]*

[Note that in Q&A 13, passage of the *HOPE Act* changed the contribution options beginning in 2007 for individuals who gain HSA eligibility mid-year, though the methodology outlined there remains accurate for individuals who lose eligibility during the year.]

Becoming HSA-eligible during the year. Individuals who become HSA-eligible after Jan. 1 but no later than Dec. 1 have two options:

Option 1. Pro-rate the contribution, as in the preceding example.

Option 2. Utilize the Last-Month Rule, which allows HSA owners to contribute up to the statutory maximum annual contribution for the contract type. Your clients who choose this option (and most will, based on your advice) must then remain HSA-eligible through the end of the *following* calendar year (the "testing period"). If they lose eligibility before the end of the testing period for any reason other than disability or death, they must include any excess contribution (the amount greater than the pro-rated maximum) and any earnings on that excess contribution in their taxable income for the year when they fail to remain eligible through the testing period. They also must pay an additional 10% tax as a penalty. The penalty applies to both the excess contribution and the earnings on it.

Example: *Beatriz graduates from college in May and starts her new job June 17, 2019. She enrolls in a self-only HSA-qualified medical plan and is covered immediately. She becomes HSA-eligible July 1, the first day of the first month that she satisfies all eligibility requirements. Beatriz can contribute up to 6/12 of the $3,500 statutory maximum contribution (a total of $1,750) into her HSA. Alternatively, she can contribute up to the full $3,500, as long as she remains HSA-eligible through the end of December 2020.*

Beatriz loses her HSA eligibility when she leaves the company on the first anniversary of her start date. She must include the portion of her 2019 contribution in excess of her pro-rated amount ($1,750) and earnings on that amount (let's assume 0.1% interest for 12 months, or $1.75) as taxable income. She must also pay a penalty in the form of a 10% additional tax of $175.18 on the excess contribution and earnings attributable to it (a total of $1,926.93) when she files her 2020 personal income tax return.

Individuals who become HSA-eligible Dec. 2 or later can't contribute to an HSA for that year, since they aren't HSA-eligible as of the first day of any month during the year. *[See IRC Section 223(c)(1)(A)(i); HOPE Act, Section 305; IRS Notice 2004-2, Q&A 2;* and *IRS Publication 969, published annually.]*

Contributing in excess of the pro-rated amount. People who don't expect to remain HSA-eligible through the testing period (for example, due to enrollment in Medicare or loss of HSA-qualified coverage) and want to avoid the penalty shouldn't contribute more than the pro-rated amount. For many of your clients, however, the Last-Month Rule is an opportunity to further reduce taxable income and either build HSA balances for future use, or pay high current qualified expenses with pre-tax dollars to gain an immediate tax advantage.

Here are some examples of when it makes sense to employ the Last-Month Rule and risk remaining HSA-eligible through the testing period:

The Last-Month Rule is an opportunity to further reduce taxable income.

- Your client incurs high expenses.

Example: *Sophia is under age 55 and is enrolled in a self-only contract. She becomes HSA-eligible Nov. 1, 2018 and enrolls in a non-interest-bearing HSA. She incurs $2,575 in qualified expenses during December.*

Sophia can contribute no more than $575 (two months of HSA eligibility) in 2018 if she adopts the pro-rating approach. By contributing an additional $2,000 into her HSA to pay her claims, she saves about $600 in taxes. If Sophia loses eligibility before the end of the testing period, the $2,000 is included in her taxable income and she pays an extra $200 as a penalty. The $2,000 would have been taxed if she hadn't made the additional contribution, so her net loss is the $200 additional tax (penalty). In effect, she puts $200 at risk as a potential penalty to save about $600 in taxes.

- Your client doesn't foresee losing his HSA eligibility due to loss of employer-based coverage through the end of next year. In this case, he can use the Last-Month Rule to maximize his reduction in taxable income.

Example: *Trajan becomes HSA-eligible Nov. 1, 2018, and contributes the entire $3,450 self-only maximum into his non-interest-bearing HSA.*

He saves an additional $850 in taxes (assuming 30% federal FICA and income taxes and state income taxes and a $2,875 additional contribution beyond the pro-rated amount). If Trajan doesn't remain eligible through the testing period, the $2,875 excess contributions and any earnings on that amount are included in his taxable income (which is the case had he not made the excess contribution in the first place). He pays an extra $287.50 in taxes as a penalty. Thus, Trajan puts less than $300 at risk as a potential penalty to save about $850 in taxes.

Pro-rating and catch-up contributions. People don't pro-rate their catch-up contribution based on when their birthday falls during the year. For example, a client who turns age 55 Oct. 6 (two months of HSA eligibility—November and December) doesn't have to limit contribution to 2/12 ($166.67) of the maximum catch-up contribution. Instead, she can contribute up to the full $1,000 catch-up contribution maximum, as long as she is HSA-eligible all 12 months.

Individuals must follow the rules just outlined if they're not HSA-eligible all 12 months of the calendar year. Thus, if your client loses her HSA eligibility during any calendar year after she turns age 55, she must pro-rate her catch-up contribution, just as she does her statutory contribution. If she becomes HSA-eligible during any year that she's age 55 or older, she can either pro-rate her catch-up contribution *or* adopt the Last-Month Rule, make the full $1,000 contribution, and remain HSA-eligible through the testing period to avoid a penalty. *[See IRS Publication 969, published annually.]*

Losing eligibility temporarily during the year. Individuals who receive certain non-preventive care through VA (veterans) or IHS (Native Americans) coverage lose their HSA eligibility for three full months following the month that they receive care. Their contribution limits and options depend on when they receive care and when they regain HSA eligibility.

> **Complete a course of treatment before Sept. 1**: They aren't HSA-eligible for September, October, or November of Year 1, then regain HSA eligibility Dec. 1.
>
> Example: *Lissa, complaining of migraine headaches, submits to an MRI and diagnostic tests at a VA facility in mid-July 2019.*
>
> *She loses her HSA eligibility for three months (August, September, and October). Because she regains her HSA eligibility before Dec. 1, she can use the Last-Month Rule and contribute up to the maximum in 2019. She must remain HSA-eligible through the end of the testing period (end of 2020) to avoid taxes and penalties on her 2019 contribution. Alternatively, she can pro-rate her 2019 contribution, depositing no more than 9/12 of her maximum contribution in her HSA.*
>
> **Complete a course of treatment during September**: They don't regain HSA eligibility by Dec. 1, so they can't take advantage of the Last-Month Rule.

Example: *Sally undergoes hip-replacement surgery in mid-September 2019 at a VA facility.*

She loses her HSA eligibility for October, November, and December. She therefore can't use the Last-Month Rule to make a full annual contribution. She must pro-rate her contribution, depositing no more than 9/12 of the maximum contribution in her HSA. She regains HSA eligibility as of Jan. 1, 2020, so her 2020 contribution limit isn't affected by this surgery.

Complete a course of treatment after Oct. 1: Not only do these individuals not regain HSA eligibility by Dec. 1 of Year 1, they don't become eligible before Feb. 1 (or later) of Year 2.

Example: *Carrie undergoes plantar fascia surgery at her local VA facility to relieve chronic foot discomfort in November 2019.*

She then loses her HSA eligibility for December, January, and February. She must pro-rate her 2019 contribution, depositing no more than 11/12 of her maximum contribution in her HSA. Her 2020 contribution is also affected, since she's not HSA-eligible during the first two months of the year. She can either pro-rate her contribution (no more than 10/12 of the maximum) or apply the Last-Month Rule to her 2020 contribution (assuming she's HSA-eligible as of Dec. 1, 2020). If she chooses the latter course, she must remain eligible through the testing period that ends Dec. 31, 2021.

Contributions and Family Members

Maximum contribution and multiple HSAs. Some people own more than one HSA, for a variety of reasons (some of which will be discussed later). The statutory maximum annual contribution is their total limit for the year, regardless of how many HSAs they own or into how many HSAs they direct contributions. *[See IRS Notice 2004-50, Q&A 64.]*

Contribution limits when both spouses are HSA-eligible on a family HSA-qualified medical plan. Though families typically have only one HSA owned by one spouse, it's legal (and sometimes appropriate) for both spouses to own HSAs. When both spouses are HSA-eligible, they can't contribute a combined amount in excess of the statutory maximum annual contribution for a family contract. They can split that amount between their two (or more)

HSAs as they choose. *[See IRC Section 223(b)(5)(A)* and *IRS Notice 2004-50, Q&A 32.]*

Here's a scenario in which both spouses' owning HSAs can be important:

- Reuben plans to retire at age 65, remain covered on his employer's medical plan, and enroll in Medicare (disqualifying him from additional HSA contributions) effective April 1, 2019.
- Reuben's wife, Louisa, age 63, plans to continue her coverage on Reuben's employer-sponsored medical plan. Louisa satisfies all HSA eligibility requirements.

How much can they contribute to their HSAs for 2019?

- Reuben can contribute $250 (3/12 of $1,000) to his HSA as a catch-up contribution.
- Louisa can contribute $1,000 to her HSA as a catch-up contribution.
- Reuben is eligible to contribute only through March 31. The maximum amount of the $7,000 contribution for family coverage that he can contribute is $1,750 (3/12 of $7,000).
- Only Louisa is eligible to contribute after March 31. She can contribute up to 9/12 of the $7,000 family contribution limit ($5,250), plus the remainder of the $1,750 for January through March that Reuben doesn't contribute to his HSA.

The maximum contribution between them is:

Description	Whose HSA?	How Much?
Reuben's catch-up (pro-rated)	Reuben's	$250.00
Louisa's catch-up	Louisa's	$1,000.00
Pro-rated family coverage (Jan—Mar)	Reuben's or Louisa's	$1,750.00
Pro-rated family coverage (Apr—Dec)	Louisa's	$5,250.00
TOTAL		**$8,250.00**

[See IRS Notice 2004-50, Q&A 32.]

Contribution limits when each spouse is covered on a self-only HSA-qualified medical plan. Each spouse can contribute no more than the statutory maximum annual contribution for self-only coverage. In addition, each can make a $1,000 catch-up contribution, if eligible, to his or her own HSA.

Contribution limits when domestic partners or ex-spouses are enrolled in a family HSA-qualified medical plan. The law is clear about the treatment of HSA contributions and married couples (see preceding discussion). What about contribution limits when domestic partners or ex-spouses are covered on a family contract? They're not married, so they don't fall under the provisions of the law that limit married partners to a single family contribution maximum, split between their respective HSAs as they choose.

Leading benefits attorneys and HSA administrators conclude that in this case, *each* individual can contribute up to the maximum family contribution (less any adjustments for eligibility in fewer than 12 months during the calendar year).

It's important to understand that the IRS hasn't published formal guidance on domestic partner contribution limits. So, what guidance is available?

> The IRS hasn't published formal guidance on domestic partner contribution limits.

IRS officials are invited regularly to professional organizations' meetings to provide insight based on their understanding of the law. In 2010, at an annual meeting of the American Bar Association (ABA), an IRS official was confronted with this scenario: Subscriber and domestic partner are enrolled in family coverage. They're not married to each other and both have family coverage. The ABA posited that in this situation, each of them can contribute up to the family maximum.

The IRS official, answering based on his understanding of the rules and not on behalf of the IRS, agreed with the ABA's conclusion. Your clients should check with their legal or tax counselor to assess the potential risk of adopting this approach in the absence of clear IRS guidance. *[See Appendix E, Informal Guidance on Contribution Limits for Domestic Partners.]*

Contribution limits when adult children are enrolled in a family HSA-qualified medical plan. Children who remain your clients' tax dependents can't open their own HSAs (and your clients can reimburse their qualified expenses tax-free from their HSAs, as you'll see in Chapter 19, *HSA Distributions*). If a child is no longer your client's tax dependent and satisfies all HSA eligibility requirements, she can open her own HSA. Because she's covered on a family contract and not married to anyone with whom she must split a family maximum contribution, leading benefits attorneys and HSA administrators conclude that she can contribute up to the maximum family contribution (less any pro-rating that may apply), irrespective of what other family members contribute.

Contributions to the daughter's HSA don't affect your client's ability to contribute up to the $7,000 statutory maximum family contribution to his HSA in 2019. As with the earlier domestic partner situation, the conclusion that the daughter can contribute up to the statutory family maximum is based on an IRS official's *unofficial* statements at the 2010 ABA meeting.

Your clients should seek legal or tax counsel to evaluate the potential risk of following this guidance in the absence of clear IRS guidance. *[See Appendix E, Informal Guidance on Contribution Limits for Domestic Partners.]*

Contribution Caveats

Contributions are in cash only. All HSA contributions must be made in cash. Your clients can't transfer stocks or other assets to their HSAs without first converting them to cash. *[See IRC Section 223(a)* and *IRS Notice 2004-2, Q&A 16.]*

Contributions aren't limited to earned income. Unlike contributions to certain retirement accounts, contributions to HSAs can come from any legal source, including dividends, unemployment benefits, lottery or gambling winnings, and proceeds from the sale of assets and gifts. This is an important and often-overlooked feature that distinguishes HSAs from most other tax-advantaged opportunities. People without sufficient earned income for whatever reason—illness, unemployment, commitment to an unpaid opportunity, early retirement—can still contribute to their HSAs.

Anyone can contribute to your clients' HSAs. Though typically only an employer, an HSA owner, and perhaps the owner's spouse contribute to an HSA, anyone else can make contributions as well, including a parent or other relative, a neighbor, or a total stranger. If the source of the contributions is anyone but the employer, the account owner—your client—receives the tax deduction. *[See IRS Notice 2004-2, Q&A 11* and *Q&A 18* and *IRS Notice 2004-50, Q&A 28.]*

Contribution limits aren't reduced based on income. Your clients can make the full contributions to which they're entitled under federal tax law, regardless of their taxable income. Contribution amounts aren't reduced or phased out with higher income, as they are with certain retirement plans like IRAs. Your clients, Jeff Bezos, and Warren Buffett can all contribute the same amount to their respective HSAs without a phase-out of the tax deduction based on income.

Contributions through a Cafeteria Plan are subject to nondiscrimination testing. Employers who allow employees to elect to receive a portion of their compensation in the form of tax-free HSA contributions must conduct annual nondiscrimination testing. These tests ensure that the program doesn't disproportionately benefit highly compensated employees.

If the plan is tested early in the plan year and fails, the employer can reduce high-income employees' pre-tax payroll deductions through the Cafeteria Plan to a level such that their participation doesn't result in failure of the plan. For example, the employer may impose a $2,500 limit on self-only contributions and $5,000 limit on family contributions through the Cafeteria Plan.

Your clients, Jeff Bezos, and Warren Buffett can all contribute the same amount to their respective HSAs.

Nondiscrimination testing is also required on other components of Cafeteria Plans, including Health FSAs and DCRAs. In those cases, high-income employees may have to reduce their annual elections as well if the plan fails when tested early in the year.

When elections to Health FSAs and DCRAs are reduced for nondiscrimination issues, participants lose the tax deduction tied to the amount of the lost election. They have no way to realize these tax savings except through the Cafeteria Plan.

In contrast, your high-income clients whose company HSA plans fail nondiscrimination testing can reduce their Cafeteria Plan pre-tax contributions and make additional personal (after-tax) contributions to their HSAs. They then can deduct these contributions from their taxable income via an above-the-line deduction (on page 1 of Form 1040, which reduces adjustable gross income) when they file their personal income tax return.

The deduction effectively returns to them the federal income taxes and state income taxes (in all states that tax personal income, except Alabama, California, and New Jersey) paid on the funds when earned. They can't escape FICA taxes, which means that the first $130,500 (2018 figure) of taxable income is subject to a 7.65% (employee share) payroll tax for Social Security and Medicare Part A premium taxes. Above the $130,500 figure, only the 1.45% (employee share) of the Medicare payroll tax is applied.

Paying the full 7.65% payroll tax results in a higher reported income to the Social Security Administration for calculating Social Security benefit. Depending on their income during their 35 highest-earning years, this additional reported income may affect future Social Security benefits. *[See IRS Notice 2004-2, Q&A 16, Q&A 19,* and *Q&A 33.]*

Contribution deadline. Your clients can contribute via pre-tax payroll through the end of the calendar year (so that the contributions are reflected accurately in Box 12 of their Form W-2s) and make personal contributions up to the due date of their personal income tax return (generally April 15). This extended contribution period allows them to direct a year-end bonus payable early the following year into their HSAs as a contribution credited to the prior year. It also allows them to make a last-minute reduction in their taxable income as they complete their personal income tax return. *[See IRS Notice 2004-2, Q&A 21.]*

Contributions and Cafeteria Plans

HSA payroll deductions. You and your clients are probably familiar with Health FSAs and the requirement that they make a binding prospective annual election. Your clients can't change this election based on qualified expenses above or below that amount. A key feature of HSAs that you've already explored is that HSA owners don't commit to a binding annual contribution level. Instead, your clients can adjust their pre-tax HSA payroll contributions prospectively throughout the year (at least monthly). *[See IRS Notice 2004-2, Q&A 16, Q&A 19,* and *Q&A 33.]*

> Your clients can adjust their pre-tax HSA payroll contributions prospectively throughout the year.

Contribution flexibility. Your clients can contribute to their HSAs at any time in any amount (up to the maximum contribution to which they're entitled). They can make consistent contributions per payroll period through their employer's Cafeteria Plan if the employer makes this option available, as most do. They can use a year-end bonus paid at the end of January to front-load that year's contribution or back-load the prior year's contribution. They can make payroll deductions for a certain number of months and then stop payroll deductions. They can contribute nothing at the beginning of the year and then start deductions. They can reduce their contribution during months when their income is lower (or expenses higher) and increase it again when their income is higher (or expenses lower). Your clients alone (perhaps with your guidance) determine the timing and amount of their contributions to their HSAs. *[See IRS Notice 2004-2, Q&A 21.]*

Employer restrictions on payroll changes. Though employees can change their pre-tax payroll contributions regularly, the law doesn't spell out how often they can make changes. A good rule of thumb for employers is to allow employees to make changes *at least* monthly because HSA eligibility is determined month-to-month. Your clients should review their employers' policies and create a strategy for amount and timing of contributions based on those policies. *[See IRS Notice 2004-50, Q&A 58.]*

Excess Contributions

Excess Contributions. Mistakes happen. Your client switches jobs mid-year and contributes above the statutory limit to her two HSAs. Another client makes a lump-sum contribution for the year in February, then switches jobs and enrolls in non-HSA-qualified coverage beginning in May. A third client takes advantage of the Last-Month Rule to increase his contributions one year, then loses his job and enrolls in Medicare effective Feb. 1.

These clients want to remove the excess contributions to avoid taxes and penalties. *Fortunately, they can.* They contact their HSA administrator, which provides instructions—usually directing your clients to a form that they can download, complete, and submit—on how to remove the excess contribution (and earnings attributable to it, which in today's interest-rate environment is typically minimal). Your clients must include the excess contribution amounts and any gains on the excess contributions as taxable income for the year. If they make contributions through pre-tax payroll, they need to contact their employer, which then must adjust their Form W-2 to reflect their compensation accurately. *[See IRS Notice 2004-50, Q&A 35.]*

HSA owners can't reverse non-excess contributions tax-free. You may at some point have a client who funds his HSA and then, for whatever reason, determines that he needs or wants the funds for another purpose. The law doesn't permit an HSA owner to simply change his mind about contribution levels retroactively and try to reverse or erase a contribution or multiple contributions. Withdrawal of contribution amounts below the annual contribution limit is included in your client's taxable income and subject to a 20% penalty if he is under age 65 and not disabled. *[See IRC Section 223(f)(3)* and *IRS Notice 2004-50, Q&A 35.]*

Counseling Your Clients

- ✓ Be sure that your clients understand their applicable contribution limits, based on both their contract type and the number of months that they're HSA-eligible during a calendar year.

- ✓ If they contribute to more than one HSA (most common when they switch jobs), make sure their total contributions don't exceed their limits for that year.

- ✓ If a client becomes HSA-eligible between Jan. 2 and Dec. 1, weigh carefully with her the costs and benefits of pro-rating contributions versus using the Last-Month Rule to increase her contributions up to the statutory limit for her contract type (and the $1,000 catch-up contribution if she's age 55 or older). In many cases, the benefits of using the Last-Month Rule to increase contributions outweigh the risks of losing eligibility during the testing period, especially with no known risk of loss of eligibility on the horizon.

- ✓ If a client covers one or more family members who are HSA-eligible on his medical plan, be sure that he understands whether and how contributions by other family members to their HSAs affect his contribution to his HSA.

- ✓ If your client isn't HSA-eligible yet and is interested in the financial advantages that an HSA offers, explore whether her spouse can satisfy HSA eligibility requirements. If so, she can enjoy the benefits of an HSA program through her spouse's HSA. They can make personal (tax-deductible) contributions to her spouse's HSA, build medical equity, and reimburse qualified expenses tax-free.

CHAPTER 19

HSA Distributions

To enjoy the full range of tax advantages associated with an HSA, owners must ensure that they limit distributions—or withdrawals—to qualified expenses. To determine whether a product or service is a qualified expense, they must ask (and answer correctly) three questions:

- What is the product or service, and is it defined under federal tax law as a qualified expense?
- Who incurred the expense, and what was that person's relationship to the HSA owner at the time of the expense?
- What's the date of purchase of the product or service?

This chapter explores how the answers to these three questions determine whether a distribution from an HSA is tax-free.

Qualified expenses. Expenses are qualified for tax-free distribution if they diagnose, mitigate, or treat an injury, illness, or condition. Unfortunately, the IRS doesn't provide a comprehensive list of services that qualify for tax-free distribution. Instead, it updates and distributes annually a document entitled *IRS Publication 502,* which lists and defines the products and services that taxpayers can deduct as medical expenses to reduce their taxable income. This list is nearly identical to the list of qualified expenses. Most HSA administrators maintain a short, fairly comprehensive—but not exhaustive, as it evolves over time—list to which account owners can refer.

These expenses are tax-free only to the extent that individuals bear financial responsibility for them.

> Example: *Brian purchases a C-PAP machine for $1,000. His medical insurer reimburses 80% of the cost, or $800. He can reimburse up to the $200 that he owes tax-free from his HSA.*

[See IRC Section 223(d)(2)(A) and *IRS Notice 2004-2, Q&A 25* and *Q&A 26.]*

Non-qualified expenses. HSA owners can take distributions from their HSA at any time for any reason. They aren't limited to reimbursing only qualified expenses, as are participants in a Health FSA or HRA program.

Your clients who withdraw HSA funds for non-qualified expenses must report the distribution as taxable income when they complete their individual tax returns. They must pay a penalty in the form of an additional tax equal to 20% of the distribution. They can avoid the penalty (but not the treatment of the distribution as income) once they turn age 65 or become disabled or die.

Example: *Charlotte and her sisters decide to go on a dream cruise vacation to celebrate her retirement. She withdraws a total of $2,000 from her HSA to pay for the trip, making $1,000 withdrawals in the years that she turns age 64 and age 65.*

Charlotte must include the first year's $1,000 distribution as taxable income and pay an additional tax of 20%, or $200. Assuming she is in the 35% tax bracket, her total tax is $550. Because she withdraws the second $1,000 after she turns age 65, Charlotte must include it in her taxable income, but she pays no additional tax as a penalty.

Your clients can avoid the penalty altogether if they have incurred a matching amount of qualified expenses that they haven't reimbursed from their HSAs.

Example: *Analyn withdrew the $2,000 in the preceding example. She also incurred $1,500 of qualified dental expenses and purchased new bifocals for $500 during the past three years, when she was HSA-eligible. She paid her dentist and optician with personal funds. Because she paid for those qualified expenses with personal funds, she can withdraw funds without tax liability and subsequently match those expenses against her distributions if the IRS audits her personal income tax return.*

[See IRC Section 223(f)(2) and *Section 223(f)(4)*, and *IRS Notice 2004-2, Q&A 25* and *Q&A 26.]*

Limiting frequency of reimbursements. The IRS imposes no limits on how often your clients can make distributions from their HSA and sets no minimum distribution. HSA administrators can set limits or minimum distributions. Though HSA administrators can do so, they are in the business of satisfying customers who have many choices in the market. You and your clients would be hard-pressed to find an administrator who imposes a limit on number of transactions per month or sets a minimum dollar figure below which your clients can't make a distribution. *[See IRS Notice 2004-50, Q&A 80.]*

Prescriptions, authorizations, or physician orders are generally not required. In most cases, a qualified expense is a qualified expense—period. In many cases, a medical, dental, or vision insurer may require referrals, authorizations, or physician orders before insurance covers an expense. Those requirements don't factor into whether an expense is qualified for tax-free reimbursement from an HSA.

> Example: *Olivia injures her knee getting out of the pool after teaching a water aerobics class. Her orthopedic surgeon diagnoses a torn meniscus and recommends surgery.*
>
> *The surgeon neglects to seek approval from Olivia's insurer before the 20-minute procedure. After reviewing the claim, the insurer denies coverage because its guidelines call for patients in that situation to go through a course of physical therapy before scheduling surgery. Even though the insurer didn't approve the claim, surgery is an appropriate treatment for a torn meniscus. Olivia can reimburse this expense tax-free from her HSA.*

[See IRS Notice 2004-2, Q&A 25 and *Q&A 26.]*

Over-the-counter drugs and medicine. The exception to this no-prescription rule involves over-the-counter drugs and medicine. Under an unpopular provision of the ACA, HSA owners need a prescription (or a letter of medical necessity) signed by a state-authorized prescriber to reimburse over-the-counter drugs and medicine (except insulin) tax-free. (This requirement applies to Health FSAs as well.) HSA owners don't present the prescription to purchase the over-the-counter drug. Instead, they retain it in their files if they claim tax-free distributions to purchase cough elixir, allergy pills, sleep aids, antacid medication, and other common over-the-counter remedies.

This prescription requirement applies to over-the-counter drugs and medicine only. HSA owners can purchase over-the-counter equipment and supplies (such as contact-lens solution, bandages, carpal-tunnel splints, reading glasses, crutches, and C-PAP supplies) tax-free without a prescription.

In addition, they need a prescription or letter of medical necessity in their files if they claim a tax-free distribution for certain drugs and medicine that typically are considered to affect general health only and therefore aren't qualified for tax-free distribution. Examples are pre-natal vitamins, vitamin B-12 supplements for patients after certain bariatric surgeries, massage therapy to treat a musculoskeletal condition, and a new health club membership as part of a weight-loss regimen overseen by a physician.

A prescription doesn't automatically make an expense qualified for tax-free distribution. A prescription or letter of medical necessity doesn't guarantee that the IRS will accept the expenses as medically necessary in the event of a personal income tax return audit if that expense isn't described in *IRS Publication 969*. Some medical professionals prescribe services, equipment, and regimens that they believe are medically necessary but that the IRS hasn't reviewed and approved. Examples are an herbal cleansing regimen to reduce bloating or a monthly massage to reduce stress. When an HSA owner ventures into a gray area, a prescription or letter of medical necessity may merely alter the shade of gray rather than turn it black or white.

As an IRS agent once explained to the author, "Any quack can write a prescription for anything." The item prescribed must satisfy the IRS standard for a qualified expense for the purpose that the patient is using it.

Your clients don't need to provide documentation (prescription or letter of medical necessity) when they purchase the product or service. They do need to retain a copy in their records to justify a tax-free distribution if the IRS audits their personal income tax return and questions an HSA distribution.

An HSA owner can reimburse eligible family members' qualified expenses tax-free, even if the family member isn't HSA-eligible herself or enrolled in the account owner's coverage.

Eligible family members. HSA owners can reimburse their own, their spouse's, and their tax dependents' qualified expenses tax-free from their HSAs. **These individuals don't have to be enrolled in the HSA owner's medical plan, nor do they have to be HSA-eligible themselves**, for the owner to reimburse their qualified expenses tax-free.

This point bears repeating because it's one of the most misunderstood concepts in the HSA world: An HSA owner can reimburse eligible family members' qualified expenses tax-free, even if the family member isn't HSA-eligible herself or enrolled in the account owner's coverage.

Be sure to review with your clients which individuals enrolled in their medical plans aren't on this list. Domestic partners' and ex-spouses' qualified expenses can't be reimbursed tax-free from your clients' HSAs, even if these individuals remain covered on the HSA owner's medical plan. Nor can expenses incurred by your clients' children who no longer qualify as their tax dependents under Section 152 of the IRC, even if they're enrolled in your clients' medical coverage. The implications of these situations are explored later in this chapter. *[See IRS Notice 2004-2, Q&A 25* and *Q&A 26* and *IRS Notice 2004-50, Q&A 36.]*

Neither employers who sponsor an HSA program nor administrators can limit distributions to qualified expenses. Under federal tax law, employers have latitude in limiting qualified expenses reimbursed through a Health FSA or HRA that the employer sponsors. HSAs, however, aren't employer-sponsored plans. Neither an employer nor an HSA administrator can limit the list of qualified expenses for tax-free reimbursement from employees' HSAs. *[See IRS Notice 2004-2, Q&A 29* and *Q&A 30.]*

HSA distributions to reimburse a domestic partner's qualified expenses. Expenses incurred by an HSA owner's domestic partner aren't qualified for tax-free reimbursement from the HSA, even if the domestic partner is covered on the HSA owner's medical insurance and the expenses are HSA-qualified. Any distributions from your client's HSA for a domestic partner's expenses are included in the HSA owner's taxable income in the year of distribution and subject to an additional 20% penalty unless your client—not her domestic partner—is age 65 or older or disabled.

A domestic partner, if otherwise HSA-eligible, can open her own HSA. Anyone (including your client) can contribute to her HSA, and the domestic partner can reimburse her own and her tax dependents' qualified expenses tax-free from her HSA. See Chapter 25, *Different Family Structures—Different Rules,* for more information.

[Note: If your client's domestic partner is her tax dependent under Section 152 of the IRC, distribution from her HSA for that partner's qualified expenses may be tax-free. It's rare for a domestic partner to be a tax dependent.]

HSA distributions to reimburse an ex-spouse's qualified expenses. The qualified expenses of your client's ex-spouse aren't qualified for tax-free distribution from your client's HSA, even if your client by court order must cover his ex-spouse on his medical insurance or assume financial responsibility for her out-of-pocket medical costs. A family-court judge can set the financial arrangements associated with divorce but can't overrule federal tax law. Any distributions for an ex-spouse's qualified expenses with a date of purchase or service on or after the date of a court order of separate maintenance (or the equivalent document in other jurisdictions that's a precursor to a divorce) are included in your client's taxable income. They're also subject to an additional 20% tax unless your client is age 65 or older or disabled.

Ex-spouses and divorce decrees that require the HSA owner to transfer a portion of an HSA balance. A judge can order your client to transfer a portion of his HSA balances to an ex-spouse as part of a divorce settlement. In this case, the ex-spouse can open her own HSA in her name. She doesn't have to be HSA-eligible to open the account to receive this transfer. Your client can move the funds to the ex-spouse's HSA as a transfer (no tax implications) rather than as a taxable distribution from his account.

If the ex-spouse is HSA-eligible, she can make additional contributions to her own HSA. If not, she can spend the balance but can't make additional deposits into the account.

If your client is required to assume financial responsibility for a portion of her out-of-pocket expenses, he can either pay them with personal (after-tax) funds or contribute to her HSA if she is HSA-eligible so that she can pay those expenses with tax-free funds. In the latter case, she receives the tax deduction. You might counsel a client in this situation to negotiate an agreement with his ex-spouse to contribute a lesser sum than the court order into her HSA. Your client saves money and the ex-spouse receives a tax deduction, which increases the purchasing power of the lesser contribution to more than the value of the reimbursement outside the HSA.

An ex-spouse, if otherwise HSA-eligible, can open an HSA in her name. Anyone (including your client) can contribute to that HSA, and the ex-spouse can reimburse her (and her dependents') qualified expenses tax-free.

If the ex-spouse is your client's tax dependent under Section 152 of the IRC (which is rare), distributions from your client's HSA for the ex-spouse's qualified expenses may be tax-free. *[See IRC Section 223(f)(7)* and *Chapter 25,* Different Family Structures, Different Rules, *for more information.]*

HSA distributions to reimburse a non-dependent child's qualified expenses. If a child no longer satisfies the definition of a dependent under Section 152 of the IRC, an HSA owner can't reimburse any of the child's expenses tax-free from his HSA, even if the child remains covered on the parent's medical plan. The parent can at any time reimburse tax-free any qualified expenses that the child incurred while still a tax dependent.

The non-tax-dependent child, if otherwise HSA-eligible, can open an HSA in her name. Anyone (including your client) can contribute to her HSA, and she can reimburse her (and, if applicable, her tax dependents') qualified expenses tax-free. The child receives the tax deduction for any contributions made to the HSA (other than by the child's employer), including contributions made by a parent.

Note that this provision is different from other accounts. Employees who participate in a Health FSA or HRA can reimburse qualified expenses incurred by children to age 26, whether or not those children are the employee's tax dependents. Health FSAs and HRAs follow the ACA rules for coverage under a medical plan, while HSA rules follow IRS rules for tax deductibility of a family member's expenses based on whether or not the family member qualifies as the HSA owner's tax dependent.

Distributions to reimburse qualified expenses incurred by a tax-dependent child not enrolled in the HSA owner's medical plan. The child's medical coverage doesn't determine whether his expenses are qualified for tax-free reimbursement through his parent's HSA. As long as the child remains your client's tax dependent, your client can reimburse the child's qualified expenses tax-free. Remember also that as long as the child remains a tax dependent, he can't open an HSA in his name.

Distributions to reimburse a child's qualified expenses when an ex-spouse claims the child as a tax dependent. In a divorce settlement, only one spouse can claim a minor child as a tax dependent in a given year. Whether or not your client can claim the child as a tax dependent, if the child satisfies the definition of a dependent child under Section 152, your client can reimburse the child's qualified expenses tax-free from his HSA. *[See IRS Notice 2008-59, Q&A 33.]*

Distributions for qualified expenses incurred by a spouse or child enrolled in a non-HSA-qualified medical plan. A spouse's or child's medical coverage is *not* relevant to whether your client can reimburse that family member's qualified expenses tax-free from his HSA. As long as the account owner and spouse are married at the time of the service or purchase, the HSA owner can distribute funds tax-free from his HSA to pay the bill.

A spouse's or child's medical coverage is *not* relevant to whether your client can reimburse that family member's qualified expenses tax-free.

Distributions for qualified expenses incurred by a spouse or child enrolled in Medicare. Again, the family member's medical coverage does *not* matter. What's relevant is the person's relationship to the HSA owner. As long as the account owner and the spouse are married at the time of the service or purchase or the child qualifies as a tax dependent, the HSA owner can reimburse his spouse's or child's qualified medical, dental, vision, and over-the-counter expenses tax-free from his HSA. *[See IRS Notice 2004-50, Q&A 36.]*

Spouses' reimbursing each other's expenses. It's not uncommon for spouses, particularly when both are age 55 or older and eligible to make catch-up contributions, to each own an HSA. In this situation, each spouse can reimburse his or her spouse's qualified expenses tax-free. The law doesn't restrict two-HSA couples to reimbursing only their own—but not their spouse's—expenses. *[See IRS Notice 2004-50, Q&A 38.]*

Distributions to reimburse medical premiums. Premiums for employer-sponsored medical coverage generally aren't qualified expenses for tax-free distributions from an HSA. In most cases, employers adopt a Cafeteria Plan that allows employees to pay their portion of premiums through pre-tax payroll deductions. People who purchase insurance in the nongroup market, whether through an ACA marketplace, through another reseller, or directly from an insurer, may qualify for an income tax credit to offset a portion of their premium costs.

The prohibition against tax-free reimbursement of premiums doesn't extend to all medical premiums, however. Your clients who continue coverage by exercising their COBRA rights can pay COBRA premiums tax-free through their HSA. COBRA coverage isn't considered group coverage, even though COBRA participants continue coverage on their old employer-sponsored plan. And people collecting unemployment benefits can reimburse their medical premiums tax-free from their HSAs.

In both of these situations, having built medical equity in an HSA allows your clients to afford the high cost of nongroup coverage at a time when they may be in financial transition. *[See IRC Section 223(d)(2)(C)(i)* and *223(d)(2)(C)(iii)* and *IRS Notice 2008-59, Q&A 31* and *Q&A 32.]*

Distributions to reimburse a spouse's Medicare premiums. There is one caveat to the rule that an HSA owner can reimburse all HSA-qualified medical expenses incurred by a spouse. Under a little-understood provision, your client can't reimburse tax-free her husband's Medicare premiums before she reaches age 65. She can reimburse her husband's qualified medical, dental, vision, and over-the-counter expenses. She can reimburse all his Medicare cost-sharing, including his Part A deductible, his Part B deductible and coinsurance, and his varied cost-sharing on Part D. She can't, however, reimburse his, her own, or anyone else's Medicare premiums tax-free until she—the HSA owner—turns age 65. This is true even if she enrolls in Medicare coverage before age 65 due to a specific condition like end-stage renal disease or Lou Gehrig's disease.

This provision requires some planning by your client's family. Let's say your client is the account owner, her spouse is older than she is, and they want to reimburse the spouse's Medicare premiums. The spouse, if HSA-eligible, must open his own account. He can fund it with a $1,000 annual catch-up contribution. They can also allocate part of their maximum contribution for a family contract into his, rather than her, HSA.

Example: *Rebecca, the medical plan subscriber, is 12 years younger than her husband, Emil Philip (EP). When EP turned age 55, he opened his own HSA and contributed his $1,000 annual catch-up contribution. They also agreed to make a personal contribution of an additional $1,500 of their family contribution maximum into his HSA (so, for example, in 2019, they deposit $1,500 of the $7,000 maximum contribution into EP's HSA and the $5,500 balance into Rebecca's).*

After 10 years, EP has built a balance of $33,000 in medical equity in his HSA through contributions and investment gains.

He uses his balances to reimburse his Medicare premiums tax-free, while they reimburse his out-of-pocket expenses from Rebecca's HSA (balance: $75,000) to ensure that his account remains funded until Rebecca turns age 65 and can reimburse both her own and EP's Medicare premiums tax-free.

[See IRC Section 223(d)(2)(C)(iv); IRS Notice 2004-50, Q&A 45; and *IRS Notice 2008-59, Q&A 29* and *Q&A 30.]*

Distributions to reimburse long-term care insurance premiums. You've probably counseled many of your clients to purchase long-term care insurance to preserve their assets in the event that they are admitted to a nursing home for custodial care. Premiums may seem unaffordable, even to your younger clients who purchase coverage in their 30s or 40s to lock in lower premiums.

HSA owners can make tax-free distributions to reimburse long-term care insurance premiums. Like the tax deduction, the tax-free reimbursement is capped depending on your client's age. The IRS sets this limit annually for each 10-year age span.

An HSA may be an attractive source of funds to purchase insurance and provide a tax benefit as well. On the other hand, distributions for long-term care premiums reduce medical equity at a time when it may make more sense financially to preserve and grow HSA balances tax-free. A more prudent course for your client may be to purchase long-term care insurance with after-tax funds and deduct premiums when she files her personal income tax return.

Note that this provision applies to long-term care *premiums.* Expenses associated with long-term custodial care (such as nursing-home charges) aren't eligible for tax-free distribution. *[See IRC Section 223(d)(2)(C)(ii)* and *IRS Notice 2004-50, Q&A 40.]*

Distributions to reimburse long-term care expenses. Long-term care expenses are generally custodial in care and don't qualify for tax-free distributions from an HSA. If long-term care fees include qualified expenses (for example, a patient receives outpatient therapy services that are billed separately from the custodial fee), those expenses can be reimbursed tax-free from an HSA. This breakdown of expenses is rare and generally not an option for patients. *[See IRS Notice 2004-50, Q&A 42.]*

Going back in time to reimburse qualified expenses tax-free. Your client can reimburse tax-free any qualified expense that he, his spouse, or his tax dependents incur on or after the day that he "established" his HSA (see next paragraph). This is an important feature of an HSA, particularly when it comes to cash flow. An HSA owner who incurs a high expense early in his coverage under an HSA-qualified plan can negotiate repayment terms with his provider, then make those future payments from his HSA with funds contributed after he incurs the high expense. HSA owners never lose the ability to reimburse a qualified expense tax-free merely because they don't have a sufficient HSA balance at the time of the service. *[See IRS Notice 2004-50, Q&A 39.]*

HSA owners never lose the ability to reimburse a qualified expense tax-free merely because they don't have a sufficient HSA balance at the time of the service.

Establishing an HSA. The IRS defers to state trust law to determine when an HSA owner establishes his HSA. Though trust law varies from state to state, in most states an account owner must do the following to open a trust (an HSA is a trust):

1. Signal intent to open a trust (such as signing an application or accepting terms and conditions online).

2. Name a beneficiary of the trust so that it passes to the HSA owner's designee in the event of his death.

3. Place corpus, or an item of value, within the trust. The amount can be as little as a penny in most cases.

Most HSAs are established when the account is open and the first funds are deposited. The date of funding may be after the first payroll cycle following the effective date of coverage, which means that any expenses incurred before the date of funding can't be reimbursed tax-free—ever—through the HSA.

> Example: *Himari enrolls in an HSA-qualified medical plan April 1, 2019, and becomes HSA-eligible immediately. Her first payroll deposit after April 1 is the second Friday of April—April 12. Himari can't reimburse tax-free any expenses*

that she incurs prior to April 12, now or in the future. Those expenses count toward her medical plan deductible if they're covered services, but Himari can't take advantage of tax-free reimbursements through her HSA.

Special note on HSAs governed by Utah state trust law: In 2009, the Utah legislature passed a bill to amend the state's trust law. Under this law, your client can establish an HSA retroactively as far back as the day that she enrolls in an HSA-qualified medical plan [see following examples] provided that she opens the account and makes an initial contribution of any amount before the earlier of the date that (1) she files her personal income tax return for that year or (2) the deadline, without extensions, for filing a personal income tax return (generally April 15).

Example: *Same circumstances as previous example, but Himari establishes an HSA governed by Utah law. As long as Himari opens and places an initial deposit in her HSA before filing her 2019 personal income tax return in mid-April 2020, she can reimburse tax-free all qualified expenses incurred with dates of service or purchase on or after April 1, 2019.*

If Himari doesn't open and fund her HSA before the April 2020 deadline, she loses her ability to reimburse tax-free any qualified expenses that she incurs between April 1 and Dec. 31, 2019. She can reimburse qualified expenses tax-free that she incurs on or after Jan. 1, 2020, as long as she establishes her HSA by April 15, 2021.

[See IRS Notice 2004-50, Q&A 39 and *IRS Notice 2008-59, Q&A 38* and *Q&A 39.]*

The Utah legislature can't overrule federal tax law. HSA owners with accounts governed by Utah law can, under Utah state trust law, *establish* their HSAs back to the date that they enrolled in an HSA-qualified plan. They can't, however, reimburse expenses incurred before the first day of the first month that they satisfy federal HSA eligibility requirements.

Example: *Lisa, an HSA owner whose account is governed by state trust law in a state other than Utah and whose coverage begins April 24, 2019, doesn't become HSA-eligible until May 1. She can't establish an HSA before that date or reimburse tax-free any expenses incurred prior to May 1 (or later, depending in many states on the date of the initial contribution to the account).*

Her best friend Tonica's HSA is governed by Utah trust law. Tonica also enrolled in an HSA-qualified plan with an effective date of coverage of April 24, 2019 and met all other HSA eligibility requirements that day. She can establish her HSA retroactively back to April 24, but she can't reimburse tax-free any expenses that she incurs before the date that she satisfies federal eligibility requirements. If Tonica undergoes day surgery April 27, she won't be able to reimburse that expense tax-free from her HSA—ever—even though she can establish her HSA back to April 24 because she isn't HSA-eligible under federal law until May 1.

[See H.B. 195, Utah Uniform Probate Code—Trust Amendments, 2009 General Session, State of Utah.]

Out-of-pocket expenses in excess of HSA balances. Although the thrust of this book is about strategies to build HSA balances by paying for qualified expenses with personal (after-tax) funds to preserve HSA balances in a tax-free environment, some HSA owners may run into a situation where the only feasible alternative is to make distributions from their HSA. But what happens when even their HSA balance isn't sufficient to reimburse the qualified expense?

HSA owners have several options in these situations:

- In most cases, they can negotiate repayment terms with a medical provider. This strategy doesn't work with pharmacies, who demand full payment at the time of purchase and pick-up. If HSA owners use personal funds to cover a shortfall in their HSA balances, they needn't fret. They *never* lose the ability to reimburse tax-free any qualified expense that they (or a spouse or tax dependent) incur on or after the latter of the date that they become HSA-eligible or establish their HSA. They can reimburse themselves after they make future contributions to their HSA. That's right. Your clients can repay today's expenses not only with yesterday's contributions (a positive account balance), but also with tomorrow's (future) contributions when their current balances are insufficient.

- They can pay with personal funds and reimburse themselves with subsequent contributions. In fact, some HSA owners leave their debit card at home, pay for all qualified expenses with an incentive personal credit card (to accumulate points or miles), and then pay the personal credit card bill with a distribution from their HSA. It's all perfectly legal.

- They can access a line of credit if their HSA administrator offers this feature (and, if applicable, their employer extends the program to its employees). Under this arrangement, your client can tap funds to pay bills that exceed her HSA balance. In a typical model, the employer funds a separate account that advances the money to the HSA owner/employee, who then repays the loan. These arrangements can be designed to comply with HSA rules when the account itself isn't used as collateral to secure the loan. A growing number of administrators offer this type of program to reduce a major psychological barrier to HSA acceptance.

Employers can offer at least one of these two options as well:

- Accelerate employer contributions into individual employees' HSAs based on claims incurred.

- Offer payroll loans. This program is separate from the HSA. The employer extends the loan, which the employee repays through taxable payroll deductions. The employee can then reimburse herself through her HSA, using pre-tax dollars to achieve the same tax benefit as if she had withdrawn the money originally and paid the provider directly.

[See IRS Notice 2004-50, Q&A 39 and *Q&A 60.]*

Deadline for reimbursement. HSA owners face no deadline to reimburse an expense tax-free or lose that opportunity forever. Once your client has established her HSA, she can reimburse any qualified expense tax-free at any point in the future. In this case, she can use future contributions to reimburse a qualified expense that she's incurred already, as long as the date of service is on or after the date that the HSA was established.

HSA owners face no deadline to reimburse an expense tax-free or lose that opportunity forever.

Example: *Anika is aggressively building medical equity by not reimbursing qualified expenses tax-free from her HSA. She has retained her receipts for $37,000 of qualified expenses that she has incurred during the prior nine years while she was HSA-eligible. Anika has an opportunity to accompany her sister on a European vacation after her sister's friend backed out, but she needs to come up with $8,000 tomorrow.*

Anika can reimburse expenses incurred during her first five years of coverage tax-free from her HSA.

This reimbursement-timing flexibility is very different from a Health FSA or HRA, which requires prompt submission of all reimbursement requests within a defined period—usually 90 days from the end of the plan year. *[See IRS Notice 2004-50, Q&A 39.]*

Gaps between HSA eligibility. As HSAs become more mainstream products, a growing number of account owners disenroll from HSA-qualified plans, move to companies that don't offer an HSA program, and subsequently re-enroll in HSA-qualified coverage. In these cases, they may be able to reimburse all qualified expenses incurred during the gap in HSA eligibility.

An HSA owner who maintains a positive balance in an old HSA up until 18 or fewer months before she enrolls in her current HSA program is deemed to have a continuously established HSA. She can reimburse tax-free any qualified expense that she, her spouse (and it doesn't have to be the same spouse as before), and her tax dependents incur. The gap between periods of HSA eligibility can be much longer than 18 months. It can be 10 years or more, as long as she had a positive balance in an HSA as long ago as 18 months before she regains HSA eligibility.

Here are two scenarios of breaks in HSA eligibility and their impact on tax-free distributions:

- If the account balance in the old HSA was greater than zero at some point during the 18 months before your client establishes a new HSA, the new HSA is deemed to have been established as of the date that the previous HSA was established.

Example: *Sully had an HSA when he worked for his old company between 2005 and 2010. He kept a small balance in that account, though monthly administrative fees ate away the balance. By Feb. 1, 2018, his balance reached zero. His new employer introduces an HSA program effective April 1, 2019. Sully enrolls and makes his first HSA deposit with the April 12 payroll.*

Because Sully funded a new HSA within 18 months of exhausting the balance in the old HSA, his new HSA is deemed to have been established in 2005. Sully can reimburse all qualified expenses that he incurred since 2005 from his future contributions to his new HSA.

- If the gap is more than 18 months and the account had no balance at any point beyond the last 18 months, then the HSA is reestablished as of the date that the new HSA is established. Your client can't use funds in the new HSA to reimburse tax-free any qualified expenses incurred before he established the new HSA.

Example: *Jared participated in an HSA program between 2012 and 2014. He never contributed much to the account. He exhausted his balance by early 2016 and his administrator closed the account later that year. He works with Sully now and also enrolled in the company's HSA program effective April 1, 2019.*

Since Jared had no HSA balances during the prior 18 months (dating back to Oct. 1, 2017), his new HSA is established as of the April 12, 2019, payroll deposit (the HSA isn't covered by Utah trust law). Jared can't go back to the date that he established his initial HSA and reimburse expenses that he incurred since then with new contributions.

[See IRS Notice 2008-59, Q&A 41.]

Counseling Your Clients

- ✓ Make sure your clients understand the importance of establishing their HSAs as soon as they can. It's not enough to be HSA-eligible—they must establish the accounts under federal tax law before they can begin to reimburse qualified expenses tax-free.

- ✓ Encourage clients who lose HSA eligibility non-permanently (such as changing jobs and not having access to an HSA-qualified medical plan versus a permanent situation like enrolling in Medicare) to maintain a positive balance in their HSA. That way, if they become HSA-eligible again, they can open a new HSA with an establishment date going back to the original HSA establishment date. They can then reimburse all intervening qualified expenses tax-free with contributions to their new HSA. This one simple strategy allows your clients to reimburse potentially thousands of dollars tax-free from their new HSA with contributions made long after they incurred those expenses. Make sure that your clients take into account the impact of HSA maintenance fees that the administrator withdraws automatically from the account. They must ensure that their best-laid plans of maintaining a balance in the old HSA aren't foiled by monthly administrative fees withdrawn from the account.

- ✓ Make sure your clients understand whose expenses they can reimburse. And emphasize that a family member's relationship to them, not the family member's coverage or eligibility to open her own HSA, determines whether distributions to cover her qualified expenses are tax-free.

- ✓ Help your clients understand not only the qualified expenses that they can reimburse tax-free today, but also those that they can reimburse tax-free in the future, like Medicare premiums. This knowledge should motivate them to build medical equity.

CHAPTER 20

HSA Administration

Your clients must open and establish their HSAs with a bank or other IRS-approved HSA administrator. These administrators process contributions and distributions, maintain records, and offer certain services, such as an investment platform and annual tax reporting. They also provide general educational information to account owners.

HSA administrators don't offer legal or compliance advice, nor do they generally offer investment advice directly. Their compliance responsibilities are very narrow, with the remainder left squarely in the hands of your clients.

> HSA administrators don't offer legal or compliance advice.

The best way to understand an HSA administrator's role is to compare it to a bank's or other financial institution's. It provides an account into which the owner deposits and from which the owner withdraws funds. It tracks all transactions accurately. It safeguards cash balances. It provides a debit card and other forms of withdrawal. It maintains a portal that the owner can visit to review transactions and balances. It produces forms to assist the owner in completing his personal income tax return.

What the financial institution doesn't do is review deposits to see whether they're from legal enterprises. It doesn't check withdrawals to see whether they're made for qualified expenses or represent good value to the consumer. And it doesn't question account owners after the fact about their withdrawals or demand follow-up documentation.

This chapter focuses on

- which services a typical administrator offers, and which ones it doesn't;
- what factors to review when choosing an administrator;

- guard rails that the administrator may or may not place on debit cards to limit inadvertent distributions for expenses that aren't HSA-qualified;
- HSA investment options, fees, and strategies;
- the level of protection afforded to HSA balances; and
- means of correcting excess contributions and mistaken distributions from an HSA.

HSA administrators. Any business can perform administrative functions, such as recordkeeping and moving money, to support an HSA program. An administrator must work with a bank or other IRS-approved financial institution that holds HSA deposits in trust. These institutions are either HSA-specific banks or financial or insurance companies that have experience administering IRAs (whose rules and processes are the basis for much of the administration of HSAs). *[See IRS Notice 2004-50, Q&A 72.]*

Trustees, custodians, and administrators. Though the terms "trustee" and "custodian" have distinct meanings in the legal profession, the differences in the HSA world are indistinguishable for the average account owner. HSA trustees and custodians are institutions that hold balances in trust.

HSA administrators, in contrast, are companies that perform routine administration services such as providing customer service and education, issuing debit cards, processing contributions and distributions, and maintaining an online portal through which account owners can track activity.

Most of the largest HSA firms serve as both trustees (hold deposits) and administrators (process activity and maintain records). These trustees are typically banks that have broadened their services from traditional personal and commercial banking relationships with individuals and companies to include employee benefits. Some trustees/administrators were founded specifically to support medical reimbursement programs like HSAs, Health FSAs, and HRAs.

The other common model is to have these functions split in a turnkey program in which an administrator (often a third-party administrator, or TPA, that manages FSAs, HRAs, and other employer-sponsored benefit programs) contracts directly with a financial institution that acts as the trustee. These TPAs already have a benefits relationship with employers. They become the middlemen between employers and employees on the one hand and financial institutions on the other.

An HSA is a trust. Your clients can't merely designate a financial account at a local bank as an "HSA" and enjoy the tax advantages of an HSA program. They must open an account with an approved HSA trustee or custodian, either directly or through an HSA administrator that works with an approved trustee or custodian. The trustee creates the HSA as a trust with compliant supporting documents. *[See IRS Notice 2008-59, Q&A 38.]*

Owning more than one HSA. Your clients can own and manage as many HSAs as they wish. Most individuals own only one because owning multiple HSAs doesn't increase either their contribution limits or the number of family members whose expenses they can reimburse tax-free from their HSA.

There are times when it's appropriate for someone to own more than one HSA.

> Example 1: *Jafari opens an HSA with his old employer, leaves the company, and several years later enrolls in his new employer's HSA with a different administrator. Though he can roll over his HSA balance to his new employer's administrator, he likes the investment options and low fees that his old employer's administrator offers.*

> Example 2: *Nora doesn't like her employer's preferred administrator for any number of reasons (such as poor investment options or a fee charged for each distribution). She can open a second HSA with an administrator of her choice and make regular trustee-to-trustee transfers to move balances from her employer's preferred administrator to her own.*

> Example 3: *Francisco wants to build medical equity, but he knows that he'll be tempted to spend his HSA balances if he incurs a high expense. He regularly makes trustee-to-trustee transfers from his employer's HSA to his chosen HSA. He then cuts up the debit card to his chosen HSA to reduce his ability to access funds.*

[See IRS Notice 2004-50, Q&A 64.]

> An HSA is an individually owned account.

No joint HSAs. An HSA is an individually owned account, like a retirement account. Most administrators, at the owner's request, issue a debit card to a spouse or child. The debit card may be in the account owner's name or her spouse's or child's, depending on that administrator's policy. She also can share log-in information with her spouse. The trust itself, however, is owned by the beneficiary (HSA owner) alone. *[See IRS Notice 2004-50, Q&A 63* and *IRS Notice 2008-59, Q&A 28.]*

Employers' preferred HSA administrators. Employers are permitted to work with a single HSA administrator for administrative convenience. Otherwise, an employer or its payroll company might need to link electronically with a dozen or more HSA trustees to satisfy all employees' preferences. An employer can tell employees that if they want to receive an employer contribution or make pre-tax payroll contributions through a Cafeteria Plan, they must open an HSA with the employee's chosen administrator.

Though this provision may seem limiting, it actually helps employees. Employers often receive lower fees than individual employees could negotiate. And, left on their own, many employees would fail to open HSAs promptly, because either they don't get around to it, don't know where to start, or don't understand the urgency of establishing an HSA. *[See Department of Labor Field Assistance Bulletin 2006-2, Q&A 2.]*

Employee flexibility to choose an HSA administrator different from an employer's. Though employers may decide to work with a single administrator for administrative ease, employees are free to work with whomever they choose. If your client doesn't like the employer's administrator for any reason, she has several options:

- Open her own HSA with her preferred administrator and forego her employer contribution and pre-tax payroll contributions entirely. She can make post-tax contributions to her HSA—perhaps through her company's payroll system, just as she directs post-tax pay into multiple personal checking and savings accounts—and deduct contributions from her taxable income when she files her personal income tax return. With this approach, she loses her employer contribution and FICA tax savings (up to $260 with self-only coverage and up to more than $500 with family coverage when making the statutory maximum annual contribution) and can bypass her employer's preferred HSA administrator completely. Given the financial opportunity that she must forego, this strategy is generally not recommended.

- Open two HSAs—one with her employer's preferred administrator and a second with her chosen administrator. As her employer contribution and employee pre-tax payroll contributions are deposited in an HSA with her employer's preferred administrator, she can direct that money to her preferred HSA administrator via a trustee-to-trustee transfer. She may even be able to set up regular automatic sweeps—perhaps monthly—implemented by her preferred administrator. With this approach, she maximizes her HSA deposits (receiving her employer's contribution), minimizes taxes (avoiding FICA levies), and moves her balances to her preferred HSA administrator. She must beware of potential fees associated with transfers.

Most employees don't open a second HSA. But most employees aren't counseled by an advising professional like you. While the employer's HSA administrator may be an acceptable option for many HSA program participants, you may find another HSA administrator that offers superior investment options. Or you may encourage your clients to direct their HSA contributions designated for long-term savings and investing into a second HSA. In those cases, opening a second HSA may be an appropriate strategy.

Administrative services provided. Administrators handle transactions (contributions, distributions), keep records, issue required tax documents, generate regular statements, give owners online access to their account, provide multiple means of withdrawing money from an HSA (typically some combination of debit card, checkbook, electronic transfer, and electronic billpay), and provide customer service.

Capping contributions. Though not required to do so, HSA administrators who follow industry best practices place a cap on the amount that an owner can contribute in a given calendar (tax) year. If the administrator knows whether your client is enrolled in self-only or family coverage (either through self-reporting or a file from the medical insurer), it sets the contribution ceiling to the statutory maximum annual contribution for that contract type. Otherwise, the administrator typically defaults to the statutory maximum annual contribution for a family contract as the contribution ceiling.

If your client is identified as being age 55 or older (again, either by personal attestation or insurer report), the administrator increases the contribution ceiling by $1,000 to reflect a catch-up contribution.

The administrator's cap on contributions doesn't guarantee that your client won't exceed her contribution limit. For example, a cap doesn't protect a client who

- contributes to a second HSA,
- receives non-preventive, non-service-related-disability care through the VA,

- receives non-preventive care though IHS,
- is covered on a spouse's general Health FSA, or
- changes coverage during the year from family to self-only.

All of these situations (and others) affect her contribution limit for the year, yet the administrator has no knowledge of these situations.

The burden of compliance always rests with your clients.

The burden of compliance always rests with your clients. They must understand the rules to ensure that they don't exceed their maximum contribution for a given year.

[See IRS Notice 2004-50, Q&A 73, Q&A 74, and *Q&A 75.]*

Withdrawing HSA funds. Your HSA administrator determines the means of distribution from your HSA. Most administrators issue a debit card (and additional cards to family members at your client's request). The card typically is coded in one of three ways:

- No restrictions—The account owner can use it to purchase any item at any time or withdraw cash from her account. Some administrators issue unrestricted debit cards because HSA owners can withdraw funds for any purpose (subject to adverse tax consequences if the expense isn't HSA-qualified). Moreover, a consumer can reimburse herself from her HSA for a qualified expense that she paid with another form of tender by purchasing a non-qualified item with her HSA debit card. These administrators don't want to deprive HSA owners of the flexibility and choice that a wide-open configuration allows.

- No retail restrictions—The account owner can use it to purchase any item at any time but can't withdraw cash from her account at a bank or ATM. This approach is designed to protect HSA owners from making withdrawals that have no paper trail linking them to qualified expenses.

- Restricted—The card is coded so that the account owner can purchase only HSA-qualified items or use it only at retail locations that sell mostly HSA-qualified items (like optometrist shops, pharmacies, and chiropractic offices). Administrators who adopt this approach are trying to protect HSA owners from the risk of inadvertent use of the card for a non-qualified expense. Cards with this type of restriction also offer superior protection against fraud because their acceptance is limited. Health FSA cards usually work this way, since distributions are limited to qualified expenses.

Your clients' HSA administrators or employers determine how the card is coded. The more restrictive the debit card, the less likely your clients are to use it for an expense that isn't HSA-qualified. Restrictive coding doesn't eliminate all potential distributions for non-qualified expenses, but it helps keep HSA owners in compliance.

If an administrator restricts the card to HSA-qualified items, it must provide HSA owners with another means to access funds, since owners are allowed to use their balances for non-qualified items (subject to income taxes and perhaps penalties).

Examples of other means of withdrawing funds include checkbooks (a less popular option, particularly among millennials, who are used to moving funds electronically and may never have written a check), electronic billpay, and electronic transfer into a personal financial account like a checking or savings account. *[See IRS Notice 2008-59, Q&A 27.]*

No administrator substantiation permitted. Account owners alone are responsible for managing their HSAs. HSA administrators aren't allowed to request documentation to determine whether an expense is or isn't qualified for tax-free distribution. Employers can't require substantiation as a condition for participating in an HSA program, either.

> Employers can't require substantiation as a condition for participating in an HSA program.

In this sense, an HSA works very differently from a Health FSA. Health FSA distributions are limited to qualified expenses. In contrast, HSA owners can make withdrawals for any purpose (subject to taxes and penalties for non-qualified expenses). Your client is responsible for reporting total distributions and the portion for qualified and non-qualified expenses on Form 8889 (more later in this chapter) when he files his personal income tax return.

The IRS may require him to produce substantiation records if his personal income tax return is subject to audit. Encourage clients to keep receipts to satisfy any potential audit. Many HSA administrators allow account owners to upload receipts into an "electronic shoebox." While this approach reduces clutter, owners may lose their electronic records if they subsequently change HSA administrators.

The *traditional* "shoebox" approach may work best. You may have clients who hesitate to stuff receipts into an empty shoebox or similar receptacle. You may want to advise them to purchase a three-ring binder with page protectors or cardstock pockets that they label (for example, "2018" or "2Q 2019," depending on volume). They don't need to organize their receipts, insurance Explanations of Benefits, or other documentation beyond that. If they face a personal income tax return audit, they can produce the appropriate documents and organize them. *[See IRS Notice 2004-50, Q&A 79.]*

Account Administrative Fees

HSA account fees. Most administrators charge monthly administrative fees that typically range from $2.50 to $5.00 to maintain the account. Some administrators waive these fees if the account owner maintains a minimum cash balance during the month. In many arrangements, your client's employer pays the fees directly to the administrator as long as she remains an active employee enrolled in the underlying HSA-qualified medical coverage. If she switches medical plans at renewal or terminates employment, her employer (or former employer) may stop paying the administrative fee for her.

In addition, administrators may charge other standard banking fees. Typical fees include:

- fee to print checks;
- fee to issue a bank check to the account owner, a provider, or another HSA administrator if, for example, your client transfers some or all of her balance;
- fee to receive monthly account statements in paper form (rather than electronic);
- fee to receive annual tax documents in paper form (rather than electronic);
- standard bank fees for stop-payment on a check, insufficient account balance to cover a check, and account research (such as retrieving a copy of an old check); and
- fee to close an account.

Paying account fees directly from the HSA. Some administrators withdraw monthly administrative fees directly from the account. While this process is convenient, your clients lose medical equity because their maximum contributions aren't adjusted upward to reflect these distributions for administrative expenses. On the other hand, the payment is made with pre-tax funds. It's important to understand not only the fees, but how they're paid. *[See IRS Notice 2004-50, Q&A 69.]*

Paying fees outside the HSA. If an administrator allows fees to be paid outside the HSA, this feature helps your clients preserve medical equity. Paying fees from funds other than those contributed to an HSA doesn't affect your clients' annual HSA contribution limit. *[See IRS Notice 2004-50, Q&A 71.]*

Building Balances

Interest on deposits. Most HSA administrators pay interest on account balances, though some offer basic accounts that don't pay interest and have low or no monthly administrative fees. In today's low-rate environment, HSA owners can't expect to earn more than a fraction of a percent (typically 0.05% to 0.50%) on low balances. Some administrators pay a uniform rate of interest regardless of balance. Others offered tiered interest structures that pay a higher percentage on larger balances. Your clients may be able to earn 1.0% to 1.5% on high balances ($10,000 or more). Terms vary by HSA administrator.

Though it's nice to have an account that pays interest, be sure to advise your clients to weigh interest income and administrative expenses. An average daily balance of $1,000 at a 0.05% interest rate earns a total of $5 annually. If your client has a choice between an account that pays a low rate of interest with a monthly fee and an account that pays no interest with a much lower fee, she is likely to be better off financially with the latter account.

Investment options. Most—but not all—HSA administrators offer investment options available to account owners once they reach a certain cash balance (which varies by administrator and typically is set between $1,000 and $2,500). Every HSA administrator offers a different investment menu. Most offer anywhere from about a dozen and a half to four dozen mutual fund, bond, and money-market options. They choose their menu with a goal of giving clients a variety of funds in different asset classes without an overwhelming number of options. With too many choices, some owners may suffer from "paralysis by analysis," spending their time comparing hundreds of funds rather than investing in some best-in-class options.

You can provide invaluable advice to your clients when they choose a primary or second HSA. One administrator's investment menu may be far better suited to your client and her investment strategy than another's. *[See IRS Notice 2004-50, Q&A 65.]*

Auto-investment. Many HSA administrators have systems that allow owners who have met the investment threshold to direct all future contributions right to investments in proportions that the owner has set. For example, if your client chooses to have future contributions invested equally in four funds (25% contribution to each fund), the administrator automatically processes these trades with each new contribution to the account.

You may advise your clients that, as performance varies in each investment over time, they need to rebalance the portfolio. And you certainly will advise them to look at their HSA investment portfolio not merely in isolation, but also as part of an overall portfolio that includes retirement accounts and taxable investments. An "unbalanced" HSA investment portfolio (for example, heavily weighted toward foreign growth stocks) may be perfectly appropriate if, when combined with your clients' other investments, it results in a balanced approach to investing total long-term assets.

Investment fees. Some HSA administrators charge investment fees in the form of a monthly charge for access to the investment platform or a per-trade levy. Many don't. This is an important variable that you and your clients need to evaluate when choosing an HSA administrator. High investment fees reduce investment gains and magnify losses.

High investment fees reduce investment gains and magnify losses.

Investment advice. HSA administrators don't offer investment advice. The investment platform vendor (such as Charles Schwab or TDAmeritrade) typically employs licensed investment professionals with whom account owners can consult to review financial goals, discuss other long-term investments (like assets invested in retirement accounts), and guide them in assembling an appropriate portfolio of investments.

As more HSA owners accumulate higher balances (nationally, HSA owners who invest a portion of their balances have an average HSA balance of

$14,000), a nascent trend in the industry is for the administrator itself to offer portfolio advice and services for an additional fee. These services can range from simple advice to the account owner (who then decides whether to execute the recommended transactions) to the administrator's active management of the owner's account.

Prohibited transactions. This topic is explored in detail in Chapter 11, *Self-Directed HSAs*. Most HSA administrators allow investment only in a subset of publicly traded instruments, including select mutual funds and bonds as standard investment options and perhaps stocks or exchange-traded funds. These investments are all permitted under IRS regulations. When individual HSA owners venture beyond these instruments to invest in real estate, businesses, and issuance of private debt, they run the risk of engaging in prohibited transactions.

Other potential transactions include an owner's pledging an HSA as collateral for a loan, a bank's lending money to an individual's HSA, or an owner's borrowing directly from his HSA. An HSA administrator can ensure that it doesn't extend a loan to an HSA and that owners don't make prohibited transactions within their HSAs, but it can't monitor accounts and account owners to ensure that they avoid all potential prohibited transactions.

The penalty for prohibited transactions is steep. The entire balance is distributed immediately. That amount is subject to income taxes and, if applicable, a 20% additional tax as a penalty. *[See IRS Notice 2004-50, Q&A 67* and *Q&A 68* and *IRS Notice 2008-59, Q&A 34, Q&A 35, Q&A 36,* and *Q&A 37.]*

Asset Protection

Asset protection from bank failure. Most HSA balances are held in accounts protected by FDIC insurance up to $250,000. FDIC insurance gives HSA balances the same degree of protection that their owners enjoy with other bank accounts. Some HSAs may be administered by state-chartered banks that offer state-level protection similar to—or perhaps better than—the FDIC program.

Asset protection in cases of divorce. Like any other asset, HSA balances are assets subject to a settlement in a divorce proceeding. A judge can order that your client give a portion of her HSA balances to a soon-to-be ex-spouse. In these cases, the spouse opens his own HSA (whether or not he is HSA-eligible) and your client transfers a portion of her HSA balances into that HSA. The transfer isn't subject to taxes because it isn't a distribution. See Chapter 25, *Different Family Structures, Different Rules*, for more information about transferring HSA balances as part of a divorce settlement.

Asset protection and bankruptcy. HSAs currently do not enjoy the same bankruptcy protection as many retirement plans under federal law. In a Chapter 7 bankruptcy, a bankruptcy trustee can order distributions from HSAs and use them to repay unsecured creditors.

States also have a role in defining which assets are exempt from bankruptcy proceedings. Some states, such as Virginia, have granted this protection to HSAs. In most jurisdictions, though, HSA balances, like most other personal assets, are available to fund a settlement. *[See in re Leitch, 49 BR 918 (B.A.P., Eighth Circuit, July 16, 2013).]*

HSAs and escheatment. There is no federal standard to determine when an HSA is considered abandoned property. State law governs this feature of HSAs. In general, HSAs are less likely than retirement accounts to be considered abandoned because owners can tap funds from these accounts tax-free at any time and thus generate more activity in these accounts. In contrast, retirement account assets typically aren't spent until age 59½ or later, so it's not uncommon for owners of a small IRA to forget about the account in the course of several relocations and changes in banking relationships. Still, HSAs are subject to applicable state escheatment laws.

Correcting Errors

Reversing excess contributions. Administrators aren't required to help HSA owners correct excess contributions, but nearly all do. If your client has contributed in excess of the statutory annual maximum to his HSA, advise him to contact his HSA administrator (and employer, if he contributed through pre-tax payroll contributions) promptly to begin the process of reversing the error. He can withdraw the excess contribution amount (and any earnings on it) before he files his personal income tax return that year with no penalty.

If he doesn't reverse the excess contribution by then, your client must include the excess contribution (and earnings on it) in his taxable income for the year that he made the excess contribution—filing an amended personal income tax return if necessary—and pay a 6% excise tax on the excess contribution (and earnings on it). And he must withdraw the funds from the account. *[See IRS Notice 2004-2, Q&A 22.]*

Reversing non-excess contributions. The rules are different for HSA owners who want to reverse a non-excess contribution to spend funds not needed to reimburse qualified expenses on something else. In that case, the reversal isn't permitted.

Example: *Rosa funds her HSA to the self-only contribution limit in early March after she receives her year-end bonus. She incurs very low out-of-pocket expenses and decides that the bonus money is better spent on a quick getaway to the Caribbean during Thanksgiving week.*

Rosa seeks information from her HSA administrator and learns that she can't withdraw the funds without including the withdrawal in her taxable income (which she expected) and paying the 20% penalty for a distribution for a non-qualified expense (which she didn't expect).

Reversing contributions without penalty can occur only when the amount of the reversal represents a contribution above an HSA owner's statutory maximum contribution for the year. *[See IRS Notice 2004-50, Q&A 35.]*

Reversing mistaken distributions. Administrators aren't required to perform this service, but again nearly all do. After all, an HSA owner is a customer—and a customer with account balances that the administrator can lend to generate income.

The reversal isn't automatically approved. The rules state clearly that the mistake must be "as the result of a mistake of fact due to reasonable cause." The author's interpretation: Your client paid a provider from his HSA, and his medical plan later reprocesses the claims and reverses his financial responsibility—probably OK. . . . Your client "accidentally" paid his mortgage from his HSA for the fourth time in six months because his biweekly paycheck schedule didn't line up with his mortgage due date—probably not OK.

A mistake must be "as the result of a mistake of fact due to reasonable cause."

Here are typical situations in which HSA owners make a mistaken distribution:

- they pay for some non-qualified items along with qualified items while shopping at the pharmacy with an HSA debit card that isn't coded to restrict their purchases to HSA-qualified items,

- their insurer reprocesses a claim and reduces or eliminates their financial responsibility for the service, or

- they pay for a service at the time of service (such as an emergency room at an out-of-network facility or dental services) and an insurer subsequently pays some or all of the financial responsibility after they file a claim.

In these cases, your client needs to contact her HSA administrator or visit its Web site. Administrators typically have a short form that the account owner completes, indicating the amount of and reason for the mistaken distribution. Your client submits that form, along with a check to return the funds to the account. As long as the mistake appears to be inadvertent, the administrator probably will accept the funds and adjust the account balance accordingly. *[See IRS Notice 2004-50, Q&A 37.]*

Counseling Your Clients

✓ Make sure your clients understand the limits of their administrator's compliance responsibility.

✓ Help your clients who seek an independent TPA (rather than one chosen by an employer) evaluate their options.

✓ Determine whether your client should open a second HSA either to segregate balances to preserve for tax-free distributions for qualified expenses in retirement or to take advantage of account features like better investment options or lower fees.

✓ Help your clients understand their HSA investment options and integrate their HSA investments into their overall long-term investment strategy and portfolio.

✓ Be sure that your clients understand HSA rules. Their HSA administrator isn't responsible for keeping HSAs in compliance with IRS regulations. Administrators provide basic information and some safeguards, but not legal or compliance advice.

- ✓ Help your clients understand HSA fees. Be sure that they minimize what they pay to maintain their accounts. Many administrators now charge a fee to send printed monthly statements (vs. free delivery of electronic copies) and distributions by paper checks (vs. free delivery by electronic transfer). The statement fees can be avoided easily by selecting electronic delivery. Your clients must find out how to do so if their administrator's default method of delivery is paper statements.

- ✓ Be sure your clients maintain a record of receipts in case the IRS audits their personal income tax return. Remember, unlike a Health FSA, in which the plan administrator requests records to substantiate purchases, HSA administrators don't verify that withdrawals are for qualified expenses. Your clients must know what expenses are qualified for reimbursement, report this activity when they file their personal income tax return, and maintain adequate records in case the IRS reviews their activity as part of an audit of their personal income tax return.

- ✓ Suggest that your clients review information in their HSA administrator's educational library. These libraries typically contain multi-media resources to help HSA owners understand how to manage their HSAs to remain in compliance with IRS regulations and to maximize their balances.

- ✓ Help your clients work with their HSA administrators to correct excess contributions or mistaken distributions before filing their personal income tax return for that year. The sooner they address these issues, the better.

CHAPTER 21

Moving Money Between Accounts

Most HSA owners own and manage only a single account. This strategy makes sense when that one account—often chosen by a current or former employer—meets the owner's needs and preferences. In the case of a more sophisticated owner or an account with high fees or limited investment options, owners may want to move funds from one HSA to another account as either a one-time or a recurring transaction.

At the same time, an HSA is a health-reimbursement as well as a long-term savings account. Owners may have balances in other accounts that they can transfer into their HSAs. They need to know which accounts' balances can be rolled to an HSA and the rules associated with each transaction.

This chapter discusses

- two methods of moving funds from one HSA to another,
- whether your clients can move funds from an employer's Health FSA or HRA to a new HSA, and
- the rules for, benefits of, and potential pitfalls associated with moving funds from an IRA to an HSA.

HSA administrators aren't required to accept rollovers. While HSA owners can roll over funds from one HSA to another, HSA administrators aren't required to accommodate your clients' attempts to move balances to an account that they administer. It's unlikely, however, that an administrator would actually deny that transaction. Administrators and their affiliated financial institutions are in the business of attracting assets; to deny a transfer robs them of balances that they otherwise would hold. Further, the rollover process is well established in the IRA world and works seamlessly, thus providing HSA administrators with a detailed blueprint to create a simple process. *[See IRS Notice 2004-2, Q&A 23* and *IRS Notice 2004-50, Q&A 78.]*

Moving funds between two HSAs when the owner is no longer HSA-eligible. HSA owners who are no longer eligible to make contributions to their HSA don't lose their ability to open new HSAs or to move funds from one HSA to another. This flexibility is important as your clients' needs change over time. Your recently retired clients may want to consolidate their finances by moving their HSA balances from their former employer's preferred administrator to an HSA administered by their personal bank or investment platform. In retirement, they may want to move funds from their current investment-focused HSA to another account that helps them preserve their accumulated medical equity with lower fees and higher interest rates on CDs. *[See IRS Notice 2008-59, Q&A 20.]*

Moving funds between two HSAs via rollover. HSA owners can make one rollover per year from one HSA to another HSA, as long as they own both accounts. The process is straightforward. The owner requests a distribution from her HSA, takes possession of the funds, and then deposits the money in another HSA within 60 days of receipt. But this action has been dubbed *playing with fire* for decades in the IRA world because any funds not deposited within 60 days are considered a distribution for non-qualified expenses. The distribution is then included in taxable income and subject to an additional 20% tax. *[See IRS Notice 2008-59, Q&A 20.]*

Moving funds between two HSAs via trustee-to-trustee transfer. HSA owners can make an unlimited number of transfers between two HSAs that they own. In this process, your client works with one administrator (usually the receiving firm) and completes paperwork to initiate the transfer. The administrator then contacts the other HSA administrator to move the money. This process has been well established for decades in the IRA world. Because your client never takes possession of the funds, this form of transfer removes the risk of *playing with fire.*

Owners can make an unlimited number of transfers between two HSAs that they own.

Trustee-to-trustee transfers can be an important strategy in a number of situations:

- Your client is locked into an employer's HSA administrator. She can receive employer and her own pre-tax payroll contributions into one HSA and then move her balances regularly to the HSA of her choice.
- Your client wants to segregate her HSA balances that she's accumulating as medical equity. If she wants to ensure that she doesn't spend balances but instead preserves the funds to reimburse qualified expenses tax-free in retirement, she can transfer the balances into a second HSA that she doesn't tap.
- Your client changes jobs and begins to participate in an HSA program with a new administrator. She can work with the old and new administrators to move her balances to simplify her HSA management and compliance responsibility without running the risk of "playing with fire."

The first two strategies—owning more than one HSA—may result in multiple administrative fees, multiple minimum balances, and possible fees to execute transfers. The third strategy typically involves account closing fees that usually run between $18 and $30. *[See IRS Notice 2008-59, Q&A 20.]*

Administrators aren't required to accept rollovers or transfers. As with excess contributions and mistaken distributions (refer to Chapter 20, *HSA Administration*), administrators don't have to accept rollovers or transfers. It's hard to imagine why one wouldn't, however, as the result is increased assets under management through a simple process that's been well tested for more than four decades with IRAs. An administrator does *not* have the option of not complying with a rollover or transfer request to move money from that administrator to another. *[See IRS Notice 2004-50, Q&A 78* and *IRS Notice 2008-59, Q&A 20.]*

Moving funds between an MSA and an HSA. HSA owners can move funds between an MSA, the forerunner of HSAs, and an HSA via either a rollover or a trustee-to-trustee transfer. The reverse isn't true: An HSA owner can't transfer or roll over balances to an existing MSA. If you have an HSA-eligible client with an old MSA, she should move her balances to an HSA to consolidate balances and reduce her administrative and compliance burden. She will enjoy more flexibility and features with an HSA than with an MSA. *[See IRS Notice 2004-50, Q&A 78.]*

Moving Health FSA balances into an HSA. Individuals who end a Health FSA plan year with a balance are *not* permitted to move those funds to an

HSA. The HOPE Act, passed in late 2006, allowed individuals to make a one-time transfer between 2007 and 2011. Few HSA owners were able to transfer unused Health FSA balances because the law severely restricted those who were eligible.

If your client is shifting from a Health FSA to an HSA and has a balance near the end of the Health FSA year, it's important to understand the design of the Health FSA. If it has a grace period or a limited carryover, those features may affect her ability to open and contribute to an HSA. Be sure to read Chapter 23, *Health FSAs and HSA Eligibility*, for this critical information.

Moving HRA balances into an HSA. HRA owners are **not** allowed to roll over balances to an HSA. Rollovers were allowed between 2007 and 2011, though restrictive rules limited the number of people who were actually eligible to execute a rollover.

Moving 401(k) plan funds into an HSA. HSA owners can't roll over funds from a traditional or Roth 401(k) plan to an HSA. If they can move those funds from a 401(k) plan to an IRA, they can then make a one-time rollover from an IRA into an HSA. See Chapter 8, *Rolling an IRA Balance to an HSA*, to learn more.

Moving IRA funds to an HSA. HSA owners who are HSA-eligible can make a once-per-lifetime rollover from a traditional or Roth IRA (though a Roth rollover doesn't make sense financially) to an HSA. This opportunity may be appropriate for your clients who want to move retirement funds from a tax-deferred to a tax-free account.

It comes with some opportunity costs and risk. The rollover counts against that year's maximum contribution, so your clients who roll over an IRA balance forfeit immediate tax savings that they would otherwise enjoy on contributions. They face a risk if they take possession of the funds rather than have the two administrators transfer the balance. If they take possession of the IRA funds and don't make the deposit in the HSA within 60 days, the entire transfer becomes a premature withdrawal from an IRA. It is then included in taxable income and subject to an additional 10% tax as a penalty.

A key point here is that the HSA owner who executes a balance transfer from an IRA to an HSA must be HSA-eligible when she moves the funds from her IRA to her HSA and must subsequently remain HSA-eligible for 12 full months after the transfer. These rules are covered in more detail in Chapter 8, *Rolling an IRA Balance to an HSA*.

Counseling Your Clients

- ✓ Review your clients' HSA strategies to determine whether they need to open another HSA or replace a current HSA by rolling over balances into a new HSA.
- ✓ Make sure your clients who currently participate in their employer's Health FSA or HRA program understand that they can't build HSA balances quickly by transferring unused balances from either current program into their new HSAs.

CHAPTER 22

HSA Tax Reporting

Compliance with federal tax law is a critical responsibility for your clients who own HSAs. The burden may seem daunting at first to clients familiar with Health FSAs. These clients are accustomed to relying on FSA administrators, who assume most of the responsibility for gathering the information to ensure compliance. In contrast, HSAs are self-administered plans that place the compliance responsibility squarely on the shoulders of owners.

Tax reporting is one feature of compliance that Health FSA participants don't face. Though the mention of tax compliance may draw a visceral reaction from some clients, the truth is that HSA tax reporting is fairly straightforward.

This chapter reviews

- how your clients' tax-reporting responsibilities as HSA owners differ from Health FSA and HRA participants',
- where and how your clients report HSA activity on a personal income tax return,
- what information your clients' HSA administrators provide to help them prepare their tax return, and
- what calculations they need to make to determine any tax liability that results from HSA distributions.

With the additional freedom that HSAs allow versus Health FSAs and HRAs comes another level of participant/owner responsibility. Health FSAs and HRAs are employer-sponsored benefit plans, and the employer (as the plan sponsor) and its contracted third-party administrator are largely responsible for compliance. They ensure that participants' elections don't exceed the annual IRS limit, distributions are for qualified expenses only, and the program complies with rules designed to ensure that it doesn't disproportionately benefit higher-paid employees.

In contrast, HSAs are financial accounts owned by individual employees. Employers and their administration partners have few responsibilities to ensure that employees manage their accounts consistent with federal law.

Here's a quick breakdown of some of the most relevant responsibilities.

Ensure that employees don't exceed annual election/ contribution limits:

- Health FSAs and HRAs are offered only through employers. Employers ensure that employees don't make a Health FSA election in excess of the IRS annual limit and that HRA participants receive the proper account balance credit in their notional accounts.

- In contrast, your clients can contribute to an HSA either through pre-tax payroll or with funds from a personal account. An employer can monitor contributions through a Cafeteria Plan to flag contributions in excess of the IRS limit based on level of coverage (self-only or family contract) and age (additional $1,000 catch-up contribution for employees age 55 or older). But the employer may not know whether the employee had a disqualifying event that didn't make her HSA-eligible all 12 months and certainly can't monitor an employee's personal contributions made outside the Cafeteria Plan.

Ensure that distributions are for qualified expenses:

- Health FSA and HRA funds are available for qualified expenses only, as set by the federal tax code (with additional restrictions by the employer permitted). Plan administrators must substantiate all distributions to ensure that they are for qualified expenses only.

- In contrast, HSA owners can make account distributions for any expense, though withdrawals for non-qualified expenses are subject to income taxes and possible penalties. Neither an employer nor an HSA administrator can require substantiation as a condition of withdrawals from an HSA.

Ensure that account information is reported correctly to the IRS:

- Health FSA and HRA participants don't file any additional forms with their federal personal income tax return because the programs are employer-sponsored and substantiation is ongoing. Tax issues related to these arrangements are handled through existing employer documentation. For example, if a Health FSA or HRA participant fails to substantiate an expense, the administrator may inform the employer, who then can add that amount to the employee's taxable income through Form W-2.

- In contrast, HSA owners receive certain tax forms from their HSA administrator and must use some of this information to complete a form that they include in their personal income tax return filing.

Form 1099-SA. Your clients receive annual Form 1099 statements that reflect activity in other financial accounts. They receive one when they have an HSA as well. The form has an "SA" suffix to reflect the fact that the statement summarizes HSA activity.

Form 1099-SA provides a single figure: annual distributions from the HSA. Form 1099-SA doesn't identify distributions as being for qualified or non-qualified expenses. It can't, since HSA administrators don't substantiate distributions as qualified. And it doesn't break them down by debit card, HSA paper check, and direct deposit in the participant's personal bank account. It merely reflects total withdrawals from the account during the prior calendar year.

Form 1099-SA doesn't identify distributions as being for qualified or non-qualified expenses.

HSA administrators must send this document by Jan. 31. HSA owners then use this information to help them complete their personal income tax return. They must review their records to determine how much of their total distributions were for qualified expenses and how much were for non-qualified items. The sum of those figures must equal the total distributions reported on Form 1099-SA.

Your clients should retain Form 1099-SA for their records, just as they do their other Form 1099s for other investments, their Form W-2s, and other tax documents. The IRS receives a copy from the administrator to compare with your clients' tax return.

Form 5498-SA. Administrators are required to issue this form no later than May 31 of the following calendar year (for example, by May 31, 2019, for the 2018 calendar year) to both account owners and the IRS. This form shows total contributions to the account from all sources and the fair market value of the HSA as of the date the form is issued.

Administrators aren't required to issue the form until May 31 because your clients can make elections to their HSA for a particular tax year up to the due date (without extensions) of federal income tax returns (by April 16, 2019, for 2018 tax returns). Some administrators issue an unofficial preliminary Form 5498-SA by Jan. 31 to help HSA owners complete their income tax return. As long as your clients don't make additional contributions after Dec. 31 for a given tax year, they can rely on that form.

Your clients can also rely on other sources of information to calculate total contributions. If their only deposits are through pre-tax payroll at work, they can refer to Box 12 on the Form W-2 that their employers provide by Jan. 31. That figure includes both employer contributions (if any) and employee contributions through pre-tax payroll. These two sources are summed into a single figure labeled "employer contribution." Don't worry—the source is irrelevant, as Form 8889 (more in a moment) asks for total contributions from all sources on Line 2.

Another means of determining total contributions is to ask the HSA administrator. In fact, the figure may appear as a line item on your clients' online portals. The portal also probably includes a record of all transactions, including contributions, that your client or his tax professional can sum to calculate this figure.

As with Form 1099-SA, your clients keep this form in their tax files rather than submit it with their personal income tax return. The administrator sends a duplicate copy to the IRS.

Form 8889. Your clients need to complete this form and submit it with their personal income tax return if they make any contributions to or take any distributions from their HSAs in a given calendar year. The form is slightly longer than a page. Most clients need to fill in no more than half a dozen boxes and then reflect no tax liability (so long as all distributions were for qualified expenses).

Tax software packages ask buyers whether they have an HSA. If they answer affirmatively, the software walks them though the questions required to complete Form 8889.

Counseling Your Clients

- ✓ Make sure your clients retain the tax forms that their administrators send in their tax files as back-up in case of an audit.

- ✓ Counsel your clients to make sure that they complete Form 8889 and submit it with their personal income tax return.

SECTION V

Special Compliance Issues

INTRODUCTION TO SECTION V

The compliance discussion in Section IV was organized by broad subject area, such as eligibility, contributions, and distributions. Now, it's time to merge some of that information and go into greater depth to review compliance issues under certain circumstances.

This section applies rules for HSA eligibility, contribution, and distribution to specific situations, such as unmarried life partners, clients enrolled in partners' employers' Health FSA or HRA programs, adult children who are no longer the parent's tax dependents, and clients who are approaching (or have already reached) age 65 and their eligibility to enroll in Medicare.

This section is designed to bring all the compliance rules for any of these situations under one roof so that you and your clients can understand the role that family members' coverage and family structures play in determining your clients' (and their family members') HSA eligibility.

CHAPTER 23

Health FSAs and HSA Eligibility

Tens of millions of Americans are enrolled in their employers' Health FSA programs, and Health FSAs cover about 100 million Americans in a typical year. As discussed previously, Health FSAs provide tax benefits and cash-flow advantages to participants, who can pay for qualified expenses with pre-tax dollars and access their entire election for the year at any point in the year, irrespective of how much the employer has deducted from their paychecks.

Employees who understand and participate in Health FSAs are natural candidates for a transition to HSAs, which have all the tax advantages of a Health FSA with the additional benefit of a long time horizon that allows owners to build medical equity. Unfortunately, in some cases, these ideal candidates aren't eligible to open and contribute to an HSA when their employers first offer the program because their Health FSA participation creates an HSA eligibility issue.

This chapter reviews

- why a Health FSA is a qualified employer-sponsored benefit (like employer-sponsored medical coverage) and the implications for HSA eligibility;
- different "extenders" that employers can use to give Health FSA participants more time to spend their balances, and how those extenders may delay their ability to open and contribute to an HSA; and
- what steps participants and employers can take to minimize the HSA eligibility issue.

Health FSA Defined

A Health FSA is an employer-sponsored benefit plan that allows employees to elect to receive a portion of their pay in the form of tax-free reimbursement of certain health-related expenses. Health FSAs are popular with employees who face out-of-pocket expenses, including medical cost-sharing (copays, deductibles, and coinsurance), dental (such as fillings, restorative treatment, and orthodontia), vision (such as prescription glasses and sunglasses, contact lenses, and vision correction surgery), and certain over-the-counter drugs and medicine (reimbursable only with a valid prescription) and equipment and supplies.

Participating employees make a binding annual election that they can change only with a qualifying life event (such as birth, marriage, adoption, or divorce), not with a sudden change in actual or projected expenses. Their employer then divides the election by the number of pay periods and deducts that amount from each paycheck during the year, regardless of the pace at which the participant spends the funds.

The plan automatically covers the employee, her spouse, her tax dependents, and children to age 26 (whether or not those children remain her tax dependents). All of these family members' qualified expenses can be reimbursed from the Health FSA, even if these individuals aren't enrolled in her employer-sponsored medical coverage.

Participants derive two major benefits from the program.

First, employers deduct participants' Health FSA elections with pre-tax dollars, which means that no FICA taxes and no federal (and, if assessed, state) income taxes are withheld. The Health FSA gives these participants, in effect, an average 25% discount coupon on every qualified item that they purchase.

Second, participants can spend their entire election at any time during the year. This provision, called uniform coverage, allows participants with high medical expenses early in the year to sleep well at night, since funds are available for immediate spending. And some participants are able to negotiate prompt-payment discounts because the funds are available immediately. For example, the author's family received a $500 discount on each of two restorative dental procedures and a $400 discount on vision correction surgery—in addition to tax savings—by paying at the time of service with a Health FSA debit card loaded with the full annual election.

Federal tax law defines Health FSAs as a self-insured, limited-benefit plan, similar in some respects to a medical plan. Participants pay a fixed premium per pay period for coverage, just as they do for medical coverage. The coverage is limited, and each participant chooses her own limit. It's self-insured because the employer assumes liability for all claims. Employees pay a premium, but the premium isn't always equal to the benefit derived (participants can leave employment mid-year having spent more or less than they contributed, while a participant who remains employed may simply not spend her entire election).

The fact that a Health FSA is considered a benefit plan is relevant to you and your clients for two reasons.

First, a Health FSA must abide by some important ACA rules that apply to other employer-sponsored plans, such as covering children to age 26 whether or not they remain the subscriber's tax dependent.

Second, its status as a benefit plan must be considered when you and your clients review certain potential strategies to further reduce their taxable income and increase their accumulation of medical equity.

Health FSAs and HSAs

Individuals who enroll in their employer's general Health FSA aren't HSA-eligible. HSA eligibility rules place restrictions on other coverage to which individuals may have access and still be HSA-eligible. In this case, the individual is enrolled in an employer-sponsored medical plan and a separate benefit plan, both of which must satisfy the design requirements of an HSA-qualified plan in order for the individual to be eligible to contribute to an HSA. A Health FSA that reimburses the first dollar (no deductible) of medical expenses is disqualifying coverage. *[See IRS Rev. Rul. 2004-45, Situation 1.]*

A Health FSA that reimburses the first dollar (no deductible) of medical expenses is disqualifying coverage.

Individuals whose *spouses* enroll in their employer's general Health FSA program aren't HSA-eligible, either. Under federal tax law, a Health FSA automatically covers the employee, the employee's spouse, and the employee's tax dependents and children to age 26 unless the employer restricts this list (which is rare). Thus, if your client is enrolled in an HSA-qualified medical plan at work and doesn't enroll in her employer's Health FSA program, but her husband enrolls in his employer's general Health FSA, his enrollment disqualifies both of them (and anyone else on the medical plan, such as a non-tax-dependent child who otherwise might be HSA-eligible) from opening, contributing to, or receiving an employer contribution to an HSA. *[See IRS Rev. Rul. 2004-45, Situation 1.]*

Wanting to become HSA-eligible isn't a qualifying event to terminate Health FSA coverage. Health FSA participants can't disenroll from or alter their election into a Health FSA without a qualifying life event. A desire to open and contribute to an HSA promptly upon enrolling in an HSA-qualified medical plan isn't a qualifying life event to terminate participation in a Health FSA. These individuals can't become HSA-eligible before the end of their Health FSA plan year—or perhaps even later if their plan has a provision allowing them to reimburse qualified expenses that they incur after the end of the 12-month plan year.

Spending the entire election doesn't terminate Health FSA coverage. A Health FSA participant remains enrolled in the plan during the entire plan year, even if she exhausts her entire annual election before the end of the year. She can't become HSA-eligible while the Health FSA plan year is still running, even if she has spent her annual balance.

Non-aligned medical plan and Health FSA plan years create eligibility issues. It's not unusual for employers to choose different renewal dates for their medical plans and Health FSAs. This timing is problematic. For example, if the employer introduces an HSA-qualified medical plan for an effective date of Oct. 1, employees who participate in the Health FSA program that runs on the calendar year can't become HSA-eligible to open or contribute to an HSA before Jan. 1.

> Example: *Banu works for a municipality with a July 1 anniversary date for medical coverage. She wants to enroll in the new HSA program effective July 1, 2019. She participates in the municipality's general Health FSA, which runs on the calendar year.*

Banu can enroll in the HSA-qualified medical plan, but she can't open (and therefore can't accept an employer contribution or make employee contributions) to an HSA before Jan. 1, 2020. She can reimburse any qualified expenses that she incurs between July 1 and Dec. 31, 2019, from her Health FSA, though she can't increase her election to cover anticipated expenses during this time period. She can't reimburse any of those expenses from her HSA because she can't establish her HSA before Jan. 1, 2020.

This issue becomes more problematic the longer the two plans overlap. And it's magnified because employees who understand the tax-saving advantages of a Health FSA are the most likely candidates to enroll in an HSA program.

Participating employees can't resolve this issue themselves. Employers do have some options—grace periods and carryovers—but each one is a bitter pill that can affect everyone enrolled in the Health FSA program. Let's look at these options next.

Health FSAs with grace periods can negatively affect HSA eligibility. Employers are allowed to attach a grace period to Health FSAs—an additional 2½ months during which participants can continue to incur qualified expenses and reimburse them from their Health FSA. This extension of the plan year, which overlaps a new Health FSA plan year, allows participants to "double up" on reimbursements if, for example, they want to reimburse the entire cost of vision correction surgery or pay the full bill for orthodontic care up front to receive a prompt-pay discount.

Under federal tax law, if a participant enters the grace period with any remaining cash balance in her general Health FSA, she doesn't become HSA-eligible any earlier than the first day of the first month following the end of her grace period. In most cases, that translates to the first day of the fourth month after the end of the 12-month Health FSA plan year.

Example: *Zhang Min has $141 remaining in her 2018 Health FSA as of Jan. 1, 2019, the beginning of her plan's grace period. She enrolls in her employer's HSA plan as of Jan. 1, 2019.*

She can reimburse qualified expenses that she incurs between Jan. 1 and March 15, 2019, from her 2018 Health FSA. She can't reimburse tax-free any qualified expenses that she incurs between March 16 and March 31, 2019. Beginning April 1, 2019, as long as Zhang Min satisfies all HSA eligibility requirements, she can establish her HSA, contribute to her account (and accept employer contributions), and reimburse tax-free qualified expenses.

There is no limit to the amount of her annual election that a participant can spend during the grace period. Think of the grace period as allowing an *unlimited rollover* for a *limited period of time.*

Fortunately, there are some measures that participants or employers can take so that the grace period doesn't delay their opening and contributing to an HSA.

Health FSA carryovers can negatively affect HSA eligibility. Employers can permit participating employees to carry over up to $500 into a new Health FSA plan year. This feature, like the grace period, makes Health FSAs more attractive because it reduces the likelihood that participants forfeit unused balances at the end of the plan year.

There is no limit to the amount of her annual election that a participant can spend during the grace period.

At the same time, the carryover can create even bigger eligibility issues for participants who don't understand the rules and plan accordingly. If your clients carry over any balance (even a penny) in a general Health FSA into the following plan year, they are disqualified from opening or contributing to an HSA during that entire Health FSA plan year.

Example: *Kaito didn't make an election into his employer's Health FSA for 2019 because he wanted to enroll in the HSA program. He didn't realize that the 2018 Health FSA had a carryover provision. His employer carried over the $15 balance—money that Kaito thought he had forfeited—into a general Health FSA for use in 2019.*

Kaito can remain enrolled in the HSA-qualified medical plan, but he can't open or contribute to an HSA before the end of the 2019 Health FSA plan year. He can apply the $15 carryover balance to any cost-sharing that he incurs on his HSA-qualified medical plan (as well as dental, vision, and certain over-the-counter expenses), but he can't reimburse tax-free any other qualified expenses that he incurs in 2019 when he opens and funds his HSA in 2020.

There is no time limit on spending funds that carry over from a prior plan year. Think of the carryover as allowing a *limited carryover* of unused funds for an *unlimited period of time.*

Fortunately, there are some measures that your clients or their employers can take so that the carryover doesn't delay a participant's opening and contributing to an HSA.

Solving the Health FSA/HSA Eligibility Issue

Some of the HSA eligibility issues that Health FSAs create can be erased with proper identification and planning. Others can't. Let's review what can and can't be overcome.

Non-aligned plan years. If your client participates in her employer's Health FSA with one anniversary date and the employer introduces an HSA program with another anniversary date, your client will have an eligibility issue that she can't solve painlessly herself. As noted earlier, she can't open or contribute to an HSA (or accept an employer contribution) as long as she's covered on a general Health FSA. And she's covered on her Health FSA through at least the end of the plan year, regardless of when she exhausts her election.

She and her employer each have two options in this situation. None is ideal.

First, her employer can prospectively terminate the general Health FSA as of the day prior to the effective date of the HSA program. But this change affects every Health FSA participant, not just those who want to enroll in the HSA program. Every participant will be either a winner or a loser, depending on whether she has spent more than she has deposited (she wins; the employer covers the shortfall) or she has deposited more than she has spent (the employer wins; she forfeits her remaining balance to her employer, who can't return the funds to her).

Second, and a little less drastic, her employer can convert the general Health FSA prospectively to a Limited-Purpose Health FSA to reimburse dental and vision expenses only. This option allows participants to spend their elections, but on a much narrower range of services. It too creates winners and losers, depending on participants' remaining balances and their projected use of funds.

Third, she can delay enrollment in the HSA program for a year, decline to participate in the general Health FSA at renewal, and then enroll in the HSA program. This option robs her of a year of paying lower premiums. It also leaves her with a period of time between the end of the Health FSA plan year and the effective date of the HSA program during which her incurred expenses aren't qualified for reimbursement from either tax-advantaged account.

Fourth, she can enroll in the HSA-qualified plan, delay opening her HSA, and reimburse qualified expenses through her general Health FSA. She can then open her HSA on the first day of the first month that she satisfies HSA eligibility requirements (presumably the first day of the first month after the end of the Health FSA plan year). She reaps the benefit of lower premiums, can open and contribute to her HSA sooner, and eliminates a gap between reimbursement programs. She may not have elected a sufficient sum in her Health FSA, however, to cover potential out-of-pocket responsibility under the HSA-qualified coverage.

The best option is for an employee (or benefits advisor, third-party representative, or insurer representative) to be proactive and discuss aligning the Health FSA and medical-plan anniversary dates before introduction of an HSA program. When the medical plan and Health FSA share the same effective date of coverage, employers and employees avoid choosing from among these four less attractive alternatives.

Grace period. Your client who is enrolled in a general Health FSA with a grace period can become HSA-eligible on the first day after the regular plan year (the first day of the grace period) if she spends her entire election before the grace period commences. To do so, she must have a zero balance with the Health FSA administrator; it's not enough to have qualified expenses that she has incurred but for which she hasn't sought reimbursement. As long as her account with the Health FSA administrator shows a zero balance as of the end of the last day of the 12-month plan year, she becomes HSA-eligible the following day as she begins coverage on her HSA-qualified medical plan and satisfies all other HSA eligibility requirements.

Employers can aid participants as well by altering the Health FSA program prospectively (before the end of the plan year). Here are two approaches:

- **Eliminate the grace period.** If the employer prospectively reverts to a 12-month plan year, the Health FSA won't overlap with the new medical plan year. General Health FSA participants can gain HSA eligibility immediately as long as they satisfy all other eligibility requirements. The downside of this approach is that some participants may be preserving balances for expenses during the grace period. A common example is a participant who plans to use one year's grace period and the following year's plan year to pay for vision correction surgery on both eyes at once (whose price tag may exceed the $2,650 maximum election allowed in 2018). If the employer terminates the grace period, this participant can't use her election as she had planned and forfeits those funds to the employer who changed the plan mid-year.

- **Change the grace period to make it HSA-compatible.** An employer can prospectively change the grace period to limit reimbursement to dental and vision expenses (a Limited-Purpose Health FSA during the grace period). Participants continue to have access to their Health FSA balances during the grace period and also gain eligibility to open and contribute to an HSA. The downside is that participants who had planned to spend their election on medical expenses during the grace period (say, for a planned maternity stay or surgical procedure) can't do so. They risk forfeiting their balances.

The grace period is a continuation of the plan year. Employers do not have the option to split their Health FSA participant population during a plan year. Employers can't limit reimbursements in the grace period to dental and vision expenses only for employees seeking to gain HSA eligibility during the grace period. Any change in the grace period—eliminating it or limiting reimbursement to dental and vision—applies equally to all participants, whether or not an individual participant's goal is to become HSA-eligible immediately after the end of the 12-month Health FSA plan year.

Employers do not have the option to split their Health FSA participant population during a plan year.

The ideal solution to this issue is for your client's employer (or HSA administrator) to educate employees who want to become HSA-eligible during the grace period to spend their entire balance before the beginning of the grace period. This approach avoids the collateral damage to other participants when an employer prospectively redesigns its Health FSA program.

Limited carryover. Employers can design a Health FSA to allow participants to carry over up to $500 of unused funds into the following Health FSA plan year. This feature increases employee participation and elections because it reduces the fear of forfeiting unused balances. At the same time, it poses certain potential HSA eligibility risks.

Your client can eliminate the potential risk of carrying over unused funds into a year in which she wants to establish HSA eligibility by spending down her balance and submitting all requests for reimbursement to the Health FSA administrator before the end of the general Health FSA plan year. If she has no balances to carry over, she has no risk that a carryover will disqualify her from opening and contributing to an HSA.

Employers can take two actions to ensure that balance carryovers don't affect employees' HSA eligibility:

- **Prospectively eliminate the carryover provision.** General Health FSA participants can gain HSA eligibility immediately as long as they satisfy all other eligibility requirements. The downside of this approach is that some employees who aren't concerned with HSA eligibility may have purposely funded their Health FSAs in excess of anticipated expenses to carry over $500 to apply to a large expense the next year. An example is a dental implant and crown that cost a total of $3,000. The participant can carry over $500 and then apply the following year's $2,650 election to pay for the service in full.
- **Allow employees to carry over the unused funds into a Limited-Purpose Health FSA.** An employer can offer a Limited-Purpose Health FSA, which reimburses dental and vision expenses only, and carry over unused funds into that account. This approach allows employees to continue to have access to those unused funds, although for a more limited range of services.

In the grace-period discussion, you saw that employers can't split their Health FSA participant population into two distinct groups: those who seek HSA eligibility and those who don't. The rules are different for carryovers because the unused funds carry over into a *new* plan year. Participants can enroll in either a general or a Limited-Purpose Health FSA the following year. Thus, your clients who participate in a general Health FSA this year can carry over unused funds into a Limited-Purpose Health FSA (if their employer offers this product) and gain immediate HSA eligibility (assuming they satisfy all other requirements).

Though the transition from a Health FSA with a carryover provision to an HSA can be smoother than the transition from a Health FSA with a grace period, it's potentially more dangerous. If the carryover isn't executed properly into a Limited-Purpose Health FSA and instead is deposited in a general Health FSA, your client can't become HSA-eligible before the end of the Health FSA plan year—typically 12 months later. She can enroll in the HSA-qualified plan and reimburse her qualified medical, dental, vision, and over-the-counter expenses tax-free from her Health FSA, but she's locked into that general Health FSA—and therefore isn't HSA-eligible—for a full year. And to reemphasize a point made earlier, Health FSA coverage remains in place even when a participant exhausts the current year's election. Thus, spending the carryover balance quickly isn't an option to regain HSA eligibility during the general Health FSA plan year.

Your clients can gain HSA eligibility at the beginning of the plan year either by spending their entire balance during the year, so that there is no carryover, or by accepting a carryover into a Limited-Purpose Health FSA if the employer offers that option. Their key to success is to understand their options and act accordingly.

A spouse's Health FSA. Remember, your client is covered by his spouse's Health FSA unless his employer has restricted the list of eligible enrollees to exclude spouses (which is very rare).

If the spouse's general Health FSA plan offers a grace period, your client must work with his spouse to spend the entire balance before the end of the 12-month plan year. Otherwise, your client won't be HSA-eligible until the first day of the first month following the end of the grace period (typically three full months).

If the spouse's plan offers a carryover feature, your client's spouse must see whether her employer offers a Limited-Purpose Health FSA (which won't be automatic, since her employer has no indication that she's covered on your client's medical plan and therefore seeks to become HSA-eligible). If so, her employer can move her carryover amount to the Limited-Purpose Health FSA. Otherwise, she can solve the HSA eligibility issue by spending her entire election before the end of the year so that she has no balance to carry over.

These opportunities are available only when your client's medical plan and his spouse's Health FSA have the same effective dates. If the spouse's Health FSA plan year runs past the effective date of the HSA-qualified medical plan, your client (and his spouse) can't become HSA-eligible before the end of the 12-month Health FSA plan year at the earliest.

Counseling Your Clients

- ✓ Guide your clients through a discussion of their Health FSA to determine whether a grace period or carryover of unused funds may affect their HSA eligibility. If their HSA eligibility may be affected, help them understand what they or their employer can do so that they can gain HSA eligibility at the beginning of the medical plan year.

- ✓ Make sure your clients understand the impact of a spouse's general Health FSA on their HSA eligibility.

CHAPTER 24

HRAs and HSA Eligibility

Employers who offer medical plans with high deductibles often combine them with a reimbursement account to help employees manage their out-of-pocket financial responsibility. HRAs are one such option.

This chapter

- defines an HRA, explains why it's defined as a benefit, and explores the implications for HSA eligibility;
- reviews the levers that employers control in designing their HRA programs; and
- discusses when HRAs affect HSA eligibility—and when they don't.

Since the IRS provided initial guidance in 2002, HRAs have become an effective tool for many employers in their efforts to control medical costs.

What is an HRA? In the simplest terms, it's a self-insured, limited-benefit plan that's integrated with a deductible-based medical insurance plan to help employees manage their out-of-pocket medical costs. It's labeled *self-insured* because it's funded entirely by employers, with no employee money directly or indirectly flowing into the account. And it's a *limited-benefit* plan because, regardless of the claims costs incurred by a covered employee or dependent, the HRA is financially responsible for only a defined portion of those expenses—expressed as an annual value.

Here's how an employer might deploy an HRA:

Old program: Medical plan with a $2,000 deductible ($5,400 annual premium).

New program: Medical plan with a $4,000 deductible ($4,200 annual premium) and an HRA that reimburses the final $2,000 of the deductible.

Do you see the potential advantages of this approach?

First, the employer is guaranteed to save $1,200 in the annual premium per employee.

Second, the employees' net financial responsibility doesn't change. Under either plan, they're responsible for the first $2,000 in deductible expenses. After that, either the insurer (old program) or the employer and then the insurer (new program) assume financial responsibility.

The potential issue is that the employer assumes an additional $2,000 in financial responsibility (for claims between $2,000.01 and $4,000) with only $1,200 savings. So, why would an employer adopt this program? The employer is in effect betting that the costs (administrative fees and reimbursements) of running the HRA program are less than the premium savings.

Is this a reasonable bet? It usually is. The answer depends on the size of the employer group and the insurer's rating methodology. Employers need to evaluate the situation annually by comparing premiums at renewal for the lower-deductible (higher-premium) medical plan versus the sum of the renewals for the higher-deductible (lower-premium) medical plan and the reimbursement and administrative costs of the HRA.

Third, the employer can back a promise of a dollar with an actual outlay typically in the range of $0.25 to $0.65. How is this possible? An HRA is a notional account. The employer gives each employee a virtual IOU that promises to pay any deductible expenses between $2,000.01 and $4,000 in this case. The employee is happy because someone else (the employer) pays these bills. The employer is happy because it knows that it reimburses no claims for (typically) more than half its employees and, depending on the HRA plan design, almost always pays less than 50 cents in actual reimbursement for every dollar of promised benefit.

Fourth, employers have wide latitude in designing an HRA program to fit their budgets and their employee recruitment, retention, and satisfaction goals. Employers can design the following elements of the program:

- **Expenses reimbursed.** Employers typically limit the list of qualified expenses to deductible expenses and, if applicable, coinsurance amounts for which employees are responsible.

- **Dollar value.** Employers determine the total dollar amount of HRA reimbursement that they offer employees. That amount can vary from year to year. The IRS doesn't set a minimum or maximum benefit.

- **Payment order.** Employers decide when the HRA begins to pay expenses. In the preceding example, the employer requires employees to pay the first $2,000 of expenses before the HRA begins to reimburse their claims. Employers can allocate the same $2,000 to a plan that pays the *first* $2,000 of expenses or pays 50% of each of the $4,000 of deductible claims. Each of these designs has an impact on both employers' and employees' medical budgets and on employees' satisfaction with the medical coverage.

- **Whether to allow carryover.** Employers determine whether employees who don't use all their funds during a plan year can carry over some or all of their balance into the following year, in effect allowing employees to use their good claims history in one year to buy down their financial responsibility in a future year of high claims.

- **Amount of carryover.** Employers who allow a carryover decide whether to allow employees to carry over the entire balance or make them forfeit some of it.

HRAs and HSA Eligibility and Contributions

Employees who have access to HRA balances may or may not be HSA-eligible, depending on the design of the HRA. HSA eligibility rules require that when a person is enrolled in more than one form of coverage (including medical insurance and a benefit plan), *all* coverage must satisfy the design requirements for an HSA-qualified plan. Thus, employees enrolled in an HSA-qualified medical plan whose employer also offers an HRA can become HSA-eligible (assuming they satisfy all other eligibility requirements) to open and contribute to an HSA only in the following circumstances:

- They choose not to enroll in the HRA, either because they select a medical plan without the HRA or they specifically refuse the HRA integrated with the underlying medical plan;

OR

- The HRA itself isn't disqualifying.

There are four types of *limited* HRAs in which employees like your clients can participate without compromising their HSA eligibility:

Post-Deductible HRA. This design, the most common of the limited HRAs, has a deductible no less than the statutory minimum annual deductible for an HSA-qualified medical plan ($1,350 for self-only and $2,700 for family coverage in 2018 and 2019). Employers can choose a higher HRA deductible. In the example earlier, an HRA that reimburses the final $2,000 of a $4,000 deductible on a self-only plan qualifies as a Post-Deductible HRA because the employee is responsible for the first $2,000 of deductible expenses—well above the $1,350 minimum—before the HRA begins to pay.

An HRA that reimburses the final $2,000 of a $4,000 deductible on a self-only plan qualifies as a Post-Deductible HRA.

In contrast, the HRA isn't HSA-qualified if the family deductible is $4,000 and the HRA reimburses all deductible expenses after $2,000, since the HRA begins to reimburse employees before they satisfy the statutory minimum annual deductible for a family contract. *[See IRS Rev. Rul. 2004-45, Situation 4.]*

Limited-Purpose HRA. This design limits reimbursement to qualified dental and vision expenses (plus a handful of preventive services that aren't covered in full under federal law). Employers typically use this HRA design as a stand-alone substitute for dental or vision insurance, rather than integrate it with a high-deductible medical plan (which typically covers only a narrow range of dental and vision services). This HRA design doesn't disqualify employees from opening and contributing to an HSA because, under federal tax law, dental and vision coverage are permitted coverage. *[See IRS Rev. Rul. 2004-45, Situation 2.]*

Retirement HRA. Employers can create a second HRA that collects the spill-over of unused funds from an active employee's HRA and preserves them for future use. For example, an employer allows employees to carry over unused HRA funds into the following plan year. Once they reach the maximum balance that their employer allows, additional unused balances are deposited in a second HRA. Employees can tap funds in the Retirement HRA only when they leave employment and satisfy certain other requirements (often including number of years worked, age, and account balance).

This plan design doesn't disqualify employees from becoming HSA-eligible because they can't access Retirement HRA balances while they remain actively employed. *[See IRS Rev. Rul. 2004-45, Situation 5.]*

Suspended HRA. This design is similar to the Retirement HRA in that excess unused balances spill over into this second HRA. Employees can't withdraw funds from their Suspended HRA. Employers typically set up a Suspended HRA program when they offer a choice of high-deductible medical plans with either an HRA or an HSA. If employees have built an HRA balance sufficient to cover most of their deductible, they may be reluctant to enroll in an HSA program. Walking away from that financial cushion would leave them with more net out-of-pocket exposure.

The Suspended HRA allows employees to preserve those excess HRA balances in a suspended state, enroll in an HSA program during open enrollment, and then switch back to the HRA program with access to the suspended balances at a future open enrollment. The Suspended HRA reduces employees' cost of switching plans by allowing employees to return to the HRA program later without having forfeited their accumulated HRA balances.

As with the Retirement HRA, this design doesn't disqualify employees from becoming HSA-eligible because they don't have access to their Suspended HRA balances while they're enrolled in the HSA program. *[See IRS Rev. Rul. 2004-45, Situation 3.]*

Counseling Your Clients

✓ Make sure your client's benefit program doesn't disqualify him from opening and contributing to an HSA. Your client's employer should be designing an HRA that's integrated with a medical plan to ensure that the program doesn't disqualify enrollees from becoming HSA-eligible, but it never hurts to verify.

CHAPTER 25

Different Family Structures, Different Rules

Nontraditional family structures and situations create a great deal of misunderstanding when it comes to medical coverage, HSA eligibility, HSA contribution limits, and items qualified for tax-free distribution from an HSA. This chapter sorts through all these issues.

Specifically, this chapter explores

- differences in the rules that govern certain family members' eligibility to enroll in a medical plan and eligibility to open and contribute to an HSA;
- why your client can't reimburse tax-free from her HSA an expense incurred by her domestic partner or ex-spouse and how the expense may give her a tax benefit anyway;
- IRS tax treatment of same-sex spouses' qualified expenses;
- why your client can't reimburse tax-free from her HSA qualified expenses incurred by adult children who are no longer her tax dependents—and the options available to them; and
- the impact of divorce on your client's ability to reimburse his children's qualified expenses tax-free from his HSA.

As a starting point, it's important to understand the difference between medical coverage and HSAs.

Fully insured medical coverage is regulated by the federal and state governments. Self-insured medical coverage has an ERISA exemption, which means that state rules—including benefit mandates—are superseded by federal law and therefore don't apply. *Federal* regulations and mandates, two growth industries during the past two decades and particularly since the introduction of the ACA, do apply. Medical coverage eligibility is determined by a combination of federal and state (for fully insured coverage) laws and mandates, as well as insurers' policies and employers' preferences where applicable.

Judges in some states can require that an ex-spouse be covered on your client's medical coverage. Some insurers give employers the option to allow employees to cover domestic partners on the employer-sponsored medical plan. These are examples of eligibility requirements for medical coverage. The key point is that *medical-plan eligibility* is determined by a combination of federal and state government laws and regulations, insurer rules, and employer rules and practices.

Medical-plan eligibility is determined by a combination of federal and state government laws and regulations, insurer rules, and employer rules and practices.

In contrast, HSAs are regulated almost exclusively by federal tax law. There are some exceptions. First, states can decide whether to honor the same tax advantages that the federal government extends to HSAs. All states that levy a personal income tax except Alabama, California, and New Jersey allow a deduction for HSA contributions. Tennessee and New Hampshire (two states without an income tax) don't allow unlimited tax-free accumulation of account balances.

Second, state trust law determines when an HSA is established. This is an important concept, since, as you've already learned, expenses incurred before an HSA is established can't be reimbursed tax-free from an HSA. States define the laws that apply to trusts established under their jurisdiction. They can alter their trust laws (as Utah did in 2009)—refer back to Chapter 19, *HSA Distributions,* for more information—to provide specific provisions for HSAs. Otherwise, HSAs follow the law for all other trusts subject to that state's jurisdiction. In most cases, the trust law in the state in which the *trustee* is domiciled—not the administrator, employer, or employee—governs your clients' HSAs.

Third, HSAs follow state bankruptcy rules. HSAs aren't exempt from seizure to satisfy the judgment of a bankruptcy court, unlike many retirement plan assets. Some states extend protection to HSAs, but most don't.

Fourth, state laws regarding escheatment (disposition of unclaimed property) apply to HSAs. The federal government hasn't created a uniform escheatment policy with respect to HSA assets deemed abandoned.

Beyond these areas, state governments, insurers, and employers are largely powerless to regulate HSAs. None of these entities can impose tighter (or looser) eligibility requirements, change contribution limits, expand or limit the range of services qualified for tax-free distributions, or impose any other privileges, responsibilities, or restrictions on HSA owners.

Here are some important rules to follow when you are trying to understand the implications of nontraditional family structures and arrangements on HSAs:

- Medical plan enrollment does not affect whose expenses an HSA owner can reimburse tax-free from her HSA.
- The *relationship* between the HSA owner and another family member determines whether the other person's qualified expenses can be reimbursed tax-free from the owner's HSA.
- People who are covered on the medical plan and whose expenses aren't qualified for tax-free reimbursement from the HSA owner *may* be eligible to open and contribute to their own HSAs and reimburse their own (and their tax dependents', if applicable) qualified expenses tax-free.
- Spousal actions that might affect your client's HSA eligibility (such as a spouse's enrolling in a general Health FSA) have no impact on HSA owners who aren't legally married to their life partner.

Let's apply these rules to specific family situations.

Domestic Partner

As noted earlier, some insurers and employers allow employees to add domestic partners to their medical coverage, often subject to affidavit or evidence of a level of commitment. Federal tax law doesn't recognize domestic partners, however. So, although domestic partners may be covered on the medical plan, they aren't recognized by federal tax law as it's applied to HSAs.

Domestic partners' expenses aren't qualified for tax-free distribution. Although domestic partners can incur qualified expenses, including those applied to your client's medical plan and subject to cost-sharing, their expenses aren't qualified for tax-free distribution from your client's HSA. Any distributions from your client's HSA for a domestic partner's expenses are included in your client's taxable income. If your client is under age 65 and not disabled, the distribution is subject to an additional 20% tax as a penalty.

Domestic partners may be eligible to open their own HSA. HSA eligibility is determined person-by-person; it isn't limited to medical-plan subscribers. It's not unusual for more than one person on a family contract to satisfy HSA eligibility requirements. In the case of the domestic partner, the issue is whether that person satisfies the eligibility requirements to open and contribute to her own HSA:

- Is she enrolled in an HSA-qualified medical plan? See Chapter 16, *HSA-Qualified Medical Plan*.
- Does she have disqualifying coverage? See Chapter 17, *HSA Eligibility*.
- Does she qualify as a taxpayer's tax dependent under Section 152 of the IRC?

If the answers to these questions are yes, no, and no, respectively, the domestic partner is eligible to open and contribute to her own HSA. Once she opens and funds her own HSA (and funding can come from any source, including your client), she can reimburse her own and her tax dependents' qualified expenses tax-free.

Domestic partners may contribute up to the statutory limit of the relevant contract type—probably. So, how much can a domestic partner contribute to her HSA in this case? The IRS has not issued definitive guidance. In the 2010 annual meeting of the American Bar Association, ABA officials asked an IRS agent for his personal view on a domestic partner's contribution limit when the medical-plan subscriber was also HSA-eligible. The IRS agent, answering based on his knowledge of the law and not speaking for the IRS in an official capacity, agreed with the committee's belief that the domestic partner could deposit up to the statutory maximum contribution into her own HSA, irrespective of contributions made by anyone else who is covered on the contract.

Implication: Though married couples are limited to a total contribution of $7,000 between the spouses in 2019, domestic partners can *each* contribute up to $7,000 into their respective HSAs, even though they're covered on one family HSA-qualified medical plan with a total deductible between them as low as $2,700 in 2019.

Let's look at the financial implication of this interpretation:

	Married Couple	Domestic Partners
Medical plan deductible	$3,000	$3,000
Total contributions	$7,000	$14,000
Contribution in excess of deductible	$4,000	$11,000

Same-Sex Spouse

The information in this section provides a brief history of how HSA law evolved for same-sex spouses. The bottom line: Today, they are treated as opposite-sex couples under federal tax law.

Prior to the Supreme Court's *Windsor* ruling in 2013 and subsequent IRS interpretation (IRS Notice 2013-17), federal tax law didn't recognize same-sex spouses. Thus, same-sex spouses were treated like domestic partners when it came to tax treatment of their HSAs. Today, as a result of the *Windsor* decision and subsequent IRS guidance, same-sex couples are extended the same tax treatment as opposite-sex married couples. *[See* United States. v. Windsor, executor of the Estate of Spyer, et al., *Case No. 12-307, argued before the Supreme Court March 27, 2013 and decided June 26, 2013.]*

This change extended some advantages that same-sex couples hadn't enjoyed prior to the *Windsor* ruling. Perhaps the most important is the ability to reimburse each other's qualified expenses tax-free. At the same time, it eliminated their option to make double total contributions to their respective HSAs, as just outlined in the domestic partner discussion.

Adult Children Who Are No Longer Tax Dependents

The ACA under Section 152 of the IRC allows parents to continue to cover children who are no longer their tax dependents to age 26. This feature has turned out to be one of the most popular provisions of the ACA, as it has allowed adult children to begin their careers with employers who don't offer insurance or to forego their employer's coverage until age 26 to increase their take-home pay. On the other hand, in some cases this access to coverage may reduce a young adult's incentive to find employment with benefits. And it certainly has had an impact in ACA marketplaces, removing millions of young, overwhelmingly healthy potential consumers from purchasing their own policies to balance the risk pool.

While these children remain covered on a parent's plan, as discussed earlier, medical coverage and HSA rules aren't identical. When a child is no longer a tax dependent, your client can no longer reimburse his expenses tax-free from her HSA. Distributions for the child's expenses (HSA-qualified or non-qualified) after the child no longer qualifies as a tax dependent are included in your client's taxable income and, unless she's age 65 or older or disabled, are subject to an additional 20% tax as a penalty.

When a child is no longer a tax dependent, your client can no longer reimburse his expenses tax-free from her HSA.

What's a parent to do, especially when the child remains on the family medical plan and incurs HSA-qualified cost-sharing or dental, vision, or qualified over-the-counter expenses? Let's go back to one of the guiding principles established at the beginning of the chapter: HSA eligibility is determined on an individual basis. Therefore, the same test can be applied as for domestic partners:

- Is the non-dependent adult child enrolled in an HSA-qualified medical plan? See Chapter 16, *HSA-Qualified Medical Plan*.

- Does he have disqualifying coverage? See Chapter 17, *HSA Eligibility*.

- Does he qualify as a taxpayer's tax dependent under Section 152 of the IRC?

If the answers are yes, no, and no, respectively, the adult child is eligible to open his own HSA. And who can contribute to his HSA? He can. So can your client—and anyone else. If his employer sponsors an HSA program and the employer's Cafeteria Plan allows the employer to make tax-free employer contributions to employees who are HSA-eligible through coverage not offered by the employer, his employer can contribute as well. The child receives the tax deduction for any contributions made by anyone other than his employer.

Example: *Chris covers his son, Anthony, age 24, on his HSA-qualified medical plan. Anthony is no longer Chris's tax dependent. Anthony ends up in the hospital and satisfies $4,600 of the family's $6,000 annual deductible. Chris can't reimburse those expenses tax-free from his HSA. Instead, he helps Anthony open his own HSA. Anthony has little money, so Chris funds the account with $4,000.*

Chris then tells Anthony to negotiate repayment terms with the hospital and to find $600 to pay on the back-end of the payment schedule. Chris tells Anthony that he'll help him complete his income tax return to ensure that he takes the full HSA contribution deduction (which will lower Anthony's taxable income enough to pay his $600 share of the hospital bill without cutting into his disposable income). Anthony is the financial winner here. Chris can't pay Anthony's expenses with pre-tax dollars, but he does get to preserve his HSA balances for future qualified expenses and use Anthony's tax deduction for Chris's HSA contribution. This tactic reduces the amount that Chris must pay Anthony to satisfy the bill without reducing Anthony's standard of living.

This situation is a win-win. Chris was fortunate that he received clear guidance from someone who understands HSAs and how to use—not bend, merely use—the existing rules to open a second door to a family tax advantage when the first door was bolted shut.

Ex-Spouses

Ex-spouses are treated the same under HSA rules as domestic partners. See that discussion for more information.

In some situations, judges can require one party in the divorce to continue to offer coverage to the other party. That ruling binds the employee, the employer, and the insurer to extend that coverage. It does not, however, change federal tax law. Family court judges can't change federal tax law. Any distributions from the employee's HSA for expenses, whether those items or services are qualified expenses or not, incurred by the ex-spouse are included in the employee's taxable income and, unless he has attained age 65 or is disabled, subject to an additional 20% tax as a penalty.

As with domestic partners, if the ex-spouse satisfies all eligibility requirements, she can open her own HSA and reimburse her own and her tax dependents' qualified expenses tax-free.

In the course of disposition of assets during a divorce, medical equity accumulated in an HSA during the marriage is fair game. A judge can order one party to give a portion of his HSA balances to the other party. When this happens, the recipient spouse doesn't need to be HSA-eligible to open an HSA. Transfers ordered as part of a divorce pass from one HSA owner to the other without tax implications for either. The distributing HSA owner's withdrawal isn't subject to tax or penalty, and the recipient account owner can't claim an income tax deduction. Once the recipient HSA owner's account is funded, she enjoys the same benefits and is subject to the same rules as any other HSA owner. *[See IRS Publication 969 for more information.]*

Divorce and Children

It's not uncommon for minor children to be impacted by divorce. In most cases, an HSA owner can reimburse a tax-dependent child's qualified expenses tax-free, even if the other parent (the ex-spouse) has legal custody of the children or claims the children on her federal income tax return. Make sure that your client checks with a tax advisor versed in this area of tax law to ensure compliance. *[See IRS Notice 2008-59, Q&A 33* and *IRS Publication 969.]*

Counseling Your Clients

✓ Be sure your clients understand how their current family situation influences their HSA strategy, eligibility, contribution limits, and distributions.

✓ When your clients have family members who can open and contribute to their own HSAs, review with them the financial opportunities that they can exercise. It may or may not make sense for a client to fund an HSA owned by a domestic partner, an ex-spouse, or an adult child who's no longer a tax dependent. Your client needs to be aware of the options and, if she chooses, obtain appropriate counsel to make the best financial decision for the family.

✓ Be sure to emphasize to your clients the importance of HSA considerations if their family situation changes. Their eligibility to open and contribute to an HSA, their contribution limits, and whose expenses they can reimburse tax-free may be altered with a change in family situation or structure. Each client needs to seek counsel and factor HSA considerations into the content and timing of any such changes.

✓ If your client is going through a divorce, be sure to counsel her to understand the role that HSA assets can play in a divorce settlement. Divorce lawyers, even those who understand the tax and financial implications of the disposition of most financial assets, often don't understand the role of HSAs in divorce. You may be able to help your client (and her lawyer) gain asymmetric information in negotiations.

SECTION VI

Stay Tuned

CHAPTER 26

Proposed Changes to HSA Rules

Medical treatment and coverage are dynamic, and laws often don't keep up with these changes. Government rules by definition are static and rigid. Congress hasn't changed HSAs via legislation since the *HOPE Act* in December 2006, although the House passed some HSA expansion provisions in its *American Health Care Act of 2017*, which never reached the floor of the Senate for a vote. And the IRS hasn't published comprehensive HSA guidance since 2008, although it has issued some narrow guidance on specific topics since that time. As a result, HSA rules are in most cases a decade behind the rapid innovation in the field of medical-service delivery.

In this chapter, you'll find

- some of the areas in which emerging technology create gray areas for HSA eligibility,
- a discussion of current legislative action designed to expand HSAs, and
- an exploration of how one proposal backed by the Trump administration and soon to be introduced in the Senate may dramatically reduce the need for future regulations and interpretation.

There are two ways that the federal government can attempt to keep up with changes in a regulated industry like medical insurance.

First, the executive branch can issue new regulations when the original legislation grants it this power. For example, in the 2,700-page bill that became the ACA, the phrases "the Secretary shall" and "the Secretary may" appear 1,442 times. This wording is an invitation for the executive branch to write detailed regulations within a loose framework set by Congress in the legislation.

The original HSA legislation gives the IRS the authority to index the statutory minimum annual deductible, the statutory out-of-pocket maximum, and the statutory maximum annual contribution figures. In addition, the IRS responds to specific inquiries from within the industry to clarify points in the law, such as when an HSA is considered *established* legally and how the design of a plan deductible (*aggregate* or *embedded*—see Chapter 16, *HSA-Qualified Medical Plan* as a refresher) affects HSA eligibility.

Second, Congress can amend the law. In 2017, Congress passed the *Tax Cuts and Jobs Act*. Among other provisions, this law reduced the penalty under the ACA for an individual who failed to purchase appropriate medical coverage to $0.

With passage of the *HOPE Act* in 2006, Congress changed the calculation of HSA contribution limits that it had set in the original 2003 bill. It removed language limiting contributions to the lesser of (1) the deductible or (2) the statutory maximum annual contribution. The *HOPE Act* allowed all HSA-eligible individuals to contribute up to the statutory maximum annual contribution.

Congressional action is also sometimes necessary to overturn executive branch regulations. Regulators are reluctant to change regulations that their offices have issued previously. Sometimes Congress steps in to make changes that an industry or interest group proposes, even when the executive branch could make the changes on its own.

Most legislative proposals don't become law, and the following list undoubtedly won't be an exception to this rule. Some of the proposed legislation that has bipartisan support may reach the floor intact (or with only slight modification) for a formal vote. That's true for the bills that focus on one specific issue.

Many of the issues listed were addressed in legislation that includes multiple provisions to expand and enhance HSAs, particularly the *Hatch-Rubio-Paulsen* and *Kelly-Blumenauer* bills. These bills were sponsored by Sen. Orrin Hatch (R-UT), Sen. Marco Rubio (R-FL), and Rep. Erik Paulsen (R-MN) and by Reps. Mike Kelly (R-PA) and Earl Blumenauer (D-OR). Many of their provisions were incorporated into two bills, the *Increasing Access to Lower Premium Plans and Expanding Health Savings Accounts Act of 2018* and the *Restoring Access to Medication and Modernizing Health Savings Accounts Act of 2018.* The House of Representatives passed both bills in late July 2018. They failed to become law when the Senate took no action before the 115th Congress adjourned in December 2018.

The prospects for positive action on any of these issues is cloudy in the era of divided government beginning in January 2019, when Democrats assumed control of the House and Republicans retained the majority in the Senate. The best hope is that one or more of these provisions is included in a broader bill that addresses taxes of medical coverage, care, and financing.

Actuarial Value

The author has been working with a legislative assistant to a U.S. senator and a member of the Trump administration to draft legislation to create a second path to designing an HSA-qualified plan. The proposal would automatically designate any plan with an actuarial value (AV) less than a certain threshold (70%, 75%, or 80%) as an HSA-qualified plan.

In simple terms, AV represents the expected split of financial responsibility between patients and insurers, based on the plan design. For example, the insurer is responsible for, on average, 70% of the total cost of covered services received on a plan with an AV of 70, while the patient assumes responsibility for the remaining 30% on average.

This proposal offers three distinct benefits.

First, this proposed legislation immediately extends HSA eligibility to somewhere between 15 million and 40 million families (the exact number depends on the AV chosen) who are enrolled in plans with high deductibles that have one or more disqualifying features—typically office visits or prescription drugs covered in full after a copay. These families face the burden of high deductibles and additional coinsurance responsibility without the benefit of a tax-advantaged reimbursement account. The AV proposal would allow them to, in effect, receive an average 25% discount on all out-of-pocket expenses that they pay through an HSA.

This proposed legislation immediately extends HSA eligibility to somewhere between 15 million and 40 million families.

Second, the AV option simplifies HSA eligibility rules. Regulations have not kept up with changes in medical delivery during the past decade. The IRS hasn't yet provided further guidance on a number of issues, such as telemedicine, employer onsite clinics, preventive prescription drugs, and direct primary-care arrangements. These issues represent gray areas that may affect HSA eligibility. With the AV option, these issues are irrelevant. As long as the plan design satisfies the AV standard, it's an HSA-qualified plan.

Third, state legislators and regulators have the power to disqualify fully insured HSA-qualified plans in their states—either intentionally or, more likely, inadvertently—with mandates that conflict with current law. The State of Maryland, for example, passed a law in 2017 providing gender equality in contraception coverage by mandating full coverage for vasectomies. Federal tax law doesn't recognize vasectomies as a preventive service, as it does female contraception. So, under this law, no one covered by a fully insured plan regulated by Maryland (including women) could open or contribute to an HSA—even people who didn't undergo the procedure.

The state appealed to the IRS, which confirmed that vasectomies aren't a preventive service. The IRS issued a "safe harbor" ruling through the end of 2019 to give Maryland (and, as it turns out, four other states) time to change their laws or disqualify all HSA-qualified plans beginning in 2020.

The AV approach ensures that state laws don't affect HSA eligibility in those states. As long as the coverage satisfies the AV target, it's an HSA-qualified plan.

HSAs and Chronic Care

Under current rules, all non-preventive care must apply to the deductible on an HSA-qualified plan. This design requirement limits HSA adoption, for several reasons.

First, HSA-qualified plans typically aren't appropriate coverage for people with chronic conditions that require regular diagnostic care and treatment, particularly employees whose company offers another plan option. The strategy of accepting the certainty of lower premiums in exchange for the possibility of higher out-of-pocket responsibility is compromised when higher claims costs are a certainty. These individuals instead choose coverage with a higher premium that reduces both their out-of-pocket costs and their incentive to become more effective medical consumers.

Second, employers are often reluctant to adopt an HSA-qualified plan or offer one as their only coverage option if they know of specific employees who would be disproportionately burdened by the high out-of-pocket cost of chronic care. This reluctance is especially common among small employers, who typically know more about their employees' personal situations. Retaining a higher-premium plan may hinder the company's ability to invest in other aspects of its business, including higher pay, other employee benefits, more efficient machines, or a program to increase sales.

A coalition of organizations, led by the American Benefits Council, is spearheading an effort to allow insurers the option to design HSA-qualified plans that cover chronic care below the deductible. These plans are similar to Value-Based Insurance Design (V-BID or VBID) plans that insurers build to remove financial barriers to services that manage chronic conditions. A diabetic with a $3,000 deductible might have routine podiatric and ophthalmic care covered in full, for example, while the $3,000 deductible applies to an MRI, joint replacement, outpatient therapy, and other services unrelated to the patient's chronic condition.

US Sens. John Thune (R-SD) and Tom Carper (D-DE) and US Reps. Diane Black (R-TN) and Earl Blumenauer (D-OR) introduced the bipartisan *Chronic Disease Management Act of 2018* in their respective chambers early in 2018 to allow HSA-qualified plans to cover chronic care under the deductible. The *Restoring Access to Medication and Modernizing Health Savings Accounts Act of 2018* included a weakened provision that allows up to $250 for self-only and $500 of family coverage of high-value care to be covered below the deductible. The ceiling is far below what's necessary to design a meaningful, effective chronic-care approach within an HSA program.

HSAs and Working Seniors

Medicare is disqualifying coverage. That's bad news for the many Americans who continue to work past age 65. The Social Security Administration reports that 58% of men and 64% of women—many of whom remain active at work—begin to collect Social Security benefits before age 65. Under current law, as discussed earlier, these individuals are enrolled in Medicare Part A and Part B as of the first day of the month of their 65th birthday. They are then no longer eligible to contribute to an HSA.

Imagine for a moment two 65-year-olds. Rich is a manager at a service company and earns $80,000 annually. His income covers his current needs, so he chooses to defer Social Security benefits to receive a higher monthly benefit when he begins to draw benefits. He remains covered on his employer's HSA-qualified plan. He makes HSA contributions to reimburse his current and future qualified expenses tax-free. His HSA balance grows until he's no longer eligible to make additional contributions.

Poor lost his job at a manufacturing plant at age 61 when the plant shut down. He ended up working in a convenience store at one-third of his former pay. He applied for Social Security benefits at age 62 to supplement his income. He enrolled in HSA-qualified coverage and contributed enough to his HSA to reimburse his current expenses.

At age 65, Poor loses his HSA eligibility because he's enrolled automatically in Medicare. He still has out-of-pocket expenses. He can't make additional contributions to his HSA to cover those expenses. His options are to pay with after-tax dollars (which means that he loses about a 25% discount that he enjoyed with his HSA) or begin to deplete his HSA balance to enjoy tax benefits (thus reducing funds available to reimburse qualified expenses later in life).

As you can see, current law disproportionately affects lower-income workers. They are more likely to apply for Social Security benefits before Full Retirement Age, which affects their HSA eligibility. Higher-income workers can defer collecting Social Security benefits, which allows them to continue to contribute to their HSA and build medical equity (as well as collect a higher Social Security benefit when they do apply).

A coalition (which includes the author) is working in Washington, DC to change the rules. Though proposals differ slightly, the most promising approach is to allow people who are enrolled in Medicare Part A or Part B (or both) to remain HSA-eligible as long as they satisfy all eligibility requirements (including remaining enrolled in their employer's HSA-qualified coverage).

This proposal has powerful advantages.

First, it would allow individuals to continue to contribute to their HSA when they're enrolled in Part A or Part B (or both). They continue to receive tax advantages when they incur qualified expenses. For people with $5,000 of out-of-pocket expenses, the tax savings amount to somewhere between $1,000 and $1,500 (depending on their tax situation). And they can continue to build medical equity by contributing more than they withdraw. This medical equity helps them manage their medical, dental, and vision out-of-pocket costs and Medicare premiums during retirement.

Second, it actually saves the government money. Today, most people who are enrolled in Medicare and can also remain covered on their employer's insurance drop the employer plan and retain Medicare as their only coverage. After all, they can no longer make HSA contributions or accept an employer contribution to their HSA. Medicare becomes a more attractive financial option for them. Medicare, as their only coverage, assumes responsibility for their claims.

Under this proposal, individuals like Poor could remain HSA-eligible while enrolled in Medicare. Poor would probably waive Part B (he can opt out of Part B, but not Part A) to avoid the $134 monthly premium, remain enrolled in his employer's plan, accept an employer HSA contribution, and make additional contributions to his HSA. And assuming that his company has at least 20 employees, his employer-sponsored coverage would remain the primary payer. Medicare, as secondary payer, would pay little.

Section 3 of the *Increasing Access to Lower Premium Plans and Expanding Health Savings Accounts Act of 2018* went halfway toward solving this issue by allowing working seniors who enrolled in Part A to remain HSA-eligible. The proposal ended discrimination based on income (lower-paid working seniors who rely on Social Security to supplement their incomes would remain HSA-eligible). It didn't end discrimination based on employer size (working seniors in companies with fewer than 20 employees who are forced by their insurer to enroll in Part A and Part B would be disqualified).

HSA Option within Medicare

A growing number of the 10,000 Americans who turn age 65 every day have been covered by an HSA-qualified plan for five years, a decade, or longer. They're comfortable with the concept. They're willing to accept higher out-of-pocket costs in exchange for tax savings. They've become better consumers of medical care, researching options, asking their doctors pointed questions, and choosing courses of treatment that they believe are most cost-effective.

Then they enroll in Medicare. They no longer have the option to enjoy tax savings. The fruits of their expertise as consumers flow primarily to their insurer (Medicare) rather than to them. In short, the value of the skills that they have developed over years as consumers of medical care provide them with little financial advantage in traditional Medicare.

What's the solution? Offer an HSA-qualified option in Medicare Advantage. Private insurers can design Medicare Advantage plans that mirror their HSA-qualified commercial plans. Individuals who enroll in Medicare would have the same choices that they enjoy today *plus* the option to remain HSA-eligible and continue to contribute to an HSA.

> Individuals who enroll in Medicare would have the same choices that they enjoy today *plus* the option to remain HSA-eligible and continue to contribute to an HSA.

That option isn't available today. Medicare does have a Medical Savings Account (MSA) option, but it's far less advantageous than a robust HSA program. Under the MSA program, the government funds the MSA up to a portion of the deductible. Enrollees can't make additional contributions to cover their current or future qualified expenses.

An HSA option within Medicare Advantage would give Medicare enrollees the incentive to continue to be active consumers of medical care (with benefits accruing not only to themselves as patients, but also to Medicare as the payer).

The *Hatch-Rubio-Paulsen* bill included this provision (Section 202). It was not included in either bill that the House passed in late July 2018.

Increased Contribution Limits

Early HSA-qualified plans had low deductibles (typically $1,000 to $2,000 for self-only coverage and twice those amounts for family coverage) and full or nearly full coverage after the deductible. A typical plan had a self-only deductible between $1,250 and $1,500, with financial responsibility after the deductible limited to copays for office visits, emergency services, and prescription drugs.

HSA rules allowed individuals to contribute up to the lower of the deductible or the statutory annual contribution limit. Beginning in 2007, contribution limits were set at the statutory annual contribution limit, regardless of plan deductible.

Since then, out-of-pocket costs have risen dramatically, for many reasons. The cost of medical care continues to rise at twice the level of general prices, so increasing out-of-pocket financial responsibility is a means of moderating premium increases. The ACA prohibited insurers from pricing individual or small-group coverage based on expected utilization or on projected costs based on age. To manage risk, insurers increased deductibles and coinsurance.

Now, as you learned earlier, Silver and Bronze plans in ACA marketplaces impose out-of-pocket responsibility in excess of $10,000 for the average covered family. Today's HSA contribution limits ($3,500 for self-only coverage and $7,000 for family coverage in 2019) don't cover this additional responsibility.

The *American Health Care Act*, which the House of Representatives approved in 2017 (but died when the Senate didn't consider it) included a provision to increase the contribution limit to the statutory out-of-pocket maximum ($6,650 for self-only coverage and $13,300 for family coverage in 2018). This proposal, which has been included in other legislation that has been filed but not yet considered by Congress, would ensure that people who face extremely high costs would have the opportunity to pay those expenses with pre-tax dollars.

The *Increasing Access to Lower Premium Plans and Expanding Health Savings Accounts Act of 2018,* included a provision in Section 4 to allow contributions up to the statutory out-of-pocket limit.

Disqualifying Coverage

As discussed in Chapter 17, *HSA Eligibility*, people lose their HSA eligibility if they are covered under or receive care through a number of other programs, including Indian Health Services, TRICARE, and sharing ministries, or they are patients in a direct primary-care practice.

In late July 2018, the House passed the *Native American Health Savings Improvement Act of 2018.* This bill permits Native Americans who receive care through the Indian Health Services system to remain HSA-eligible. The bill expired at the end of the 115th Congress.

Health FSA and HRA Transition Relief

Not all employers align their benefits, as discussed in Chapter 23, *Health FSAs and HSA Eligibility.* And employers and employees in this situation face some less-than-ideal options.

Section 6 of *The Restoring Access to Medication and Modernizing Health Savings Account Act of 2018* addressed this issue. Employers could roll over Health FSA participants' balances into an HSA or split the Health FSA population mid-year so that employees who enrolled in an HSA-qualified plan could convert to a Limited-Purpose Health FSA.

Additional Qualified Expenses

Various proposals seek to expand the list of expenses that are qualified for tax-free reimbursement from an HSA (and also a Health FSA and HRA). Among the items are health-club memberships, exercise equipment, and vitamins and nutritional supplements. These provisions can gain grassroots support with the efforts of more than 36,000 health clubs and thousands of supplement manufacturers and retailers. Approving any of these items as qualified expenses represents a break from current law. Today, products and services that diagnose, treat, cure, or mitigate an injury, illness, or condition are qualified expenses. These items are designed for general health to *prevent* injuries, illnesses, and conditions.

A provision to expand the list of qualified expenses to include fitness-club memberships, the cost of fitness-related classes, and certain fitness equipment was included in the *Restoring Access to Mediation and Modernizing Health Savings Accounts Act of 2018.*

Paying Medical Premiums

Today, HSA owners can reimburse commercial (non-Medicare) medical premiums tax-free from their HSAs only if they're continuing coverage through COBRA or are receiving unemployment benefits.

Individuals who purchase insurance today through their employers generally receive more favorable tax treatment than those who buy coverage in the nongroup market, either directly from insurers or through ACA marketplaces. Advocates for equality of treatment of group and nongroup enrollees favor a change in the law that expands the list of qualified expenses to include nongroup premiums.

This concept isn't without its skeptics. The debate is philosophical. One camp believes the primary purpose of HSA programs is to empower patients as consumers by giving them financial incentives to choose care based on cost and quality. Another camp sees the purpose of HSAs as helping individuals manage medical costs, which include not only their out-of-pocket responsibility but premiums as well.

One camp believes the primary purpose of HSA programs is to empower patients as consumers by giving them financial incentives to choose care based on cost and quality.

This provision would apply only to people who don't qualify for advance premium tax credits ("premium subsidies") under the ACA and who purchase HSA-qualified coverage. The *Hatch-Rubio-Paulsen* bill (Section 302) included this provision, but it wasn't addressed in either of the bills that the House passed in late July 2018.

This approach is a rather clumsy means of addressing a fundamental disparity in the federal tax code. The different tax treatment is more appropriately addressed in broader tax-law reform. Nevertheless, this provision is attractive politically. Members of Congress may want to support a benefit for the growing number of Americans who are independent contractors in the gig economy and must purchase coverage in the nongroup market.

Reimbursing Adult Children's Expenses

HSA owners can reimburse their children's expenses only if the children qualify as tax dependents. This provision is widely misunderstood, and many HSA owners undoubtedly are out of compliance because they assume that they can reimburse tax-free any qualified expenses incurred by a child who remains covered on their medical plan. Under the ACA, a child can remain covered on a parent's plan until age 26, even if the child is no longer the parent's tax dependent, even if the child has access to employer-sponsored insurance, and even if the child is married.

The rules may be particularly confusing to HSA owners who have participated in Health FSAs in the past (and may currently participate in a Limited-Purpose

Health FSA to increase their tax savings). Health FSAs are subject to the provision in the ACA that covers children to age 26, whether or not they qualify as a parent's dependent.

Both the *Hatch-Rubio-Paulsen* (Section 207) and *Kelly-Blumenauer* (Section 5) bills addressed this issue by adopting the Health FSA standard for HSAs. The provision wasn't included in the two bills that the House passed in late July 2018.

Spouse's Catch-Up Contributions

Under current law, an HSA-eligible spouse of an HSA plan subscriber who wants to make a $1,000 catch-up contribution must open her own HSA to accept the contribution. This provision often increases costs (the second HSA may impose monthly administrative fees) and complexity (spouses must search for an HSA if the subscriber's employer's HSA administrator doesn't have a program that makes it easy for a spouse to open an account).

Section 5 of the *Increasing Access to Lower Premium Plans and Expanding Health Savings Accounts Act of 2018* included this provision.

COBRA as Group Coverage

While this issue isn't specific to HSAs, the definition of COBRA as nongroup coverage affects people who delay enrollment in Medicare, as discussed in Chapter 14, *Timing Medicare Enrollment*. Because individuals who continue their employer coverage through COBRA aren't deemed to have employer-sponsored coverage, they face penalties and potential gaps in coverage when they subsequently enroll in Medicare.

Several organizations who advocate for older Americans are prepared to support legislation that defines COBRA as group coverage. If this definition is adopted, individuals who move from COBRA coverage to Medicare are entitled to a Special Enrollment Period (and thus no gap in coverage) and face no penalties for delaying Medicare enrollment without group coverage.

Afterword

By reading this book and understanding its contents, you have armed yourself with knowledge that your market competitors lack (unless they too have read this book). Some of us in the HSA world have been shouting for years about the benefits of an HSA as a long-term savings-and-investment account. Our voices rarely carried into the world of long-term investing and retirement planning.

Only recently—say, since early 2017—have HSAs begun to receive the attention that they deserve as a long-term account. The financial press and even popular press have started to run articles touting the advantages of HSAs. A growing number of financial, investment, and retirement advisors conferences are now including break-out sessions on integrating HSAs into long-term investment planning. Others are bringing this concept to the main stage at these industry gatherings.

The way that financial and retirement planners—and, increasingly, their clients—are viewing HSAs is changing. Most HSA owners still use their accounts like Health FSAs—setting contribution levels at their expected annual qualified expenses and then reimbursing current expenses as incurred. But a growing number are beginning to understand the additional flexibility that HSAs provide in building medical equity—a superior form of wealth. They want to explore this concept further with an advising professional who truly understands the concepts and issues and can provide guidance integrated into their overall long-term strategies.

If you've truly absorbed the key lessons contained in this book, you qualify as an informed advisor who can explain and illustrate the benefits of an HSA. You can enjoy the satisfaction of helping, and perhaps reap well-earned additional revenue from, grateful clients whose lives in retirement are richer and more fulfilling because they, with your guidance, built medical equity and navigated the compliance path successfully.

If I have succeeded in my mission:

- you have a much better understanding of HSAs and how your clients can use these accounts to increase their wealth.

- you see how HSAs differ in their tax treatment from other long-term tax-advantaged accounts and can guide your clients in a discussion of how incorporating HSAs into their portfolio can turbocharge their medical-equity accumulation.

- you understand the basic compliance issues around HSA eligibility, contributions, distributions, and balance transfers between multiple HSAs owned by the client to minimize your clients' compliance risk.

- you recognize the interplay between Medicare and HSAs.

- you understand the key questions that you and your clients must address to ensure that they make the right decisions to maximize their individual financial position. Decisions seemingly unrelated to HSAs—for example, when to begin to collect Social Security benefits—have important implications for your clients' continued HSA eligibility.

- you can show your clients how redirecting their current levels of long-term savings, without committing additional current income to retirement savings if that action represents an unreasonable financial burden, can result in greater spending power in retirement.

- you can counsel your clients on how to balance the immediate tax advantages of an HSA (pre-tax contributions and tax-free distributions for current expenses) with the long-term tax advantages (pre-tax contributions, tax-deferred/free accumulation of medical equity, and tax-free distributions for qualified expenses incurred in retirement versus reimbursing the same expenses through a traditional IRA or 401(k) plan from which the distribution is included in your client's taxable income).

- you and your clients understand that different HSA administrators offer different product features and benefits, and an HSA that was appropriate while they were working for one employer may not be optimal in retirement on features ranging from fees to investment options.

- you and your clients realize that just as they can use self-directed IRAs to fund private investments (in real estate, business, and equipment, for example), they can manage self-directed HSAs in the same manner. These opportunities don't appeal to most individuals, but you may have clients with special expertise who can leverage that knowledge to force appreciation in certain investments.

William G. (Bill) Stuart
Rockland, Massachusetts
January 2019

APPENDIX A

Test Your Knowledge

The best way to learn—to really learn—material is to test your knowledge. This exam is designed to reinforce the material presented in this book. You can complete this exam by yourself after you read the book and refer back to it periodically to identify topics that you need to review.

1. Which of the following is *not* a great reason for Charles Taft to own an HSA?

A. Account owners build medical equity.

B. HSA owners enjoy triple-tax-free benefits.

C. HSA owners can roll over up to $500 of remaining balances to spend the following plan year.

D. HSAs are inheritable.

2. Which of the following is *not* an advantage of HSAs over Health FSAs?

A. Unlimited rollover of unused funds.

B. Immediate access to the entire annual election.

C. Pre-tax payroll contributions.

D. Tax-free reimbursement of medical plan out-of-pocket costs.

3. Which of the following is *not* a characteristic of an HRA?

A. It's usually integrated with a medical plan.

B. Participants receive reimbursement only when they incur qualified expenses.

C. The employer determines the value of the HRA.

D. Employee contributions are tax-free.

4. What is medical equity?

A. Deductible credits that offset future out-of-pocket expenses.

B. Coverage after satisfying the plan's out-of-pocket maximum in a given year.

C. Funds saved and invested in a tax-free account for future tax-free distribution for qualified expenses.

D. The requirement under Title IX that hospitals and clinicians treat patients equally, regardless of sex, race, color, age, sexual orientation, country of origin, or primary language.

5. Which plan(s) allow participants to make prospective changes to their pre-tax payroll contributions during the year?

A. Health FSA.

B. HRA only.

C. Health FSA and HSA.

D. HSA only.

6. Which plan(s) don't require an administrator to follow up promptly to substantiate all reimbursements to ensure that they're for qualified expenses?

A. HSA only.

B. HRA only.

C. Health FSA and HSA.

D. HRA and HSA.

7. Which of the following features of an HRA can an employer *not* design?

A. Dollar value of the HRA.

B. Whether unused funds can roll over.

C. Limit on employee contributions.

D. Whether the employee or the HRA pays the first dollars of deductible expenses.

8. Which of these benefit plans is (are) owned by employees?

A. HSA only.

B. HSA and Health FSA only.

C. Health FSA only.

D. Health FSA and HRA only.

9. Which of these accounts allow Edward Gorman to make pre-tax or tax-deductible contributions?

A. HRA and traditional IRA.

B. Traditional 401(k) plan and Roth IRA.

C. HSA and traditional 401(k) plan.

D. HSA, HRA, traditional 401(k) plan, and traditional IRA.

10. Which of these plans offer tax-free distributions?

A. HRA and traditional IRA.

B. Traditional 401(k) plan and Roth IRA.

C. HSA (if distributions are for qualified expenses) and Roth IRA.

D. HSA (if distributions are for qualified expenses), Roth 401(k) plan, and traditional IRA.

11. Which of the following features of Tom Gourlay's family medical coverage disqualifies him from contributing to an HSA?

A. The out-of-pocket maximum is $6,000.

B. Select preventive care is covered outside the deductible.

C. The plan has a $5,000 family deductible, with each family member capped at $2,500.

D. Certain preventive prescription drugs are covered outside the deductible, subject to copay.

12. John DeBonay's employer offers employees the option to participate in a Health FSA. How does this plan affect John's HSA eligibility?

A. He's not HSA-eligible merely because his employer offers this plan.

B. He's not HSA-eligible if he enrolls in the plan and it's not a limited Health FSA.

C. He's not eligible unless it's a limited Health FSA or he signs a contract binding him to seek reimbursement for dental and vision expenses only.

D. He's not HSA-eligible unless the FSA doesn't also offer a Dependent Care Reimbursement Account.

13. George Spear wants to remain enrolled in his employer's medical coverage, but his employer consolidated plans and now offers only an HSA-qualified plan. George is already enrolled in Medicare. Can George enroll in the HSA-qualified medical plan?

A. No, because his enrollment in Medicare disqualifies him from opening an HSA.

B. Yes, because being HSA-eligible isn't a requirement for being eligible to enroll in a medical plan.

C. No, because individuals can't be covered on two medical plans.

D. Yes, but he forfeits his right to enroll in Part C or Part D in the future.

14. Courtland Hess's employer's medical plan has an embedded $3,000/$6,000 family deductible and a $7,000 non-embedded family out-of-pocket maximum. Based on this information alone, can the coverage be an HSA-qualified plan?

A. No, because it has an embedded deductible, which is prohibited by the ACA.

B. Yes, because the out-of-pocket maximum is at least $1,000 higher than the deductible.

C. No, because a plan that has an embedded deductible must have an embedded out-of-pocket maximum.

D. Yes, because the individual deductible exceeds the statutory minimum annual deductible for a family contract and the family out-of-pocket maximum is less than the ACA individual out-of-pocket maximum.

15. George Parkhurst offers his employees an HSA-qualified self-only medical plan with a $5,000 self-only deductible in 2019. He then offers an HRA that reimburses all deductible expenses after $1,500. Can his employees who enroll open and contribute to an HSA based on this design?

A. No, because employees enrolled in an HRA aren't HSA-eligible.

B. No, because the HRA reimburses more than half the deductible.

C. Yes, because George's deductible responsibility is more than the statutory minimum annual deductible ($1,350 in 2019).

D. Yes, because HRA designs have no impact on HSA eligibility.

16. Helen Truman visits her local VA center to be fitted for a new prosthetic. She lost her left leg in an IED explosion outside Basra during the first Gulf War. How does this visit affect her HSA eligibility?

A. She loses HSA eligibility for three months.

B. It doesn't affect her HSA eligibility because Helen's condition is service-related.

C. She loses her HSA eligibility for the remainder of the year.

D. Receiving VA care doesn't affect Helen's HSA eligibility because veterans who saw active combat remain HSA-eligible when they receive any care that they've earned through the VA.

17. John Wright turns age 65 Oct. 6. He continues to work, is covered on his employer's HSA-qualified plan, and hasn't enrolled in Medicare. Can he remain HSA-eligible?

A. Yes. Turning age 65 doesn't affect his HSA eligibility.

B. No. He automatically loses HSA eligibility at age 65.

C. No. He must enroll in Social Security at age 65, which makes him ineligible to contribute to an HSA.

D. Yes. Individuals who are age 65 and are covered by an employer's HSA-qualified plan are automatically HSA-eligible, regardless of whether they enroll in Medicare.

18. James Gifford's wife is enrolled in a general Health FSA. Does her enrollment affect his HSA eligibility?

A. No. A spouse's benefits don't affect the other spouse.

B. Yes. James can't become HSA-eligible because he's automatically covered on her general Health FSA unless her employer specifically excludes spouses (rare).

C. No. As long as James signs an affidavit swearing that he won't reimburse any expenses from her general Health FSA, he doesn't lose his HSA eligibility.

D. Maybe. Only one of them can be HSA-eligible if she participates in a general Health FSA. They must choose which one of them will contribute to an HSA.

19. **Kittie Brink's husband enrolls in Medicare at age 65. He remains covered on her HSA-qualified medical plan. Does his Medicare enrollment affect her HSA eligibility?**

    A. No, it doesn't disqualify Kittie because she can't draw benefits from his Medicare coverage.

    B. Yes, it disqualifies her from contributing to an HSA until the beginning of the following calendar year.

    C. Yes, it disqualifies Kittie forever, unless her husband disenrolls from Medicare.

    D. Maybe. It disqualifies her only if he enrolls in Part B or Part D, but not Part A only.

20. **H.B. Phillips is covered on his wife's low-deductible HMO plan. He's also enrolled in his employer's HSA-qualified plan. Is he HSA-eligible?**

    A. Yes, because his employer's coverage is primary.

    B. No, because if he wants to be HSA-eligible and is covered by more than one medical plan, all plans must be HSA-qualified.

    C. No, because individuals can't be covered on more than one medical plan.

    D. Yes, because HSA eligibility rules ignore a spouse's coverage.

21. **James Lamb's medical plan has a $5,000 family deductible with an individual $2,500 deductible. This plan design is consistent with HSA-qualified medical coverage.**

    True.

    False.

22. **Albert King began to receive Social Security benefits at age 64. He loses his HSA eligibility as of the month of his 65th birthday.**

    True.

    False.

23. **Individuals who enroll in a general Health FSA and sign an affidavit binding them to reimburse only dental and vision expenses can contribute to an HSA while participating in the Health FSA.**

    True.

    False.

24. John Lutz is HSA-eligible. His spouse enrolls in Medicare. John can continue to contribute to his HSA.

True.

False.

25. Employers who offer a free-standing (not integrated with the medical plan) telemedicine program may inadvertently disqualify their employees from opening or contributing to an HSA.

True.

False.

26. Laura Keene, age 42, enrolls in her employer's self-only HSA-qualified medical plan effective May 6. How much can she contribute to her HSA in 2019?

A. No more than 7/12 of $3,500.

B. No more than 8/12 of $4,500.

C. No more than 7/12 of $4,500.

D. Either up to 7/12 of $3,500 or up to the full $3,500 if she uses the Last-Month Rule.

27. Edwin Brink, who is HSA-eligible all 12 months this year, turns age 55 July 31. How much of a catch-up contribution can he make this year?

A. $1,000.

B. 6/12 of $1,000.

C. 7/12 of $1,000.

D. $0. He can't make a catch-up contribution until the first year that he is 55 the entire year.

28. Louis Carland, age 62, loses his HSA eligibility when he leaves his job and his self-only coverage Oct. 6, 2019. How much can he contribute to his HSA in 2019?

A. Up to 9/12 of $3,500.

B. Up to 9/12 of $4,500.

C. Up to 10/12 of $4,500.

D. Up to 10/12 of $4,500 or up to the full $4,500 if he uses the Last-Month Rule.

29. John Mathews, who just turned 40, enrolls in his employer's HSA-qualified family coverage with a $5,000 deductible and a Post-Deductible HRA that reimburses the final $2,000 of his deductible. What's the maximum amount that he can contribute to his HSA in 2019 if he is eligible all 12 months?

A. $7,000.

B. $7,000 less the $2,000 reimbursed from the HRA.

C. $0. He isn't eligible to contribute to an HSA if he's covered by an HRA.

D. $7,000 less whatever of the HRA he actually receives as reimbursement for deductible expenses.

30. Jeannie Gourlay Struther's employer contributes $1,000 to her HSA. What impact does the employer contribution have on Jeannie's HSA contribution?

A. No impact. Jeannie can still make pre-tax payroll deductions for the full statutory maximum for her contract type.

B. She can't contribute to her HSA in a year that her employer contributes.

C. Jeannie can contribute up to the statutory maximum for her contract type less the $1,000 that her employer contributes.

D. She can contribute no more than the amount of the employer contribution.

31. Individuals who contribute to both a workplace retirement plan and an HSA must reduce their retirement plan maximum contribution by a dollar for every dollar that they contribute to their HSA.

True.

False.

32. Individuals who lose HSA eligibility during the year can pro-rate their contributions or use the Last-Month Rule to contribute up to the statutory maximum for their contract type.

True.

False.

33. Individuals can't make HSA contributions after Jan. 31 of the following year.

True.

False.

34. When both a husband and wife own HSAs, each can contribute up to the statutory maximum annual contribution for a family contract.

True.

False.

35. When a single mother covers her two young daughters, who are her tax dependents, on her HSA-qualified medical plan, she can contribute no more than the self-only maximum contribution because she's the only individual on the contract who's HSA-eligible.

True.

False.

36. Which of the following is *not* relevant when determining whether Henry Raybold's distribution from an HSA is tax-free?

A. Who incurs the expense.

B. Date of service.

C. The cost of the service.

D. Whether the service diagnoses, mitigates, or treats an injury, illness, or condition.

37. What is the annual limit that Joe Simms faces on distributions from his HSA in 2019?

A. $3,500 for self-only coverage or $7,000 for family coverage.

B. No limit.

C. Distributions are limited to contributions that year.

D. $5,000 for self-only coverage and $10,000 for family coverage.

38. An HSA owner can reimburse which of the following expenses?

A. His domestic partner's vision correction surgery.

B. Emergency-room services incurred by his 25-year-old son, a full-time firefighter.

C. His wife's aromatherapy and massage at a local spa.

D. His teen-age son's dental implant.

39. Under the trust law of most states, when is an HSA established?

A. When the individual enrolls in an HSA-qualified plan.

B. When the individual completes his paperwork to open the account.

C. When the first deposit is made into the account.

D. The first day of the first month after the administrator processes all paperwork.

40. Why is the date of establishment so important for HSA owners?

A. They can't reimburse any expenses tax-free with dates of service before that date.

B. If they die before that date, they can't pass their HSA intact to a spouse.

C. They can't begin to invest funds until at least 30 days after they establish their HSA.

D. Their contributions aren't pre-tax or tax-deductible before the establishment date.

41. Employers can require that employees limit distributions of the employer contribution to an HSA to qualified expenses.

True.

False.

42. John Withers can reimburse his 25-year-old son's inpatient expenses tax-free from his HSA if the child remains his tax dependent.

True.

False.

43. HSA owners face a one-year deadline to reimburse all qualified expenses tax-free.

True.

False.

44. An HSA owner can't reimburse his wife's expenses if she's not covered on his HSA-qualified medical plan.

True.

False.

45. Once an HSA owner is no longer HSA-eligible, she can't reimburse qualified dental and vision expenses tax-free, but she can always reimburse qualified medical expenses tax-free.

True.

False.

46. An employee doesn't like the HSA administrator that his employer has chosen. Which of the following is *not* an option?

A. He can file Form 8889, requesting that his employer make contributions directly to an HSA at another institution.

B. He can forego employer and employee pre-tax contributions entirely.

C. He can move funds from his employer's preferred HSA administrator to a second HSA.

D. He can open his own HSA with another administrator and make personal contributions that he can deduct on his personal income tax return.

47. Which of the following forms is *not* part of annual HSA tax reporting?

A. Form 8889.

B. Form 5498-SA.

C. Form 1099-SA.

D. Schedule D.

48. Which of the following statements is *not* true about excess contributions to an HSA?

A. Administrators aren't required to work with HSA owners to correct excess contributions.

B. HSA owners can avoid penalties by removing the excess contribution and all earnings associated with the excess contribution before filing their personal income tax return for the year of the excess contribution.

C. Uncorrected excess HSA contributions are included in taxable income and subject to an additional tax.

D. Owners who fail to correct excess contributions can't make tax-free distributions the following year.

49. Which of the following is the only issue affecting John Buckingham's maximum HSA contribution that his HSA administrator can know for certain?

A. Whether he's eligible to make a catch-up contribution (based on his age as reported by him to the administrator).

B. Whether John receives care at the local VA hospital.

C. Whether he makes additional contributions in a given year to another HSA.

D. Whether John has a disqualifying event that may reduce his maximum contribution for that year.

50. Which of the following statements is false?

A. An HSA is a trust.

B. An individual can own a dozen or more HSAs if she chooses.

C. An HSA owner can designate a regular checking account as an HSA if her bank doesn't offer a formal HSA, as long as she pledges to reimburse only qualified expenses.

D. There are no joint HSAs, although an owner can give a spouse or child authority to withdraw funds from her HSA.

51. An individual can own more than one HSA.

True.

False.

52. Husbands and wives can own a joint HSA only if both are eligible to make catch-up contributions.

True.

False.

53. If a judge orders Harry Hawk, an HSA owner, to pay half his ex-wife's medical expenses as part of a divorce settlement, he can pay those expenses—and only those expenses that she incurs—tax-free from his HSA.

True.

False.

54. HSA administrators can offer debit cards that allow HSA owners to withdraw funds at any time for any purpose, including withdrawing cash at ATMs.

True.

False.

55. HSAs enjoy the same bankruptcy protection as retirement accounts.

True.

False.

56. Ned Emerson's Health FSA has a grace period. Which action will *not* allow him to become HSA-eligible as of the end of the 12-month Health FSA plan year?

A. He spends his entire balance before the beginning of the grace period.

B. His employer turns the grace period into a Limited-Purpose Health FSA for all participants.

C. His employer eliminates the grace period for all participants.

D. He reimburses only dental and vision expenses that he incurs during the grace period.

57. Kate Evans's employer participates in her employer's Dependent Care Reimbursement Account, which ends Dec. 31. Her employer offers an HSA program effective July 1. Which of these statements is true?

A. Kate can enroll in the HSA program and open an HSA immediately if she satisfies all other HSA eligibility requirements.

B. She can't open an HSA before the end of the DCRA plan year.

C. Kate can enroll in the HSA program and open an HSA immediately only if she terminates her DCRA participation with 30 days' notice to the employer.

D. She can't simultaneously contribute to her HSA and make elections to her DCRA.

58. Which of the following steps can Jake Rittersbach's employer *not* take to allow employees participating in a Health FSA with a rollover feature to become HSA-eligible immediately after the end of the Health FSA plan year?

A. Prospectively terminate the rollover program.

B. Roll the balance into a Limited-Purpose Health FSA the following year.

C. Roll the funds into a Retirement Health FSA.

D. Instruct participants to spend their entire election so that they don't have balances to roll over.

59. Which of the following is *not* a limited HRA that allows an employee to open and contribute to an HSA?

A. Limited-Purpose HRA.

B. Post-Deductible HRA.

C. Retirement HRA.

D. Dependent Care HRA.

60. What's the minimum deductible for a Post-Deductible HRA tied to family coverage in 2019?

A. $1,350.

B. $2,700.

C. $7,000.

D. The value of the medical plan deductible less $2,700.

61. Which of the following characteristics is *not* true for Johnny Evans's Health FSA grace period?

A. Johnny's employer can change his grace period to a Limited-Purpose grace period because Johnny wants to become HSA-eligible, while his co-workers' grace period continues to allow reimbursement for medical, prescription drug, dental, vision, and certain over-the-counter expenses.

B. Johnny has up to 75 days during which he can spend the prior year's unspent balances and also spend the current year's election.

C. The grace period disqualifies Johnny from opening or contributing to an HSA if it's a general Health FSA and he didn't exhaust his entire election before the beginning of the grace period.

D. If Johnny wants to become HSA-eligible, he must spend his entire balances prior to the grace period.

62. When an employer offers an HSA program for the first time, employees have a once-per-lifetime opportunity to terminate their participation in a Health FSA.

True.

False.

63. Individuals enrolled in a spouse's general Health FSA are HSA-eligible as long as they're not enrolled in the spouse's employer's primary medical plan.

True.

False.

64. Charles Byrne's employer carries over Charles's small remaining balance into the following year's general Health FSA. Charles can open an HSA on the first day of the first month after he has spent his carryover.

True.

False.

65. A grace period allows for an *unlimited* carryover of remaining balances for a *limited* period of time.

True.

False.

66. Joseph Hazelton covers his domestic partner, his two adult children (no longer his tax dependents), and his two college-aged (still tax dependents) children on his medical plan. How many of the family members are potentially HSA-eligible?

A. One. Joseph only.

B. Two. Joseph and his domestic partner.

C. Three. Joseph and his two adult children.

D. Four. Joseph, his domestic partner, and his two adult children.

67. Will Ferguson is required by a divorce agreement to reimburse his ex-spouse's medical expenses. Which of the following statements is *not* true?

A. Will can reimburse her qualified expenses tax-free from his HSA if the divorce decree orders him to pay her expenses.

B. If she's HSA-eligible, she can open an HSA. Will can contribute to her HSA, but she is entitled to the tax deduction for that contribution.

C. She can open her own HSA to reimburse her qualified expenses tax-free.

D. Will can reimburse her expenses from his HSA, subject to income taxes and potential penalties.

68. Henry Rathbone covers his 24-year-old son, a self-employed plumber who's doing well financially, on his HSA-qualified medical plan. Which of the following statements is true?

A. Since the son isn't the medical plan subscriber, he can't open his own HSA.

B. Henry can reimburse his son's expenses tax-free because the son is covered on Henry's medical plan.

C. The son, if otherwise eligible, can open his own HSA.

D. The son can't open his own HSA unless Henry doesn't open one, because families are limited to a single HSA.

69. John Dyott has been divorced from his wife for two years. They have two children, whom she claims as tax dependents on her personal income tax return. Because the children are her tax dependents, he can't reimburse their expenses tax-free from his HSA.

True.

False.

70. Though the IRS hasn't provided guidance on this topic, many administrators advise HSA owners that they and their domestic partners who are HSA-eligible and covered on the same medical plan may *each* be able to contribute up to the family maximum.

True.

False.

71. Ned Spangler turns age 65 May 29. Which of the following statements is true?

A. He's automatically enrolled in Medicare Part A as of June 1.

B. Ned doesn't have to enroll in any Part of Medicare at age 65 unless he's collecting Social Security or Railroad Retirement benefits.

C. He must enroll in Part A at age 65 if he worked enough employment quarters to qualify for premium-free coverage, but enrollment in Part B and Part D is optional.

D. Ned must enroll in either Part A or Part C as of the first day of the month that he turns 65.

72. Which of the following services are covered by Medicare Part A?

A. Inpatient services and home health care.

B. Inpatient services and follow-up office visits related to the surgery for six months.

C. Inpatient services and retail prescriptions.

D. All dental and vision services, as well as certain over-the-counter drugs and medicine.

73. What do the Medicare secondary payer rules do?

A. Determine whether a particular service is covered by Part A or Part B.

B. Determine which coverage pays first when a Medicare enrollee is covered by another non-Medicare plan as well.

C. Allocate claims costs between Part A and Part C for an inpatient stay.

D. Determine whether a drug is covered by Part A or Part D.

74. Which of the following isn't a Medicare enrollment period?

A. Initial Enrollment Period.

B. Special Enrollment Period.

C. General Enrollment Period.

D. Qualified Enrollment Period.

75. Which of these situations triggers a Part B penalty for John "Buck" Buckingham?

A. Buck's employer-based coverage prior to enrolling in Part B didn't satisfy the MCC standard.

B. He retired three months before his 65th birthday and continued his employer-sponsored plan through COBRA for 18 months before enrolling in Part B.

C. Buck remained employed and on his employer's plan until he enrolled in Medicare during his Special Enrollment Period.

D. He started receiving Social Security benefits at age 63.

76. Individuals who are covered after their 65th birthday by a prescription-drug plan that's not as rich as Medicare are subject to penalties for the rest of their life once they enroll in Part D.

True.

False.

77. By far the most common Part of Medicare subject to penalties is Part A.

True.

False.

78. Individuals who enroll in Part C don't have to pay Part A or Part B premiums, since all Part C plans replace traditional Medicare.

True.

False.

79. MCC stands for Medical Care Cooperatives, which are not-for-profit provider groups that deliver Medicare-approved care to patients.

True.

False.

80. John Selecman must pay a Medicare penalty, but the penalty expires after a certain number of years. His penalty applies to which Part(s) of Medicare?

A. Part A.

B. Part B.

C. Part D.

D. Parts B and D.

81. Jimmie Maddox, who's HSA-eligible, can make a one-time rollover from which retirement accounts to an HSA?

A. SEP, SIMPLE, or Roth IRA.

B. Traditional IRA or Roth IRA.

C. Traditional 401(k) plan or traditional IRA.

D. Any employer-sponsored retirement plan.

82. Which of the following statements is *not* true for a rollover of funds from an IRA to an HSA?

A. It counts against the annual HSA contribution limit.

B. An employer must approve the rollover if the HSA owner is participating in an employer's HSA program.

C. The HSA owner must remain HSA-eligible during the testing period, which lasts 12 full months from the month of the rollover.

D. Only one rollover per lifetime is permitted (with one exception).

83. Which of the following is *not* a reason for John Frederick Parker to roll over funds from an IRA to an HSA?

A. Distributions for qualified expenses are tax-free from the HSA but would have been taxed if distributed for the same expenses from a traditional IRA.

B. HSA distributions aren't subject to Required Minimum Distributions.

C. HSA distributions aren't considered when calculating provisional income.

D. HSAs enjoy bankruptcy protections that IRAs don't.

84. Rollovers can be made from traditional or Roth IRAs, though generally a rollover from a traditional IRA is more advantageous from the perspective of tax treatment of distributions, required mandatory distributions, and provisional income.

True.

False.

85. If Henry James rolls over funds from an IRA to an HSA and doesn't remain HSA-eligible through the testing period, the entire rollover is classified as a premature withdrawal from his IRA.

True.

False.

86. Which of the following statements about HSA investments is *not* true?

A. HSA owners can invest once they satisfy the minimum threshold in their cash accounts set by their administrator or employer.

B. HSA administrators typically offer compliance and investment advice.

C. HSA administrators usually offer a select menu of mutual fund options.

D. Administrators may allow HSA owners to set up an auto-investment program so that all contributions above the cash threshold are automatically invested in funds according to the HSA owner's directive.

87. Which of the following investments is *not* permitted in Charles Leale's self-directed HSA?

A. Investing in commercial real estate.

B. Flipping residential real estate.

C. Purchasing insurance contracts.

D. Lending money to a business.

88. Which of the following statements is *not* true with respect to Billy Otis's self-directed HSA investments?

A. They subject Billy to compliance risks that the administrator doesn't help him address.

B. They allow Billy to leverage his specific knowledge to build his HSA balances.

C. If the IRS determines that an investment isn't permitted, Billy's HSA is liquidated and the balance is deemed an immediate distribution for non-qualified expenses, subject to taxes and penalties.

D. Self-directed HSAs like Billy's have become more common today than traditional HSAs with mutual-fund investments.

89. Under HSA rules, George Brainerd Todd can't begin to invest funds in his HSA until he has accumulated a cash balance of at least $1,000, and his administrator or employer can set a higher figure.

True.

False.

90. HSA owners can own more than one HSA for investment (or any other) purposes.

True.

False.

91. Which of the following is *not* a consideration for Mary Hart as she determines when to enroll in Medicare?

A. Her current prescription-drug coverage doesn't satisfy the MCC standard.

B. Medicare premiums are much lower than her commercial coverage.

C. She hasn't worked enough employment quarters to qualify for premium-free Part B coverage.

D. Her current doctors providing treatment for an acute condition may not accept Medicare assignment of benefits.

92. James Ferguson has coverage through his company as an active employee. He retires at age 68 after 45 years with his company and enrolls in Medicare immediately during his Special Enrollment Period. On which Part of Medicare might he pay penalties in the form of a premium surcharge for the rest of his life?

A. Part A.

B. Part B.

C. Part D.

D. None.

93. Helen Muzzy turns age 65 July 3. Which of the following is *not* true?

A. She will automatically be enrolled in Medicare, as all Medicare-eligible individuals are enrolled in Part A and Part D at age 65.

B. Helen will be enrolled in Medicare Part A and Part B if she is drawing Social Security benefits or if she applies for Medicare coverage.

C. Her birthday triggers an Initial Enrollment Period.

D. Helen will not face any future penalties if she enrolls around her 65th birthday.

94. John Miles remains HSA-eligible as he approaches his 70th birthday. His daughters are encouraging him to retire. Which of the following statements is true?

A. John can continue to delay enrollment in Medicare and Social Security. The longer he continues to delay enrollment in Social Security past age 70, the higher his monthly benefit when he finally begins to collect his benefit.

B. John can continue to defer Social Security and thus remain HSA-eligible, but he won't boost his monthly Social Security benefit by deferring past his 70th birthday.

C. He must begin to collect Social Security benefits at age 70.

D. He automatically loses his HSA eligibility at age 70, so John's best bet is to enroll in Medicare at that time.

95. Which of the following is *not* a key decision point that affects Joseph Stewart's current or future HSA eligibility?

A. Age 62, when Joseph can begin to collect early Social Security benefits.

B. Age 65, when he's eligible to enroll in Medicare.

C. Age 67, when he can apply for his full Social Security benefit.

D. Age 70½, when Joseph must begin to make Required Minimum Distributions from his traditional 401(k) plan and IRA plans.

96. Clara Harris amassed medical equity of more than $76,000 in her HSA before she retired in 2017. For which services can Clara *not* make tax-free reimbursements from her HSA in retirement?

A. Medicare Part D premiums.

B. Medicare deductibles, copays, and coinsurance.

C. Long-term care insurance premiums.

D. Nursing home charges.

97. How does being covered on COBRA after age 65 affect Billy Withers when he finally enrolls in Medicare?

A. Because COBRA doesn't constitute group coverage, Billy could pay Part A, Part B, and Part D penalties.

B. Because COBRA isn't MCC coverage, he could pay Part A and Part D penalties for a period of twice the number of years that he had COBRA coverage after age 65.

C. Because COBRA isn't considered group coverage, Billy faces a Part B penalty of a 10% premium surcharge for every 12 full months of COBRA coverage between his 65th birthday and when he finally enrolls in Medicare.

D. COBRA has no impact on future Part A or Part B premiums, but he may have to pay a lifetime surcharge on Part D premiums.

98. Joseph Sessford is age 68 and is enrolled in his employer's HSA-qualified plan and Medicare Part A. His company employs more than 100 workers. Which of the following statements is true?

A. His employer coverage is primary for all services.

B. Joseph's employer coverage is primary for inpatient services, while Part A is primary for all physician office visits and other outpatient services.

C. His providers determine which plan—the employer coverage or Medicare—offers a better reimbursement and submit a claim to the richer plan.

D. Medicare covers Joseph's inpatient services and prescription drugs, while his employer's plan covers physician and other outpatient services.

99. You are Maggie Gourlay's advising professional. She is age 70 and was enrolled in an HSA program for 12 years. She needs $17,500 quickly to avoid foreclosure on a rental property she owns. She asks four advisors for their advice. Which (correct) statement is attributable to you?

A. "Maggie, any distributions that you make from your HSA are included in your taxable income and subject to an additional 20% tax."

B. "Maggie, you can withdraw $17,500 and match it against qualified expenses that you've incurred since you established your HSA and haven't reimbursed previously; you avoid taxes and penalties on the amount of deferred reimbursement."

C. "You can withdraw funds from your HSA at age 65 and avoid taxes, Maggie, but the 20% penalty always applies."

D. "You can't make distributions for any non-qualified expenses from your HSA, period, Maggie. You need to find another source of funds or you are out of compliance with HSA rules. I want to help you avoid fines and a possible prison sentence."

100. Joseph "Peanut John" Burroughs, now age 72 and covered by Medicare, has three HSAs from old jobs. He asks the same four advising professionals for direction. Which (correct) advice to you provide?

A. "You can consolidate your three HSAs into one. In fact, you should do so—it would be 'nuts' not to do it—to avoid admin fees on three accounts. You can make two trustee-to-trustee transfers to move the funds."

B. "You've missed your window to consolidate accounts, Peanut John. You must be HSA-eligible to move funds from one HSA to another. I'm sorry your former advisor didn't inform you."

C. "You're allowed one lifetime trustee-to-trustee transfer of funds from one HSA to another. If you haven't used that one transfer, you can consolidate down to two HSAs, but not one."

D. "You can consolidate balances into one account. The transfer amounts are subject to taxes, but not penalties. To minimize the tax bite, Peanut John, transfer the two accounts with the lowest balances into the HSA with the highest balance."

Quiz Answers:

1. C. Limited rollovers are a feature of some Health FSA programs. HSA funds roll over without a dollar limit. *See Chapter 23.*

2. B. "Uniform coverage," the concept of immediate access to an annual election, is a feature of a Health FSA but not an HSA. HSA owners don't make a binding annual election, so they can't spend funds before the money is deposited in their HSA. *See Chapter 4.*

3. D. Employees can't make direct or indirect contributions to HRAs. *See Chapter 4.*

4. C. *See references throughout the book and Appendix B.*

5. D. HSAs only. Health FSA elections are binding absent a qualifying event. Employees can't contribute to an HRA. *See Chapter 4.*

6. A. Health FSA and HRA reimbursements are limited to qualified expenses, so administrators must document that reimbursements are for qualified expenses. Neither administrators nor employers can require immediate substantiation of HSA distributions. *See Chapter 5.*

7. C. Employees can't contribute to HRAs. *See Chapter 5.*

8. A. Health FSAs and HRAs are benefit plans owned and administered by employers. HSAs are individually owned financial trusts. *See Chapter 5.*

9. C. All other answers include at least one account into which employees can't make contributions (HRA, answers A and D) or accounts that accept only post-tax contributions (Roth IRA, answer B). *See Chapter 5.*

10. C. All other answers include a traditional IRA or traditional 401(k) plan. Distributions from these accounts are included in taxable income in the year of distributions. *See Chapter 3.*

11. C. A plan isn't HSA-qualified if anyone covered on a family plan can access benefits before the statutory minimum annual deductible for a family contract ($2,700 in 2018 and 2019) is met. *See Chapter 16.*

12. B. Individuals enrolled in a Health FSA aren't HSA-eligible unless the Health FSA is either a Limited-Purpose or Post-Deductible Health FSA. *See Chapter 23.*

13. B. Eligibility to enroll in a medical plan is entirely separate from eligibility to open and contribute to an HSA. *See Chapter 17.*

14. D. *See Chapter 17.*

15. C. George is covered by two medical plans. Neither the primary plan nor the HRA reimburses any expenses below the statutory minimum annual deductible. *See Chapter 17.*

16. B. Accessing VA preventive care or care related to a service-related disability doesn't affect Helen's HSA eligibility. *See Chapter 17.*

17. A. HSA eligibility is affected by disqualifying coverage, not age. As long as John doesn't enroll in disqualifying coverage like Medicare, he remains HSA-eligible. See *Chapter 17.*

18. B. A Health FSA is a benefit plan in which spouses are automatically enrolled unless the Health FSA plan sponsor (employer) limits participation. A plan that isn't designed as a limited Health FSA disqualifies all participants from opening or contributing to an HSA. *See Chapter 17.*

19. A. Medicare issues individual policies only. One spouse's enrollment in Medicare doesn't affect the other spouse's HSA eligibility. *See Chapter 17.*

20. B. When an individual is covered by more than one medical plan, all plans must be HSA-qualified or the individual can't open or contribute to an HSA. *See Chapter 17.*

21. False. An HSA-qualified plan can't pay any benefits until the family has incurred financial responsibility equal to at least the statutory minimum annual deductible ($2,700 in 2018 and 2019). *See Chapter 16.*

22. True. Individuals who receive Social Security benefits before age 65 are automatically enrolled in Part A and Part B as of their 65th birthday. Enrollment in any Part of Medicare is a disqualifying event. *See Chapter 17.*

23. False. A Health FSA doesn't become a Limited-Purpose Health FSA unless plan documents limit reimbursement to dental and vision expenses. *See Chapters 17 and 23.*

24. True. This individual isn't covered by his spouse's Medicare policy. Medicare offers individual coverage only. *See Chapter 17.*

25. True. Though the IRS hasn't issued formal guidance on this issue, a program that offers diagnostic and treatment services outside the deductible may be disqualifying. *See Chapter 17.*

26. D. She can contribute for the seven months (June through December) that she is eligible as of the first day of the month. She can also use the Last-Month Rule and contribute up to the maximum as long as she is HSA-eligible Dec. 1. *See Chapter 18.*

27. A. HSA contributions aren't pro-rated based on when a birthday falls during the year. As long as he is HSA-eligible all 12 months, he can make the full catch-up contribution. *See Chapter 18.*

28. C. He is HSA-eligible on the first day of 10 months (January through October) and is old enough to make a $1,000 (pro-rated) catch-up contribution. The Last-Month Rule doesn't apply when an individual isn't HSA-eligible as of Dec. 1. *See Chapter 18.*

29. A. The Post-Deductible HRA has no impact on his contribution limit. He can contribute up to the statutory maximum annual contribution for a family contract. *See Chapter 18.*

30. C. The statutory maximum annual contribution includes contributions from all sources. Employer contributions reduce employee contributions dollar-for-dollar. *See Chapter 18.*

31. False. HSA contribution limits are independent of retirement plan contribution limits. *See Chapter 18.*

32. False. The Last-Month Rule applies only to individuals who are HSA-eligible as of Dec. 1. *See Chapter 18.*

33. False. HSA owners can contribute to their HSA for a given tax year until the earlier of the date that they file their personal income tax return or the due date for income tax returns. *See Chapter 18.*

34. False. Spouses are limited to the statutory maximum annual contribution to a family contract, which they can split between their two HSAs as they wish. *See Chapter 18.*

35. False. Her contribution limit depends on the contract type (self-only or family coverage), regardless of how many covered family members are HSA-eligible themselves. *See Chapter 18.*

36. C. *See Chapter 19.*

37. B. HSA distributions aren't subject to annual or lifetime limits. *See Chapter 19.*

38. D. The other expenses are incurred by ineligible individuals (domestic partner and child who's no longer a tax dependent) or represent a non-qualified expense (aromatherapy and massage). *See Chapter 19.*

39. C. *See Chapter 19.*

40. A. *See Chapter 19.*

41. False. Neither administrators nor employers can require that distributions from an HSA be made for qualified expenses only. *See Chapter 19.*

42. True. *See Chapter 19.*

43. False. Owners face no deadline. They can reimburse qualified expenses tax-free decades later, as long as they incurred the expenses after they established their HSA. *See Chapter 19.*

44. False. Her medical coverage is irrelevant. Her relationship to the HSA owner determines whether he can make tax-free distributions for her qualified expenses. *See Chapter 19.*

45. False. An HSA owner can reimburse all qualified expenses tax-free at any time in the future, as long as she incurred the expenses after she established her HSA. *See Chapter 19.*

46. A. Form 8889 is paperwork filed with a personal income tax return that summarizes HSA contribution and distribution activity during the tax year. *See Chapter 22.*

47. D. *See Chapter 22.*

48. D. *See Chapter 18.*

49. A. *See Chapter 18 and Chapter 20.*

50. C. An HSA must be established as a trust and follow all HSA rules. *See Chapter 18.*

51. True. *See Chapter 18.*

52. False. There are no joint HSAs. If each spouse is eligible to make a catch-up contribution, each must open an individual HSA. *See Chapter 20.*

53. False. An HSA owner can't reimburse an ex-spouse's qualified expenses tax-free from his HSA, even if he is ordered to pay her expenses. *See Chapter 19.*

54. True. Some administrators limit the cards to work only at merchants who typically sell HSA-qualified services. Other can and do offer unrestricted debit cards. *See Chapter 20.*

55. False. *See Chapter 20.*

56. D. The grace period must be a Limited-Purpose Health FSA, with plan documents and administration that reimburse only qualified dental and vision expenses. *See Chapter 23.*

57. A. A Dependent Care Reimbursement Account (also called a Dependent FSA or DCRA) has no impact on HSA eligibility. *See Chapter 23.*

58. C. There is no such thing as a Retirement Health FSA.

59. D. *See Chapters 17 and 24.*

60. B. A Post-Deductible HRA must not begin to reimburse any expenses before the statutory minimum annual deductible. *See Chapter 24.*

61. A. Employers can't split their Health FSA populations at any point during the year, including during the grace period. *See Chapter 23.*

62. False. They are locked into their Health FSA for the balance of the plan year (including grace period, if applicable). Enrolling in an HSA-qualified plan isn't a qualifying event to terminate Health FSA coverage. *See Chapter 23.*

63. False. A spouse's participation in a Health FSA excludes all family members from becoming HSA-eligible. *See Chapter 23.*

64. False. He is covered by the Health FSA the entire following year. He can't become HSA-eligible during that period, even if he spends his rollover balance quickly and made no election to that year's Health FSA. *See Chapter 23.*

65. True. *See Chapter 23.*

66. D. *See Chapter 25.*

67. A. Family-court judges can't overrule tax law. An HSA owner can't reimburse tax-free any expenses incurred by an ex-spouse. *See Chapter 25.*

68. C. More than one family member on the contract may be HSA-eligible. Henry's son is no longer Henry's tax dependent. He satisfies other eligibility requirements, so he can open his own HSA. *See Chapter 25.*

69. False. In most cases, both parents can reimburse their children's qualified expenses, even if one parent can claim them as dependents on his or her personal income tax return. *See Chapter 25.*

70. True. *See Chapter 25 and Appendix E.*

71. B. *See Chapter 13.*

72. A. *See Chapter 13.*

73. B. *See Chapter 13.*

74. D. *See Chapter 13.*

75. B. *See Chapter 13.*

76. True. *See Chapter 13.*

77. False. Anyone who worked 40 employment quarters and earned a minimal amount each quarter receives Part A premium-free and penalty-free. *See Chapter 13.*

78. False. *See Chapter 13.*

79. False. MCC stands for Medicare Creditable Coverage, which measures whether a commercial medical plan offers a prescription drug benefit at least as rich as Medicare coverage. *See Chapter 13.*

80. A. For the few individuals who pay Part A penalties, the premium surcharge is levied for twice the number of years that they delayed enrollment after their 65th birthday. Part B and Part D penalties are permanent. *See Chapter 13.*

81. B. All rollovers from retirement accounts to an HSA must come from a traditional or Roth IRA. *See Chapter 8 and Appendix D.*

82. B. These rollovers are independent of the employer. *See Chapter 8.*

83. D. *See Chapter 8.*

84. True. *See Chapter 8.*

85. True. *See Chapter 8 and Appendix D.*

86. B. Administrators may offer the services of licensed investment agents, either directly or through their investment platform partner, but they don't typically offer advice on investments. They also don't offer compliance guidance. *See Chapter 10.*

87. C. *See Chapter 11.*

88. D. *See Chapter 11.*

89. False. Neither the original legislation nor subsequent formal guidance from IRS places minimum thresholds on investments. *See Chapter 10.*

90. True. *See Chapter 10.*

91. C. Part B is never premium-free. *See Chapter 13.*

92. C. If his prescription-drug plan doesn't satisfy MCC standards, he's subject to a Part D penalty. Because he was entitled to a Special Enrollment Period, he doesn't face a Part B penalty. And he earned enough during a 45-year career to satisfy the requirement that he work 40 employment quarters to earn Part A premium-free. *See Chapters 13 and 14.*

93. A. *See Chapters 13 and 14.*

94. B. *See Chapter 14.*

95. D. RMDs don't affect HSA eligibility. *See Chapter 15.*

96. D. *See Chapter 12.*

97. C. Maintaining employer-sponsored coverage until triggering a Special Enrollment Period is critical to avoiding Part B penalties. It's irrelevant to Part A and Part D penalties. *See Chapter 14.*

98. A. *See Chapters 13 and 14.*

99. B. *See Chapters 12 and 19.*

100. A. *See Chapter 21.*

APPENDIX B

Glossary of Terms

Affordable Care Act (ACA). The landmark legislation signed into law by President Obama on March 23, 2010, that increases federal regulation over medical insurance products and markets. Its formal name is the Patient Protection and Affordable Care Act, or PPACA, though the full name is rarely used. It's often referred to as "ObamaCare."

Allowable charge. The maximum amount that an insurer reimburses for a covered expense. Inside the insurer's network, the allowable charge is negotiated between the insurer and provider. Outside the network, the insurer typically pays a percentage of the Medicare reimbursement or a certain percentile of the prevailing charges within the geographic area.

Balance-bill. The amount above the insurer's allowable charge that a non-network provider charges a patient. The balance-bill amount is the patient's financial responsibility and isn't applied to the deductible or out-of-pocket maximum.

Benefit period (for Medicare Part A): The period of time beginning with a patient's admission into an acute-care hospital or skilled-nursing facility (SNF, pronounced "sniff") and ending when the patient hasn't received inpatient hospital or SNF care for 60 consecutive days. Patients pay a deductible of $1,340 (2018 figure) per benefit period.

Centers for Medicare and Medicaid Services (CMS). The agency within the U.S. Department of Health and Human Services that's responsible for overseeing Medicare and Medicaid.

Coinsurance. A fixed percentage of the allowable charge that the patient and medical insurer split. Example: An $80 physician visit for a Medicare Part B enrollee is split 80%/20% so that Medicare pays $64 and the patient is responsible for the $16 balance.

Consumer-Driven Health (CDH). Generally defined as medical coverage with a deductible of at least $1,000 per individual and $2,000 per family. Because patients are responsible for the initial covered services each year, they have incentives to behave as consumers to determine which services they need and where they receive their care based on cost and quality.

Coordination of benefits. The behind-the-scenes activity in which two or more insurers engage when they cover an individual who generates a claim. These rules are well established among insurers.

Copay. A fixed dollar amount typically paid by the patient at the point of service. The balance of the allowable charge is paid by the medical insurer. Examples: a $35 copay for a physician visit and a $15 copay for generic drugs.

Cost-sharing. The portion of allowable charges that are the patient's financial responsibility. These charges are expressed as coinsurance, copays, and deductibles.

Deductible. The amount of allowable charges for which a patient is responsible before a medical insurer begins to reimburse a portion of claims. Examples: Patients enrolled in Medicare are responsible for the first $1,240 in allowable charges for inpatient care during each benefit period (after which Medicare pays allowable charges in full for a period of time) and for the first $183 of Part B outpatient services (after which Medicare pays 80% of allowable charges and the patient is responsible for the remaining 20%).

Effective date of coverage. The day on which a medical policy begins to cover a policyholder. Medicare's effective date of coverage is always the first day of the month. Most commercial plans also are effective on the first day of the month, but others are effective the 15th, 25th, or other day of the initial month of coverage.

Employee Retirement Income Security Act (ERISA). A sweeping 1974 law. In the context of HSAs, the law exempts self-insured medical plans from state regulations, including benefit mandates.

Employment quarter. A calendar quarter during which an employee earns at least $1,320 (2018 figure—prior years' figures are less) to earn one of the 40 employment quarters necessary to receive Medicare Part A premium-free at age 65 or later.

Full Retirement Age. The age at which an individual can apply to receive Social Security benefits and receive his full (not a discounted) benefit. The age is 66 years and no months for individuals born between 1943 and 1954, then increases by two months per year until anyone born in 1960 or later receives full benefits at age 67.

Health Flexible Spending Arrangement (Health FSA). An employer-sponsored, limited-benefit medical plan that allows employees to receive a portion of their income in the form of tax-free funds to reimburse qualified medical, dental, and vision, and certain over-the-counter expenses.

Health Maintenance Organization (HMO). Medical coverage in which members must receive care within a specific network of participating providers. Care is usually coordinated by a primary-care physician. The plan usually (but doesn't always) require referrals to receive specialty care.

Health Reimbursement Arrangement (HRA). An employer-sponsored, limited-benefit medical plan that allows employers to give employees tax-free funds to reimburse qualified medical expenses. An HRA is usually integrated with a medical plan so that the HRA reimburses a portion of employee cost-sharing.

Health Savings Account (HSA). A triple-tax-free financial account that is the subject of this book.

High Deductible Health Plan (HDHP). The name given to HSA-qualified medical coverage in the original legislation. In 2003, a plan with a $1,000 self-only or $2,000 family deductible was considered "high deductible." Today, those deductible levels are common (and below the average in small businesses). And many plans with high deductibles don't satisfy other requirements that coverage must include for individuals covered on the plan to become HSA-eligible. For this reason, these plans are referred to as "HSA-qualified coverage" throughout this book.

Medicare Advantage (Medicare Part C). An alternative to traditional Medicare (Part A and Part B, plus Part D) offered by private insurers regulated by CMS. About 30% of Medicare enrollees currently receive their care through these plans, which resemble HMOs and often offer additional benefits and value-added programs that traditional Medicare doesn't provide.

Medicare Secondary Payer. A set of rules that determines whether Medicare is the primary payer or secondary payer when a patient is covered by Medicare and at least one other policy.

Medicare Supplement. A private insurance plan that reimburses providers for most of the Medicare deductibles and coinsurance for which Medicare enrollees are financially responsible. Medicare enrollees (sometimes with financial assistance from their former employers) pay a monthly premium for this optional additional coverage.

Out-of-Pocket Maximum. The total amount that a patient pays during a plan year for deductibles, coinsurance, and copays for covered services (but not including premiums). HSA-qualified medical plans and most other commercial coverage have out-of-pocket maximums to cap patient financial responsibility. Medicare Part B is an example of coverage that doesn't have a maximum, so patients are exposed to unlimited financial responsibility.

Point-of-Service plan (POS). Medical coverage that allows members to choose at the time that they receive care whether to stay within the insurer's network (typically with lower cost-sharing) or seek care outside that network (with higher cost-sharing). Members usually have to work with a primary-care physician to coordinate their care with in-network providers to receive the highest level of benefits (lowest cost-sharing).

Preferred Provider Organization (PPO). Medical coverage that gives members maximum freedom to receive care from any provider. Members usually don't have to work with a primary-care physician or seek referrals for specialty care. The insurer's level of reimbursement depends on whether a preferred (contracted) or non-preferred (non-contracted) provider delivers the care.

Primary payer. The insurer to which claims are submitted first when an individual is covered by more than one plan.

Primary-Care Physician (PCP). A provider who works with a patient to develop a health strategy, delivers preventive care, monitors and treats simple conditions, and refers patients to specialty care when appropriate. PCPs usually practice pediatrics, internal medicine, or family medicine. They are referred to as "gatekeepers" in many HMO and POS plans because they manage access to specialty care.

Provisional Income. A calculation that determines the percentage of an individual's Social Security benefits that is subject to federal income taxes. Most retiree income, including wages, traditional IRA and 401(k) plan withdrawals, and stock dividends are included in the calculation. HSA distributions aren't.

Required Minimum Distribution (RMD). The amount that owners of certain retirement plans must distribute annually from their accounts beginning no later than the year that they turn age 70½. If distributions fall short of this figure, the difference between the RMDs and actual distributions is taxed at 50%.

Secondary payer. The insurer to which claims are submitted after the primary payer has processed the claim and made payment according to its contract. The secondary payer may or may not reimburse a portion of the patient's remaining financial responsibility, depending on the terms of its contract.

APPENDIX C

Internal Revenue Code Section 223

26 U.S. Code § 223—Health savings accounts

(a) DEDUCTION ALLOWED

In the case of an individual who is an eligible individual for any month during the taxable year, there shall be allowed as a deduction for the taxable year an amount equal to the aggregate amount paid in cash during such taxable year by or on behalf of such individual to a health savings account of such individual.

(b) LIMITATIONS

(1) IN GENERAL The amount allowable as a deduction under subsection (a) to an individual for the taxable year shall not exceed the sum of the monthly limitations for months during such taxable year that the individual is an eligible individual.

(2) MONTHLY LIMITATION The monthly limitation for any month is 1/12 of—

(A) in the case of an eligible individual who has self-only coverage under a high deductible health plan as of the first day of such month, $2,250.

(B) in the case of an eligible individual who has family coverage under a high deductible health plan as of the first day of such month, $4,500.

(3) ADDITIONAL CONTRIBUTIONS FOR INDIVIDUALS 55 OR OLDER

(A) In general—In the case of an individual who has attained age 55 before the close of the taxable year, the applicable limitation under subparagraphs (A) and (B) of paragraph (2) shall be increased by the additional contribution amount.

(B) Additional contribution amount—For purposes of this section, the additional contribution amount is the amount determined in accordance with the following table:

For taxable years beginning in:	The additional contribution amount is:
2004	$500
2005	$600
2006	$700
2007	$800
2008	$900
2009 and thereafter	$1,000

Author's note: The HOPE Act of 2006—see Appendix F—provides an additional opportunity for individuals who become HSA-eligible mid-year. As long as they're HSA-eligible by Dec. 1, they can contribute up to the statutory maximum contribution (plus the full catch-up contribution) for the calendar year. They then must remain HSA-eligible through the end of the following calendar year. For a description of this concept, called the Last-Month Rule, see Chapter 18, HSA Contributions.

(4) COORDINATION WITH OTHER CONTRIBUTIONS The limitation which would (but for this paragraph) apply under this subsection to an individual for any taxable year shall be reduced (but not below zero) by the sum of—

(A) the aggregate amount paid for such taxable year to Archer MSAs of such individual,

(B) the aggregate amount contributed to health savings accounts of such individual which is excludable from the taxpayer's gross income for such taxable year under section 106(d) (and such amount shall not be allowed as a deduction under subsection (a)), and

(C) the aggregate amount contributed to health savings accounts of such individual for such taxable year under section 408(d)(9) (and such amount shall not be allowed as a deduction under subsection (a)).

Subparagraph (A) shall not apply with respect to any individual to whom paragraph (5) applies.

(5) SPECIAL RULE FOR MARRIED INDIVIDUALS In the case of individuals who are married to each other, if either spouse has family coverage—

(A) both spouses shall be treated as having only such family coverage (and if such spouses each have family coverage under different plans, as having the family coverage with the lowest annual deductible), and

(B) the limitation under paragraph (1) (after the application of subparagraph (A) and without regard to any additional contribution amount under paragraph (3))—

(i) shall be reduced by the aggregate amount paid to Archer MSAs of such spouses for the taxable year, and

(ii) after such reduction, shall be divided equally between them unless they agree on a different division.

(6) DENIAL OF DEDUCTION TO DEPENDENTS
No deduction shall be allowed under this section to any individual with respect to whom a deduction under section 151 is allowable to another taxpayer for a taxable year beginning in the calendar year in which such individual's taxable year begins.

(7) MEDICARE ELIGIBLE INDIVIDUALS
The limitation under this subsection for any month with respect to an individual shall be zero for the first month such individual is entitled to benefits under title XVIII of the Social Security Act and for each month thereafter.

(8) INCREASE IN LIMIT FOR INDIVIDUALS BECOMING ELIGIBLE INDIVIDUALS AFTER THE BEGINNING OF THE YEAR

(A) In general—For purposes of computing the limitation under paragraph (1) for any taxable year, an individual who is an eligible individual during the last month of such taxable year shall be treated—

(i) as having been an eligible individual during each of the months in such taxable year, and

(ii) as having been enrolled, during each of the months such individual is treated as an eligible individual solely by reason of clause (i), in the same high deductible health plan in which the individual was enrolled for the last month of such taxable year.

(B) Failure to maintain high deductible health plan coverage

(i) In general—If, at any time during the testing period, the individual is not an eligible individual, then—

(I) gross income of the individual for the taxable year in which occurs the first month in the testing period for which such individual is not an eligible individual is increased by the aggregate amount of all contributions to the health savings account of the individual which could not have been made but for subparagraph (A), and

(II) the tax imposed by this chapter for any taxable year on the individual shall be increased by 10 percent of the amount of such increase.

(ii) Exception for disability or death
Subclauses (I) and (II) of clause (i) shall not apply if the individual ceased to be an eligible individual by reason of the death of the individual or the individual becoming disabled (within the meaning of section 72(m)(7)).

(iii) Testing period
The term "testing period" means the period beginning with the last month of the taxable year referred to in subparagraph (A) and ending on the last day of the 12th month following such month.

(c) DEFINITIONS AND SPECIAL RULES For purposes of this section—

(1) ELIGIBLE INDIVIDUAL

(A) In general—The term "eligible individual" means, with respect to any month, any individual if—

(i) such individual is covered under a high deductible health plan as of the 1st day of such month, and

(ii) such individual is not, while covered under a high deductible health plan, covered under any health plan—

(I) which is not a high deductible health plan, and

(II) which provides coverage for any benefit which is covered under the high deductible health plan.

(B) Certain coverage disregarded Subparagraph (A)(ii) shall be applied without regard to—

(i) coverage for any benefit provided by permitted insurance,

(ii) coverage (whether through insurance or otherwise) for accidents, disability, dental care, vision care, or long-term care, and

(iii) for taxable years beginning after December 31, 2006, coverage under a health flexible spending arrangement during any period immediately following the end of a plan year of such arrangement during which unused benefits or contributions remaining at the end of such plan year may be paid or reimbursed to plan participants for qualified benefit expenses incurred during such period if—

(I) the balance in such arrangement at the end of such plan year is zero, or

(II) the individual is making a qualified HSA distribution (as defined in section 106(e)) in an amount equal to the remaining balance in such arrangement as of the end of such plan year, in accordance with rules prescribed by the Secretary.

(C) Special rule for individuals eligible for certain veterans benefits
An individual shall not fail to be treated as an eligible individual for any period merely because the individual receives hospital care or medical services under any law administered by the Secretary of Veterans Affairs for a service-connected disability (within the meaning of section 101(16) of title 38, United States Code).

(2) HIGH DEDUCTIBLE HEALTH PLAN

(A) In general—The term "high deductible health plan" means a health plan—

(i) which has an annual deductible which is not less than—

(I) $1,000 for self-only coverage, and

(II) twice the dollar amount in subclause (I) for family coverage, and

(ii) the sum of the annual deductible and the other annual out-of-pocket expenses required to be paid under the plan (other than for premiums) for covered benefits does not exceed—

(I) $5,000 for self-only coverage, and

(II) twice the dollar amount in subclause (I) for family coverage.

(B) Exclusion of certain plans
Such term does not include a health plan if substantially all of its coverage is coverage described in paragraph (1)(B).

(C) Safe harbor for absence of preventive care deductible
A plan shall not fail to be treated as a high deductible health plan by reason of failing to have a deductible for preventive care (within the meaning of section 1871 of the Social Security Act, except as otherwise provided by the Secretary).

(D) Special rules for network plans—In the case of a plan using a network of providers—

(i) Annual out-of-pocket limitation
Such plan shall not fail to be treated as a high deductible health plan by reason of having an out-of-pocket limitation for services provided outside of such network which exceeds the applicable limitation under subparagraph (A)(ii).

(ii) Annual deductible

Such plan's annual deductible for services provided outside of such network shall not be taken into account for purposes of subsection (b)(2).

(3) PERMITTED INSURANCE The term "permitted insurance" means—

(A) insurance if substantially all of the coverage provided under such insurance relates to—

(i) liabilities incurred under workers' compensation laws,

(ii) tort liabilities

(iii) liabilities relating to ownership or use of property, or

(iv) such other similar liabilities as the Secretary may specify by regulations,

(B) insurance for a specified disease or illness, and

(C) insurance paying a fixed amount per day (or other period) of hospitalization.

(4) FAMILY COVERAGE

The term "family coverage" means any coverage other than self-only coverage.

(5) ARCHER MSA

The term "Archer MSA" has the meaning given such term in section 220(d).

(d) HEALTH SAVINGS ACCOUNT For purposes of this section—

(1) IN GENERAL—The term "health savings account" means a trust created or organized in the United States as a health savings account exclusively for the purpose of paying the qualified medical expenses of the account beneficiary, but only if the written governing instrument creating the trust meets the following requirements:

(A) Except in the case of a rollover contribution described in subsection (f)(5) or section 220(f)(5), no contribution will be accepted—

(i) unless it is in cash, or

(ii) to the extent such contribution, when added to previous contributions to the trust for the calendar year, exceeds the sum of—

(I) the dollar amount in effect under subsection (b)(2)(B), and

(II) the dollar amount in effect under subsection (b)(3)(B).

(B) The trustee is a bank (as defined in section 408(n)), an insurance company (as defined in section 816), or another person who demonstrates to the satisfaction of the Secretary that the manner in which such person will administer the trust will be consistent with the requirements of this section.

(C) No part of the trust assets will be invested in life insurance contracts.

(D) The assets of the trust will not be commingled with other property except in a common trust fund or common investment fund.

(E) The interest of an individual in the balance in his account is nonforfeitable.

(2) QUALIFIED MEDICAL EXPENSES

(A) In general
The term "qualified medical expenses" means, with respect to an account beneficiary, amounts paid by such beneficiary for medical care (as defined in section 213(d) [1] for such individual, the spouse of such individual, and any dependent (as defined in section 152, determined without regard to subsections (b)(1), (b)(2), and (d)(1)(B) thereof) of such individual, but only to the extent such amounts are not compensated for by insurance or other wise. Such term shall include an amount paid for medicine or a drug only if such medicine or drug is a prescribed drug (determined without regard to whether such drug is available without a prescription) or is insulin.

(B) Health insurance may not be purchased from account Subparagraph (A) shall not apply to any payment for insurance.

(C) Exceptions. Subparagraph (B) shall not apply to any expense for coverage under—

(i) a health plan during any period of continuation coverage required under any Federal law,

(ii) a qualified long-term care insurance contract (as defined in section 7702B(b)),

(iii) a health plan during a period in which the individual is receiving unemployment compensation under any Federal or State law, or

(iv) in the case of an account beneficiary who has attained the age specified in section 1811 of the Social Security Act, any health insurance other than a medicare supplemental policy (as defined in section 1882 of the Social Security Act).

(3) ACCOUNT BENEFICIARY
The term "account beneficiary" means the individual on whose behalf the health savings account was established.

(4) CERTAIN RULES TO APPLY Rules similar to the following rules shall apply for purposes of this section:

(A) Section 219(d)(2) (relating to no deduction for rollovers).

(B) Section 219(f)(3) (relating to time when contributions deemed made).

(C) Except as provided in section 106(d), section 219(f)(5) (relating to employer payments).

(D) Section 408(g) (relating to community property laws).

(E) Section 408(h) (relating to custodial accounts).

(e) TAX TREATMENT OF ACCOUNTS

(1) IN GENERAL
A health savings account is exempt from taxation under this subtitle unless such account has ceased to be a health savings account. Notwithstanding the preceding sentence, any such account is subject to the taxes imposed by section 511 (relating to imposition of tax on unrelated business income of charitable, etc. organizations).

(2) ACCOUNT TERMINATIONS
Rules similar to the rules of paragraphs (2) and (4) of section 408(e) shall apply to health savings accounts, and any amount treated as distributed under such rules shall be treated as not used to pay qualified medical expenses.

(f) TAX TREATMENT OF DISTRIBUTIONS

(1) AMOUNTS USED FOR QUALIFIED MEDICAL EXPENSES
Any amount paid or distributed out of a health savings account which is used exclusively to pay qualified medical expenses of any account beneficiary shall not be includible in gross income.

(2) INCLUSION OF AMOUNTS NOT USED FOR QUALIFIED MEDICAL EXPENSES
Any amount paid or distributed out of a health savings account which is not used exclusively to pay the qualified medical expenses of the account beneficiary shall be included in the gross income of such beneficiary.

(3) EXCESS CONTRIBUTIONS RETURNED BEFORE DUE DATE OF RETURN

(A) In general—If any excess contribution is contributed for a taxable year to any health savings account of an individual, paragraph (2) shall not apply to distributions from the health savings accounts of such individual (to the extent such distributions do not exceed the aggregate excess contributions to all such accounts of such individual for such year) if—

(i) such distribution is received by the individual on or before the last day prescribed by law (including extensions of time) for filing such individual's return for such taxable year, and

(ii) such distribution is accompanied by the amount of net income attributable to such excess contribution.

Any net income described in clause (ii) shall be included in the gross income of the individual for the taxable year in which it is received.

(B) Excess contribution
For purposes of subparagraph (A), the term "excess contribution" means any contribution (other than a rollover contribution described in paragraph (5) or section 220(f)(5)) which is neither excludable from gross income under section 106(d) nor deductible under this section.

(4) ADDITIONAL TAX ON DISTRIBUTIONS NOT USED FOR QUALIFIED MEDICAL EXPENSES

(A) In general
The tax imposed by this chapter on the account beneficiary for any taxable year in which there is a payment or distribution from a health savings account of such beneficiary which is includible in gross income under paragraph (2) shall be increased by 20 percent of the amount which is so includible.

(B) Exception for disability or death
Subparagraph (A) shall not apply if the payment or distribution is made after the account beneficiary becomes disabled within the meaning of section 72(m)(7) or dies.

(C) Exception for distributions after medicare eligibility
Subparagraph (A) shall not apply to any payment or distribution after the date on which the account beneficiary attains the age specified in section 1811 of the Social Security Act.

(5) ROLLOVER CONTRIBUTION An amount is described in this paragraph as a rollover contribution if it meets the requirements of subparagraphs (A) and (B).

(A) In general
Paragraph (2) shall not apply to any amount paid or distributed from a health savings account to the account beneficiary to the extent the amount received is paid into a health savings account for the benefit of such beneficiary not later than the 60th day after the day on which the beneficiary receives the payment or distribution.

(B) Limitation
This paragraph shall not apply to any amount described in subparagraph (A) received by an individual from a health savings account if, at any time during

the 1-year period ending on the day of such receipt, such individual received any other amount described in subparagraph (A) from a health savings account which was not includible in the individual's gross income because of the application of this paragraph.

(6) COORDINATION WITH MEDICAL EXPENSE DEDUCTION
For purposes of determining the amount of the deduction under section 213, any payment or distribution out of a health savings account for qualified medical expenses shall not be treated as an expense paid for medical care.

(7) TRANSFER OF ACCOUNT INCIDENT TO DIVORCE
The transfer of an individual's interest in a health savings account to an individual's spouse or former spouse under a divorce or separation instrument described in subparagraph (A) of section 71(b)(2) shall not be considered a taxable transfer made by such individual notwithstanding any other provision of this subtitle, and such interest shall, after such transfer, be treated as a health savings account with respect to which such spouse is the account beneficiary.

(8) TREATMENT AFTER DEATH OF ACCOUNT BENEFICIARY

(A) Treatment if designated beneficiary is spouse

(i) In general—If, by reason of the death of the account beneficiary, any person acquires the account beneficiary's interest in a health savings account in a case to which subparagraph (A) does not apply—

(I) such account shall cease to be a health savings account as of the date of death, and

(II) an amount equal to the fair market value of the assets in such account on such date shall be includible if such person is not the estate of such beneficiary, in such person's gross income for the taxable year which includes such date, or if such person is the estate of such beneficiary, in such beneficiary's gross income for the last taxable year of such beneficiary.

(ii) Special rules

(I) Reduction of inclusion for predeath expenses
The amount includible in gross income under clause (i) by any person (other than the estate) shall be reduced by the amount of qualified medical expenses which were incurred by the decedent before the date of the decedent's death and paid by such person within 1 year after such date.

(II) Deduction for estate taxes

An appropriate deduction shall be allowed under section 691(c) to any person (other than the decedent or the decedent's spouse) with respect to amounts included in gross income under clause (i) by such person.

(g) COST-OF-LIVING ADJUSTMENT

(1) IN GENERAL—Each dollar amount in subsections (b)(2) and (c)(2)(A) shall be increased by an amount equal to—

(A) such dollar amount, multiplied by

(B) the cost-of-living adjustment determined under section 1(f)(3) for the calendar year in which such taxable year begins determined by substituting for "calendar year 1992" in subparagraph (B) thereof—

(i) except as provided in clause (ii), "calendar year 1997", and

(ii) in the case of each dollar amount in subsection (c)(2)(A), "calendar year 2003".

In the case of adjustments made for any taxable year beginning after 2007, section 1(f)(4) shall be applied for purposes of this paragraph by substituting "March 31" for "August 31", and the Secretary shall publish the adjusted amounts under subsections (b)(2) and (c)(2)(A) for taxable years beginning in any calendar year no later than June 1 of the preceding calendar year.

(2) ROUNDING

If any increase under paragraph (1) is not a multiple of $50, such increase shall be rounded to the nearest multiple of $50.

(h) REPORTS The Secretary may require—

(1) the trustee of a health savings account to make such reports regarding such account to the Secretary and to the account beneficiary with respect to contributions, distributions, the return of excess contributions, and such other matters as the Secretary determines appropriate, and

(2) any person who provides an individual with a high deductible health plan to make such reports to the Secretary and to the account beneficiary with respect to such plan as the Secretary determines appropriate.

The reports required by this subsection shall be filed at such time and in such manner and furnished to such individuals at such time and in such manner as may be required by the Secretary.

(Added Pub. L. 108–173, title XII, § 1201(a), Dec. 8, 2003, 117 Stat. 2469; amended Pub. L. 109–135, title IV, § 404(c), Dec. 21, 2005, 119 Stat. 2634; Pub. L. 109–432, div. A, title

III, §§ 302(b), 303(a), (b), 304, 305(a), 307(b), Dec. 20, 2006, 120 Stat. 2949, 2950, 2953; Pub. L. 111–148, title IX, §§ 9003(a), 9004(a), Mar. 23, 2010, 124 Stat. 854; Pub. L. 114–41, title IV, § 4007(b)(1), July 31, 2015, 129 Stat. 466; Pub. L. 115–97, title I, §§ 11002(d)(1)(V), 11051(b)(3)(E), Dec. 22, 2017, 131 Stat. 2060, 2090.)

APPENDIX D

IRS Guidance on IRA-to-HSA Rollovers

Part III—Administrative, Procedural, and Miscellaneous

Health Savings Accounts

Notice 2008-51

Section 307 of the Health Opportunity Patient Empowerment Act of 2006 (the Act) added § 408(d)(9) to the Internal Revenue Code. The Act is part of the Tax Relief and Health Care Act of 2006, enacted December 20, 2006, Pub. L. No. 109-432. This notice provides guidance on a qualified HSA funding distribution from an individual's Individual Retirement Account (IRA) or Roth IRA to a Health Savings Account (HSA). The qualified HSA funding distribution is a one-time transfer from an individual's IRA to his or her HSA and generally excluded from gross income and is not subject to the 10 percent additional tax under § 72(t).

BACKGROUND

Eligible individuals

Generally, only eligible individuals (as defined in § 223(c)(1)) may contribute to HSAs. Maximum annual HSA contributions are based on an individual's eligibility, age, and health plan coverage.

General rules on taxation of distributions from IRAs

A distribution from an IRA under § 408 generally is included in gross income. If an IRA owner made nondeductible contributions to the IRA, those contributions are recovered on a *pro-rata* basis and the distribution is partly included in and partly excluded from gross income under the rules of § 408(d) and § 72(e)(8).

A nonqualified distribution from a Roth IRA under § 408A is included in gross income only to the extent that earnings are distributed. A qualified Roth IRA distribution (as defined in § 408A(d)) is excluded from gross income.

If a distribution from an IRA or Roth IRA is made before the IRA or Roth IRA account owner attains age 59½, the distribution also is subject to a 10 percent additional tax under § 72(t) unless an exception applies. These exceptions include distributions made on account of death or disability, and distributions made as part of a series of substantially equal periodic payments for the life expectancy of the IRA holder.

HEALTH OPPORTUNITY PATIENT EMPOWERMENT ACT OF 2006

Tax treatment of qualified HSA funding distributions

Section 408(d)(9) provides, in general, that a qualified HSA funding distribution from an individual's IRA or Roth IRA to that individual's HSA is not included in gross income, if the individual is an eligible individual under § 223(c)(1). Moreover, notwithstanding the pro-rata basis recovery rules under § 72, for purposes of determining the basis in any amount remaining in an IRA or Roth IRA following a qualified HSA funding distribution, the qualified HSA funding distribution is treated as included in gross income to the extent that such amount does not exceed the aggregate amount which would have been so included if there were a total distribution from the IRA or Roth IRA owner's accounts. For example, suppose an individual who has $200 of basis in an IRA with a fair market value of $2,000 makes a qualified HSA funding distribution of $1,500 from the IRA. Immediately after the qualified HSA funding distribution, the individual retains $200 of basis in an IRA that has a fair market value of $500.

If a qualified HSA funding distribution from an individual's IRA or Roth IRA exceeds the aggregate amount which would have been included in gross income if there were a total distribution from that individual's IRA or Roth IRA accounts, the individual's basis in the excess amount (i.e., the amount that would have been excluded from gross income in a distribution to which § 408(d)(9) did not apply) does not carry over to the HSA.

A qualified HSA funding distribution is not subject to the 10 percent additional tax under § 72(t). However, if the qualified HSA funding distribution results in a modification of a series of substantially equal periodic payments that, prior to the modification, qualify for the exception to the 10 percent additional tax under § 72(t)(2)(A)(iv), and such modification results in the imposition of the recapture tax under the rules of § 72(t)(4), the recapture tax applies to the payments made before the date of the qualified HSA funding distribution.

The amount contributed to the HSA through a qualified HSA funding distribution is not allowed as a deduction and counts against the individual's maximum annual HSA contribution for the taxable year of the distribution. In addition, the taxability of these distributions is subject to the testing period rules in § 408(d)(9)(D), discussed below.

Qualified HSA funding distribution only from certain types of IRAs

A qualified HSA funding distribution may be made from a traditional IRA under § 408 or a Roth IRA under § 408A, but not from an ongoing SIMPLE IRA under § 408(p) or an ongoing SEP IRA under § 408(k). For this purpose, a SEP IRA or SIMPLE IRA is treated as ongoing if an employer contribution is made for the plan year ending with or within the IRA owner's taxable year in which the qualified HSA funding distribution would be made.

After the death of an IRA or Roth IRA account owner, a qualified HSA funding distribution may be made from an IRA or Roth IRA maintained for the benefit of an IRA or Roth IRA beneficiary. This distribution will be taken into account in determining whether the required minimum distribution requirements of §§ 408(a)(6), 408(b)(3), and 408A(c)(5) have been satisfied.

Maximum amount of qualified HSA funding distribution

For purposes of § 408(d)(9)(C)(i), a qualified HSA funding distribution from the IRA or Roth IRA of an eligible individual to that individual's HSA must be less than or equal to the IRA or Roth IRA account owner's maximum annual HSA contribution. The maximum annual HSA contribution is based on (1) the individual's age as of the end of the taxable year and (2) the individual's type of high deductible health plan (HDHP) coverage (self-only or family HDHP coverage) at the time of the distribution. For example, in 2008, an IRA owner who is an eligible individual with family HDHP coverage at the time of the distribution and who is age 55 or over by the end of the year is allowed a qualified HSA funding distribution of $5,800, plus the $900 catch-up contribution. An IRA or Roth IRA owner who is an eligible individual with self-only HDHP coverage, and who is under age 55 as of the end of the taxable year, is allowed a qualified HSA funding distribution of $2,900 for 2008.

One-time qualified HSA funding distribution

Generally, only one qualified HSA funding distribution is allowed during the lifetime of an individual. If, however, the distribution occurs when the individual has self-only HDHP coverage, and later in the same taxable year the individual has family HDHP coverage, the individual is allowed a second qualified HSA funding distribution in that taxable year. Both distributions count against the individual's maximum HSA contribution for that taxable year. The distributions must be from an IRA or Roth IRA to an HSA owned by the individual who owns the IRA or Roth IRA or, in the case of an inherited IRA, for whom the IRA or Roth IRA is maintained (i.e., a qualified HSA funding distribution cannot be made to an HSA owned by any other person, including the individual's spouse). IRA or Roth IRA owners are not required to make the maximum qualified HSA funding distribution or to make any qualified HSA funding distribution.

If an individual owns two or more IRAs, and wants to use amounts in multiple IRAs to make a qualified HSA funding distribution, the individual must first make an IRA-to-IRA transfer of the amounts to be distributed into a single IRA, and then make the one-time qualified HSA funding distribution from that IRA.

No deemed distribution date

A qualified HSA funding distribution relates to the taxable year in which the distribution is actually made. The rules in § 223(d)(4)(B) and § 219(f)(3) (contributions made before the deadline for filing the individual's federal income tax return are deemed to be made on the last day of the preceding taxable year) do not apply to qualified HSA funding distributions.

Procedures for making the transfer from an IRA to an HSA

An individual must be an eligible individual (as defined in § 223(c)(1)) at the time of the qualified HSA funding distribution. The distribution must be a direct transfer from an IRA or Roth IRA to an HSA. For example, if a check from an IRA or Roth IRA is made payable to an HSA trustee or custodian and delivered by the IRA or Roth IRA account owner to the HSA trustee or custodian, the payment to the HSA will be considered a direct payment by the IRA or Roth IRA trustee, custodian or issuer to the HSA for purposes of § 408(d)(9).

Testing period rules

If a qualified HSA funding distribution is made from the individual's IRA or Roth IRA to the individual's HSA under § 408(d)(9) and the individual remains an eligible individual during the entire testing period, the amount of the qualified HSA funding distribution is excluded from the individual's gross income and the 10 percent additional tax under § 408(d)(9)(D) does not apply. The testing period begins with the month in which the qualified HSA funding distribution is contributed to the HSA and ends on the last day of the 12th month following that month. Each qualified HSA funding distribution allowed in § 408(d)(9)(C)(ii)(II) has a separate testing period. For testing period purposes, an eligible individual who changes from family HDHP coverage to self-only HDHP coverage during the testing period remains an eligible individual. If at any time during the testing period the individual ceases to meet all requirements to be an eligible individual, the amount of the qualified HSA funding distribution is included in the individual's gross income. The qualified HSA funding distribution is included in gross income in the taxable year of the individual in which the individual first fails to be an eligible individual. This amount is subject to 10 percent additional tax (unless the failure is due to disability, as defined in § 72(m)(7), or death). See § 408(d)(9)(D). Earnings on the amount of the qualified HSA funding distribution are not included in gross income. Amounts included in the IRA or Roth IRA owner's gross income under § 6 408(d)(9)(D) are not also included in gross income under § 408(d)(1) or (2), nor do the § 72 rules apply (including the additional tax under § 72(t)).

No interaction between testing periods

Section 223(b)(8)(B) provides generally that if an individual fails to remain an eligible individual during the § 223(b)(8) testing period, an amount is included in the individual's gross income (computed by subtracting the sum of the monthly contribution limits that the individual would otherwise have been entitled to under § 223(b)(1) and (2) from the amount actually contributed). The testing period rules in § 223(b)(8)(B) do not apply to amounts contributed to an HSA through a qualified HSA funding distribution. Thus, if an individual remains an eligible individual during the entire § 408(d)(9) testing period, then no amount of the qualified HSA funding distribution is included in income and the 10 percent additional tax under § 223(b)(8)(B) does not apply.

Application of § 223(b)(8)(B) testing period to contributions which are not qualified HSA funding distributions

If an HSA account beneficiary's contributions to his or her HSA in a taxable year include both a qualified HSA funding distribution (or distributions) and other contributions subject to § 223(b)(8), the § 408(d)(9)(D) testing period rules apply to qualified HSA funding distribution (or distributions) and the § 223(b)(8)(B) testing period rules apply to the other contributions. If the individual fails to remain an eligible individual during the § 223(b)(8)(B) testing period, but does remain a qualified individual during the § 408(d)(9)(D) testing period, the amount included in the individual's gross income is the lesser of:

(1) the amount that would otherwise be included under the § 223(b)(8)(B) rules; or

(2) the amount of contributions to the HSA for the taxable year other than the amount contributed through qualified HSA funding distributions.

HSA distributions not used for qualified medical expenses

An HSA distribution not used for qualified medical expenses (as defined in § 223(d)(2)) is included in gross income under § 223(f)(2) and subject to the 10 percent additional tax under § 223(f)(4) (with certain exceptions), regardless of whether the amount contributed to the HSA under the qualified HSA funding distribution is included in the account beneficiary's income and subject to the additional tax under § 408(d)(9)(D). See Notice 2007-22, 2007-10 I.R.B. 670, regarding the consequences of distributions from HSAs.

EXAMPLES

The following examples illustrate these rules. It is assumed in the examples that no previous qualified HSA funding distributions have been made by the individual, and that all distributions are from IRAs and are otherwise included in the IRA owner's gross income. None of the IRAs are ongoing SEP IRAs described in § 408(k), or ongoing SIMPLE IRAs described in § 408(p). For purposes of § 223(f)(4) and § 408(d)(9)(D)(ii), none of the IRA owners or HSA account beneficiaries are disabled. None of the exceptions to the 10 percent tax under § 72(t) apply.

Example 1. Individual A, age 45, enrolls in family HDHP coverage on January 1, 2008, is otherwise an eligible individual (as defined in § 223(c)(1)) as of that date and through December 31, 2009. A's maximum annual HSA contribution for 2008 is $5,800. A owns an IRA with a balance of $2,000. A direct trustee-to-trustee transfer of $2,000 is made from A's IRA trustee to A's HSA trustee on April 2, 2008.

The $2,000 distribution is a qualified HSA funding distribution, and accordingly is not included in A's gross income and is not subject to the additional tax under § 72(t). A's testing period with respect to the qualified HSA funding distribution begins in April 2008 and ends on April 30, 2009. After the qualified HSA funding distribution of $2,000, $3,800 of A's 2008 HSA maximum annual contribution remains.

Example 2. Same facts as Example 1, except that A ceases to be an eligible individual on January 1, 2009. Under § 408(d)(9)(D), in 2009 A must include $2,000 in gross income, the amount of the qualified HSA funding distribution, plus an additional tax of $200 (10 percent of the amount included in income).

Example 3. Individual B, age 57, enrolls in self-only HDHP coverage effective January 1, 2008, is otherwise an eligible individual as of that date and through December 31, 2009. B's maximum annual HSA contribution for 2008 is $3,800 ($2,900 plus the $900 catch-up contribution). B owns an IRA with a balance of $13,550. A direct trustee-to-trustee transfer of $3,800 is made from B's IRA trustee to B's HSA trustee on June 4, 2008.

The $3,800 distribution is a qualified HSA funding distribution. The distribution from B's IRA is not included in B's gross income and is not subject to the additional tax under § 72(t). The qualified HSA funding distribution of $3,800 equals B's 2008 maximum annual HSA contribution. B's testing period with respect to the qualified HSA funding distribution begins in June 2008 and ends on June 30, 2009.

Example 4. Individual C, age 38, enrolls in self-only HDHP coverage on January 1, 2008, is otherwise an eligible individual on January 1, and remains an eligible individual through December 31, 2009. C owns an IRA with a balance of $12,550. A qualified HSA funding distribution of $2,800 is made from C's IRA trustee directly to C's HSA trustee on June 4, 2008.

On August 1, C enrolls in family HDHP coverage. A transfer of $3,000 is made from C's IRA trustee directly to C's HSA trustee on August 15, 2008.

The $2,800 and $3,000 distributions are qualified HSA funding distributions. The distributions from the IRA are not included in C's gross income and are not subject to the additional tax under § 72(t). The qualified HSA funding distributions of $5,800 ($2,800 + $3,000) equal C's 2008 maximum annual HSA contribution. C's testing period for the first qualified HSA funding distribution begins in June 2008 and ends on June 30, 2009 and the testing period for the second qualified HSA funding distribution begins in August 2008 and ends on August 31, 2009.

Example 5. Individual D, age 43, enrolls in family HDHP coverage on January 1, 2008, is otherwise an eligible individual on January 1, and remains an eligible individual through December 31, 2009. D owns an IRA with a balance of $17,500. A qualified HSA funding distribution of $5,800 is made from D's IRA trustee directly to D's HSA trustee on March 18, 2008.

On June 1, D changes from family HDHP coverage to self-only HDHP coverage. The $5,800 distribution from the IRA is not included in D's gross income and is not subject to the additional tax under § 72(t). The qualified HSA funding distribution of $5,800 equals D's maximum annual HSA contribution at the time the transfer occurred. D's testing period begins in March 2008 and ends on March 31, 2009.

Example 6. Individual E, age 50, begins family HDHP coverage and is first an eligible individual on June 1, 2008. E owns an IRA with a balance of $20,000. A direct trustee-to-trustee transfer of $3,500 is made from E's IRA trustee to E's HSA trustee on June 4, 2008. On June 4, 2008 E also contributes $2,300 in cash to his HSA for a total contribution of $5,800. On July 1, 2009, E ceases to be an eligible individual.

The $3,500 distribution is a qualified HSA funding distribution, is not included in E's gross income, and is not subject to the additional tax under § 72(t). E's testing period with respect to the qualified HSA funding distribution begins in June 2008 and ends on June 30, 2009. E remains an eligible individual during the qualified HSA funding distribution testing period. No amount of the $3,500 distribution is included in E's gross income.

The testing period for the $2,300 contribution begins in December 2008 and ends on December 31, 2009. E's full contribution limit under § 223(b)(8) for 2008 is $5,800. E's sum of the monthly contribution limits is $3,383 (7/12 times $5,800). E's maximum annual contribution for 2008 is $5,800, the greater of $5,800 or $3,383.

The amount included in E's gross income and subject to the 10 percent additional tax under § 223(b)(8)(B) in 2009 is $2,417 ($5,800–$3,383). The cash contribution to E's HSA is $2,300. The amount included in E's gross income and subject to additional tax is $2,300, the lesser of $2,417 or $2,300.

Example 7. Same facts as Example 6, except that the distribution from E's IRA to E's HSA is $1,000 and E contributes $4,800 in cash for a total HSA contribution of $5,800 in 2008.

E remains an eligible individual during the qualified HSA funding distribution testing period. No amount of the $1,000 distribution is included in E's gross income.

E's full contribution limit under § 223(b)(8) for 2008 is $5,800. E's sum of the monthly contribution limits is $3,383 (7/12 times $5,800). E's maximum annual contribution limit for 2008 is $5,800, the greater of $5,800 or $3,383.

The amount included in E's gross income and subject to the 10 percent additional tax under § 223(b)(8)(B) is $2,417 ($5,800–$3,383). The cash contribution to E's HSA is $4,800. The amount included in E's gross income and subject to the additional tax in 2009 is $2,417, the lesser of $2,417 or $4,800.

Example 8. Same facts as Example 6, except that E ceases to be an eligible individual on May 1, 2009. The $3,500 distribution is a qualified HSA funding distribution, is not included in E's gross income in the year of the distribution, and is not subject to the additional tax under § 72(t). E's testing period with respect to the qualified HSA funding distribution begins in June 2008 and ends on June 30, 2009. E ceases to be an eligible individual during the qualified HSA funding distribution testing period. The $3,500 distribution is included in E's gross income. In addition, the 10 percent additional tax ($350) under § 408(d)(9)(D)(II) applies to the amount.

The testing period for the $2,300 contribution begins in December 2008 and ends on December 31, 2009. E's full contribution limit under § 223(b)(8) for 2008 is $5,800. E's sum of the monthly contribution limits is $3,383 (7/12 times $5,800). E's maximum annual contribution limit for 2008 is $5,800, the greater of $5,800 or $3,383.

The amount included in E's gross income and subject to the 10 percent additional tax in 2009 under § 223(b)(8) is $2,417 ($5,800–$3,383). The cash contribution to E's HSA is $2,300. The amount included in E's gross income and subject to additional tax is $2,300, the lesser of $2,417 or $2,300.

Example 9. Individual F, age 47, has family HDHP coverage and is first an eligible individual on January 1, 2008. F's maximum annual HSA contribution for 2008 is $5,800. F owns an IRA with a balance of $10,000. A direct trustee-to-trustee transfer of $10,000 is made from F's IRA trustee to F's HSA trustee on September 26, 2008.

The $10,000 contribution exceeds F's $5,800 contribution limit. In 2008, $4,200 ($10,000–$5,800) is included in F's gross income under § 408 as a taxable IRA distribution. The $4,200 is also subject to additional tax under § 72(t), as well as an excise tax on excess HSA contributions under § 4973.

Example 10. Individual G, age 32, has self-only HDHP coverage and is first an eligible individual on January 1, 2007. G remains an eligible individual through December 31, 2009. G's maximum annual HSA contribution for 2007 is $2,850 and $2,900 for 2008. G owns an IRA with a balance of $4,500. A direct trustee-to-trustee transfer of $1,000 from G's IRA trustee to G's HSA trustee is made on September 6, 2007.

Another direct trustee-to-trustee transfer of $1,500 from G's IRA trustee to G's HSA trustee is made on April 28, 2008. G makes no other contributions to his HSA for 2008.

The $1,000 contribution to G's HSA in September 2007 is a qualified HSA funding distribution, is not included in G's gross income, and is not subject to the additional tax under § 72(t). G's testing period with respect to this contribution begins in September 2007 and ends on September 30, 2008.

The $1,500 contribution to G's HSA in April 2008 is not a qualified HSA funding distribution, is included in G's gross income for 2008 under § 408 as a taxable IRA distribution, and is subject to the additional tax under § 72(t). However, the $1,500 contribution to G's HSA is allowed as a deduction under § 223(a) in 2008, because G remains an eligible individual in 2008 and has not otherwise made contributions to the HSA or had contributions on G's behalf made to an HSA in excess of $1,400 for 2008. No testing period under § 408 applies to the $1,500 contribution.

REPORTING AND WITHHOLDING

Employers are not responsible for reporting whether an employee remains an eligible individual during the testing period.

A qualified HSA funding distribution is not subject to withholding under § 3405 because an IRA or Roth IRA owner that requests such a distribution is deemed to have elected out of withholding under § 3405(a)(2). For purposes of determining whether a distribution requested by an IRA or Roth IRA owner satisfies the requirements of § 408(d)(9), the IRA or Roth IRA trustee may rely upon reasonable representations made by the account owner.

EFFECTIVE DATE

Sections 408(d)(9) and 223(b)(4)(C), allowing qualified HSA funding distributions from IRAs to HSAs, are effective for taxable years beginning after December 31, 2006.

DRAFTING INFORMATION

The principal author of this notice is Leslie R. Paul of the Office of Division Counsel/Associate Chief Counsel (Tax Exempt and Government Entities). For further information regarding this notice contact Ms. Paul at (202) 622-6080 (not a toll-free call). For information regarding the rules applicable to IRAs, contact Cathy V. Pastor at (202) 622-6090 (not a toll-free call).

APPENDIX E

Informal Guidance on Contribution Limits for Domestic Partners

AMERICAN BAR ASSOCIATION
SECTION OF TAXATION
MAY MEETING 2010

COMMITTEE ON EMPLOYEE BENEFITS
JOINT COMMITTEE ON EMPLOYEE BENEFITS
INTERNAL REVENUE SERVICE
MAY 6-8, 2010

1. § 223—Contributions to Health Savings Account

An employee elects family coverage for himself and his domestic partner under a high deductible health care plan (HDHP) for a calendar year. The domestic partner is not the employee's dependent. The fair market value of the health coverage for the domestic partner is imputed as income to the employee.

Question A: What amount can the employee contribute to a health savings account (HSA) during the year such coverage is elected, disregarding any "catch-up contribution" that may be available to the employee?

Question B: Does the special rule for married individuals that limits the contribution amount that a husband and wife can make to an HSA apply to the employee and his domestic partner?

Question C: What amount can the employee's domestic partner contribute to an HSA during the year such coverage is elected, disregarding any "catch-up contribution" that may be available to the employee's domestic partner?

Proposed Response A: Since the employee has elected family coverage defined in Section 223(c)(4) of the Code as "any coverage other than self-only coverage" and Notice 2004-50 confirms that family HDHP coverage is HDHP coverage for one HSA-eligible individual and at least one other individual (whether or not the other individual is an HSA-eligible individual), the employee is treated as having family HDHP coverage and is eligible for contributions up to the HSA contribution limit for family HDHP coverage.

Proposed Response B: No. The HSA contribution limits imposed on married individuals do not apply to domestic partners. The Defense of Marriage Act provides that domestic partners will not, for federal tax purposes, be considered each other's "spouse." 1 U.S.C. § 7. Thus, the employee and his domestic partner are not subject to the contribution limits imposed on married individuals.

Proposed Response C: The employee's domestic partner is eligible to contribute up to the HSA contribution limit for family HDHP coverage for the same reason that the employee is eligible to contribute up to the HSA contribution limit for family HDHP coverage.

IRS Response A: The Service representative agrees with the proposed response.

IRS Response B: The Service representative agrees with the proposed response.

IRS Response C: The Service representative agrees with the proposed response.

APPENDIX F

Health Opportunity Patient Empowerment Act of 2006

Author's note: Only the sections of the law relevant to this book are included in this appendix.

H.R. 6111

Tax Relief and Health Care Act of 2006
[Enrolled as agreed to or Passed by Both House and Senate]

Title III—HEALTH SAVINGS ACCOUNT

SEC. 301. SHORT TITLE.

This title may be cited as the 'Health Opportunity Patient Empowerment Act of 2006'.

SEC 303. REPEAL OF ANNUAL DEDUCTIBLE LIMITATIONS ON HSA CONTRIBUTIONS

(a) In General—Paragraph (2) of section 223(b) (relating to monthly limitations) is amended—

(1) In subparagraph (A) by striking 'the lesser of—' and all that follows and inserting '$2,250.', and

(2) In subparagraph (B) by striking 'the lesser of—' and all that follows and inserting '$4,500.'.

(b) Conforming amendment Section 223(d)(1)(A)(ii)(I) is amended by striking 'subsection (b)(2)(B)(ii)' and inserting 'subsection (b)(2)(B).'

(c) Effective Date—The amendments made by this section shall apply to taxable years beginning after December 31, 2006.

SEC 305. CONTRIBUTION LIMITATION IS NOT REDUCED FOR PART-YEAR COVERAGE

(a) Increase in Limit for Individuals Becoming Eligible Individuals After Beginning of the Year—Subsection (b) of Section 223 (relating to limitations) is amended by adding at the end the following paragraph:

'(8) INCREASE IN LIMIT FOR INDIVIDUALS BECOMING ELIGIBLE INDIVIDUALS AFTER THE BEGINNING OF THE YEAR—

'(A) IN GENERAL—for purposes of computing the limitation under paragraph (1) for any taxable year, an individual who is an eligible individual during the last month of such taxable year shall be treated—

'(i) as having been an eligible individual during each of the months in such taxable year, and

'(ii) as having been enrolled, during each of the months such individual is treated as an eligible individual solely by reason of clause (i), in the same high deductible health plan in which the individual was enrolled for the last month of such taxable year.

'(B) FAILURE TO MAINTAIN HIGH DEUCTIBLE HEALTH PLAN COVERAGE—

'(i) IN GENERAL—If, at any time during the testing period, the individual is not an eligible individual, then—

'(I) gross income of the individual for the taxable year in which occurs the first month in the testing period for which such individual is not an eligible individual is increased by the aggregate amount of all contributions to the health savings account of the individual which could not have been made but for subparagraph (A), and

'(II) the tax imposed by this chapter for any taxable year on the individual shall be increased by 10 percent of the amount of such increase.

'(ii) EXCEPTION FOR DISABILITY OR DEATH—Subclauses (I) and (II) of clause (i) shall not apply if the individual ceased to be an eligible individual by reason of the death of the individual or the individual becoming disabled (within the meaning of section 72(m)(7).

'(iii) TESTING PERIOD—The term 'testing period' means the period beginning with the last month of the taxable year referred to in subparagraph (A) and ending on the last day of the 12th month following such month.'.

(b) Effective date—The amendments made by this section shall apply to taxable years beginning after December 31, 2006.

SEC 307. ONE-TIME DISTRIBUTION FROM INDIVIDUAL RETIREMENT PLANS TO FUND HSAs.

(a) In General—Subsection (d) of section 408 (relating to the taxability of beneficiary of employees' trust) is amended by adding at the end the following new paragraph:

'(9) DISTRIBUTION FOR HEALTH SAVINGS ACCOUNT FUNDING—

'(A) IN GENERAL—In the case of an individual who is an eligible individual (as defined in section 223(c)) and who elects the application of this paragraph for a taxable year, gross income of the individual for the taxable year does not include a qualified HSA funding distribution to the extent such distribution is otherwise includible in gross income.

'(B) QUALIFIED HSA FUNDING DISTRIBUTION—For purposes of this paragraph, the term 'qualified HSA funding distribution' means a distribution for an individual retirement plan (other than a plan described in subsection (k) or (p)) of the employee to the extent that such distribution is contributed to the health savings account of the individual in a direct trustee-to-trustee transfer.

'(C) LIMITATIONS—

'(i) MAXIMUM DOLLAR LIMITATION—The amount excluded from gross income by subparagraph (A) shall not exceed the excess of—

'(I) The annual limitation under section 223(b) computed on the basis of the type of coverage under the high deductible health plan covering the individual at the time of the qualified HSA funding distribution, over

'(II) In the case of a distribution described in clause (ii)(II), the amount of the earlier qualified HSA funding distribution.

'(ii) ONE-TIME TRANSFER—

'(I) IN GENERAL—Except as provided in subclause (II), an individual may make election under subparagraph (A) only for one qualified HSA funding distribution during the lifetime of the individual. Such an election, once made, shall be irrevocable.

'(II) CONVERSION FROM SELF-ONLY TO FAMILY COVERAGE—If a qualified HSA funding distribution is made during a month in a taxable year during which an individual has self-only coverage under a high deductible health plan as of the first day of the month, the individual may elect to make an additional qualified HSA funding distribution during a subsequent month in such taxable year during which the individual has family coverage under a high deductible health plan as of the first day of the subsequent month.

'(D) FAILURE TO MAINTAIN HIGH DEDUCTIBLE HEALTH PLAN COVERAGE—

'(i) IN GENERAL—If, at any time during the testing period, the individual is not an eligible individual, then the aggregate amount of all contributions to the health savings account of the individual made under subparagraph (A)—

'(I) shall be includible in the gross income of the individual for the taxable year in which occurs the first month in the testing period for which such individual is not an eligible individual, and

'(II) the tax imposed by this chapter for any taxable year on the individual shall be increased by 10 percent of the amount which is so includible.

'(ii) EXCEPTION FOR DISABILITY OR DEATH—Subclauses (I) and (II) of clause (i) shall not apply if the individual ceased to be an eligible individual by reason of the death of the individual or the individual becoming disabled (within the meaning of section 72(m)(7).

'(iii) TESTING PERIOD—The term 'testing period' means the period beginning with the month in which the qualified HSA funding distribution is contributed to a health savings account and ending on the last day of the 12th month following such month.

'(E) APPLICATION OF SECTION 72—Notwithstanding section 72, in determining the extent to which an amount is treated as otherwise includible in gross income for purposes of subparagraph (A), the aggregate amount distributed from an individual retirement plan shall be treated as includible in gross income to the extent that such amount does not exceed the aggregate amount which would have been so includible if all amounts from all individual retirement plans were distributed. Proper adjustments shall be made in applying section 72 to other distributions in such taxable year and subsequent taxable years.'.

(b) Coordination With Limitation on Contributions to HSAs—Section 223(b)(4) (relating to coordination with other contributions) is amended by striking 'and' at the end of subparagraph (A), by striking the period at the end of subparagraph (B) and inserting ', and', and by inserting after subparagraph (B) the following new subparagraph:

(C) The aggregate amount contributed to health savings accounts of such individual for such taxable year under section 408(d)(9) (and such amount shall not be allowed as a deduction under subsection (a)).'.

(c) Effective Date—The amendments made by this section shall apply to taxable years beginning after December 31, 2006.

Index